A

HISTORY

OF

BATH

BLADUD SON OF LUDHUDIBRAS
EIGHTH KING OF THE BRITANS,
FROM BRUTE, A GREAT PHILOSOPH
ER
& MATHEMATICIAN, BRED AT
ATHENS & RECORDED THE FIRST
DISCOVERER, AND FOUNDER OF
THESE BATHS, EIGHT HUNDRED
SIXTY THREE YEARS, BEFORE,
CHRIST, THAT IS TWO THOUSAND
FIVE HUNDRED SIXTY TWO YEAR
TO THE PRESENT YEAR 1699

BATH
IMAGE AND REALITY

Graham Davis
and
Penny Bonsall

 Carnegie Publishing

supported by CPI Bath Press

front cover
Aerial view of Royal
Crescent and the
King's Circus, two
of Bath's showpiece
architectural
attractions.
PHOTOGRAPH BY DAE SASITORN/
WWW.LASTREFUGE.CO.UK

back cover
top Head of Minerva.
BY COURTESY OF BATH AND
NORTH EAST SOMERSET COUNCIL,
ROMAN BATHS MUSEUM

centre Panoramic view
of Bath from Beechen
Cliff, 1846.
BY COURTESY OF BATH CENTRAL
LIBRARY, BATH & NORTH EAST
SOMERSET COUNCIL

frontispiece
A seventeenth-
century sculpture of
Bladud, set in a niche
overlooking the King's
Bath. In a marvellously
imaginative reworking
of the Bladud myth,
the inscription
reads: 'Bladud son
of Ludhudibras,
King of the Britans
[sic], from brute a
great philosopher &
mathematician, bred
at Athens & recorded
the first discoverer,
and founder of these
Baths, eight hundred
sixty three years before
Christ that is two
thousand five hundred
sixty two years to the
present year 1699'.
PHOTOGRAPH: CARNEGIE, 2005

Also published by Carnegie:
Prof. David Hey, *A History of Yorkshire: 'County of the Broad Acres'* (2005)

Other town and city histories available from Carnegie:
Prof. John K. Walton, *Blackpool*
Peter Aughton, *Bristol: A People's History*
Dr John A. Hargreaves, *Halifax*
Dr Andrew White (ed.), *A History of Lancaster*
Peter Aughton, *Liverpool: A People's History*
Prof. Alan Kidd, *Manchester*
Dr Jeffrey Hill, *Nelson*
Prof. David Hey, *Sheffield*

Forthcoming town and city histories:
Prof. Carl Chinn, *Birmingham*
Dr Derek Beattie, *Blackburn*
Dr John Doran, *Chester*
Dr John A. Hargreaves, *Huddersfield*
Dr Andrew White, *Kendal*
Anthea Jones, *Cheltenham*
Dr Trevor Rowley, *Oxford*
Dr Mark Freeman, *St Albans*
Prof. Bill Sheils, *York*

Full details on www.carnegiepublishing.com

A history of Bath: image and reality

Copyright © Graham Davis and Penny Bonsall, 2006

First published in 2006 by Carnegie Publishing Ltd,
Chatsworth Road,
Lancaster LA1 4SL
www.carnegiepublishing.com

British Library Cataloguing-in-Publication data
A catalogue record for this book is available from the British Library

ISBN 10: 1-85936-112-9
ISBN 13: 978-1-85936-112-2

Designed, typeset and originated by Carnegie Publishing
Printed and bound in Bath by CPI, Bath Press

The publishers are grateful to CPI Bath Press, printers in Bath for 160 years,
for generously supporting this book by bearing part of the cost of printing and binding.

Contents

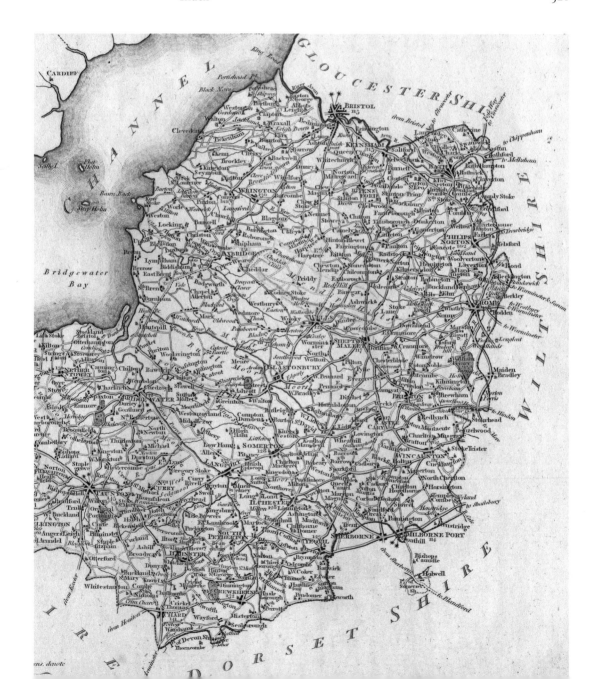

Introduction

A T THE BEGINNING of the twenty-first century Bath is one of the most popular and significant tourist destinations in Britain. Visitors from all around the world arrive by car, coach or train to visit the much-renovated and tidied up Roman Baths, to marvel at the sites of this World Heritage city, or to meander through its now carefully conserved eighteenth-century streets. For a few hours before they are whisked away to Stratford-upon-Avon, Edinburgh or London, they absorb the carefully presented image of Bath as ancient spa, elegant Georgian city and haunt of the likes of Richard 'Beau' Nash or Jane Austen. The adventurous might take a look at the excavated cellars of Sally Lunn's – Bath's 'oldest building' – after sampling one of the establishment's famous buns; or climb down into the abbey's vaults to view the medieval artefacts on display; or visit, perhaps, one of the many themed museums which have been established to cater for the 4 million or so visitors who make their way to Bath each year. Bath has always been good at presenting a favourable image to the world.

It goes without saying that the true picture of Bath throughout its long and varied history is much fuller, more interesting and varied than the façade presented to casual visitors. The history of Bath is, in fact, one which has encompassed many changes of both image and function over the centuries. From its earliest known history as spa during the Roman period, Bath transformed itself into Saxon monastic town and subsequently Norman cathedral city. It developed into a regional market and – perhaps surprisingly – a centre of the woollen trade during the Middle Ages, before becoming perhaps the most significant national health resort of the sixteenth and seventeenth centuries. Thereafter rapid expansion in the Georgian period created an enduring architectural legacy and made Bath the foremost fashionable resort of the eighteenth century, attracting increasing numbers of visitors. From the later 1700s, the city experienced some years of relative decline, from which it emerged as a favoured place of genteel residence in the nineteenth and twentieth centuries. Recently Bath has reflected many national trends and developments, and has become a World Heritage Site and conservation area. This theme of constant re-invention now sees Bath attempt to become a 'festival city', in the market for cultural tourism, while the long-anticipated opening of a new thermal spa should bring a new lease of life to the hot springs which, of course, represent Bath's very oldest attraction, and in many ways its very *raison d'être*.

This book differs from most histories of Bath in two principal ways. Firstly, it is a social history, in which deliberate emphasis is given to the lives of ordinary

opposite Cary's map of Somerset, 1787. Throughout its history Bath has been of importance to a wide surrounding area, as a trading place and market which also attracted rural migrants in search of work. Today many people from outside the city commute into Bath for work, but it also serves as a cultural centre and a regional shopping centre. The close relationship between Bath and its hinterland was acknowledged in the formation of the Bath and North East Somerset Council, when unitary authorities were established under local government reforms in the late twentieth century.

PRIVATE COLLECTION

I

citizens as well as to important individuals who have made their mark on the city through the ages. Secondly, while recognising the undoubted importance of Roman Bath and Georgian Bath, due recognition is also given to the long centuries which encompass the Saxon period, the Middle Ages and the early modern city and the two centuries which have elapsed since the great eighteenth-century building boom. Additionally the spotlight is also turned on to the post-Georgian city, to life in Bath in the Victorian period, and to important developments in the twentieth century when for the ordinary citizens of Bath the quality of life was transformed.

From around 1700 it becomes possible to reconstruct the lives of Bath citizens in ever more detail, so that the contrast between the wealthy and the labouring poor becomes self-evident: the gulf between the elegance of the Georgian townhouses and the poor housing down by the river; the smart social set within the Pump Room compared with the social problems of a surprisingly industrialised city; the contrast, in short, between image and reality. A process of camouflage disguised less attractive features in the interests of a public image which changed over time according to historical circumstances. A complex, often surprising history is revealed through the issues explored in this book, one beyond the usual emphasis on Bath as an affluent or fashionable spa resort.

Bath has a long and glorious history which is rightly cherished by its inhabitants and visitors alike. We would suggest, however, that the true nature of this remarkable and chequered history is not always fully understood or respected. In few other cities has the commercial exploitation of the city's history, to serve the needs of the tourist industry, had such a distorting effect on popular

A HISTORY OF BATH

At the very centre of the modern tourist city are the Roman Baths. Despite its classical, antique façade, what is now the visitors' reception hall actually dates from 1897 when it was opened as a concert hall extension to the Grand Pump Room, designed by J. M. Brydon.

PHOTOGRAPH: CARNEGIE, 2005

understanding. The selective emphasis on its most saleable assets – Roman remains, Georgian architecture, and famous visitors – presents Bath history in an attractive 'gift-wrapped' package, devoid of its contemporary context and in many respects ignoring their proper historical significance. We hope that this is a more rounded story, identifying where possible the role of all its citizens, including the labouring poor, as well as that of the various social elites.

Over the last few decades archaeologists have explored and explained Bath's growth and function in the Roman period and they have also contributed significantly to the growing understanding of the city in medieval times. Historians have also made their contribution in numerous books on aspects of Bath's history with an abiding focus on the eighteenth century. There is some truth in the observation that the received social history of Bath 'is architectural first, medical and literary next, and all about Bath as a social melting pot.'[1]

Chapter one examines the origins and early history of Bath up to the fairly arbitrary date of the Norman Conquest in 1066. It opens with a description of the local topography, and the natural resources that shaped the development of the city, before moving on to an account of the prehistory of the Bath area. Bath's first age of fame, as the Roman spa, Aquae Sulis, is then explored, followed by an explanation of its fate during the so-called Dark Ages after the Roman departure, and its emergence as an important Christian site in Saxon times.

Chapter two takes the narrative on from the Norman Conquest, and the subsequent growth of Bath as a cathedral city, through the centuries in which it was primarily a centre of the woollen industry. Thereafter, the renewed interest in the curative properties of the hot springs is discussed, and life in Bath as described in the seventeenth century is reconstructed.

Chapter three examines the spectacular growth of Bath in the Georgian period and its glorious peak of fame as the finest resort in all England. At this time Bath became the model for continental spas to emulate. This chapter also examines how the extravagant building of Bath was organised and financed, including the role of credit and speculation. In discussing the presence of wealthy visitors and the Bath season, we show how Bath became the butt of satirical writers and cartoonists as the *parvenus* came to rub shoulders with the fashionable company.

Chapter four explores the important role of the labouring poor in eighteenth-century Bath, not only in supplying the workforce for the building of Bath,

Number 1 Royal Crescent. At the east end of the Crescent, this house was the first to be completed and acted as the model for the rest. The house was given to the Bath Preservation Trust in 1968.
PHOTOGRAPH: CARNEGIE, 2004

but also in providing all the services enjoyed by visitors. Equally important is the recognition that in attracting the wealthy to Bath, many other undesirables – beggars, tramps, prostitutes and thieves – came in search of rich pickings in the city. Many Bath charities grew up in response to the problems posed by unwanted visitors and by the presence of the resident poor.

Chapter five is the first of three on the Victorian and Edwardian periods. It explains how the need to attract a new clientele – the middle classes – after the loss of the fashionable set, led to the creation of a new public face for Bath, what we describe as 'the making of genteel Bath'. Guide books propagated a new image designed to bring respectable folk to live in the city, rather than merely to visit. Chapter six features the world of work and shows that the propaganda of the guide books was unashamedly a piece of social camouflage and selective focus. It is argued that far from being only a city of 'elegance and refinement', without the vulgar intrusion of commerce or industry, it is evident

The steps leading down from the Paragon to Walcot Street. In Victorian times the passageway was dimly lit by gas lamps.
PHOTOGRAPH: CARNEGIE, 2005

that Bath was in fact an industrial city during the nineteenth century. Small-scale crafts allied to retailing outlets, rather than large factories, formed the staple of Bath industries, and it is clear that the majority of Bath's citizens belonged to the working classes. Chapter seven challenges the view that Bath was merely a conservative backwater, especially after its radical politics of the Chartist period. A great deal of important building and social progress took place in Victorian Bath, not least an experiment with the politics of the 'civic gospel' led by Jerom Murch, arguably the leading political figure of the period, and a man who had a finger in every sphere of the city's life and institutions.

Chapter eight takes a serious look at Bath in the twentieth century and recognises the huge improvements in the condition of its citizens through national policies on health, welfare and education, despite the inter-war depression and the wartime damage inflicted in the Bath blitz. This was a time when changing economic structures and the growth of modern tourism provided the basis of a new prosperity.

Chapter nine assesses the role of Bath as a heritage city, focusing on the long-standing conflict between the needs of visitors and those of residents. Post-war planning and the *volte-face* over development towards a strict policy of conservation have contributed to major changes in the way the city looks. Finally, we are writing at a time when a series of proposed developments will transform the city over the next twenty years, raising key questions on the future direction of Bath in the twenty-first century.

For those who live in and around Bath or who visit the city, there is no need to extol its virtues as one of the most beautiful cities in Britain. Its world heritage status confirms its pedigree as a very special place. The outstanding beauty of Bath is captured in the many handsome photographs which accompany the text of the book. A careful study of them will repay residents and visitors, showing not only the famous set pieces – the Roman baths, the abbey church, the King's Circus and Royal Crescent – but also reveal details of Bath's other history.

In walking around the city – and it is thankfully still a city which is enjoyable to walk in – observe the remnants of the city walls and note the industrial history recorded in the street names; read the inscriptions on the monuments in the abbey and other city churches; observe above shop fronts the signs that reveal a lost commercial past; notice the detail of lettering (see, for example, the Female Penitentiary in Walcot Street) or the carvings of statues set in Bath stone (for example, the little cherub above Mallory's in Old Bond Street); and enjoy the generous sense of space in the broad pavements along which both the fashionable and the 'swell mob' paraded. As well as spotting the famous names recorded on the city plaques on prominent buildings, imagine also the streets filled with sedan and bath chairmen, street vendors, beggars, pickpockets, crossing sweepers or runaway horses.

The richness and diversity of Bath history over a period of over two millennia are almost unparalleled in English history. We hope that this book will help bring it to a wide audience.

A *putto* or cherub salutes shoppers from his niche in the building at Old Bond Street. The *putto* had earlier formed part of the Melfort Cross within the Cross Bath, which was demolished in 1783, when some of its more decorative parts were acquired by the perfumer whose house in Old Bond Street this was.

PHOTOGRAPH: CARNEGIE, 2004

Origins and early history

I N his *Itinerary* of 1540 the sixteenth-century antiquarian John Leland described the geographical location of Bath, and in so doing its *raison d'être* before its expansion in the modern period:

> The citie of Bath is sette both yn a fruiteful and pleasant botom, the which is environed on every side with great hills, out of which cum many springes of pure water that be conveyed by dyverse ways to serve the cite.[1]

From a very early period, the history of Bath has been profoundly influenced by its particular geology and by its phyisical location, 'compassed almost round about, wth yᵉ River of Avon', as William Smith described it in 1588, as well as by the exploitation of the natural resources of the locality.[2] The most famous of these, the hot springs, still define Bath's image in the twenty-first century, just as they have done for over two thousand years. In fact, the springs were being used as long ago as the prehistoric period, well before the Romans created the famous spa town known as Aquae Sulis. After the Romans left Britain, the waters declined in importance to the local economy and to the image of Bath. It was as a major Christian centre that the city was best known in the Saxon age. The early growth and development of Bath is the subject of this chapter.

The natural setting and prehistory of Bath

Bath lies in its 'pleasant botom' on the River Avon at the southern end of the Cotswolds some 30 km inland from the Severn estuary, within the boundaries but right at the extremity of the historic county of Somerset. The Bath region is topographically similar to the Cotswolds although locally the country is more broken and varied. The Cotswold escarpment runs through the area from Dyrham, Tog Hill and Freezing Hill down to Little Down and Kelston Hill, but south of the Avon it degenerates into a series of peninsulas with valleys between. The area around the city is strikingly varied in relief through being dissected by the Avon and its tributaries, notably the River Frome and the Cam and Wellow brooks. Steep slopes all around Bath (although seldom exceeding 600ft in general height) rise to almost level, flat topped plateaux at Lansdown to the north-west, Charmy Down to the north-east, Bathampton, Claverton and Combe Down to the east and south-east, and Odd Down and Southdown to the south and south-west. Except at Bath itself, and around Bathford and Bathampton, there is little flat land in the stream and river valleys in the immediate region.

opposite The famous 'Gorgon's head', which was discovered in 1790 when the Pump Room was being built, represents an intriguing mixture of ancient spiritual belief. The discovery helped stimulate further the renewed interest in Bath's ancient history.

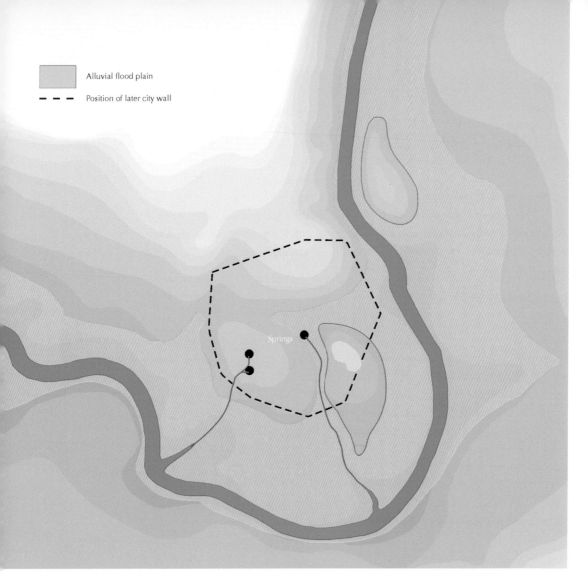

Springs

Bath lies on a low ridge within the loop of the river Avon where, coincidentally, three hot springs emerge and drain southwards into the river. The ancient city was built on the ridge, but later suburbs close to the river were, until very recently, susceptible to flooding.

DRAWN BY ADAM GREGORY, CARNEGIE

The Avon meanders across a wide flood plain at Bath, where the city is sited on a river crossing. The earliest walled settlements were located within the north–south and east–west reaches of a meander, on a river terrace formed c.60,000 BC when the Avon cut down and left part of its former floor slightly above the flood level, thus creating a dry site. The river was significant for Bath's history not only in determining early settlement but also for its later importance in developing trade with the nearby port of Bristol, and (after the building of canals) with London and other parts of the country. The river valley (spectacularly deep to the east of Bathampton Down) and its surrounding green hills were to provide an attractive setting for the 'Queen of Spas', but air tends to stagnate at the bottom of the valley where it can create a moist, rather enervating atmosphere. 'Balmy Bath' and its mild winters were promoted as one of its advantages in the eighteenth century but not all of the city's visitors appreciated the local climate. Alexander Pope described Bath as 'a sulphurous pit', and Mrs Piozzi (a friend of Dr Johnson) condemned the lower town as being like 'a stew-pot.'[3]

Complex geology underlies the local topography. It was in this region in 1792–95 (while engaged in surveying the Somerset Coal canal) that William Smith, the 'father of English geology', came to discover the fundamental principles of stratigraphy. Bath lies between the clay vales of the Triassic and Liassic rocks to the west and the Oxford clay, Purbeck beds and Gault clay of north Wiltshire to the east. The Somerset coalfield and the carboniferous limestone and the older rocks of Mendip are to the south-west, while the chalk escarpments and greensand of the Downland country of Wiltshire occur to the south-west and south-east of the city. The hills around Bath are formed of Jurassic rocks (the oolites, cornbrash and fullers earth) but in the locality of Bath itself the surface geology is overlain by slumped material of a broken, mixed nature.

Iron ores occur commonly in nearly all the strata of the region, although they have been worked only in particular formations in limited districts. Yet

A geological map of the neighbourhood of Bath, engraved and hand-coloured by John Cary c.1799, after an original drawn by William Smith.

Bath itself might have become a centre of heavy industry, according to Charles Moore, writing in the 1860s:

> In the neighbourhood of Bitton, the Middle Lias yields an average of 22 per cent metallic iron, and there are beds in the Limpley Stoke valley, and in other places around Bath, giving about 30 per cent, and it probably only arises from the accident that these beds are not quite thick enough to work profitably, that the beautiful district around that city is not converted into one for the manufacture of iron.[4]

Other natural resources were of direct benefit to Bath: the hot springs on which its fame rests primarily, the stone with which much of the city was built, and the local deposits of fullers earth. In a bend in the Avon valley, three natural springs rise out of a clay ridge, outcropping from beneath the limestone mantle. Falling as rain on Mendip, the water that reaches Bath 8,000 or more years later emerges at a rate of a third to a quarter of a million gallons per day, at a temperature (raised by the earth's internal heat) of around 40°C at what became known as the Cross Bath, rising to 46°C at the King's Bath and 49° at the Hot Bath.

The limestones which cap the hills around the city are the source of Bath stone. This was used by the Romans but then fell out of fashion until the eighteenth century when Ralph Allen (who by then had acquired the main quarries at Combe Down) became a successful advocate for its qualities. The stone is mined rather than quarried, a process that has left the Combe Down area honeycombed by underground workings. Despite its pleasant colour and texture, and the fact that it carves well, Bath stone does have several disadvantages. It is soft and easily sawn in the stone mines but must be left in the open air for weeks to 'mature' or harden and to lose its 'quarry water'. After that stage is completed, it must be stacked as it lay in the stone bed and this position must be maintained when it is built into a wall, or else it will crack and decay very rapidly.[5] When it is first used Bath stone is almost white, but its surface tends to rot as a result of weathering, and its affinity for soot (which forms a hard black scale on the exposed stone) proved to

A cross-section of part of north Somerset. The arrows show how rain falling on Mendip some 8,000–10,000 years ago has gradually found its way along the bedding planes and joints of the carboniferous limestone, picking up heat from the earth's core. The principal fault line where the water re-emerges is at Bath.

DRAWN BY ADAM GREGORY, CARNEGIE

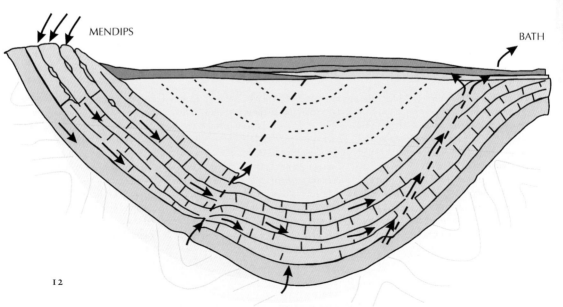

MENDIPS

BATH

The spring within the King's Bath. In the first century AD the Romans built a stone-walled reservoir to contain the spring and to supply water to the adjacent baths. No one then bathed in the spring, which was dedicated as a sacred site to Sulis Minerva. Eventually the spring was covered by a vaulted building between the temple and the baths, but by the sixth century the buildings were unused and the roof had collapsed into the spring. The water level continued to rise within the ruins, and the site became more and more derelict, although the Saxon monks might have used its waters for bathing. During the twelfth century the King's Bath – named after Henry I – was built from the remains of the Roman buildings. Still within the bounds of the monastery, it was used as a curative bath, fed with hot water from the spring directly below. Some of the bathing 'niches' in the walls can still be seen today. The brass rings in the walls were donated by grateful bathers who had been cured by the waters. After the dissolution of the monasteries in the sixteenth century the city authorities acquired the King's Bath and later built the Queen's Bath on the south side (shown on a seventeenth-century representation on pages 68–9). The King's Bath remained in use until 1939. The floor was removed for structural reasons in 1979, and the water level was lowered to its present level.

PHOTOGRAPH: CARNEGIE, 2005

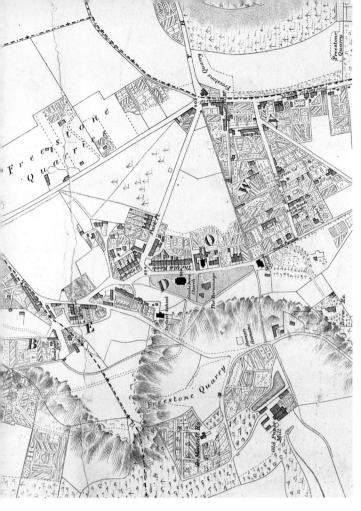

be another disadvantage. Anne Elliot, the heroine of Jane Austen's *Persuasion* (1818), dreaded 'the possible heats of September in all the white glare of Bath',[6] but by the later nineteenth century much of the city was grey or soot-blackened.

Bath's third natural resource, fullers earth (mined until the second half of the twentieth century near South Stoke, south of the city), was important in the development of the woollen industry, where it was used for extracting grease from the cloth in fulling or 'tucking' mills. The fullers earth series consists of layers of clay separated by a limestone bed. When wet, the clay is slippery and can cause landslips, such as occur quite frequently around Bath.

Stone mining at Corsham in the twentieth century.

BY COURTESY OF THE MUSEUM OF BATH AT WORK

While all of its natural resources played a part in the history of Bath, it was the presence and exploitation of the hot springs that gave 'both name and fame to the place', as Daniel Defoe noted in the 1720s.[7] Yet in further suggesting that the city would have been 'insignificant without the existence of the baths', Defoe made the commonplace error of accepting that the history of Bath is encapsulated within its dominant image. We challenge that assumption in the chapters that follow, but no account of Bath would be complete without some reference to the traditional explanation of the part the hot springs played in the origins of the city.

Bladud, a princely figure (said to be the son of King Lud and the father of Shakespeare's King Lear) is credited with discovering the healing powers of the waters. Ostracised on account of his leprosy and reduced to the lowly role of swineherd, his swine also had some skin disease but after wallowing in the muddy ground around the spring they emerged cured. Bladud, following their example, then immersed himself in the spring pool and he too was cured. In that place, the story goes, he founded a great city.

This mythical origin of Bath was widely known as early as the twelfth century and it was alive in oral tradition in Bath in the early eighteenth century. It was a major influence on the architect John Wood, whose vision of Bath was steeped in the Britannic myth of origin. According to Wood, Bath – a city the size of ancient Babylon – had been the metropolitan seat of the British Druids. In *An Essay towards a Description of Bath* (1742 and 1749), an account of his own contribution to the building of the city, he envisaged a historic landscape full of temples, altars, palaces, castles and forums, peopled with Druids, Greeks and cultured Britons. He believed that the circle was the concept of 'a Divine Architect', which had been passed by divine revelation first to the Jews and then to the Druids, and that the legendary Bladud was the first arch-Druid.[8]

John Wood's imagined past was largely fantasy, of course, but there was certainly human activity around Bath during prehistoric times, although the site of Bath itself was not permanently occupied. The most striking remains of prehistoric times in the present landscape are the banks and ditches of the Iron Age (c.600 BC – AD 43) hillforts. In the immediate vicinity of Bath there are two great, fortified settlements, at Bathampton Down and Solsbury Hill, and another smaller hillfort at Little Down. Two other sites, once identified as forts, have been re-classified. Freezing Hill or Royal Camp is now considered to be 'probably a linear earthwork' and there is 'considerable doubt', as to the former existence of Berwick Camp within the southern suburbs of Bath.[9]

Little Solsbury hillfort, showing part of the former wall and rampart. Now owned by the National Trust, the flat top at Little Solsbury was the site of an early Iron Age walled village which was occupied from about 300 to 100 BC. Substantial timber-framed and little wattle huts were protected by a 6-metre wide rampart faced with dry stone walls with rubble infill. The outer face was up to 4 metres high. Both Little Solsbury and the Bathampton Down hillforts were substantial settlements: both, indeed, covered areas similar in size to the walled city of Aquae Sulis in the valley below.

PHOTOGRAPH: CARNEGIE, 2004

Paths and trackways would have criss-crossed the countryside at this time, but little is known about early roads in the Bath region. The Jurassic ridgeway, an upland inter-regional route, is reckoned to have passed along the edge of the Cotswolds, with branches crossing the river at Bath and further west near Twerton, while other branches are tentatively suggested around Charmy Down.[10] The high road from Wells to Bath over Mendip (through Farrington Gurney, past High Littleton and Farmborough) probably follows the line of another ancient trackway.[11] The river may also have been important for communications; Aston suggests it was probably navigable to Bath at this time, and until the Middle Ages.

No major excavation has been undertaken at the Bath hillforts (and none at all using modern techniques in recent years) but a number of contemporary farmsteads around Bath have been identified, as well as a possible settlement at Sion Hill. These sites and various random finds enable us to know something of the early settlers.[12] Excavations at Charmy Down during the Second World War revealed a Middle Neolithic (*c.*2800–*c.*2400 BC) pit and a scatter of artefacts to the west of a round barrow. Later investigation at the site yielded evidence from the Beaker period (*c.*2100–*c.*1650 BC, so-called after the Beaker folk whose culture was characterised by its use of distinctively shaped vessels and by its burial customs). In a shallow pit human remains were found accompanied by grave goods: a fine long-necked beaker, a small bronze knife and a Kimmeridge shale bead. This grave had been later covered by a round barrow.

Bronze Age artefacts have been found at Solsbury Hill, and at Walcot and Twerton (both now within the boundaries of the modern city). At Monkswood, Batheaston, a horde was discovered containing torcs, arm-rings and bracelets as well as three sickles and numerous minor items. A small round barrow west of Lansdown racecourse contained a cremation, fragments of two urns, and the remains of what is known as the Lansdown 'sun disc'. Finds of a later date include a major group of Iron Age pottery from Solsbury Hill.

It is now believed that some hillforts are located on hill tops that had been occupied previously, and it seems that Bathampton Down is such an example of continuous occupation. The large site at Bathampton Down (some 32 hectares) was constructed early in the Iron Age but traces of a building have been found beneath the later rampart. Recent excavations elsewhere (notably by Professor Barry Cunliffe at Danesbury, Hampshire) have shown that in addition to their defensive functions some hill forts were centres for administration, trade, craft, industry and religion. While there is insufficient data for detailed analysis of the functions of the Bath area hill forts, there is evidence of regional trafficking of goods and raw materials, and of contact with places far distant from Bath.

No stone suitable for making axe heads occurs locally so stone axes of the Neolithic period were imported from elsewhere, either as finished pieces or in blocks of stone. Similarly, flint axes and other tools of the

Enthusiastic local archaeologists in the late nineteenth century probably destroyed a good deal while digging in barrows on Lansdown, but one remarkable find was this gilded bronze disc, measuring 172.5mm in diameter. The central motif is believed to reflect the importance of the sun in local culture in the period from 1400 to 1200 BC. Similar Bronze Age discs have been found in parts of Europe, and the sun symbol features in some of the Roman sculptures from the Sulis Minerva temple.

period originated in the flint-rich areas of Wiltshire or the Marlborough Downs. While flint for tool making was moved eastwards, pottery from the Bath/Frome area was moved westwards into Wiltshire. Four late Bronze Age socketed axes from Bath are of Irish type, believed to have been brought from south-west Ireland up the Bristol Channel. Slightly later the supply of metals switched from Ireland to North Wales for a time, but metallurgical analysis shows that from the early Bronze Age onward there were connections between the Bath/Bristol region and Brittany, as well as with parts of central Europe.

It is not known if all the hillforts near Bath are contemporary (or precisely when or for how long they were occupied), or if they were equal in status, but on the basis of the placing of the hill forts, Mick Aston has discussed some potential relationships. He has suggested that the river Avon was the boundary between the lands of Little Down, Solsbury and Bathampton and that the uplands of Lansdown and Odd Down were shared between the sites, perhaps for the grazing of sheep. Each hill fort probably had access to uplands, valley pasture and meadow land.

The inhabitants of the hill forts would have been concerned to control an area that could be exploited, for economic (principally agricultural) gain. The hot springs at Bath may have been controlled by a dominant group or perhaps shared on the site of the present-day city.[13]

A carved relief of three native mother-goddesses, found at Cleveland Walk on the slopes of Bathampton Down. Although pilgrims from throughout the empire flocked to the temple of Sulis Minerva, Celtic beliefs and traditions survived and persisted locally throughout the Roman occupation.

BY COURTESY OF BATH AND NORTH EAST SOMERSET COUNCIL, ROMAN BATHS MUSEUM

We know that early settlers made use of the waters, because excavations carried out in the 1970s around the main spring (beneath the later King's Bath) revealed a wall of the Iron Age period. The hot springs had by then already acquired religious or cult significance; a number of Celtic coins (thought to have been votive offerings) have been found and also traces of a causeway built out towards the centre of the spring.

It has been suggested that it was along this causeway that 'suppliants made their way through the alder swamp which surrounded the spring, to the point where the hot water bubbled up, there to view the most sacred spot and make their offerings to Sulis, goddess of the Spring.'[14] Such simple pilgrimage was soon to be overtaken and transformed by the Roman invasion of Britain. This led to the creation of Aquae Sulis, a complex of baths and a religious site

which were to become famous throughout Romano-Britain and over the entire Roman empire.

Aquae Sulis: the Roman spa

The Roman invasion of AD 43 advanced rapidly to occupy southern England as far west as the Bristol Channel and the river Severn. By the late autumn of that year, the Roman army had reached the Bath area, and was soon engaged in laying out the first Roman frontier in Britain. This military road, later to become known as the Fosse Way, ran diagonally across the country from the garrison fortress at Exeter to Lincoln. In the Bath region the Fosse follows the ancient north–south route along the Jurassic ridgeway.

The Fosse Way crossed the Avon at Bath, where several other major Roman roads converged: the road from London to the port of Sea Mills near Avonmouth and the Severn crossing; the road north to Gloucester; and the south-east road

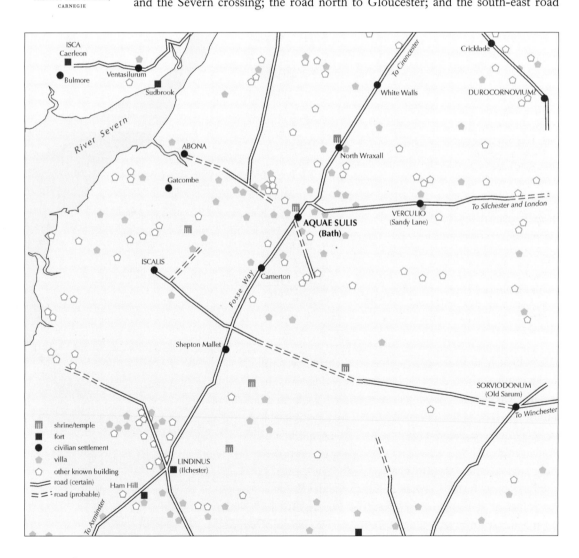

18

This life-size gilded bronze head of Minerva was once crowned with a Corinthian helmet. The head was found when a sewer trench as being dug in Stall Street in 1727, the first of many archaeological discoveries unearthed as the Georgian town was being built. The helmeted figure was probably the cult statue in the temple dedicated to Sulis Minerva, who was a conflation of Celtic and classical deities, with Sulis apparently sharing Minerva's attributes of wisdom, curative powers and martial prowess. Incorporating local gods into Roman worship made fine political sense.

BY COURTESY OF BATH AND NORTH EAST SOMERSET COUNCIL, ROMAN BATHS MUSEUM

'IN BRITAIN [THERE] ARE HOT SPRINGS ADORNED WITH SUMPTUOUS SPLENDOUR FOR THE USE OF MORTALS ... MINERVA IS PATRON GODDESS OF THESE.'

SOLINUS, 3RD CENTURY AD

across Wessex to the southern port of Hamworthy on Poole Harbour. The ford to the south of the present-day Cleveland Bridge was the principal river crossing at Bath, which expert opinion agrees would have been guarded by the military. A military presence in the vicinity is suggested by archaeological evidence from the earliest Roman period, but there is continuing speculation as to the likely site of a Roman fort. The Queen Square area has been proposed by some authorities but there is also strong support for a probable site east of the river at Bathwick.[15]

The coming of the Romans heralded the development of the hot springs into the principal settlement of its kind in Roman Britain.[16] The marshy ground around the springs was drained in successive phases of activity, and within an

A reconstruction drawing of the temple precinct as it may have looked when first laid out in the AD 60s and 70s. Four Corinthian columns supported the so-called Gorgon's Head frieze in the pediment on the temple of Sulis Minerva, which stood on a high podium towards the centre of the precinct. To the east, in the open air, stood the sacrificial altar which was set in the middle of a paved area. At this stage the sacred spring was still an open pool in the south-east corner, but it had been surrounded by a lead-lined wall which formed a watertight reservoir. The wall south of the spring formed the north wall of the great hall of the bathing establishment. The complex was altered considerably over time. A new precinct was laid out east of the temple in the early second century and late in the Roman period the spring reservoir was enclosed and roofed with a massive concrete vault. The entire bath suite, which had previously been extended, was now roofed in masonry. The sanctuary had reached almost its final form by the early third century, although some further modifications took place in the late third or early fourth century.

ILLUSTRATION BY IVAN FRONTANI, CARNEGIE

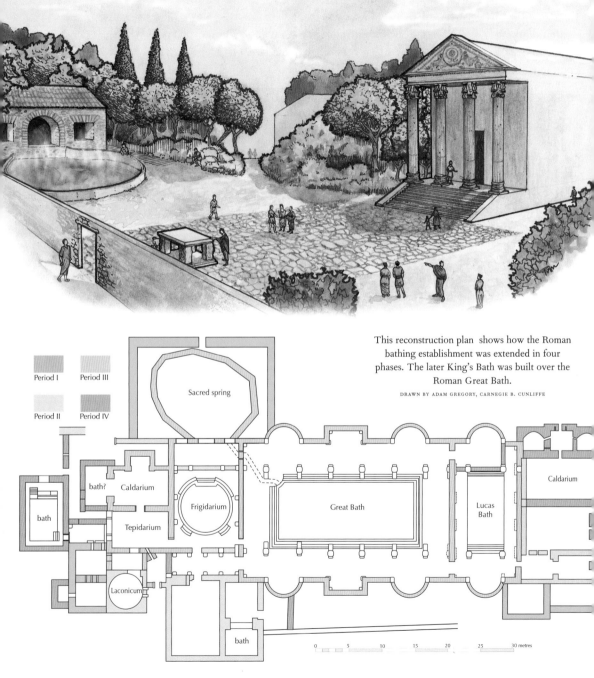

Period I Period III

Period II Period IV

Sacred spring

This reconstruction plan shows how the Roman bathing establishment was extended in four phases. The later King's Bath was built over the Roman Great Bath.

DRAWN BY ADAM GREGORY, CARNEGIE B. CUNLIFFE

bath? Caldarium

Caldarium

bath

Frigidarium

Great Bath

Lucas Bath

Tepidarium

Laconicum

bath

0   5   10   15   20   25   30 metres

area of about 10 hectares (24 acres) the Romans erected a complex of buildings including a substantial suite of baths and a temple to Sulis Minerva, who was an amalgamation of the Celtic deity and the Roman goddess Minerva. It was the Romans who gave Bath its first recorded name, Aquae Sulis.

Although substantially smaller than, for example, the Roman city of Cirencester in Gloucestershire, the importance of Aquae Sulis as a religious shrine and spa attracted pilgrims from throughout Romano-Britain and across Europe. The hot springs probably continued to be frequented by local native peoples in the early Roman period, and they may also have attracted some visitors from further afield, but the baths and the temple complex were not built until the 60s to 70s AD. Why development took place only then, some twenty years after the conquest, has never been explained. One theory is that the work was undertaken at the command of Tiberius Claudius Togidubnus (the 'client king' of a local tribe, and ally of the Romans) as a monument to the conquest of Britain, and only incidentally as a practical facility. Another suggestion is that it was built originally as an army facility.[17]

There is no evidence of significant urban activity around the main complex when it was first erected. Buildings, streets and yards dating from the first and early second centuries are believed to have related merely to the running of the temple and baths. From the later second century onwards further development was under way. Open spaces were filled in, and some houses (with under floor

The main Roman drain, into which subsidiary drains emptied at intervals along its length; several Roman manholes gave access for maintenance work. The drain still carries water from the spring down to the river Avon, a few hundred metres away to the south.

PHOTOGRAPH: CARNEGIE, 2005

A detail of Savile's early seventeenth-century map of Bath showing the area to the south of the baths complex, with the outflow from the main hot spring running, via the horse bath, to the Avon.

BY COURTESY OF M. REYNOLDS, FOTOFORUM

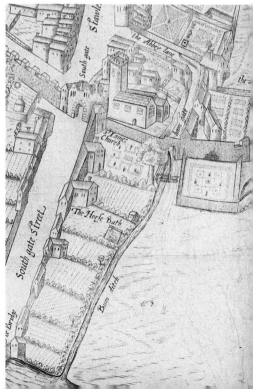

The so-called
Gorgon's head was
the centrepiece of
the pediment above
the Roman temple,
visible from the
temple precinct in
front of the sacred
spring, and clearly
of great symbolic
importance to the site.
As the mythological
Gorgon was female,
the association is
not straightforward.
With its beard and
sun-like hair, the head
obviously combines
different cultural
traditions which the
Romans thought useful
to acknowledge in this
important site.

PHOTOGRAPHS: CARNEGIE, 2004

These two figures
– Hercules Bibax and
Bacchus – stood on
either side of the main
Roman altar within the
temple precinct.

PHOTOGRAPHS: CARNEGIE, 2004

The tombstone of Lucius Vitellius Tancinus, a trooper of the Vettones cavalry regiment, who died, aged forty-six, after twenty-six years' military service. Found in the Roman cemetery along the Fosse Way north of Bath, it depicts a cavalryman trampling down an enemy.

heating and mosaic floors) were built in the central area. Shops and industry began to appear in the fourth century, when the temple precinct was partly built over. A pewter workshop existed beside the eastern boundary wall of the main baths, and a blacksmith's workshop occupied a nearby stone building.[18] This urban growth can be ascribed to the increasing popularity and wealth of the spa, which reached its peak in the late third and fourth centuries.

It is at Walcot, several hundred metres north of the hot springs, that evidence of occupation from the earliest Roman period has been found. A settlement had grown up near the river crossing by AD 50 and it spread along the road towards the springs, especially after c.AD 60. By around AD 100 there was apparently a thriving settlement at the top of Walcot Street and down by the river, with development along Walcot Street linking it at its southern end to the baths and temple complex, which were perhaps already enclosed with an earthen bank and ditch. There was both residential and industrial occupation in the Walcot area, between the street frontage and the river. Early timber structures were replaced over time by substantial masonry buildings, and good quality houses were intermingled with shops and workshops. Potters' kilns and blacksmiths' forges have also been found in Walcot.[19] By the third and fourth centuries the two sites of settlement had merged to form an urban area of about sixty acres.[20]

Within the central area, the temple of Sulis Minerva – with the sacred spring – was erected in an enclosed,

A large female head recovered from the cemetery area of Walcot, probably part of a tombstone. The woman is depicted wearing her hair in a mass of tight curls, a style that was fashionable in Rome in the late first century AD.

An altar dedicated to Loucetius Mars and Nemetona, put up by Peregrinus, a native of Trier, now in Germany.

BY COURTESY OF BATH AND NORTH EAST SOMERSET COUNCIL, ROMAN BATHS MUSEUM

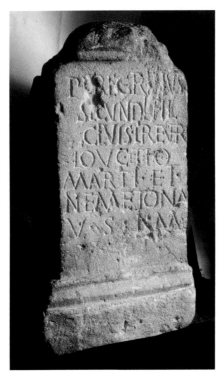

below A 'Bath curse'. Plaques of lead and pewter inscribed with messages and pleas to Sulis Minerva, usually asking the deity to punish enemies, were cast into the sacred spring by many pilgrims to the shrine. This is a good example of the type.

BY COURTESY OF BATH AND NORTH EAST SOMERSET COUNCIL, ROMAN BATHS MUSEUM

colonnaded courtyard. The main sacrificial altar was sited in the open air, in front of the temple, while many lesser altars lined the precinct. The baths lay to the south of the temple. The buildings were much modified over time, as the facilities were enlarged and improved. The Great Bath was lined with lead and fed with its supply of water from the main spring (the King's spring), which was contained within a reservoir wall and provided with an efficient sluice and drainage system. The water from the Great Bath passed on through a culvert to the Lucas Bath, from which waste water drained out into yet another bath. South-west of the main establishment (south of Beau Street) was another set of baths. These may have been associated with the healing god Aesculapius, who presided over the lesser springs that now feed the Hot Bath and the Cross Bath.[21]

The complex must have employed many people to ensure its maintenance and smooth running. The temple had its priests, augerers and lesser officials, while the baths needed administrators and numerous servants such as masseurs, perfumers,

'I CURSE HIM WHO HAS STOLEN MY HOODED CLOAK ... THAT THE GODDESS SULIS MAY AFFLICT HIM WITH MAXIMUM DEATH, AND NOT ALLOW HIM SLEEP OR CHILDREN NOW AND IN THE FUTURE, UNTIL HE HAS BROUGHT MY HOODED CLOAK TO THE TEMPLE OF DIVINITY.'

Light-weight box tiles were used in the construction of the main roof vault over the great Roman bath. Curved roof tiles on top of the box tiles formed an outer covering to protect the roof from the weather.

PHOTOGRAPH: CARNEGIE, 2005

anointers and general attendants. The visitors were a cosmopolitan crowd, coming from various parts of the empire as well as all parts of Britain. Most of them probably made a sacrifice to the goddess at the main altar, or one of the lesser ones, before moving on into the baths area. While many came to the spa because of the renowned curative properties of the waters, the bathing area was – as in later periods – something of a social scene. People met and talked, no doubt, and while some swam in the warm waters or enjoyed the 'Turkish' baths, others used the various sitting out places to view the bathing.

The sacred spring was the central focus of the religious cult and here many visitors cast votive offerings into the waters. Investigations in the 1870s exposed the Roman reservoir beneath the floor of the King's Bath and in the sludge and rubble that blocked it were found coins, jewels, pewter vessels, and two lead tablets (inscribed with a sharp metal point) which came to be known as 'Bath curses'. A larger haul was found in 1978 when the spa was closed for excavations following the death of a young girl from amoebal meningitis contracted from contaminated spring water. Deposits then yielded jewellery, over 12,000 coins of various origins, silver as well as pewter vessels, and more than 100 curse tablets. Most of the tablets were appeals to the goddess to return stolen property and punish the thief. Many seem to have been written to a formula in which the object stolen was identified, the curse elaborated and then (in some cases) a suspect named or a list of possible thieves given. Where no name or names were written it was customary to define the thief by a series of mutually exclusive pairs of alternatives, as in the curse of Docilianus: 'I curse him who has stolen my hooded cloak, whether man or women, whether slave or free, that the goddess Sulis may afflict him with maximum death, and not allow him sleep or children now and in the future, until he has brought my hooded cloak to the temple of her divinity'.[22]

That Docilianus appealed explicitly to Sulis (rather than the Roman deity Sulis Minerva) is a reminder that Celtic beliefs and traditions, inherited from the pre-Roman Iron Age, survived and flourished throughout the Roman occupation. Pagan worship continued for some years even

The altar tomb of Gaius Calpurnicus Receptus, found in the Roman cemetery at Bathwick in 1795. It reads: 'To the spirit of the departed, Gaius Calpurnius Receptus, priest of the goddess Sulis, lived 75 years; Calpurnius Trifosa, his freedwoman [and] wife had this set up.'

PHOTOGRAPH: CARNEGIE, 2005

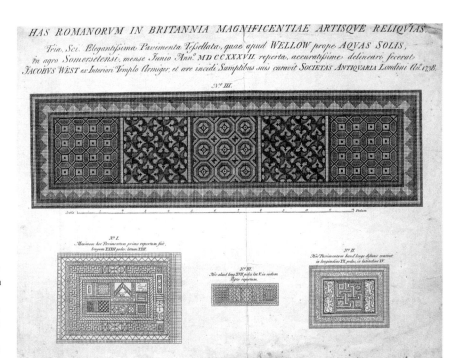

after Christianity had been established as the dominant religion, twenty years before Britain became independent of Rome in AD 410, and early Christians were not always fully committed to the new faith. Perhaps this was so with Annianus, who in the fourth century appealed to Sulis Minerva to retrieve six silver coins from an unknown thief 'whether pagan or Christian'. The wording suggests that Annianus was nominally a Christian, because 'pagans' did not refer to themselves as such.[23]

The inscription on the lead tablets give us some insight into the motives of those who visited the temple. Similarly, we can learn something of the residents of Aquae Sulis from inscriptions on monuments and tombs. Most of the funerary evidence comes from cemetery sites along Walcot Street, which can be explained by the fact that Roman law forbade adult burial within the walled area. Tombs of a stone-mason, an augerer and a sculptor have been found, but soldiers made up the largest group.

The most prestigious individual memorialized was a temple priest, Gaius Calpurnicus Receptus, who died aged seventy-five. His altar monument was discovered in what is now Sydney Gardens where it was erected by his wife, Calpurnis Trifosa, who had originally been his slave. The freeing of slaves is also recorded on two altars found within the temple precinct. They were both erected for a retired centurion, Marcus Aufidius Maximus, by two individuals both inscribed as 'his freed men'. A particularly poignant tombstone was seen c.1540 (built into the town walls) by the antiquarian John Leland. On this Vettius Romulus and Victoria Sabina had recorded the death of their daughter, Successa Petronia, aged three years, four months and nine days. In the Walcot cemetery area, the tombstone of Mercatilla, the eighteen-month-old foster daughter of Magnius, was found in 1909. It was here, too, that the young woman Vibia Jucunda, aged thirty, was buried.[24]

Some of the soldiers who died at Aquae Sulis may have been on active service, at the spa for 'rest and recreation', but others seem to have retired to the place after their careers had finished. It is likely that some were sick or wounded and came in hopes that prayers to Sulis Minerva, and the healing waters, would cure them. Perhaps this was the case with Julius Vitalis, an armourer of the Twentieth Legion who died after only nine years' service, aged twenty-nine. Vitalis belonged to a craft-guild and it was his comrades in the Guild of Armourers who paid for his cremation and tombstone.[25]

Whatever their motives for coming to Aquae Sulis, the visitors were important to the local economy. Roman Bath had special status as a spa and religious centre, and much of its wealth was dependent on its tourist trade. Yet, as in later ages, the dominant image of the city can divert attention from the realities of its diverse character.

Although Cirencester ranked higher than Bath in the hierarchy of regional urban centres, and Winchester was the main administrative centre, it is likely that Bath gained some administrative role after the early years of occupation. By the third century it was perhaps ruled by a town council, composed of a hundred ex-magistrates who had certain property qualifications.[26] The place they administered was best known as an international religious, medical and recreational centre but it also had other functions. It was a regional distribution centre for produce and goods from its hinterland, and it provided a local market for the sale or exchange of commodities. It was also in part an industrial centre. Small-scale manufacturing (such as glass working and the making of pewter vessels) was carried out within the walls, and at Lansdown.

Bath's hinterland was an agriculturally rich area, with the added advantage of mineral deposits within it or nearby. This may explain why the number of Roman villas around Bath is exceptionally high, the highest concentration in Britain.[27] There are some

ROMAN HOME COMFORTS

The Roman elite in Britain certainly enjoyed many home comforts. Just as in modern times when products such as Fortnum & Mason jams or Bovril are highly valued by expatriate Britons, so in the Roman period grapes, figs, coriander and spices were equally prized. Wine and olive oil were imported into Roman Britain from continental Europe; carpets came from Egypt; and silk and spices from the East. One important discovery on a Romano-British site at Bath in 1999 was of a peppercorn – the first to be found in Britain and only the third in the Roman world.

The Romans ate their meals from silver or pewter plates, or blue and amber glass bowls, using knives and spoons, with the table lit by candles or oil lamps. In their sleeping quarters, they had mirrors, box-wood combs, ointment jars and scent bottles, skin scrapers and manicure sets, pots of rouge, earrings and bracelets.

Pens and ink-wells were commonplace, as were dice and counters for playing games.

Sources: *Bath Chronicle*, 20 Nov. 2004; Christopher Hibbert, *The Story of England* (London: 1992), pp. 23–4.

left A nineteenth-century engraving of Roman inscriptions found at Bath.

thirty to forty villas within a 15–20km radius of Bath, yet few if any existed prior to *c*.270. One theory put forward to account for this is that opposition to the Roman conquest was so strong in the region that the lands of native peoples were confiscated as a punitive measure, and then administered as an imperial estate – perhaps with the villa at Combe Down (one of the few that predates 270) as the central administrative site. There is further conjecture that the sale of such an estate, in the latter half of the third century, would have made possible the foundation of a series of private estates, and the building of the villas for a wealthy farming class.

Most of the villas were country houses, which usually served as the centres of farmed estates, although the excavation of mosaics at Daniel Street and Norfolk Crescent (in Bath itself) suggests the presence of 'suburban' villas. They varied in size and luxuriousness, reflecting the relative wealth of the owners, but all were highly Romanised in their architectural detail and featured under-floor heating, mosaic floors and painted plaster. Those located at Box, Atworth, Wellow, Keynsham and Newton St Loe were exceptionally grand.[28]

Little is known of the form or extent of the estates around the villas, or the tenurial relationships between them, or between the villas and native farmsteads. Where two villas were sited in close proximity it is likely that one was a working farm and the other merely a country residence, perhaps maintained by town councillors or other dignitaries from Bath.[29] It is possible that a landlord based at one of the larger villas owned a number of 'satellite' villas, which contributed to the economy of the larger estate and may even have specialised in a particular type of farming.[30]

Cattle rearing, sheep farming and cereal production were the main activities in the mixed agrarian economy. Agriculture was the staple industry of Roman Britain but resources other than the fertile land were also exploited around Bath. The local stone was extracted in abundance (and used not only in Bath but in places as far distant as London), and this would have provided income for the

A mask made of tin which was found when the Roman reservoir and culvert were opened in 1878. Larger than life-size and originally backed with wood, the mask was probably used in the rites and ceremonies of the temple.

BY COURTESY OF BATH AND
NORTH EAST SOMERSET COUNCIL,
ROMAN BATHS MUSEUM

leaseholders or owners of the workings. In addition to its use as a general building material it was utilised in carved reliefs, friezes and roof finials, and also put to more functional use in gutters, tanks and coffins. Schools of craftsmen are thought to have existed, producing standard architectural 'blanks' for altars and tombs. A blank altar was found at Bathwick in 1900, with guide lines marked on it ready for inscription.[31]

Lead from the mines at Charterhouse on Mendip not only lined the Great Bath and formed the water pipes at the spa, but was also used – together with tin from Cornwall – in the manufacture of pewter. The pewter industry was particularly important in this region, located in Bath and at a major industrial village at Camerton, some 13kms (8 miles) south along the Fosse Way. The exploitation of outcrops of coal at places near Bath, such as at Priston and Newton St Loe, was another source of wealth. Nothing is known of how it was mined or traded but evidence for the use of coal is commonly found on local Roman sites. Heating the villas and the public buildings of Aquae Sulis must have required large quantities of fuel, and it also had a ritual function in the temple of Sulis Minerva, where it fuelled the perpetual fire at the main altar.[32]

The development under way in Aquae Sulis in the late third and fourth centuries, and the building of the villas, reflected an increase of prosperity throughout the province, which was especially apparent in the Bath area.[33]

ORIGINS
AND EARLY
HISTORY

A nineteenth-century photograph of the Great Bath, somewhat prosaically overlooked by the Billiard Rooms. Excavation of the baths began in the 1860s and by 1889 the Great Bath could be viewed by visitors.

PRIVATE COLLECTION, THE STAPLETON COLLECTION

Agriculture and industry flourished in the countryside while the spa reached its peak of popularity, but the fourth century was a time of ever-increasing danger as Britain faced growing threats from barbarian nations outside the Roman empire, and their allies in the native population of Britain.

The future of the spa itself became uncertain, for throughout the third and fourth centuries the sea level was rising and with it the water-table of the inland areas. This caused a series of floods, each one more severe than the last, in and around the baths and temple complex. Attempts were made to overcome the problem by raising the floor levels but because of recurring influxes of water, and the time spent clearing away mud and repairing damage, it is likely that there were periods of days or even weeks when the baths were out of use. The establishment was eventually abandoned altogether. Unrest throughout the empire made travel hazardous and this would have discouraged potential visitors to Aquae Sulis at this time. Another factor was the diminishing importance and attraction of the temple; Christianity spread and undermined pagan belief as the Roman occupation of Britain neared its end.[34]

The years AD 350–70 were a period of savage unrest. Several of the villas near Bath were attacked by piratical raiders from Ireland, who sailed up the Bristol Channel and on up the river Avon. Much of the destruction evident from this era has been attributed to the Barbarian Conspiracy of 367, when there were widespread and co-ordinated attacks on Britain. In the aftermath of these raids, urban defences were reinforced throughout the province and it may be that the wall around the central area of Bath was built at this late stage of the Roman occupation.[35]

Bath may well have been one of the major cities that petitioned the Emperor Honorius in 410 for protection, only to be told that they must look to their own defence.[36] It is likely that Bath raised its own defensive force, as many towns did in the absence of protection from the remnants of the Roman army still in Britain. The long occupation was now effectively over. A dark age was to follow, here as elsewhere, but Bath survived as a place of settlement and developed into a monastic centre in Saxon times.

Sub-Roman and Saxon Bath

Between the collapse of the Roman empire in the early fifth century and the arrival of the Saxons little is known of Bath's history. The walled area continued to be occupied but the baths, the temple and other public buildings fell into ruin. An Anglo-Saxon poem, written in the eighth or even seventh century and known as 'The Ruin',[37] is believed to refer to sub-Roman Bath although it does not name the place it describes. The poem makes specific reference to 'the hot flood of the baths', and it continues, 'wondrous is this masonry, shattered by the Fates . . . the buildings raised by giants are crumbling . . . the walls are rent and broken away, and have fallen undermined by age.' This poetic vision of the decayed city is supported by archaeological evidence, but such evidence also makes it clear that

Aquae Sulis was certainly not deserted after the Roman departure from Britain in 410.[38]

Timber buildings and stone floors were being erected in the vicinity of the springs well into the fifth century and there is evidence of continued activity around the springs and in the general baths area. The east and west baths seem to have been linked in some way, judging by 'wear patterns' between them along the walkways; Peter Davenport has suggested they might have been converted into accommodation in the fifth and sixth centuries, or that perhaps they were still partly in use as 'very reduced baths'.[39]

According to the *Anglo-Saxon Chronicle* (not an entirely reliable source), Bath was a city of sorts in the sixth century ruled over by a king. Saxon invaders swept over large parts of lowland Britain within decades of the Roman departure, and in the later part of the sixth century they began to expand their territory. They are said to have triumphed over the native British in a battle at Dyrham (10km north of Bath) in 577, when they killed three kings and captured three cities, including Bath. Whatever the accuracy or otherwise of this account, Bath thereafter came under Saxon rule. It changed hands from Wessex, kingdom of the west Saxons, to the kingdom of Mercia, and then back again; from the early tenth century Wessex and Mercia were united.

The Dyrham battle and its consequences may be the historical context in which Wansdyke was constructed. This is one of England's most impressive earthworks but its function and date have long been disputed. It was once considered to have run from Portbury or Dundry, near Bristol, to Bath, on into Wiltshire and eastward through the Savernake Forest almost to the river Kennet near Hungerford. More recently it has been recognised as two separate earthworks. The west Wansdyke ('Woden's dyke', named after a Saxon deity) ran along the high ground just south of the Avon valley, from Bath to Dundry Hill, near Bristol.

Wansdyke was a Roman-style ditch and bank with a timber facing and palisade. It might have been constructed as a boundary marker but it is more likely that it was built for defensive purposes. Where a ditch and bank exist together, the ditch is on the northern side – which indicates that it was intended to defend an area to the south. Some authorities consider it to be a boundary marker delineating areas controlled by Saxons and Britons after 577, while others have argued that it could be an earlier British defensive line, named by the Saxons who had no knowledge of its construction. Another and more plausible explanation is that Wansdyke formed part of the west Saxon defences against advancing Mercia forces from the midland regions, after a battle at Cirencester in 628.

The invading Saxons were not adherents to the Christian faith. Militant Christianity was triumphant in the final stages of the Roman occupation, having been recognised in the last twenty years of empire rule as the dominant religion, and in the aftermath of empire it seems that Bath adopted a religiously neutral name to obscure its Roman pagan title. It was known for a brief period as Aquaemann, the Old Welsh *mann* (meaning 'place') being added to the familiar

A plan and perspective drawing of the Roman baths, discovered in 1755 when the Abbot's House was demolished to make way for a new suite of baths. This drawing was made by the Bath artist William Hoare in that year, and described by him in a letter of 1762: 'my Plan and View of the Roman Baths in the state they appeared when first discovered, to which is added part of the south side of the Abbey to shew [sic] their Situation. In the Perspective View [you] will see in a Room adorned with Corinthian Pilasters an Oblong Bath with its Area and Descent by Steps and contiguous to it a smaller semicircular Bath with a descent of six very high steps ... but extremely wore [sic] by the foot. In the shaded part A is the spring and channel of the water. The other large Room has two Ludatories belonging to it, with tessellated Pavements ... In the middle between these is the Fireplace and Flue for heating the Rooms. The Floor is suspended on Pillars of square Brick, as in the drawing beneath the Plan at B. C shews [sic] the manner of the Ludatorys [sic], with their tabulated Bricks, which were continued up and long all the walls of the Room. Near one of the Ludatories the Floor is broke up to show its construction.'

'Aquae'.[40] Another name from the Saxon period is Akemannceaster, which implies that the healing potential of the waters was well known even though they were not vigorously promoted at this time.

Christianity probably survived the Saxon victory in areas held by native Britons but it does not seem to have done so around Bath, after the region was captured by the invading immigrants in 577. The faith was again established in Bath after the missionary work of St Augustine and his successors, especially through the conversion of Saxon kings, whose subordinates generally followed their example.[41]

In 675–6 Osric, king of the Hwiccas (a sub-kingdom of Mercia) granted land adjoining 'Hat Bathu', as the Saxons came to call it, to the Abbess Berta or Bertana for the founding of a nunnery. The convent's subsequent history is unknown. It may have been a 'double house', in which two communities, one male and one female, lived under one rule and one leader, usually an abbess, on the same site but strictly segregated in different parts.[42] This was not uncommon, but it sometimes happened – often after the death of an abbess – that the female side dwindled away and so what had been a double house became a male-only monastery. The monastery of St Peter may have originated in this way, as the convent disappears from the written record and there are no records of the foundation of the monastery, but in a charter of 757 Offa, king of Mercia, granted land to 'the brethren of the monastery of St Peter at Bath'. According to *The Golden Legend* (a life of the saints printed by Caxton) it was Alphege, who tradition says was born at Weston, Bath, in 953, who 'bylded ther that fayreabbaye at Bath, and endowed it, and was himself therein first abbot and founder', but this was evidently not so.[43] The Saxon abbey was one of the greatest churches in England, of such prestige that it was chosen as the place for the coronation in 973 of the first king of all England, King Edgar, but Alphege was not appointed abbot of the monastery until two years later, in 975. He may well have carried out extensions and improvements to the building.

The location of the Saxon abbey is uncertain but it might have stood on the site of the modern abbey. Another possibility is that the abbey church may be represented by the Saxon church of St James that stood west of the Abbey Green until 1279, when it was demolished and converted into the bishop's private chapel.[44] Apart from the abbey church itself there was probably a group of cells for the priests and some communal buildings.[45]

Excavations south of the abbey in 1993 unearthed complete skeletons and other bones representing thirty-three individuals, in a cemetery clearly associated with the Saxon abbey. These finds tell us something about the monastic inmates. Analysis of the bones identified an age range from seventeen to forty-five or older at the time of death. The five males whose height could be calculated were from 5ft 6½ins (168.3cm) to 6ft ¼ins (183.6cm), which suggests that

A fragment of sculpture from the Norman abbey, now on display in the Abbey Vaults. It depicts a Christian martyr suffering on the rack.

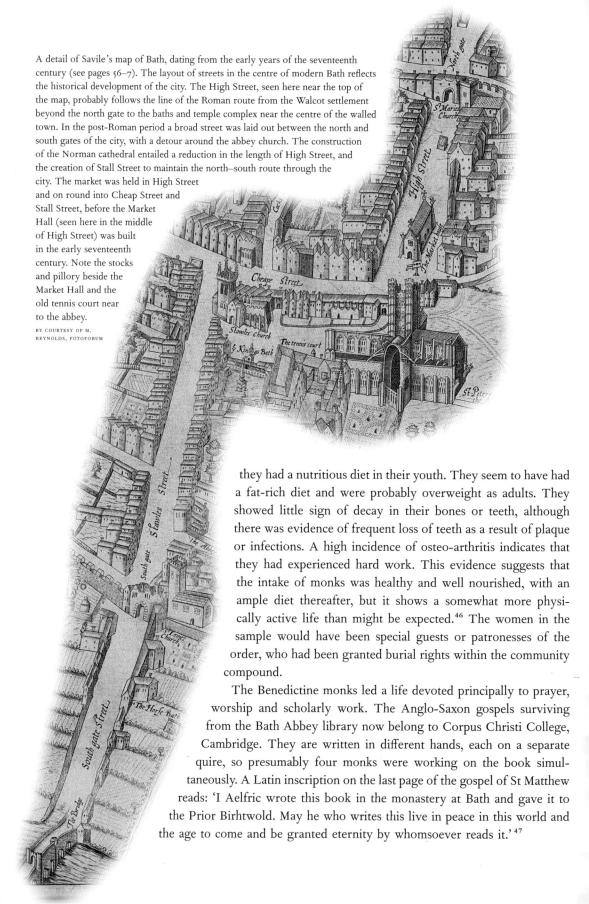

A detail of Savile's map of Bath, dating from the early years of the seventeenth century (see pages 56–7). The layout of streets in the centre of modern Bath reflects the historical development of the city. The High Street, seen here near the top of the map, probably follows the line of the Roman route from the Walcot settlement beyond the north gate to the baths and temple complex near the centre of the walled town. In the post-Roman period a broad street was laid out between the north and south gates of the city, with a detour around the abbey church. The construction of the Norman cathedral entailed a reduction in the length of High Street, and the creation of Stall Street to maintain the north–south route through the city. The market was held in High Street and on round into Cheap Street and Stall Street, before the Market Hall (seen here in the middle of High Street) was built in the early seventeenth century. Note the stocks and pillory beside the Market Hall and the old tennis court near to the abbey.

BY COURTESY OF M. REYNOLDS, FOTOFORUM

they had a nutritious diet in their youth. They seem to have had a fat-rich diet and were probably overweight as adults. They showed little sign of decay in their bones or teeth, although there was evidence of frequent loss of teeth as a result of plaque or infections. A high incidence of osteo-arthritis indicates that they had experienced hard work. This evidence suggests that the intake of monks was healthy and well nourished, with an ample diet thereafter, but it shows a somewhat more physically active life than might be expected.[46] The women in the sample would have been special guests or patronesses of the order, who had been granted burial rights within the community compound.

The Benedictine monks led a life devoted principally to prayer, worship and scholarly work. The Anglo-Saxon gospels surviving from the Bath Abbey library now belong to Corpus Christi College, Cambridge. They are written in different hands, each on a separate quire, so presumably four monks were working on the book simultaneously. A Latin inscription on the last page of the gospel of St Matthew reads: 'I Aelfric wrote this book in the monastery at Bath and gave it to the Prior Birhtwold. May he who writes this live in peace in this world and the age to come and be granted eternity by whomsoever reads it.'[47]

Bath was at this time essentially a monastic settlement with a modest set of baths, but still retaining some market function. As the fame of its abbey grew it also developed in other ways. It may have become a 'burh' or fortified place during the ninth century, as part of the defence of Wessex against Danish raiders. This was during the reign of King Alfred the Great, remembered for burning some cakes during the time he spent in refuge in the Somerset marshes, after being overwhelmed by Viking marauders at Chippenham, Wiltshire, in January 878. Using earth and timber was the quickest way to achieve some security for urban centres and at Bath a timber barricade (apparently Saxon) was found outside and parallel to the northern city wall in 1980. Within its shelter the stone wall could have been repaired, with less urgency. Roman ruins still littered parts of Bath and it was perhaps at this time that chunks of Roman carving were utilised in reinforcing the upper part of the city walls.[48]

Roman ruins were not much in evidence thereafter because Alfred and his son undertook a major reorganisation of Bath. The town was laid out with a broad street running between the north and south gates, though it had to make a detour around the abbey. The market was housed in this street – High Street – from

A reminder of Bath's glorious Roman past: a figure overlooking the baths. Bath's Roman heritage has been exploited commercially ever since the late nineteenth century when the Roman antiquities were incorporated into the Grand Pump Room extension scheme to form the Roman Baths Museum. The Great Bath itself was then enclosed in a Tuscan colonnade and terrace with statues on the parapet depicting eight Roman emperors and generals associated with Britain in some way (Julius Caesar, Claudius, Hadrian, Constantine, Vespasian; Ostorius Scapula, Paulinus (the defeater of Boudicca) and Agricola).

BY COURTESY OF BATH AND NORTH EAST SOMERSET COUNCIL, ROMAN BATHS MUSEUM

35

A piece of figurative sculpture from a screen which covered a wall behind the high altar in the Norman abbey. It dates from about 1140.

which lanes ran out to join a street circling the city, to give easy access for those defending the walls. Westgate Street was part of another important thoroughfare. It probably continued eastwards to the East or Lot gate, which led out to the town mill. The eastern stretch of Westgate Street is the modern-day Cheap Street, which is not an Anglo-Saxon name, despite the fact that the Old English *ceap* means 'market'. Before 1399 this was Sutor (shoemakers') Street. The burh of Bath gained even more importance in the early tenth century when a local mint was established. This gave Bath the status of a 'port'. Mints were confined to ports, which were market towns (both coastal and inland) and virtually synonymous with burhs but their importance rested on their trading functions, supported by the mint. It was intended that all buying and selling should be restricted to ports, where it would be witnessed by a royal official known as a reeve or portreeve. The first reeve of Bath was one Alfred, whose death in 906 was recorded in the *Anglo-Saxon Chronicle*, which suggests that Bath was a notable place.[49]

Coins from the Bath mint have been found at places in Scandinavia, perhaps taken there as part of the Danegeld – the tax imposed to raise funds with which to buy off the raiders, though all too often they simply took the money but then came back to demand more. By the later tenth century, Viking raids and campaigns were becoming increasingly troublesome and the *Anglo-Saxon Chronicle* tells us that in 1013 Sweyn Forkbeard, King of Denmark, conquered a large part of eastern England. He was crowned king of England after Ethelred (the 'Unready') fled to Normandy leaving London surrounded by Danish forces. Forkbeard then marched on to Bath where the regional governor of Wessex and the western thanes 'all bowed to Sweyn and gave hostages'.[50] The *Chronicle* gives no account of fighting in or near Bath but there is archaeological evidence of some Viking presence. A Scandinavian type of sword dateable to the late tenth / early eleventh century was found at Upper Borough Walls during excavations in 1980 and there exists in southern Sweden an eleventh-century stone inscribed in runes which reads, 'Gunkel set this stone in memory of Gunnar, his father, Rode's son. Helgi laid him, his brother, in a stone coffin in England, Bath'.[51]

> 'GUNKEL SET THE STONE IN MEMORY OF GUNNAR, HIS FATHER, RODE'S SON. HELGI LAID HIM, HIS BROTHER, IN A STONE COFFIN IN ENGLAND, BATH.'

It seems that Bath was only marginally affected by Viking raids and similarly the Norman conquest of England in 1066 made little immediate local impact. Nonetheless, Bath under Norman rule was about to undergo another change of image and function.

Norman Conquest to 1700 |

MEDIEVAL Bath was renowned as a cathedral city which attracted many pilgrims to its healing waters, but it also developed as a major urban centre of the woollen industry. Its prosperity came to rest essentially on the wool trade, until a gradual decline of this industry set in from the fifteenth century onwards. There was a growth of interest in spa treatments during the late sixteenth century, and this prompted renewed enthusiasm in Bath for commercial exploitation of the hot springs. By the end of the seventeenth century the baths were once again making a significant contribution to the wealth of the city. Meanwhile, the citizens acquired full control over their affairs, after the dissolution of the monasteries in the 1530s. The changes that followed from that event, and the rights granted to the city in a charter of 1590, were to influence aspects of life in Bath for centuries to come.

The Abbey and Abbey Churchyard, 1750. The houses in Wade's Passage were cleared away in 1825–35. The abbey dominated Bath in its medieval history.

It was the largest building by far, and its physical presence was matched by the power which the ecclesiastical authorities held over the citizens.

THE ABBEY CHURCH, BATH, 1750.
Published by H. George, Bookseller, Orange Grove. From an Original Drawing.

The Abbey Church and Orange Grove, c.1830. The Grove was the churchyard of the priory until its dissolution in the sixteenth century, but then it became an open space used for recreation and, in the eighteenth century, a fashionable shopping area.

BY COURTESY OF BATH CENTRAL LIBRARY, BATH & NORTH EAST SOMERSET COUNCIL

Cathedral city and woollen centre

Saxon Bath did not come to an abrupt end with the Norman conquest of 1066. The religious elite who dominated the city was left undisturbed, and the monastic authorities retained their land and properties. By the time of the Domesday survey in 1086 the estimated population had reached just under 1,000. Bath paid £60 and one mark of gold in taxation, considerably less than Taunton (£154) but above all other towns in Somerset.[1] The mint and some local estates, which had been held by the dowager queen Edith until her death in 1075, were now possessions of the crown. In 1087 both the Saxon abbot of the monastery and William the Conqueror died, events which marked the end of the Saxon era in Bath.

The royal estates and the strategic importance of the city's location on a river crossing attracted the unwelcome attention of armed insurrectionists in 1088, when Bath was burned and pillaged in a short-lived rebellion against the accession to the throne of William Rufus. The city was virtually destroyed

JOHN DE VILLULA OF TOURS

John de Villula (d. 1122) came from Tours in France and was commonly known as John of Tours. He was a friend as well as servant to William Rufus, and his personal physician. He is said to have bought the burnt city from William for £500. He enjoyed the company of learned men and found the English-speaking monks at Bath slow-witted dullards, which may explain why he confiscated the property of the monastery until he had assembled a new body of monks and in 1106 gave back what he had taken. He died in old age on 29 December 1122, having been suddenly seized with a pain in his heart after eating his Christmas dinner. He was buried in the presbytery of his church in Bath.

Source: *Oxford DNB* (2004), vol. 55, p. 89.

by the rebels, but once William Rufus had secured his accession he appointed John de Villula of Tours as Bishop of Wells, following the death of the Saxon incumbent, Bishop Giso.

Bath abbey came within the jurisdiction of the Bishop of Wells, but soon after his appointment John of Tours petitioned to move the see from Wells. In 1091 he was granted the city of Bath, 'that he may, with the greater honour, fix his pontifical seat there'. Bishop John became the *ex officio* abbot, although the prior took responsibility for the day to day running of the abbey. For the rest of the Middle Ages the abbey was officially a cathedral priory.[2]

The Bishop shared the Normans' disdain for all things English and considered the Saxon monks both boorish and ignorant. He took all the abbey lands and income for the see, although they were nominally separate from the bishopric, and he appointed Norman or French officials as the opportunity arose. A fellow Frenchman was installed as prior.[3]

Plans for major redevelopment in the city were soon under way. They centred on the construction of a new church, of such an enormous size that the whole of the present-day abbey would have fitted into its nave. The plans also included cloisters, a chapter house, prior's lodgings and a bishop's palace. In addition to all this, John of Tours established a collegiate school in Bath, at which the renowned medieval scholar Adelard was educated.

Implementing this building programme may have been made easier than it might have been by the devastation of large parts of the urban centre in the 1088 insurrection, but it seems likely that numerous properties were cleared of tenants to provide space for the Norman priory. The whole complex of buildings, set in gardens and orchards, surrounded by its own walls and gates, eventually came to occupy most of the south-east quarter of Bath. The Norman cathedral priory is estimated to have taken up almost twice as much land as the Saxon abbey precinct.

Topographical evidence suggests that the High Street was reduced by half its length (to its modern size), and at least one other street was closed to extend the old abbey close. A new street, Stall Street, was laid out to restore the north–south route across the city.[4] Rentable space along Stall Street provided more income for Bishop John, who needed every penny he could raise to meet the capital costs of his ambitious scheme. It was only with some difficulty that he managed to fund the project in his lifetime. He had acquired estates in Claverton (the deer park that later became the eighteenth-century Prior Park) that produced the necessary stone, and his income as lord of the city was largely devoted to the cause, but he and his successors also used funds that rightly belonged to the monks. Benefactors were encouraged to donate generously to the building fund, 'wooed by offers of spiritual rewards'.[5]

In 1106 King Henry I visited and stayed in the city. Bishop John evidently made the most of this encounter and obtained not only confirmation of his rights to the revenues of the city, but also a right to hold a fair on the feast of St Peter.

A carved head from the Norman abbey, recovered from excavations.
PHOTOGRAPH: CARNEGIE, 2005

The Christian martyr depicted on capitals from the early abbey may represent St Vincent or perhaps St Lawrence or St Bartholomew. The capitals were carved in the early twelfth century.

The fair would produce more income, from tolls and fines, and it was perhaps this new source of revenue that made it possible (and more politic) to return the income from the abbey to the priory,[6] which the bishop did at this time.

Building the Norman cathedral city was a lengthy process. Construction may have been under way in the late 1090s but the cathedral was far from completed by 1122, when John of Tours died. He was buried in front of the high altar, which suggests that work started at the east end. The Saxon abbey was perhaps retained until the new presbytery was ready to be used for religious services. Under Bishop John's successor, Bishop Godfrey (1123–35), building progressed steadily. Godfrey's successor, Robert of Lewes (1136–66), built the cloisters, chapter house, refectory, dormitory and other parts of the complex. The cathedral itself may have been completed by 1156.[7] It survived until the early sixteenth century, albeit in an increasingly dilapidated state. Maintenance costs would have been enormous and may have been so onerous that they could account for the deterioration of the building in the middle ages.[8]

All that remains visible of the great Norman church. These pillar bases can be seen through a viewing grille on the floor of the St Alphege Chapel, just north of the chancel.

John of Tours was a physician as well as an ordained priest. He had been court doctor to William Rufus at one time and he seems to have taken a particular interest in the curative powers of the Bath waters. He is credited with clearing the Roman ruins around the main spring and building a new bath, now known as the King's Bath. Leland claims there was another bath existing when he visited the city (c.1540), known as the Prior's Bath, 'in which there be no springs'. This bath was probably in the prior's lodgings, supplied by water percolating through the silted Roman Great Bath and its drainage system.[9]

The baths were under the jurisdiction of the bishop, although they were administered by the prior. No claims for miraculous cures were made but Bath was again becoming famous as a centre for healing: in the twelfth-century *Gesta Stephani* it was noted that 'sick persons from all over England go there to bathe in the healing waters, as well as the healthy, who go to see the wonderful outpourings of water and bathe in them'.[10] What John of Tours created was a Christian version of Aquae Sulis, which had flourished as a combined spa and religious centre. As a result, from Norman times to the end of the fifteenth

The pediment of the Guildhall with the city arms surmounted by a statue of Justice (not blindfolded as commonly depicted). The earliest Guildhall in Bath was situated to the east of the present site (see page 00), but by the 1620s it had been relocated to the upper storey of the Market House in the middle of High Street. By the mid eighteenth century this had become inadequate, and its island site obstructed by traffic, so the corporation resolved to build a new one 'in a more commodious place'. As well as a council chamber, mayor's parlour, banqueting hall, public rooms and the town clerk's office, the Guildhall housed a sessions court, jury room and police cells. The court was in use until the 1980s when the new Magistrates' Courts opened in North Parade Road. The present Guildhall was built between 1775 and 1779 by Thomas Baldwin, and the central dome and extensions to the north and south were added in the 1890s. The banqueting room is a particularly fine example of an Adam-style interior.

PHOTOGRAPH: CARNEGIE, 2005

century, Bath was best known as a cathedral city, controlled by the ecclesiastical authorities. Its prosperity was closely linked to the appeal of its curative waters and to increasing pilgrimage to the city.

Nonetheless, medieval Bath had other functions. Beneath the dominant image of a healing and holy city lay different realities. Despite the dominance of the Church, the secular community was beginning to acquire power through the formation of guilds, which originated in the twelfth century. The term 'guild' was used loosely in the Middle Ages, to mean any kind of urban, religious or craft organisation, although all guilds had religious affiliations and some were almost entirely religious in purpose. Craft guilds or 'companies' of clothiers, weavers, tailors, shoemakers (and lesser ones of plasterers, masons, joiners, mercers, glovers, upholsterers, butchers and bakers) emerged in later times,[11]

The Montague family crest on the great west doors of the abbey. They were given to the abbey by Sir Henry Montague, Lord Chief Justice, in 1618, in memory of two of his brothers. Another of Sir Henry's brothers was Bishop Montague, whose effigy can be seen in the abbey (see the photograph on page 52).

PHOTOGRAPH: CARNEGIE, 2005

but the original guild in Bath was a society of merchants, entrepreneurs, traders and money men. The cloth trade was the basis of their commerce but it was wealth and power, not a specific trade in itself, that gained membership of the guild.[12] The terms 'guildhall' and 'guildsmen' came to be symbolic of town government more generally. The earliest municipal charter held in Bath Record Office was granted to the merchant guildsmen of Bath by Richard I, 'the Lionheart', in 1189. The charter gave the guildsmen the right to trade unhindered and free from certain taxes, and the guild itself soon became a firmly established institution with its charter (confirmed by Henry III in 1246), its seal, its scrivener, and the power of witnessing deeds. The first written evidence of the existence of a guildhall, where the guildsmen met to conduct their affairs, is in a document of 1355, which refers to 'the appointment of the mayor in the "Gyldhalle" ...' (The medieval Guildhall is believed to have been sited immediately behind the modern building.)[13]

Considerable power still lay with the ecclesiastical authorities, but the citizens demonstrated a growing independence of spirit, both individually and collectively. In 1256 David de Berewyk, and his son William, successfully challenged the prior's denial of pasture rights on land south of the city and the 'commonality', or citizens together, challenged the Bishop in 1260 over common rights on Kingsmead. A jury reported to a royal enquiry in 1274–76 that the prior was unlawfully acting as patron of Walcot church and, furthermore, that he had allowed the king's lodgings in the priory to fall into disrepair.[14] Yet another complaint against the prior was that he 'had made with stones from the [city] walls a causeway' from the south gate to the Monks' Mill. (Carrying off stones from the walls was a common offence perpetrated by millers and a host of other small offenders.)[15]

The power struggle took a somewhat farcical turn in the early fifteenth century. It was customary for the cathedral bell to sound out the start of the

Parish boundary markers on the corner of Trim Street and Upper Borough Walls, believed to date from the eighteenth century. The letters stand for 'St Michael's Parish' and 'St Peter and Paul's Parish', the parish of the abbey.

PHOTOGRAPH: CARNEGIE, 2005

day at dawn and also the end of day curfew, when business ceased and the city gates were closed. In 1408 the townsfolk took to ringing their own bells, in the parish churches, later than that of the cathedral in the evening and earlier in the morning. This symbolic challenge to the authority of the Church was strongly resisted. The dispute went to court in 1412 but the case dragged on until 1421, when judgement went in favour of the Church.[16]

Even though the cathedral precinct physically dominated the urban area, and the clergy still had much authority over the people, Bath was more than just a cathedral city. It was also a local and regional market centre, whose economy was ever more dependent on the wool trade and the cloth industry. The earliest references to cloth manufacturers in Bath refer to 'Aylmer the Weaver', who died in 1290, and 'William the Clothmonger' in 1292, but there is archaeological evidence to show that cloth making in the city goes back to late Saxon times.[17]

The priory owned Monks' Mill (on the Avon below the later Pulteney Bridge), which was both a tucking or fulling mill and a grist mill. In the fourteenth century the priory was purchasing wool in industrial quantities, which must

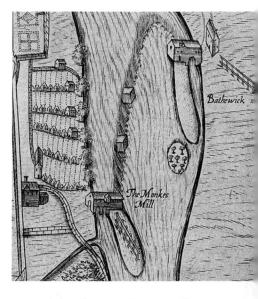

have been for spinning and weaving into cloth, although it is assumed that these processes were carried out by others rather than by the monks themselves. Prior Thomas Crist, 1332–40 (whose relative, Roger Crist, was twice mayor of Bath), bought over 900 sacks of wool from suppliers in Wiltshire in 1334.[18] Men like Alexander Dyer, mayor of Bath four times from 1332 to 1346,[19] grew rich on the woollen cloth industry, and most of the skilled workers in Bath

Two watermills are known to have taken advantage of the weired river Avon at this point near the east gate of the city: Monks' Mill and Bathwick Mill. The weir still exists below the later Pulteney Bridge, although all traces of the mills have disappeared.

BY COURTESY OF M. REYNOLDS, FOTOFORUM

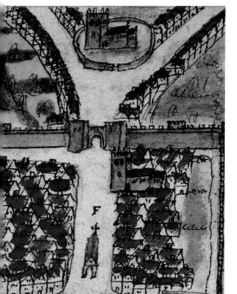

This detail from Smith's map of 1588 shows the parish church of St Michael Without just outside the city gate on the corner of Broad Street and Walcot Street. Within the gate stands the parish church of St Mary. The late Tudor market hall can be seen, but Smith's depiction of the houses is rather too sketchy to be able to identify which building was the Guildhall.

BRITISH LIBRARY

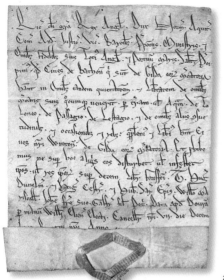

The charter of 1189, granted by Richard I, gave the guildsmen rights and powers as a body independent of the church. This marked the beginning of the emergence of a system of civic government. The charter was sealed at Dover in December 1189, a few days before the Lionheart sailed away to the Crusades.

PHOTOGRAPH: CARNEGIE, BY COURTESY OF BATH RECORD OFFICE

were engaged in the wool trade. Poll tax returns from the late fourteenth century (which suggest a total population between 1,000 and 1,100) show labourers and servants predominating among the 328 individuals whose occupations were listed, but workers in the textile industry accounted for the majority of the 106 craftsmen and tradesmen.[20]

Others were engaged in the manufacture, on a small domestic scale, of various objects made from horn and bone, and a wide range of leather goods. Excavations of rubbish pits have provided evidence of these activities, while tanners and skinners appear in several deeds and poll tax returns in the thirteenth and fourteenth centuries. Carpenters, masons and plasterers feature rarely in early records, but the churchwardens' accounts for St Michael Without (which survive, with some gaps, from *c.*1460 to the mid-sixteenth century) show that men in these trades were employed almost continuously on repairing the investment properties of the Church.[21]

The markets and fairs were also important to the local economy, bringing more trade and commerce to the city and drawing in people from the surrounding region. The market was held twice weekly, on Wednesdays and Saturdays. At least by the fifteenth century, a high cross stood in Northgate Street (the present High Street), which had become the traditional market site.[22] Stalls and booths lined the street, and on round the priory precinct into Stall Street. Cloth was sold at the markets as well as foodstuffs and household items, and the corner of Westgate Street and Stall Street was the designated corn market. For some years from 1318 the annual Cherry Fair was held from 28 July to 6 August, and another

left 'Let an olive establish the crown and a king restore the church', a dream which Bishop King interpreted as a divine message to undertake the restoration of the Norman building. This representation of the bishop's dream is on the west front of the abbey.

PHOTOGRAPH: CARNEGIE, 2004

right Statues on the west front of Bath Abbey depicting St Peter (*left*) and St Paul.

PHOTOGRAPH: CARNEGIE, 2004

annual event was the sheep fair outside Northgate, along Walcot Street.[23] There is little evidence of trade with Bristol (whether or not the river was navigable at this time is a matter of debate) but coal came into the city from the mining villages of north-east Somerset and much of the cloth woven in places such as Freshford, Wellow, or the industrial village of Twiverton-on-Avon (Twerton), was finished in Bath. One of the city's dyers, Ralph Hunt, complained to the authorities in 1405 about the theft of ten yards of blue cloth, stolen from the rack on which he had left it stretched on tenterhooks to dry.[24] For much of the fourteenth and fifteenth centuries Bath existed as a small, moderately prosperous wool town. It was of diminishing importance as a religious centre by then, and the priory was experiencing financial and other difficulties.

The priory owned considerable lands and property but its estates did not generate enough income to meet its needs, and some degree of mismanagement exacerbated the problem. By 1300 the priory estates spread across parts of Somerset, south Gloucestershire, Devon, Hampshire and Wiltshire. In addition, there were estates in Ireland. These were a constant source of trouble. The priories of Waterford and Cork were falling into ruins, and the warden to the Irish estates, Thomas Foxcote, was misusing what little income they generated. In 1334 the Bath priory obtained licence to exchange its Irish estates for lands in England, but the enactment was never effectively carried through and the difficulties continued up to the dissolution. A succession of priors, faced with mounting debts, were forced to borrow money. They obtained loans from local merchants, but also from Italian bankers. Prior Crist (1332–40) owed more than £700, which was a staggeringly large amount at the time.[25]

Prior Crist's successor, John de Iford (1340–59), took over at a crucial time, when economies and careful financial management were needed, but instead of pursuing such policies, de Iford used priory funds to provide for his relatives and friends. He was the

Statue of Henry VII in pride of place at the centre of the west front of the abbey. The king had visited Bath, with its 'ruinous church' in 1496 and again in 1497. He appointed his secretary, Oliver King, as Bishop of Bath and Wells, in 1496.
PHOTOGRAPH: CARNEGIE, 2005

Bishop Oliver King (d. 1503) was a native of London, educated at Eton and Cambridge. He combined an ecclesiastical career with royal service to several monarchs, and was sent to the Tower of London by Richard III in 1483 but reinstated in his office as secretary by Henry VII in 1485. He became Bishop of Bath and Wells in 1495 and first visited Bath in 1499. By then the abbey church was in ruins. While in the city the Bishop had a dream or vision in which he saw the Holy Trinity and a ladder with angels ascending and descending, and at the foot an olive tree supporting a crown. He heard a voice saying 'Let an olive establish the crown, and a king restore the church', which he interpreted as a divine instruction to rebuild the abbey. The ladder and angels of his dream can still be seen on the west front of the abbey, which Daniel Defoe condemned as 'almost blasphemously decorated ... the work of superstition'. John Wood later remonstrated that the flock of angels on each ladder looked like 'so many bats clung against the wall.'

Source: *Oxford DNB* (2004), vol. 31, pp. 653–4; Wroughton, *Stuart Bath*, p. 168.

cause of scandal in 1346, when he was summoned before the bishop's court on a charge of adultery with Agnes Cubbel at Hamswell, the priory's manor in Gloucestershire. Although found guilty, Prior John de Iford seems to have stayed in office – perhaps being reinstated after a brief period of suspension.[26]

Prior John may have retained his post because of a shortage of other candidates, as a result of the Black Death. This awful plague first broke out in 1348 (affecting almost all of Europe) and in 1352, with further outbreaks in 1360–62 and 1369. In Britain the main effects were felt in 1348–49, when an estimated one third or more of the total population died as a result of the epidemic. What impact it had on Bath is not known in detail but by 1377 the number of monks in the Bath priory had fallen to barely half the thirty recorded a few years before the Black Death.

The priory became poorly maintained and the monks undisciplined, as Bishop Oliver King found when he visited in 1499. There was feasting in the refectory, the monks were idle and women were often seen at 'unseemly times' in the monastery precinct.[27] Bath was gradually superseded by Wells as a focus of religious life (after the Somerset bishopric was made a joint see in the late thirteenth century) and the Norman abbey degenerated into a ruinous state.

'OF CLOTH-MAKING SHE HADD SWITCH AN HAUNT, SHE PASSED HEM OF YPRES AND OF GAUNT.'

CHAUCER, WIFE OF BATH

Bishop King decreed that this must be rectified and ordered that the running costs of the priory be reduced to pay for repairs. It was virtually a new abbey that began to be erected on the site – a building that was still incomplete in 1535.

Religious pilgrims and the sick in search of a cure still contributed to the local economy at the end of the fifteenth century, but Bath's prosperity rested fundamentally on the wool trade, on its weekly cattle and produce market, and on its three annual fairs. Chaucer's *Wife of Bath* was representative of the town's inhabitants in her occupation, if not in her enthusiasm for taking husbands. Her skill at weaving was such that 'of cloth-making she hadde switch an haunt, she passed hem of Ypres and of Gaunt'.

Change and continuity in the early modern period

It was between 1500 and 1700, centuries of political conflict and social upheaval in England, that power and authority came to be vested wholly in the corporate body. The dissolution of the monasteries in the 1530s was of particular significance for the city's future. Dominated by the medieval priory, Bath had relatively few resident gentry, and unlike other towns did not have a single great local family. The dissolution of the monasteries effected a widespread transfer from ecclesiastical authority to that of the lay corporation and resulted in significant changes in land and property ownership. The smaller monasteries were suppressed first and then the larger ones were 'investigated', far from impartially. In 1535 Dr Layton reported on Bath to Thomas Cromwell, the king's minister:

> ... we found the Prior a right virtuose man ... a man simple and not of the greteste wit, his monks worse than any I have fownde yet both in buggerie and adulterie ... the house well repared but foure hundrethe pownds in debt.[28]

Prior William Gibbs/Holloway (1525–39), who used both names, seems to have tried to curry favour with Cromwell. He sent him a pair of Irish-bred hawks

The top of the west front of Bath Abbey. Christ sits in glory about the badly eroded heavenly host. Directly beneath the Christ figure is a Tudor rose surmounted by a crown. Below this, the arms of the city of Bath are shown to the left, while those of the diocese of Bath and Wells are to the right.
PHOTOGRAPH: CARNEGIE, 2004

47

One of the two ladders to heaven on the west front of Bath abbey, with angels ascending and, in two cases, apparently descending head first. The eroded figures at the bottom of the ladders are not identifiable, but it is believed that those at the top of the ladders represent St Paul (typically holding a book) and St Peter, holding a lyre.

PHOTOGRAPH: CARNEGIE, 2005

and, on another occasion, a book from the cathedral library. Once Gibbs realised that nothing would make the King and his minister change their plans, he began to disperse the priory's property, but eventually surrendered the priory to the King's representatives on 27 January 1539. The prior was granted a pension of £80 a year and a house in Stall Street; the sub-prior and the eighteen monks who made up the community also received pensions.[29]

'[THE] MONKS [ARE] WORSE THAN ANY I HAVE FOWNDE YET BOTH IN BUGGERIE AND ADULTERIE ...'

NORMAN
CONQUEST
TO 1700

Following the dissolution, Henry VIII bestowed most of the priory's local property upon his illegitimate daughter, Etheldreda, whom he married off to John Harrington senior. (Harrington had a claim to modest fame as the inventor of a new type of water closet.) Etheldreda died young and her husband inherited her estate. The rest of the monastic lands and buildings were sold off by the crown.[30]

The still unfinished abbey and its lands were first offered to the city authorities for £500, for use as a parish church. The offer was declined, perhaps because of the money needed to complete it, although Sir John Harrington said it was turned down for fear of later being accused of defrauding the king. The building was then gutted. Lead, glass, iron and bells were removed and sold for scrap, and the shell of the church was left open to the elements. Buildings in the monastic complex, south of the church, were either sold off or demolished. The close and lands

The oldest surviving memorial plaque in Bath abbey, this monument commemorates Richard Chapman, 'Alderman of the City', who died in 1572, and his son William Chapman, 'once Mayor of the city', who died in 1627. The Chapmans were one of the families that rose to power and prominence after the dissolution of the monasteries.
PHOTOGRAPH: CARNEGIE, 2004

This elaborate tomb in the chancel of the abbey is that of Bartholomew Barnes (d.1605) and his wife. A puritan merchant from London, Barnes commissioned his own funeral monument as a way of inspiring support for the rebuilding of the abbey church. He also left a small legacy to the abbey.
PHOTOGRAPH: CARNEGIE, 2004

were bought by Humphrey Colles of Taunton, who shortly afterwards sold out to Matthew Colthurst (MP for Bath) of Wardour Castle in Wiltshire.[31] Colthurst, or his son Edmund (who also became MP for Bath), turned the prior's lodgings into a private house and made a garden of the cloister. Edmund Colthurst had financial problems, which forced him to move out in 1569, although he retained some property in Bath until 1611. Before then, in *c.*1560, he presented the roofless abbey church to the mayor and citizens to become their parish church.

The corporation was perhaps not too pleased by this gift, given the capital and operating costs which would be involved in repairing and running the abbey church. Moreover, the abbey had always been too big for the parochial needs of the city. St Michael Without served the Broad Street/Walcot Street suburb and there were four churches within the walls. St James' church had been engulfed by the Norman development and was moved to a new site near the south gate, in 1279, when the original building became the Bishop's private chapel. St Mary de Stalls (first documented in 1190) stood just north of the King's Bath, near the junction of Stall Street and Cheap Street. This was the foremost parish church, which became the church of the corporation: by 1249 masses were already being said there for the commonality. St Mary's Within was at the north gate, and St Michael Within stood near the west gate.[32]

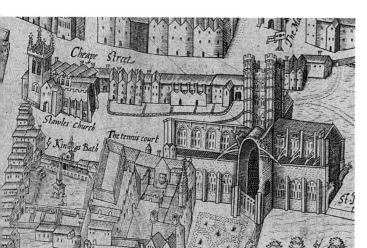

'Stawles', or St Mary de Stall's church, was where new members were admitted to the Guild and made freemen. Before the Reformation prayers for the souls of dead freemen and councillors were said in the chantry chapel within the church, which would have been endowed by the guildsmen. It was they who chose to dedicate this chantry to St Catherine, the patron saint of Bath. All chantries were dissolved during the reign of Edward VI.

BY COURTESY OF M. REYNOLDS, FOTOFORUM

The corporation did little to restore the abbey church. The impetus for renovation came from private citizens, enthused by the idea of one imposing parish church for the whole of Bath. Peter Chapman (a member of one of the families that rose to prominence after the Dissolution) was a prime mover in restoring part of the north aisle in 1572. After a visit by Queen Elizabeth, a nationwide collection was taken up and the windows and roofing in the east end were repaired. Work then slowed down somewhat. The nave was not completed until 1613, some time after the formation of the new parish and dedication of its abbey church to SS Peter and Paul in 1583.[33] The other churches of Bath were now largely redundant. St Mary's by the north gate was abandoned by 1583, leased out as a school and a prison until it disappeared in 1772. St Mary de Stalls was used as a workshop until 1593, but finally that too disappeared, in 1659. All parish churches within the walls, with the exception of St James', were abandoned for worship by the early seventeenth century, and the sites leased out for commercial use.[34]

Following the upheavals of the dissolution, the Protestant reforms of Edward VI (1547–53) made a considerable impact on religious life in Bath. Altars were replaced by communion tables, in line with the government requirement that masonry should be replaced with wooden tables, and many symbols of Catholicism were removed from the churches. When the Catholic Mary Tudor succeeded Edward VI, the churchwardens' accounts show that there was a hurried rebuilding of altars and a rapid re-introduction of Catholic practices. Protestant ideas and forms of worship then became dominant again during the reign of Elizabeth (1558–1603), 'just at the time when the Abbey was being revived not only as a building, but as a worshipping fellowship'.[35]

Another consequence of the Reformation was the decline of the medieval guilds. Their religious structure was not acceptable under the new order, and their roles were strictly curtailed. By later Tudor and Stuart times, power in Bath lay not with the guildsmen as such but with members of the leading families – the Chapmans, Sherstons, Parkers and others.[36] Meanwhile, under

letters patent of 1552, the property of the priory had been transferred to the mayor and citizens of Bath. Thereafter the corporation controlled all the city's major assets and owned four-fifths of the property within its walls; it also acquired some property outside the city, including coal works at Timsbury, Paulton and elsewhere in north-east Somerset.

The city had become a borough under a charter of 1189, but in 1590 Elizabeth I granted Bath a new charter of incorporation, under which all the powers previously held by the bishops and the prior were vested in the civic authority. The political constitution of the city rested on the 1590 charter until the Reform Act of 1832 and the Municipal Corporations Act of 1835. Power was concentrated in a small elite: the corporation was made up of a mayor, no fewer than four or more than ten aldermen, and twenty common councillors. New councillors were chosen by the existing body from the 'freemen', who otherwise had no say in the corporation's actions, but who shared in the monopoly of trade in the city up to 1765 and also in the revenue from the Freemen's Common. The mayor and aldermen were elected by the common councillors. As the governing body and the owner

The Perpendicular chancel roof of the abbey. The king's masons, Robert and William Vertue, renowned as masters of fan vaulting, were employed on the sixteenth-century rebuilding of the abbey.

PHOTOGRAPH: CARNEGIE, 2004

above The 1590 charter of incorporation granted by Elizabeth I gave the Mayor and Corporation all of the powers which had been held previously by the city's ecclesiastical authorities. As such it marked an important further stage in the secularisation of authority in the city.

below In the centre of the abbey is the tomb and effigy of Bishop James Montague, built in 1618–19. Montague was Bishop of Winchester at the time of his death, but he had been Bishop of Bath and Wells from 1608 to 1613. In his will he asked to be buried 'in the Great Church of Bath … to stir up some more benefactors to that place'.

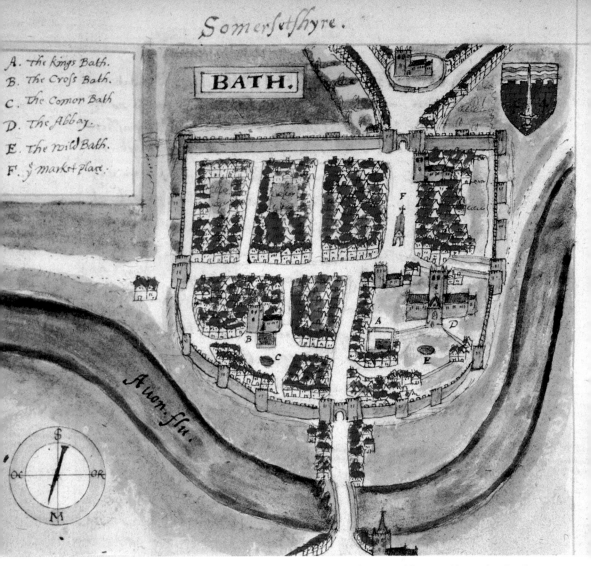

A. the Kings Bath.
B. The Croſs Bath.
C. The Comon Bath
D. The Abbay.
E. The mild Bath.
F. ye market place.

Somerſetſhyre.

BATH.

Avon flu.

William Smith's map of Bath, 1588. The earliest known map of the city, it shows the principal features of late medieval Bath, although the representation of the streets and houses is rather stylized and lacks authentic detail. The three principal city gates – north, west and south – are supplemented by an east gate which appears larger than on other depictions of the city walls and by no fewer than fifteen other towers, again not seen on other maps or plans. Smith shows the three main hot springs and their associated baths – the King's Bath on the site of the original Roman bath; the Cross Bath; and the 'Comon Bath' on the site of the later Hot Bath. The 'mild Bath' (E), just south of the abbey, might be the site of the Prior's bath mentioned by John Leland some years before this map was drawn. Three of the city's parish churches within the city walls are shown – St Michael's near the west gate; St Mary's near the north gate; and 'Stawles' (St Mary de Stall's) Church near the abbey. Outside the city walls can be seen Walcot Street and Broad Street leading away from the north gate and the church of St Michael's Without (i.e. outside the walls). Substantial suburban growth between the south gate and the bridge is delineated, but later maps suggest that fewer buildings existed along Southgate Street. The crest (top right) is that of the city, and the church at the bottom probably represents St Thomas à Becket in Widcombe which was built by Prior Cantlow in 1490–98 on the site of an earlier Norman chapel.

BRITISH LIBRARY, REF.

of much property within the city, the corporation was intimately involved in the growth and development of Bath. It derived most of its income from its property, which included the city wall, the guildhall and the market place, much of the area within the city limits, and the baths themselves.[37] These changes influenced some aspects of economic and political life for centuries to come. For example,

'BATH LYETH ON Yᴱ NORTHE[A]ST CORNER OF SOMERSETSHIRE,
COMPASSED ALMOST ROUND ABOUT, Wᵀᴴ Yᴱ RIVER OF AVON ... IT
IS BUT A LITLE CITTIE, YET ONE OF THE Yᴱ MOST ANCIENTEST IN
ENGLAND.'

WILLIAM SMITH, 1588

A HISTORY
OF BATH

the corporation's ownership of property and land, and the careful management of its assets in the eighteenth century, gave it an assured income which continued to benefit the residents of Bath right down to the twentieth century, in the form of low rates.

National events in the seventeenth century also impinged on Bath, although their effects proved to be less significant for its future than the earlier dissolution of the monastery. During the first Civil War (1642–46) Bath, like the rest of the nation, was divided in its sympathies. Some of its citizens were royalists, but parliamentarians formed the majority on the council. Ardent parliamentarians and puritans, led by Matthew Clift, usually had the support of a group of moderate puritans and so outnumbered the royalist, anti-puritan faction (led by Henry Chapman) by around 22 votes to eight.[38] The impact of the Civil War and its aftermath were less disruptive in Bath than in many other places, for there was no marked dislocation of economic life or extensive damage to property. Bath itself housed a garrison throughout the Civil War but it was not subjected to serious attack and it never came under siege from either side. In July 1643 the king's Cornish army attacked parliamentary forces holding Lansdown, but the battle ended indecisively, with the parliamentarians

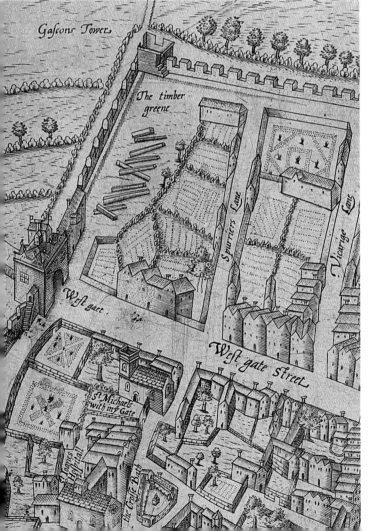

A detail of the north-west corner of the city, with Gascon's Tower on the city walls. Gascoyne or 'Gascon' was a Bath citizen who built the tower himself to repair 'a little peace of the walle that was in decay, as for a fine for a fyght that he had committed in the cyte' – an early community service order for anti-social beaviour? The 'timber greene' is still an open area, the Sawclose, where many public meetings, elections and demonstrations have been held over the years. Just outside the detailed depiction of the west gate is St Joanes Barn.

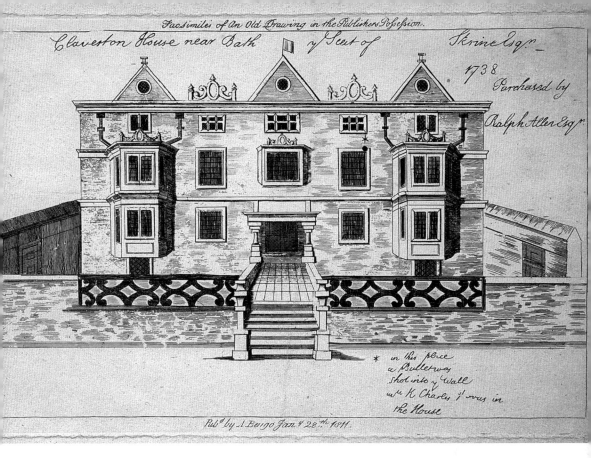

A nineteenth-century facsimile of a 1738 drawing of Claverton House, once owned by Ralph Allen. The asterisk, right foreground, marks the spot from which a bullet was shot into the wall 'when K[ing] Charles 1st was in the House'. The Jacobean house was replaced in 1819–20 by a new manor house, now the American Museum at Claverton Down.

BY COURTESY OF BATH CENTRAL LIBRARY, BATH & NORTH EAST SOMERSET COUNCIL

making a tactical withdrawal to the city, which they briefly occupied. The royalists won a decisive victory shortly afterwards, in an engagement at Roundway Down near Devizes in Wiltshire, and Bath came under royalist control from 1643 to 1645.

Throughout the conflict the council attended scrupulously to routine matters such as appointing its ale-tasters and supervisors of meat and fish. Royalist and Roundhead councillors continued to sit side by side, no matter which army was in control of the city, and the main priority was to sustain the daily flow of

overleaf The Savile map dates from some time shortly after the accession of James VI and I in 1603, and gives a very clear picture of the city in the early modern period, before the dramatic changes of the eighteenth century changed so much of the townscape. It is certainly the most important early map of the city in existence and might well have formed the basis for Speed's own map of Bath (see pages 58–9) of a few years later. Note the gardens behind many houses, and the Horse Bath off Southgate Street. St James's church, missing from Smith's 1588 map, is shown just inside the walls beside the South Gate. The 'timber greene' (top left) is now the Sawclose, while Spurrier's Lane and Vicarage Lane have become Bridewell Lane and Parsonage Lane. Cocks or Slaughterhouse Lane survives as Union Passage. Savile's lengthy commentary on both sides of the map extols the medicinal properties of the hot springs and discusses the early origins of the city and its associations with a very wide variety of real and mythical ancient kings and peoples. He is surely on firmer ground when describing the city as it was in his day: 'The Citie of Bathe ... is seated in a cheape & plentifull countrie for provision, by the river Avon, in a pleasant Valley envyroned wth high hilles yet Verie fruitfull ... It is fortified wth a high wall, wch on the insyde is rampyred wth earth allmost to ye Batlements, in which are diverse Roman antiquities both engraven & embossed ...'

BY COURTESY OF M. REYNOLDS, FOTOFORUM

DIEV ET MON DROIT

HONI SOIT QVI MALY PENSE

TO THE READER

The Citie of Bathe in the Countie of Somerset, is seated in a
cheape & plentifull countrie for prouision, by the riuer Auon, in a pleasant
Valley enuyroned wth high hilles yet Verie fruitfull, from whence many
pure springes of cold water are conueyed in pypes for the Vse thereof:
It is fortified wth a high wall, wch on the inside is rampyred wth earth allmost to
Batlements, in which are diuerse Roman antiquities both engrauen & embossed. It
hath oft Varied her names, according to ye alterations & chunges of tymes.
taking her first name (as it is thought) of ye hotte waters Ptolomeus ye ancient
Geographer writeth it Ὕδατα θερμά (i.) Aquæ calidæ; Antoninℯ noteth, that
it was called Aquæ Solis, ye waters of the Sunne. The Britons named it
Kaerbadon, Caer Badon, Caer Palladur, & Yrennaint twymin In ye time of ye
Saxons it enioyed these names viz. Bathuncestre, Hat Bathan, Cuines Accea-
manni, Accmanecestrin, & Akmanchester, wch signifieth the Citie of the
diseased, or of men troubled wth akes or aches The later Latines write it
Badiza, Badus, Badonia or Bathonia &c. There are in this well gouer-
ned Citie three principall Baths, (wch are placed twise in this mappe first as
they stand in ye Citie : then in the margent in larger forme only for the
better veiwe of the beholder) viz. the Kings bath, ye Crosse bath & ye hotte
bath, wherein are vaults & distinct seates made like chaires, for ye diseased
to rest in, wch Venerable Beda noteth to haue bene in his tyme destinguished
for both sexes And now of late years, ye Crosse bath, & hotte bath, haue bene
new Vaulted, & walled aboute, by Right-honorable benefactors. Out of two
of ye principall baths are extracted certaine others, to witt ye new bath, & the
Lazurs bath close by ye hott bath Some do coniecture ye they were first founded by Bleyden Cloyth alis Bleidd ye great Magitian & lerned Philosopher
a British King; Others do attribute it to Iulius Cesar, Solinus Polyhistor
thought ye Goddesse of these hotte waters to be Minerua or Pallas, for ye ye
Britanes called it Caer Palladur, wch signifieth ye Citie of ye Waters of Pallas; Athenæus affirmeth all hotte baths to be consecrate to Hercules : but for
further knowledg herein reade Mr Candens Britannia. Beda alledging the
Words of St Basil saith, that ye Waters of baths running through certain
mettalles, do receiue theze of such vertue of heate & they are not ely made
warme therby: but seething hott & these baths passing through mynes of sulpe
hure (as our late writers do coniecture) are neare to ye temperature, as if a
quart of cold water should be putt to a gallo of seething water : yet eche of
them differeth from other in some degrees of heate They keipe an accustom̄d
time of purging : as from 9 of ye clok in ye morning to noone, & from 9 at night

THE KINGES BATH

IHS

VIEW
BATH

The riuer Auon

Bartons farme

Gascons Tower

The timber
greene

St Ioanes harne

West gate

West gate Street

St Michaell
with ni Gate

Lateris ye Crosse Bath

The Hott
Bath

St Katherins hospitall

Chaye

Stawles Church

St Kinges Bath

The Abby lane

Lame lane

Lame
Church

Southgate Street

Stawles Street

The Horse Bath

Bum Ditch

The Bridge

Spurriers Lane

Vicarage Lane

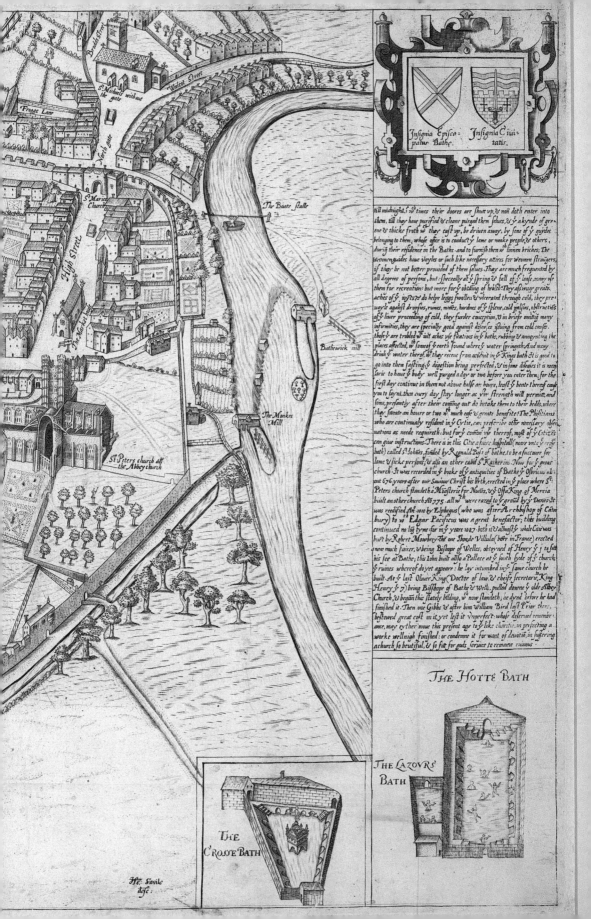

Broade Street

St Michaels without the gate

Walcot Street

Frogg Lane

North gate

St Maries Church

High Street

The Market place

St Peters church als the Abbey church

The Boate stalle

Bathewick mill

The Monkes Mill

Insignia Episcopatus Bathe.   Insignia Ciuitatis.

THE HOTTE BATH

THE LAZOVRS BATH

THE CROSSE BATH

Hr. Savile dese:

BATHE

Gascoin's Tower

West Gate

The forme of ye Kings Bath.

The forme of the New Bath.

Southgate

Ham Gate

Southgate street

The Horse

AVON FLU:

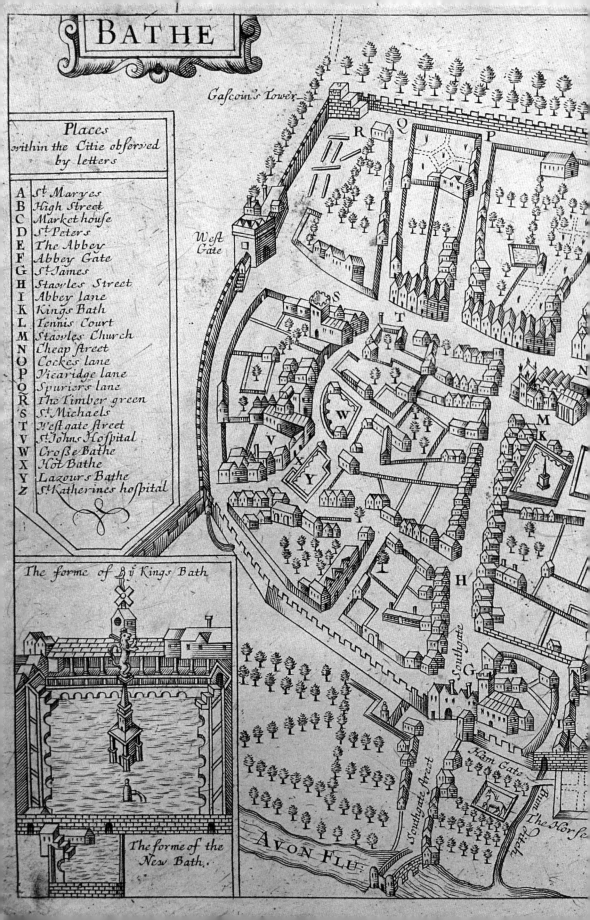

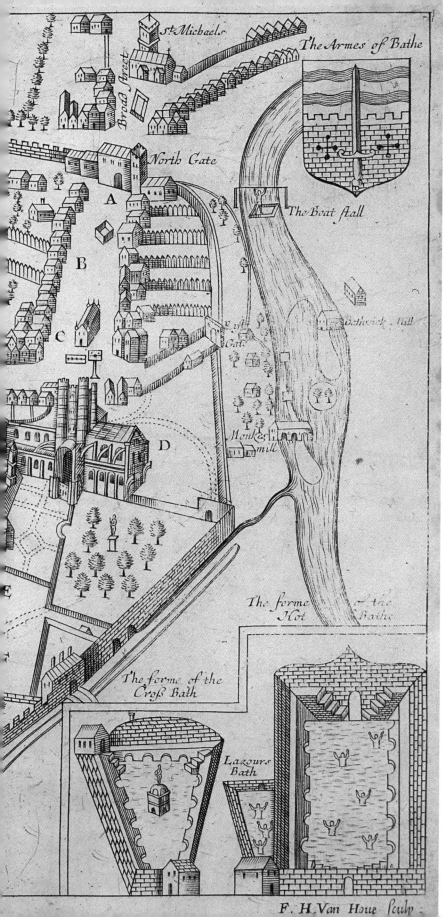

St. Michaels

The Armes of Bathe

Broad Street

North Gate

A

B

C

D

E

The Boat ſtall

Bathwick Mill

Eaſt Gate

Monkes mill

The forme of the Hot Baths

The forme of the Croſs Bath

Lazours Bath

F. H. Van Houe ſculp.

Speed's 1610 map of
Bath, seen here in an
engraving of 1676 by
F. H. van Houe, shows
the walled city in the
early post-medieval
period. The suburbs
beyond the north and
south gates are already
in evidence. The
Abbey and its grounds
occupies most of the
south-west corner
of the walled area.
Note the Ham Gate,
constructed around
the late thirteenth
century to give the
monks access to the
Ham meadows, and
nearby the Horse Bath
which was filled by
water draining from
the baths. Just east of
the Horse Bath is the
Bum Ditch, an open
sewer discharging foul
waste into the river.
The larger of the two
buildings immediately
inside the East gate has
been identified as the
early Guildhall, the site
of which now lies in
the car park behind the
modern Guildhall on
High Street.

59

Here the good LADY WALLER lyes.

The tomb of Lady Jane Waller in the south transept of the abbey. Lady Jane was the first wife of Sir William Waller, who led the parliamentarian forces at the important civil war battle of Lansdown in 1643. The alabaster figures on the monument were later damaged by royalist troops garrisoned in the abbey between 1643 and 1645.

commerce. The close family ties that existed between members of the corporation perhaps helped to foster co-operation, despite religious and political differences. The royalist Henry Chapman (innkeeper at The Sun) was brother-in-law of Matthew Clift (mercer and draper), leader of the opposing faction. A brother, a cousin and two nephews of Chapman's were also councillors, and his father was an alderman – a reminder that the corporation was a self-perpetuating oligarchy, rife with nepotism.[39]

Yet political life was inevitably strained. Although no purges of either group took place during the war years, the puritan majority reluctantly obeyed parliament's order of October 1647 to expel the royalist faction from the council.[40] Some were reinstated within months and by the time Oliver Cromwell died in September 1658 parliamentarians and royalists were more than ready to forget their differences. Hope that a lasting political settlement would create a stable climate, in which trade would improve, led to growing enthusiasm for the restoration of the monarchy. Bath was the first city in the country to proclaim Charles II as king, on 12 May 1660, and it was also the first to offer him a loyal address. Later, in the Monmouth Rebellion of 1685, Bath was staunchly behind James II.[41] Or so it seemed: the corporation had been purged of its most active whig members by then, and was fearful of the consequences of any show of disloyalty. Its support for parliament in the Civil War had not been forgotten. No man from Bath joined Monmouth's 'pitchfork rebellion' (although he had been welcomed enthusiastically to the city five years earlier) but, as a deterrent

Memorial in Bath Abbey to Sir Philip Frowde (d.1674), who served in the royalist army in the civil war. The monumental description gives more space to his marital history than to his military career, giving details of his three wives and nine children.

PHOTOGRAPH: CARNEGIE, 2004

to potential traitors, Judge Jeffreys ordered that four of the Somerset men sentenced to death at his 'Bloody Assizes' should be publicly executed in Bath. The county sheriff thoughtfully reminded the city authorities 'to provide an axe and a cleaver for the quartering the said rebels', who were butchered in the brutal manner of the times.[42]

Meanwhile, perhaps sustained by the desire for political stability, the local economy grew, but the balance of its constituent parts altered. During the sixteenth and early seventeenth centuries the city had grown slowly from an estimated population of 1,200 in 1524 to around 1,500 in 1641. Its cloth trade, however, was in decline. This was not unique to Bath, for rural competition (beginning in the fifteenth century and accelerating thereafter) was undermining the economic base of a number of textile towns, such as York, Canterbury, Gloucester and Salisbury. Personalities and local events may have played some part in Bath, where around 1527 accusations were made that William Crouch of Englishcombe had, by his violent and quarrelsome behaviour, driven two leading clothiers to leave the city – one of them said to have employed 300 people. A decade

King Edward's School (designed by Thomas Jelly, 1752). The grammar school was founded in 1552 and endowed by Edward VI. The building in Broad Street was erected on the site of the Black Swan Inn and other properties purchased by the council in 1744. More than 100 boys were taught in one large classroom; boarders slept in upstairs dormitories. The building has stood empty since 1991, when what had become King Edward's Junior School moved to purpose-built premises in North Road. The Bath city coat of arms in the pediment was carved by Joseph Plura (d.1756).

PHOTOGRAPH: CARNEGIE, 2004

or so later John Leland noted in his *Itinerary* that Bath 'hath somewhat decayed', but he attributed this to the recent deaths of three prosperous clothiers. Whatever part such contributory factors played, the effects of the slump were apparent in the startling fall in the value of property between the lay subsidies (a tax on moveable property) of 1525 and 1540. The number of citizens paying the subsidy in those years fell from 206 to thirty-one. Further evidence of the depressed state of Bath comes from its inclusion in a list of thirty-six towns and cities deemed to be so badly 'decayed' as to prompt an Act of Parliament in 1540 to enforce rebuilding,[43] but almost twenty years passed by before substantial redevelopment took place in Bath.

In the latter half of the sixteenth century there were signs of a revival in the economy. The high cross was replaced by a market hall in High Street and the corporation undertook the building of some 'new housen' in 1568–69. These were stone-built and tiled with some timber partition walls, but timber building was commonplace in Bath into the seventeenth century.[44] The potential fire hazard of timber buildings and thatched roofs led the council (which had once employed both a thatcher and a tiler) to decide in 1633 that leases on corporation property would stipulate that thatch must be replaced with tiles or slate.[45]

Because Bath had relied for its prosperity primarily on the wool trade for centuries past, it seems to have taken its people many years to recognise and adjust to structural change in the economy. The mayor was complaining, in 1622, that 'we are a very little poor City, our clothmen much decayed, and many of their workmen amongst us relieved by the city', yet it seems that Bath made little effort to retain what was seen as its staple industry. Nearby cloth towns, such as Bradford-on-Avon (Wiltshire) and Frome (Somerset) did so, partly by increasing specialisation, and the whole region benefited from the general revival of the trade after the Restoration, but within the city limits of Bath, the textile industry continued to decline. It has been said that at this time there were fifty broad looms in the parish of St Michael (outside the walls but within the city limits) and an equal number proportionately within the walls, but that the freemen's monopoly of trade within the city limits, and the regulations enforced by their companies, encouraged 'unfree' weavers to move out beyond Bath's boundaries to south of the river.[46] If this was the case, then attempts by the corporation to protect the local economy, by defending freemen's rights, actually contributed to the decline of trade within the city. Another possible explanation for change has been suggested by Sylvia McIntyre. She argues that if Bathonians did not take advantage of the regional revival in the cloth trade, it may have been because they had an alternative: rather than competing with west country cloth towns or the mercantile power of Bristol, Bath could flourish by specialising as a health and leisure resort.

That, of course, proved to be the case. The frenzy of development that gave us Georgian Bath swept away almost every trace of the earlier townscape, although (as Jean Manco points out) there are more remains from the seventeenth century than might be imagined. John Wroughton has vividly described Bath as it may have seemed to a visitor arriving from the north in the seventeenth century, and we draw below on his work to evoke a picture of the city at that time.[47] 'Passing through the now impoverished suburb of Walcot, with its many ramshackle wooden hovels, he would notice that in Walcot Street and Broad Street (just outside the city walls, where the cloth trade flourished) the housing was of a higher standard. Inside the walled area, walking around the main thoroughfares – Northgate Street, High Street, Cheap Street, Westgate Street, Stall Street and Binbury – would reveal fine stone houses packed tightly together with the city's numerous inns.' The old guildhall had by now been converted into a butchers' shambles (for the exclusive sale of meat), and in c.1625–27 the market house was demolished. In its place a new double-gabled guildhall had been built, with a council chamber and armoury on the first floor, supported by sixteen stone arches. Beneath it was the fish market, where fishmongers' stalls were set out on a paved area with open sides. In Southgate Street (which was liable to flooding) and the narrow lanes running off Westgate Street and Cheap Street (Bridewell Lane, Vicarage Lane and Cox Lane – now Union Street) there were small workshops, warehouses and poorer housing. Many undeveloped spaces existed, particularly just inside the city walls. This 'town waste' had traditionally been reserved for drying cloth on large racks. There were also plots of land behind many of the houses, used as herb and vegetable gardens, paddocks for horses or for keeping chickens or pigs.

[THE STREETS ARE] ... DUNGHILLS, SLAUGHTER-HOUSES AND PIG-STYES. THE BUTCHERS DRESS THEIR MEAT AT THEIR OWN DOORS WHILE PIGS WALLOW IN THE MIRE.

DR EDWARD JORDEN, 1631

The streets were 'most of the narrowest size, especially that nearest the centre, called Cheap-street ... the greatest eye-sore to its beauty'. They were generally well cobbled and kept in good repair, but they were not cleaned regularly until the latter half of the century, even though the corporation had powers to make by-laws over such matters. The sporadic event was recorded in the chamberlain's accounts by payments made for 'shovlinge upp the Durte in Westgate Street' or 'cleansing the way by the

Burrowalls'. Another recurring expense was the cost of clearing the ditch outside the city walls, which provided a handy tip for all sorts of rubbish, although in 1613 the council banned the practice of dumping waste from domestic privies there, or in the river.

Bath was fortunate in not having to rely upon the river for drinking water, because it had a fresh supply from springs in the surrounding hills. As Leland noted in his *Itinerary* many houses in the town had 'pipes of lead to convey water from place to place'. Stone watercourses and wooden pipes were also part of the system, which the council took responsibility for maintaining. Payments were made frequently for 'mendinge the pipes', and Thomas Burford was appointed at £2 a year to keep in good repair the watercourse from Beechen Cliff down to Southgate. The needs of residents who did not have the luxury of piped supplies were met by the provision of seven conduits at points around the city and, in addition, a well beside the North gate safeguarded supplies in time of siege.

Another council responsibility was maintaining law and order. The mayor, the recorder and two justices of the peace had power to apprehend felons, thieves and

The Cross Bath with St John's Hospital in the background. The Cross Bath probably dates back to the thirteenth century, but the earliest written description of it appeared in the 1540s. It was owned by the Church until the Dissolution, and was then in private hands for some time before the corporation acquired it in 1555. It took its name from a marble cross that once stood in the middle, but which had disappeared by 1586. Savile's map (see opposite, top left) shows the Cross Bath shortly after this date. Thomas Baldwin, the city architect, rebuilt in the Cross Bath in 1783–84, and it underwent various alterations in the nineteenth century, culminating in its conversion in 1885–86 to an enlarged, rectangular swimming pool. The roof of this was removed in 1952 and the Cross Bath became increasingly neglected until major renovations were carried out between 1999 and 2003.

PHOTOGRAPH: CARNEGIE, 2005

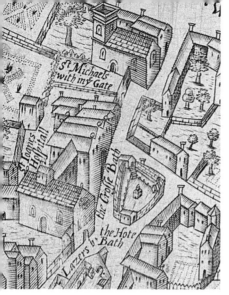

above A detail of Savile's map of around 1600, showing St John's Hospital and the church of St Michael 'within yᵉ Gate'.

top right The arms of St John's Hospital. A spate of hospital foundations in the High Middle Ages included the Hospital of St John the Baptist, founded by Bishop Reginald Fitzjocelin, between 1174 and 1180, for the support of the poor of Bath, a purpose which it still performs today.

right Chapel Court, St John's Hospital. the buildings of the hospital are arranged around the courtyard, with the main entrance from Westgate Buildings and a second one from Bath Street, behind the Cross Bath. John Wood and Elder rebuilt most of the hospital for the Duke of Chandos, *c.*1727, but the chapel itself – dedicated to St Michael – was built by William Killigrew in 1723 to replace a twelfth-century predecessor.

malefactors, and to enforce local laws by the imposition of fines. Other forms of punishment were the city pillory, erected in 1613, and the stocks; in the 1640s the tower of the disused St Mary's church, inside the north gate, was used as a prison. The city gates were locked at night and the streets patrolled by a bellman and two watchmen. In 1647 John Davis was appointed 'Bellman for this Cittie for one year next coming to walk the streets of the Cittie every night from the hours of ten of the clock till three in the morning in the summer and from one hour of nine of the clock at night till five in the morning in winter'. John Davis was paid the substantial sum of £10 annually, presumably in recognition of his responsibilities, but the watchmen received nothing but an occasional reward of free beer from the council. The town crier did rather better, for he was paid a stipend of ten shillings and provided with a special 'coate and buttons'.

The able-bodied poor of Bath (those fit for work but believed to be suffering from 'the cramp of laziness') were, under the terms of the Elizabethan Poor Law, set to work in a bridewell or house of correction but some thirty-six aged and infirm men and women were maintained in the city's almshouses at St John's Hospital near the Cross Bath, St Catherine's Hospital near the South gate, Bellot's Hospital nearby and at the almshouses at Holloway, just outside the city, which belonged to the chapel of St Mary Magdalene. The corporation also made charitable annual gifts to the poor ('To the poor in bread at Lent – £5 2s.'; 'To the poor in coal at Michaelmas – £2 8s.') and parish officers used some of the poor rate – which raised just under £30 a year – to relieve individuals in distress by means of doles of money, food or clothing. The labouring poor were hardly better off than the inmates of the almshouses. The eight men and women resident in St John's Hospital received free uniform clothing and a weekly allowance of 4s. 2d., whereas wages for manual workers ranged from about 9d. to 1s. per day. The lowest-paid workers probably earned about 5s. a week. The cost of living at this time is difficult to assess but the chamberlains' accounts record the prices of bread, rabbits, a sack of coal, boys' shoes, shirts and stockings and it seems likely that most working men would have needed the supplementary earnings of a wife and children if the family was to enjoy basic shelter with a sufficiency of food and fuel. Skilled workers, like the pump maker at the Bridewell, could earn 3s. a day, while schoolmaster Mr Mynn had an annual salary of £20 plus his board and lodging, but the truly comfortable classes of Bath were the clothiers, traders, shopkeepers, doctors, lawyers, innkeepers and lodging-house keepers. These were the men who sat on the council and generally dominated local affairs.

The size and wealth of the city in the later seventeenth century has been estimated from the Hearth Tax returns of 1664–65. Although not complete, the returns cover all the streets inside the walls and also Southgate Street, giving a total of 320 households. Allowing for missing entries and calculating on the basis of five occupants per household, plus a further allowance for inmates of the hospitals and the exceptionally large numbers of servants required to cater for the visitors, John Wroughton suggests an estimated population figure of 2,000 residents is reasonable. The number would be considerably increased by the seasonal influx of visitors. As for the distribution of wealth within Bath, and how the city compared to other places, analysis of the Hearth Tax returns reveals the Binbury area (in the south-western corner) as the most affluent sector of Bath, with an average of 7.3 hearths per household. This was followed by Westgate Street (4.8), Stall Street (4.5), Cheap Street (4.3) and Northgate Street (3.5). The over-spill areas outside the main gates were significantly poorer, especially Southgate Street with an average 1.9 hearths in each household. The incomplete returns for Broad Street and Walcot Street indicate an average of 2.8 hearths. In Bath as a whole the average per household amounted to 3.9, a figure which denotes a greater degree of affluence than was found in comparable cities such as Exeter (2.59) and York (3.2). Moreover, only 12.1 per cent of households in Bath were too poor to pay the tax, compared with

'A PRETTY GOOD MARKET-PLACE, AND MANY GOOD STREETS, AND VERY FAIR STONE HOUSES.'

SAMUEL PEPYS, 1660s

A fragment of ancient wall in Little Orchard Street, behind the Marks & Spencer store. The street name recalls the ancient abbey orchard, seen on most early maps of the city, and the wall is thought to have been part of the boundary wall which enclosed the property of the abbey.

PHOTOGRAPH: CARNEGIE, 2004

40 per cent in Exeter and 20.4 per cent in York. So Bath was evidently a fairly prosperous city in the 1660s and even though its woollen trade continued to decline it seemed to Samuel Pepys, when he visited in 1668, to have 'a pretty good market-place, and many good streets, and very fair stone houses'.

Bath had changed substantially as the Roman spa became a cathedral city, which in turn developed into a woollen town. By the late seventeenth century it was poised for further change, as it became less renowned as a manufacturing centre and better known as a watering place. 'The town and all its accommodations', remarked Celia Fiennes in the 1680s, 'is adapted to the batheing and drinking of the waters and nothing else.'[48]

The revival of the spa

The hot springs had attracted people to Bath since Roman times, but the visitors were of relatively little economic importance in the early modern period, until a fortuitous interest in the curative properties of mineral waters encouraged greater numbers to visit the spa at a time when the cloth trade was declining. In the late sixteenth century there was a spate of writings on the benefits to health of bathing in spring waters. Bath, as the possessor of one of the only two English mineral waters of note (the other being Buxton, in Derbyshire), was given much publicity in books such as that written by Dr William Turner in 1557. In his account of the spas of Germany, Italy and England, Turner specifically recommended the curative powers of the waters at Bath, but he was highly critical of the baths in their

'THE TOWN AND ALL ITS ACCOMMODATIONS IS ADAPTED TO THE BATHEING AND DRINKING OF THE WATERS AND NOTHING ELSE.'

CELIA FIENNES, 1680S

existing state and urged numerous improvements. There was no immediate response from the corporation, but in 1573 the Privy Council requested the city authorities to maintain and manage the baths better, for the reception of important visitors. The request was probably made because there were plans for Queen Elizabeth to visit Bath in the following year, although no improvements had been carried out by the time she and her retinue arrived in 1574. Yet the royal visit may have acted as a spur to those anxious to attract the wealth of the nobility and gentry to Bath, for plans were soon announced to build a new women's bath beside the King's Bath. This was to be completed by Whitsuntide

A drawing of the King's Bath, on the right, and the smaller Queen's Baths to the left, *c.*1675, by T. Johnson. Lodging houses crowd around the baths, and onlookers are entertained by watching the bathers. The naked boys on the balustrade are about to dive for coins thrown by the fashionable company.

BY COURTESY OF BATH CENTRAL LIBRARY, BATH & NORTH EAST SOMERSET COUNCIL

The key at the top of the drawing reads as follows: '(A) Kings; (B) Queens bath; (C) the kitchen [sic] under the cross; (D) this table on the wall in this Chareckter [i.e. the right-hand panel relating the Bladud legend]; (E) the dry pump; (F) Bladuds pickture [in the niche overlooking the King's Bath); (G) the parlor; (H) Francis Stoner of Stoner knight, 1624 [referring to a statue, below that of Bladud, to the Jacobean gentleman who had donated stonewotk for part of the building].' The wording on top of the building celebrates Queen Anne of Denmark, wife of James I, 1618.

'THE BATHS ARE BEAR-GARDENS, WHERE BOTH SEXES BATHE PROMISCUOUSLY; WHILE THE PASSERS-BY PELT THEM WITH DEAD DOGS, CATS AND PIGS.'

DR EDWARD JORDEN, 1631

1576, and improvements were made to the King's Bath itself in 1577–78. All this activity brought favourable comments in works such as Harrisson's *Description of England*, 1577, in which the baths were described as 'not onlie verie repared and garnished with sundrie curious peeces of workmanship ... but also better ordered, clenlier kept, and more friendlie provision made for such povertie as dailie repaireth thither.'[49] Some twenty years later, in the 1590s, the Cross Bath was enlarged and fitted out with heated changing rooms.

It was medical fashion that made the spa 'resorted unto so greatly ... the pilgrimage of health to all saints', as the Bath physician Sir John Harrington

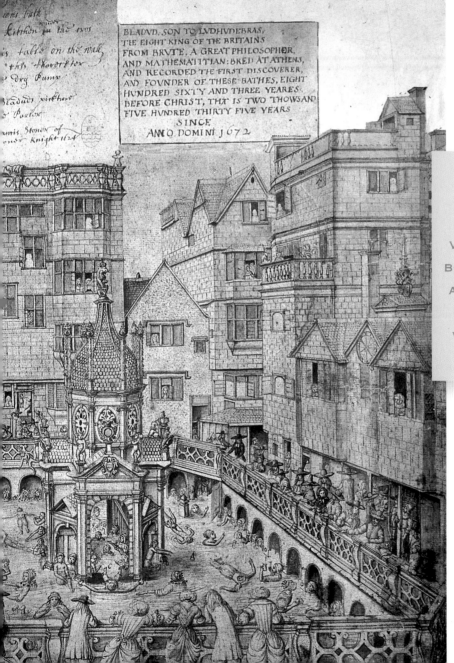

BLADVD, SON TO LVDHVDEBRAS, THE EIGHT KING OF THE BRITAINS FROM BRVTE, A GREAT PHILOSOPHER, AND MATHEMATITIAN: BRED AT ATHENS, AND RECORDED THE FIRST DISCOVERER, AND FOVNDER OF THESE BATHES, EIGHT HVNDRED SIXTY AND THREE YEARES BEFORE CHRIST, THAT IS TWO THOWSAND FIVE HVNDRED THIRTY FIVE YEARS SINCE ANNO DOMINI 1672.

'VERY MEDICINABLE, AND OF GREAT VERTU TO CURE BODIES CHARGED AND BENUMBED (AS IT WERE) WITH CORRUPT HUMOURS.'

This edition of Gilmore's of 1694 map advertises some of the city's amenities, in the list of inns in Bath and the gabled lodgings that decorate the border. At this time Bath remained predominately a walled city, with suburban extensions from Northgate into Walcot and from Southgate to the bridge across the river. The open spaces – the Abbey Garden and the Old Bowling Green – occupied part of the site of the Norman cathedral priory. In the undeveloped loop of the river on the bottom left of the map, Gilmore has provided 'ground plans' of the four baths – Cross, King's, Queen's and Hot – each with crosses at their

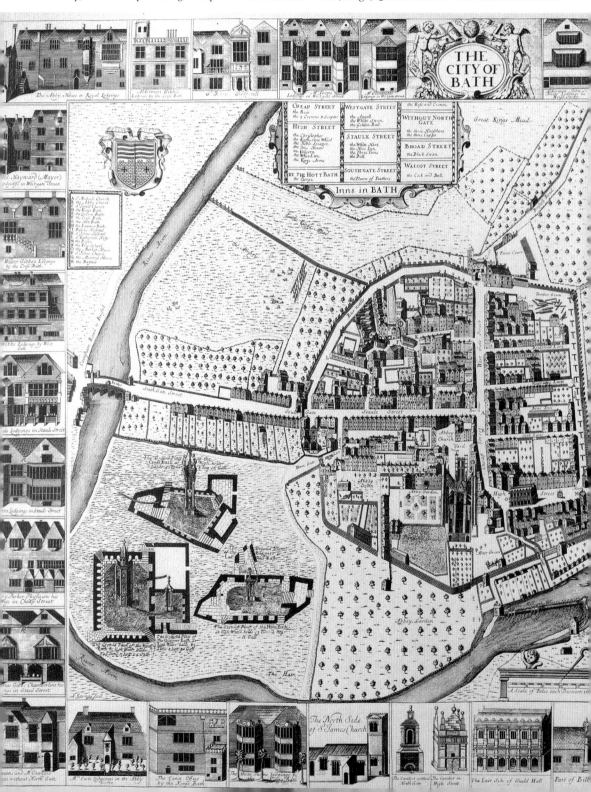

centre. Numerous drying racks for woollen cloth can be seen around the city and possibly also represented by the line of 'T's running along Upper Borough Walls. In this vicinity Spurrier's Lane has become Bridewell Lane, with the cock pit right next to the timber green on the Sawclose.

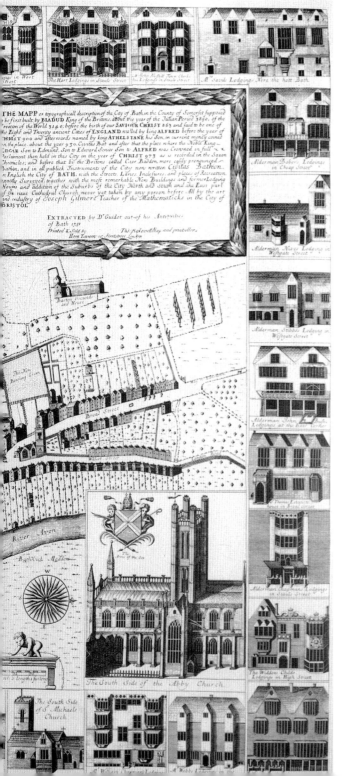

DR THOMAS GUIDOTT

Dr Thomas Guidott (1638–c.1706) was born at Lymington, Hampshire, and educated at a school in Dorchester before going up to Oxford in 1656. After graduating he undertook medical studies and qualified in 1666, whereafter he practised in the Oxford area for a year before moving to Bath where Dr John Maplet helped him to build up an extensive practice. By 1679 he is said to have lost most of his patients as a result of his 'impudence, lampooning, and libelling'. John Wood, who seems to have known Dr Guidott well, described him as 'a person of good parts, well vers'd in Greek and Latin learning, and intelligent in his profession; but so much overwhelmed with self-conceit and pride as to be in a manner sometimes crazed, especially when his blood was heated by too much bibbing.' After antagonising many of his wealthy patients, Guidott moved to London but continued to visit Bath for the summer season. He was offered professorships in medicine at both Venice and Barcelona but preferred to stay in England. He wrote and published numerous works on spa treatments in general and on the Bath waters in particular.

Source: *Oxford DNB* (2004), vol. 24, p.183.

From the panel on Gilmore's map '… Civitas Bath[i]on, in English the City of BATH, with the Streets, Lanes, Inclosures, and places of Recreation, exactly Surveyed, together with the most remarkable New Buildings and former Lodging Houses and addition of the Suburbs of the City North and South and the East part of the neat Cathedral Church never yet taken by any person before. All by the art and industry of Joseph Gilmore Teacher of the Mathematicks in the City of BRISTOL.'

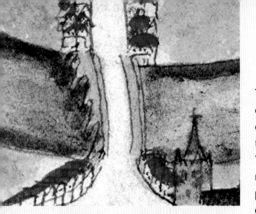

A detail of William Smith's map of Bath, 1588, a stylised view of the old bridge. He has drawn houses extending to the bridge on both banks of the river, and shows neither the gateway nor the bridge chapel.

BATH BRIDGE

The five-arched masonry bridge was built in the thirteenth century. There may have been an earlier wooden bridge at this crossing-point, where the line of Southgate was extended over the river Avon and on to what became the main road to Bristol. The bridge was subsequently rebuilt in the fifteenth century but retained such earlier features as a castellated gateway over the pier closest to the south bank and a small chapel or oratory, dedicated to St Lawrence, built into the eastern side of the parapet above the second pier from the north bank. Figures of a lion and a bear stood on pedestals at the south end of the bridge. The gateway might originally have housed a drawbridge, which was subsequently replaced by the fifth or southern arch. All these features were removed when the bridge was again rebuilt in 1754. No attempt was made to improve the flow of the river, by reducing the number of arches, and so the problem of flooding persisted. The incidence and severity of flooding had increased with the spread of new buildings on both banks by the eighteenth century, and it continued to be a problem until the flood prevention scheme of 1966–68. The site of the old Bath Bridge is now overlooked by the GWR railway bridge.

Source: R. Angus Buchanan, 'The Bridges of Bath', *Bath History*, iii (1990), pp.1–21.

With considerably more verifiable detail, Savile's map of c.1603 seems more realistic, showing gateway, chapel and flanking statues on the south bank of the river. Interestingly it also seems to show a slipway at the west side of the bridge, on the bank where the quay was later built.

below The Old Bridge, engraved by W. Watts, 1794. By this date Pulteney Bridge had been built a few hundred yards upstream and the old bridge had begun to be surrounded by more and more commercial activity. Allen's tramway reached the river nearby; considerable numbers of commercial vessels were using the river; and the quay on the north bank of the Avon (improved in the 1730s, when Avon Street was built) was getting busier.

described it in the 1590s, but the fashion that popularised spa treatments was not solely to Bath's advantage. It encouraged a search for new sources, and a multitude of springs with medicinal properties were discovered to rival Bath, although the heat and volume of its waters remained unique. These attributes, however, seemed less advantageous from the late sixteenth century, when medical opinion began to promote the idea of drinking mineral waters rather than bathing in them. Fortunately for the local economy, at Bath the warm water came to be drunk also, as a preparation for bathing. The growing enthusiasm for cold bathing in the seventeenth century was another threat to Bath, but medical writers such as the local practitioner Dr Thomas Guidott defended the hot baths successfully and the spa continued to attract the sick.[50]

The waters were claimed to be generally beneficial, as 'very medicinable, and of great vertu to cure bodies charged and benumbed (as it were) with corrupt humours'. Indeed, they were a veritable cure-all according to Dr Thomas Venner, a physician at the baths, who claimed in 1628 that 'They be of excellent efficacy against all diseases of the head and sinews, proceeding from a cold and moist cause, as rheums, palsies, lethargies, apoplexia, cramps, deafness, forgetfulness, trembling or weakness of any member, aches and swellings of the joints'. For good measure he also urged 'those that fear obesity' to resort to the baths. By now there was a 'yearly concourse in the spring and fall, of people of all sorts from all parts of this Kingdom' coming to Bath, where they were likely to fall prey to the agents of unscrupulous lodging-house keepers who were involved in something of a racket with local doctors. Agents would persuade newly arrived visitors to take lodgings in their master's house, by extolling the virtues of the bath nearest to it 'above the rest', and once 'gotten into their houses' the lodging-house keeper would recommend a physician, 'magnifying him for the best in town'.[51]

Ownership and control of the baths by the corporation was clearly an advantage in developing the resort, but it seems to have been largely as a result of the influence of physicians and apothecaries that the governing body adopted a more entrepreneurial spirit towards the spa. Some of the medical fraternity, attracted to Bath by the growing opportunities it provided for their professions, became a part of the political elite, and many others also had vested interests in the health function of the city, for example as lodging-house keepers. Sir John Harrington and Dr Oliver (inventor of the Bath Oliver biscuit, as part of his patients' dietary regime) are but two examples of medical practitioners who were absorbed into the elite and who used their influence as councillors to persuade the corporation to develop facilities for the visitors. Oliver published a pamphlet (in 1705) in which he argued the medical case for drinking the hot Bath waters all year round. This would extend the season beyond a short period in the summer, which made Bath

CATCHING A COLD
'[IS] ... ONE OF THE
WORST ACCIDENTS
THAT COULD HAPPEN TO
ANYBODY IN THE COURSE
OF DRINKING BATH
WATERS.'

DR OLIVER, 1705

in 1676 a place 'where all the people live all the winter (like Nightingales) upon the stock of their summer fat'. The lack of shelter near the baths was likely to deter invalids from drinking the waters out of the conventional season, as Dr Oliver indirectly acknowledged in his assertion that catching a cold was 'one of the worst accidents that could happen to anybody in the course of drinking Bath waters'. His pamphlet and his arguments in council were supported by another local physician, Dr Bettenson, who donated £100 towards the cost of overcoming this problem. In 1705 the corporation decided to build a pump room on the north side of the King's Bath.[52]

Through their writings, the medical fraternity 'puffed' or advertised not only the waters but also the accommodation available to visitors. As early as the 1620s Dr Thomas Venner drew attention to the convenient lodgings around the baths. By the beginning of the seventeenth century, a dozen hotel inns and many lodging houses had been established in Bath. The admittedly incomplete Hearth Tax records for 1664–65 reveal that the city had a comparatively high ratio of hearths per householder, and this reflected its specialisation as a resort. In some cases, no doubt, individuals paid for hearths in several houses but many of the more substantial tax payers (with ten to 29 hearths or, in three cases, 30 to 37 hearths) were the owners of inns or lodging houses. The medical fraternity often kept lodgings for their patients, and the surviving Hearth Tax returns record three 'Doctors of Physick' who paid tax for a total of 24 hearths in 1664.[53]

The success of Bath as a spa depended on more than the natural resources of the springs and local willingness to exploit their commercial potential. Many other English towns were becoming social centres for local gentry and the 'middling' classes in the seventeenth century, but the spas differed from other urban centres because, as Sylvia McIntyre points out, they catered primarily for people who had little connection with the town itself other than as a place of amusement. Attracting the healthy, wealthy and fashionable social elite was therefore as important – perhaps more so – than attracting the sick. Royal visits from Elizabeth I in 1574 and 1591, and from the early Stuart kings in 1613, 1615, 1628 and 1634 brought the glamour of the court to Bath and raised its status as a place of fashionable resort. The Civil War had initially a depressing impact on the spa trade but this soon picked up, as wounded soldiers began to flock to the city in the hope that the waters might heal them. Bath also attracted large numbers of military and political leaders – Roundhead and Royalist – who preferred to be based there rather than in Bristol, which was the military headquarters for both sides in turn. Bristol was said to be 'so nasty and filthy' as to be scarcely endurable. In times of drought Bristolians were reduced to pumping drinking water from the dirty river, and epidemic diseases proliferated there. Bath endured an outbreak of typhus, or 'camp fever', in 1643, but it was an essentially healthy city throughout the years of conflict. It emerged from the Civil War with its reputation enhanced.[54]

Three years after the Restoration, Charles II brought his wife Catherine to Bath in 1663, in the hope of conceiving a legitimate heir, for by then the waters were being promoted as a cure for infertility as well as dropsy, gout, skin diseases, numerous general ailments and the pox. No pregnancy occurred, and yet Catherine made a second visit to Bath as Queen Dowager in 1686. In the following year, the wife of James II (Mary of Modena) came to bathe in the Cross Bath. Her visit in 1687 was more successful than Catherine's had proved, for Mary was soon reported to be with child.

The Catholic James II was increasingly unpopular because of his pro-Catholic and absolutist policies, but there had been widespread optimism about a Protestant succession as his Catholic second wife had produced no living heir in fourteen years of marriage. All this changed with news of the royal pregnancy, which was a marvellous publicity coup for the Bath waters but less welcome to the local population in a city which had a long-standing aversion to Roman Catholicism. (There were few Catholics in Bath, but many Presbyterians and Baptists in and around the city by then.)[55] Catholics, of course, were delighted and the Secretary of State, the Earl of Melfort, commissioned an ornate marble cross for the Cross bath. The 'Melfort Cross' (decorated with three cherubim holding aloft a crown, orb and sceptre, topped with a dome supporting a crown of thorns, and bearing other Catholic iconography) was in place within three months of the birth of a prince on 10 June 1688.

The infant heir to the throne was next in line, taking precedence over the Protestant princesses. This provoked a Protestant rising and the Glorious Revolution of 1688. By the end of the year the throne had been offered to William of Orange and his wife Mary, the daughter of James II by his first marriage. The Melfort Cross therefore became an embarrassment to the corporation within months of its erection. They waited only until James had fled to the coast *en route* to France before ordering the removal of the crown of thorns, various inscriptions and 'all other superstitious things belonging thereunto'. The Protestant cause was celebrated on the coronation day of William and Mary, in April 1689, with street celebrations, patriotic banners, a Guildhall banquet and a specially commissioned song. One verse of this read:

> In Praise of him who came with Heaven's high hand
> To drive Rome's priests (those vipers) from this land
> Those locusts who to Lucifer bespoke us
> Whose mock religion is a hocus pocus.[56]

What really set the seal of royal approval on Bath was the patronage of the future Queen Anne, who came in search of a cure for her gout and dropsy in the 1680s and again in 1692. As reigning queen she made further visits to the city in the early eighteenth century. To the delight of the corporation, her frequent presence, with her court and entourage, confirmed the appeal of Bath as an exclusive resort for 'the quality'. The value of royal patronage to Bath's embryonic tourist trade was clearly recognised and exploited by the corporation. Celebrations were organised to publicise royal visits, and to encourage royal guests to return, while royal patronage was advertised through such civic

SALLY LUNN

The *Original Bath Guide* of 1917 stated that at 4 North Parade Passage, 'Sally Lunn sold the tea cakes still known by her name', and that the same house, 'an ancient shop in Lilliput Alley' was by the 1930s marked with a plaque, asserting that Sally Lunn had arrived there in 1680, earlier than previously thought, as a Huguenot refugee from France. Dorothy Hartley commenting on the story of 1831 wrote: 'We do not dispute the existence of the cook, nor the baker, but the "cry" she yelled in good west-country French was "Solet Lune! Soleilune", representing the gold top and white base of the bun. The house itself, probably built in the mid-sixteenth century, was claimed to have been a coffee house where, in Georgian times, Nash, Allen and their friends came for their morning coffee. Sally Lunn's restaurant is now one of the principal tourist attractions in modern Bath.

Source: *Oxford DNB* (2004), vol. 34, p. 774.

Sally Lunn's, North Parade Passage. The tearoom, named after the Huguenot refugee whose speciality bun is still popular with visitors, claims to be the oldest surviving house in Bath. It is a rare example in the city of any early Stuart house, built under a lease of 1622 to the carpenter George Parker. Considerably older remains dating back to the Roman period have been discovered in the cellars and can still be viewed today. The windows of the house have been much altered over the years, and what is now the ground floor was the first floor, until the ground levels were raised considerably in the late 1720s for the building of the North Parade area.
PHOTOGRAPH: CARNEGIE, 2004

improvements as the new Queen's Bath (1618) which was named in honour of Anne of Denmark, queen consort to James I.

In addition to exploiting royal visits, the corporation and individual entrepreneurs began to provide entertainments for visitors. By the mid-seventeenth century a few tree-lined walks had been laid out in the old abbey gardens, and there were bowling greens and a real-tennis court for more energetic physical exercise. Theatrical performances took place occasionally, either in the Guildhall or in the courtyards of the larger inns. Yet, as late as 1683, the Somerset justices preferred to hold the Assize Court at Wells because Bath, 'had not so good accommodation for entertainments',[57] and there were no organised social activities on the scale of those to come in the eighteenth century.

Another aspect of the positive strategy adopted to promote the spa and resort functions of Bath was the perceived need to raise and maintain its social tone. Royal visits brought the nobility and upper classes crowding into the city, but if 'the quality' were to be attracted to Bath on a regular

'... NO DISEASED OR IMPOTENT POOR PERSON LIVING ON ALMS ... SHALL RESORT OR REPAIR FROM THEIR DWELLING PLACE TO THE SAID CITY OF BATH ...'

basis then a suitable ambience of fashionable elegance was necessary. Achieving this in a city which was also a magnet for various 'undesirables' provoked an alternative or negative strategy from the authorities. Bath had been notable for its many religious and charitable foundations from the twelfth century onward. The largest of these foundations was the St John the Baptist hospital for the sick and poor, established in 1174 but given over to the corporation in 1552. The existence of such charitable institutions, plus the presence of wealthy visitors, attracted numerous poverty-stricken invalids to the city in search of a cure at the baths, and also brought beggars and vagrants looking for hand-outs to relieve their destitution. The authorities were concerned about the effects of the influx of such undesirables but showed little understanding of its causes. By the early 1570s the corporation had concluded that so many poor and diseased people were flocking to Bath that only an Act of Parliament could protect the interests of the city. The mayor therefore petitioned for an Act granting the corporation powers to ensure that: 'no diseased or impotent poor person living on alms ... shall resort or repair from their dwelling place to the said city of Bath and to the baths there for the ease of their grief unless such person be not only licensed so to do by two Justices of the Peace in the county where such person doth dwell but also provided for by the inhabitants [of their own parish].'[58] The subsequent Act of 1572 transferred the cost of supporting poor patients from the city of Bath to the parish of their origin. It also gave power to the authorities to control the numbers of undesirables entering the city. Under the terms of the Act, any sick or poor person arriving at the gates without a licence could be turned away, or treated as a vagabond and taken into custody for punishment. Attempts to restrict the numbers of the poor therefore coincided with the vigorous promotion of the spa. The need to make provision for more middle- and upper-class visitors coming to take the waters was given priority over the interests of the lower social orders. St John's Hospital, once the haven of only the poor sick, was enlarged by the corporation in the later sixteenth century to provide letting accommodation, as was the Abbey House, which had formerly been the prior's lodging.

At the end of the seventeenth century Bath remained a medieval city, encircled by a battlemented wall which was banked behind and descended to a flanking ditch. Its narrow streets and cramped buildings were dominated by the abbey church, a reminder of its monastic past. With a population approaching 3,000, it was still a small market town in which the woollen industry continued to decline, whereas the spa was attracting ever-growing numbers of visitors. Bath had always been of more than local importance but its image and primary function had undergone significant changes in times past. Its most dramatic transformation lay ahead in the eighteenth century.

Baptismal font, 1710, in the St Alphege chapel at the east end of the abbey. The lettering around the rim reads: 'Go ye teach all nations Baptizing them in the name of ye Father and of ye Son and of ye Holy Ghost.' Another, lavishly carved Victorian font from 1874 stands at the west end near the exit. Both are largely redundant, except for floral displays, as a portable font is now used for baptisms.
PHOTOGRAPH: CARNEGIE, 2004

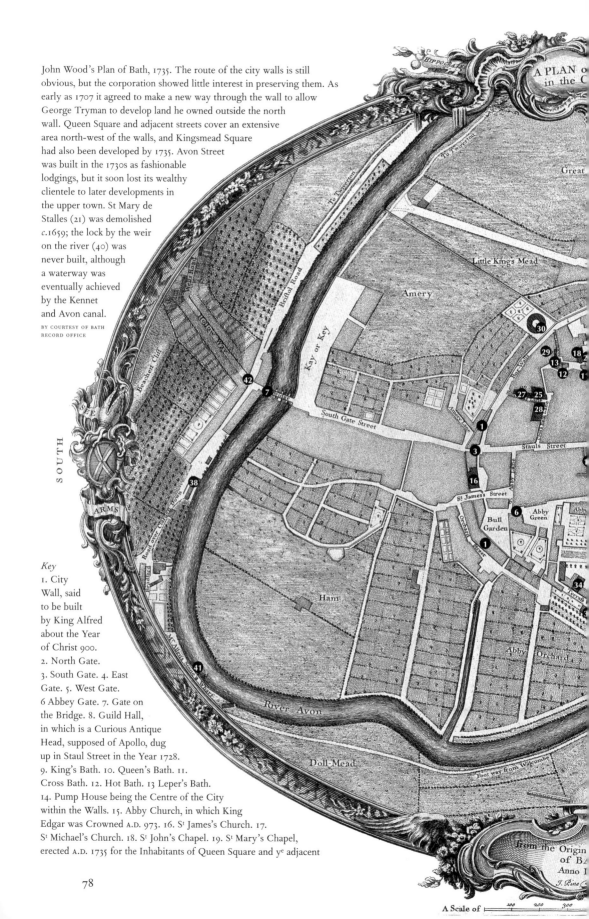

John Wood's Plan of Bath, 1735. The route of the city walls is still obvious, but the corporation showed little interest in preserving them. As early as 1707 it agreed to make a new way through the wall to allow George Tryman to develop land he owned outside the north wall. Queen Square and adjacent streets cover an extensive area north-west of the walls, and Kingsmead Square had also been developed by 1735. Avon Street was built in the 1730s as fashionable lodgings, but it soon lost its wealthy clientele to later developments in the upper town. St Mary de Stalles (21) was demolished c.1659; the lock by the weir on the river (40) was never built, although a waterway was eventually achieved by the Kennet and Avon canal.

BY COURTESY OF BATH
RECORD OFFICE

Key
1. City Wall, said to be built by King Alfred about the Year of Christ 900.
2. North Gate.
3. South Gate. 4. East Gate. 5. West Gate.
6 Abbey Gate. 7. Gate on the Bridge. 8. Guild Hall, in which is a Curious Antique Head, supposed of Apollo, dug up in Staul Street in the Year 1728.
9. King's Bath. 10. Queen's Bath. 11. Cross Bath. 12. Hot Bath. 13 Leper's Bath.
14. Pump House being the Centre of the City within the Walls. 15. Abby Church, in which King Edgar was Crowned A.D. 973. 16. St James's Church. 17. St Michael's Church. 18. St John's Chapel. 19. St Mary's Chapel, erected A.D. 1735 for the Inhabitants of Queen Square and yᵉ adjacent

A Scale of

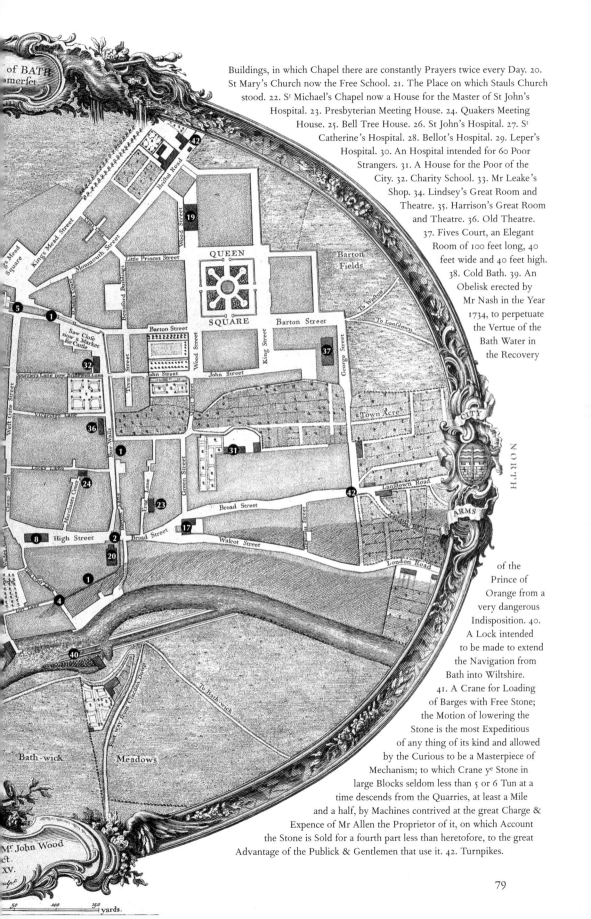

Buildings, in which Chapel there are constantly Prayers twice every Day. 20. St Mary's Church now the Free School. 21. The Place on which Stauls Church stood. 22. St Michael's Chapel now a House for the Master of St John's Hospital. 23. Presbyterian Meeting House. 24. Quakers Meeting House. 25. Bell Tree House. 26. St John's Hospital. 27. St Catherine's Hospital. 28. Bellot's Hospital. 29. Leper's Hospital. 30. An Hospital intended for 60 Poor Strangers. 31. A House for the Poor of the City. 32. Charity School. 33. Mr Leake's Shop. 34. Lindsey's Great Room and Theatre. 35. Harrison's Great Room and Theatre. 36. Old Theatre. 37. Fives Court, an Elegant Room of 100 feet long, 40 feet wide and 40 feet high. 38. Cold Bath. 39. An Obelisk erected by Mr Nash in the Year 1734, to perpetuate the Vertue of the Bath Water in the Recovery of the Prince of Orange from a very dangerous Indisposition. 40. A Lock intended to be made to extend the Navigation from Bath into Wiltshire. 41. A Crane for Loading of Barges with Free Stone; the Motion of lowering the Stone is the most Expeditious of any thing of its kind and allowed by the Curious to be a Masterpiece of Mechanism; to which Crane ye Stone in large Blocks seldom less than 5 or 6 Tun at a time descends from the Quarries, at least a Mile and a half, by Machines contrived at the great Charge & Expence of Mr Allen the Proprietor of it, on which Account the Stone is Sold for a fourth part less than heretofore, to the great Advantage of the Publick & Gentlemen that use it. 42. Turnpikes.

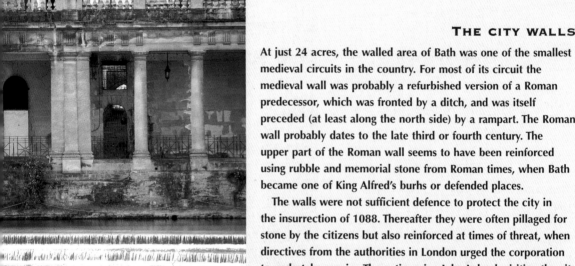

At just 24 acres, the walled area of Bath was one of the smallest medieval circuits in the country. For most of its circuit the medieval wall was probably a refurbished version of a Roman predecessor, which was fronted by a ditch, and was itself preceded (at least along the north side) by a rampart. The Roman wall probably dates to the late third or fourth century. The upper part of the Roman wall seems to have been reinforced using rubble and memorial stone from Roman times, when Bath became one of King Alfred's burhs or defended places.

The walls were not sufficient defence to protect the city in the insurrection of 1088. Thereafter they were often pillaged for stone by the citizens but also reinforced at times of threat, when directives from the authorities in London urged the corporation to undertake repairs. The antiquarian John Leland, visiting the city c.1540, described the 'noble ancient wall' built of 'a time-defying stone'. By then an extension had been built from the south-west angle to the river bank to provide additional protection for the southern part of the city. The wall and its flanking ditch were in a good state when Leland saw them; the walls he noted 'standeth almost alle, lacking but a peace about Gascoyne's tower'. Gascoyne, a Bath resident, had himself built the tower in the north-west corner to repair 'a little peace of the walle that was in decay, as for a fine for a fight that he had committed in the cyte.'

In the dangerous political times preceding the Civil War the corporation undertook an extensive programme of renovation. As early as 1641 it had spent some £36 on 'stone digginge, carryinge lyme and for making up of the Towne Wall by the prison' (the old church of St Mary, by the North gate). The walls survived the war, to be walked by Samuel Pepys in 1668, who noted that they were 'good, and the battlements all whole'.

The main gate into the town was the North gate, leading out on to the London road. Smaller postern gates existed on either side of this 'Town gate', and it was surmounted by 'a grotesque figure of King Bladud ... ten feet wide and fifteen feet high.' In 1637 Thomas Quilly was paid six shillings for 'payntinge King Bladud'. The West gate, which looked out across the common and meadows towards Bristol, was 'a very large, clumsy pile of buildings'. Over this gate there were 'some handsome apartments, occasionally used by divers of the Royal family and other persons of distinction in their visits to the city'. The South gate, which had been rebuilt in 1362, had statues of Edward III (1327–77), Bishop Ralph of Shrewsbury (1329–63) and Prior John Walcote, in a niche over the arch. The East gate (the only survivor of the city's gates) was narrower than the others, and only a subsidiary opening in the city walls, giving access to Monks' Mill and the ferry to Bathwick. It was also known as the Lot gate, from the Old English ludgate: postern. The South gate, outside of which an early suburb grew up, opened on to the old bridge across the Avon, and thence on to the road up through Holloway and Beechen Cliff onto the Fosse Way. Near the South gate there was another

A glimpse of what may have been the east gate of the city, now well below the modern street level of Grand Parade. This photograph was taken from the Bathwick side of Pulteney weir.

PHOTOGRAPH: CARNEGIE, 2004

By the time of Stukeley's panorama of the city (1723) the walls had been breached in several places, although this section still marked the limit of development towards the south-west. Part of this section survives on Lower Borough Walls.

BY COURTESY OF BATH CENTRAL LIBRARY, BATH & NORTH EAST SOMERSET COUNCIL

Trim Bridge, the arch over John Street. Originally St John's Gate, the arch was formed after 1728 to allow public passage for carriages to Queen Square.

subsidiary gate, the Ham gate, which gave direct access to the Abbey grounds.

The ancient walls were swept away in the 'rage for building' of the eighteenth century. The development of Trymme Street in 1707 (built at the initiative of George Trymme, clothier and member of the corporation) required a new way through the city walls, which was apparently negotiated without difficulty. In c.1754 the corporation decided to pull down the North and South gates, in order to facilitate private developers. A right of way through the walls was granted to developers c.1760, which resulted in the erection of Edgar Buildings in 1761, on the Town Acre, and the start of Milsom Street in 1763. Corporation land outside the city walls was given over to speculative building in 1755 and the early 1760s, and parts of the city walls were demolished to give access to this development. John Cottle, a tailor, and John Walker, a weaver, claimed they could not proceed with their development of Westgate Buildings unless 369 feet of the walls were demolished. The corporation agreed to the developers' demands, but decided that land on which the city's wall had stood for centuries should be rented out on a leasehold for one shilling per foot.

The walls measured some 10 feet (3.03m) in width at their base and were over 20 feet (6.06m) in height. Fragments remain in places, but the most easily seen section is the heavily restored length in Upper Borough Walls. Complete with its crenellations and whitewashed outer face, this stretch survived because the eighteenth-century Mineral Water Hospital's paupers' cemetery occupies the narrow patch of land in front, on the north side, which would otherwise have been built on. The restorations are considered to be quite authentic, and some idea of the difference between the inside and outside levels at the end of the medieval period can be gained here.

Sources: Cunliffe, Davenport, Wroughton and Neale, *passim*

Upper Borough Walls. Opposite the Royal Mineral Water Hospital this restored section of the city walls is the most easily viewed remnant. This section of wall was saved because of the small cemetery below which served the hospital for some years.

'The Private Concert',
one of a series of
cartoons by Thomas
Rowlandson (1756–
1827), dating from the
end of the eighteenth
century. Entitled
'Comforts of Bath',
the cartoons satirise
the polite visitors and
residents of Bath.

A panorama of Bath, 1723, from Beechen Cliff. An engraving from a drawing by the physician, naturalist and antiquarian Revd William Stukeley, dedicated to his friend Dr Richard Meade, who had accompanied him on a visit to Bath in that year. The Magdalen chapel on Holloway can be seen in the foreground.

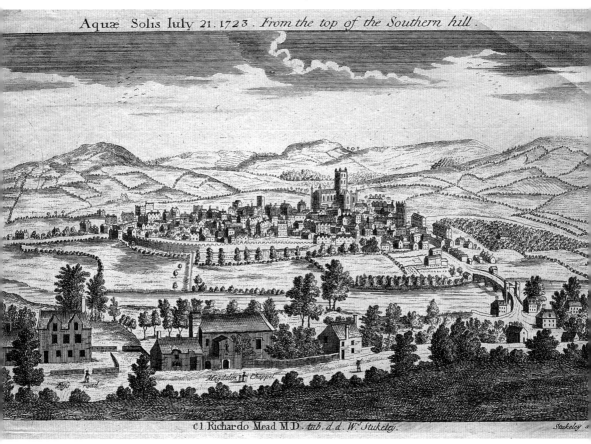

Frivolity and fashion, 1700–1820

BATH's role in the life of the nation was never to be greater or more flamboyant than it was between 1700 and the 1790s, when the city was the premier resort of frivolity and fashion.[1] In the course of the eighteenth century the enduring image of 'Georgian Bath' was created, as a place where terraces and squares formed an elegant setting for the pleasures of the nobility and the gentry. Yet even in its heyday, other realities underlay this image. In spite of increasing specialisation as a leisure resort the city nonetheless retained a mixed economy. Moreover, although 'the quality' flocked to the spa, Bath was not exclusively attractive to the wealthy and distinguished. Other less welcome visitors from the impoverished underclass were also drawn to the city. Rural migrants came, too, in search of work, while the permanent resident population included substantial numbers of the labouring classes and the lower orders of society.

Furthermore, the prevailing image of Georgian Bath to some extent obscured the dynamics of the socio-economic changes that were taking place even as that image was emerging. By the later 1700s Bath was far less fashionable than it had been in earlier decades. The social composition of the visiting company broadened, with fewer aristocrats and more members of the middle classes arriving for the season. An increasing number of the wealthy middle and upper classes chose to settle permanently in Bath, beginning the process that was to shape its later dominant image as a place of genteel residence. Simultaneously, incipient industrialisation was under way – albeit on a small scale – and this also foreshadowed developments in the decades beyond 1820.

The building of Bath

Building in Bath in the early eighteenth century was at much the same level of activity as in the country as a whole, and the capital sums involved were relatively small in comparison with later investment. Harrison's Assembly Rooms, for example, were built for £1,000 in 1708. The boom did not really take off until the late 1720s, and it reached peaks of activity in the periods 1726–32, 1753–58, 1762–71 and 1785–92. In general these periods coincided with the availability of 'cheap money', when interest rates were low.

However, two improvements in local transport acted as an additional stimulus

above 'Prior Park House Before Rebuilding' in a fan design by the artist Speren. It depicts the house at Widcombe which was replaced by Ralph Allen's new mansion. The stone tramway, featured on the right, was one of the wonders of the age, an important sight on a visit to Bath.

left An engraving of Ralph Allen, 1754, by J. Faber, after an original by T. Hudson

RALPH ALLEN (1693–1764)

Ralph Allen, postal entrepreneur and philanthropist, was baptized on 24 July 1693 in St Columb Major, Cornwall, one of four children of Philip Allen, reputedly an innkeeper in St Blazey. His early life remains obscure but certainly humble in relation to his impressive achievements. His aptitude for business showed early in Falmouth, Exeter in 1710 and then at Bath in 1712, where he became a salaried deputy postmaster. In 1720 he secured the right to farm the cross post and the bye-way post for which he agreed to pay £6,000 per annum to operate services that had an annual revenue of less than £4,000. Allen anticipated he could make great profits as the system of renewable contracts permitted an expansion of the system over England and Wales. His meticulous attention to detail and a determination to prevent fraud realized him profits of around £12,000 a year. Allen enjoyed the support of Major-General George Wade, sent to Bath to quell disaffection in the West Country over the succession of George I in 1714. Intelligence gained

to the first phase of building by reducing the costs of materials. The first of these was the Avon Navigation scheme to canalise and deepen the river between Bristol and Bath in order to lower the costs of transporting goods from the port to the city. Work began on the project in 1725. It was not completed until 1729, but the first barge reached Bath in December 1727 with a cargo made up chiefly of timber and lead for the building industry. The scheme also contributed to the development of Bath by providing an alternative means of access to the city through Allen's official duties provided information on Jacobite activities and strengthened his position through his service to the Hanoverian government. Wade became MP for Bath in 1722, and through his friendship, Allen became chief treasurer of the Avon navigation scheme in 1725 which allowed the carriage of building materials between Bristol and Bath, a vital development in support of the expanding spa resort. In the same year he became a freeman and member of the common council and its occasional banker.

On 26 August 1721 Allen married Elizabeth Buckeridge, the daughter of a London merchant, and her dowry may have contributed to his growing wealth. A house near the abbey, bought in 1726, became both office and home.

It was through his brother-in-law that Allen was able to purchase the land for the site of the mansion at Prior Park and the building stone on Combe Down. To overcome the problems posed by transporting the stone down the steep slope to the river, an ingenious wooden railway was built, equipped with wagons and cranes. From the quay the stone was shipped across the river to sites in Bath, or down the Avon for use elsewhere. Allen had a near monopoly of Bath building stone and became a major employer in the city. This profitable enterprise gave him a separate fortune, independent of his Post Office contract.

Allen's professional partnership with John Wood the elder brought a new Palladian front to his town house and then from the mid-1730s created the show-piece mansion at Prior Park, ready for occupation in 1741. Following the death of his first wife in 1736, Allen married Elizabeth Holder of the Manor House at Bathampton. Prior Park became a centre of hospitality and culture. Writers, poets and painters were regular visitors. Alexander Pope had given Allen advice on garden features and Henry Fielding commemorated his patron as Squire Allworthy in *Tom Jones* (1749) and dedicated his *Amelia* (1751) to Allen. After his death, Allen took charge of his family and the education of his children. He had a well-deserved reputation for philanthropy and concern for the less privileged. He built houses for his workmen and provided funds and stone for the building of Bath General Hospital. It is reckoned that he gave away more than a £1,000 a year.

Allen served as mayor in 1742 and acted as justice of the peace for Somerset from 1749. He remained a staunch supporter of the Hanoverians and he raised a volunteer force at the time of the 1745 rebellion. He died on 29 June 1764 at Prior Park and was buried at Claverton church. During his life he had shown a great aptitude for business allied to a largeness of spirit. While he amassed a considerable fortune, he also served the public good, and made few enemies in the process. He is traditionally credited with being one of the key figures in the making of Georgian Bath.

Sources: *Oxford DNB* (2004), vol. 1, pp. 812–14; B. Boyce, *The Benevolent Man: A Life of Ralph Allen of Bath* (1967).

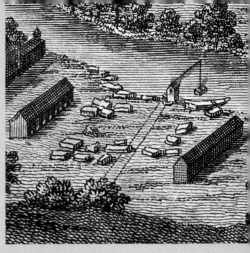

An early representation of the stone crane on the River Avon, together with associated buildings.
BY COURTESY OF BATH CENTRAL LIBRARY, BATH & NORTH EAST SOMERSET COUNCIL

at a time when the state of the roads made overland travel an uncomfortable and sometimes dangerous matter. In May 1728 the Princess Amelia (one of George II's daughters) completed her journey from London to Bath by boarding a barge, decorated in her honour, at Bristol. By 1740 there were two regular passenger boats daily each way between the port and the city of Bath.[2]

The second improvement was undertaken and financed by Ralph Allen (1693–1764) of Prior Park, one of the key figures in the development of Bath. As a shareholder in the Avon Navigation and the owner of the stone quarries at Combe Down, Allen had a strong vested interest in the growth and trade of the city. In the early 1730s he constructed a tramway almost two miles long (at a cost of £10,000) from his quarries down to the Dolemeads area beside the river. This cut the cost of stone on site in Bath and also made it economically viable for Allen to develop a small export trade. Between 1731 and 1733 some 1,800 tons of Bath stone were shipped out on the Avon Navigation.[3]

The cost of building Georgian Bath has been estimated by R. S. Neale as being in the region of £3,000,000. This figure is a rough approximation, but it suggests a surprisingly large scale of investment in speculative building at the time when the country was beginning to industrialise. The key entrepreneurs in the first half of the eighteenth century were the Duke of Chandos and the architect-developer John Wood (1704–54), while William Johnstone Pulteney was a comparable figure in the later phase of development. The corporation itself took no direct part in speculative building before the 1750s, but 'craftsmen undertakers' played a significant and sometimes underestimated role in development.[4] With the building of Pulteney Bridge (1769–74) a new town was opened up on the Bathwick estate to the eastern side of the city, with Great Pulteney Street as its centrepiece, leading majestically to Sydney Gardens. These developments to the north and east of the old medieval city were to dictate further building of squares, crescents and villa residences. Lansdown and Bathwick became the wealthiest suburbs in Bath, a process that began in the eighteenth century and matured into the nineteenth century.

The Duke of Chandos is the outstanding example of how outside money was used in developing Bath. He was at the centre of a web of national and international credit. He had made separate princely fortunes out of the lucrative post

The entrance to Pulteney Bridge from Bridge Street, in the late eighteenth century. The porticos facing outward from the square end pavilions have been long since demolished. The cattle are a reminder that even as Bath was being created as the epitome of urban sophistication, the city still had strong links with the countryside.

JAMES BRYDGES, FIRST DUKE OF CHANDOS (1674–1744)

James Brydges, politician, financier, and developer, was born at Dewsall, Herefordshire in 1674, the eldest son of James Brydges, eighth Baron Chandos (1642–1714), who held estates in Herefordshire and Radnorshire, and Elizabeth Barnard (1643–1719) who came from a successful merchant family. The young James was educated at Westminster School and New College Oxford, which he left in 1692 without a degree. After two years of study and networking at the electoral court of Hanover, and a series of indiscreet love affairs, he was recalled to England. In 1696 he married Mary Lake (1668–1712) of Cannons, Middlesex, and in 1698, through family influence in the city, he became MP for Hereford.

Between 1697 and 1702 he tirelessly pursued contacts among politicians, businessmen and courtiers, and began to invest in commercial ventures. In 1703 his connections at court secured him an appointment as a commissioner to the Admiralty, for which he was unfitted by experience or interest. In 1705, through the patronage of the Marlboroughs, he became paymaster of the queen's forces, and was able, by investing his budget during the War of the Spanish Succession, to create a fortune of £600,000 when he resigned in 1713. In 1719 he was promoted as duke of Chandos in recognition of his services to the state.

After the death of his first wife in 1712, Brydges acquired his wife's estate at Cannons and began to establish his position in the public eye with building projects and an extravagant lifestyle. He employed leading architects, Talman, Gibbs, and Vanbrugh, the best design and finest materials to furnish and decorate what became known as the finest house in England. A magnificent marble staircase, a well-stocked library, a picture gallery, and a chapel decorated in baroque style were among its striking features. Chandos, who achieved fabulous wealth through a network of credit and commercial transactions centred on London and Rotterdam, was engaged in a number of building and development projects. He bought Ormond House in St James's Square, gave it his own name and refurbished to his own taste. He had two houses built in Cavendish Square for himself and his son, and in 1726 he bought Shaw Hall near Newbury for use as a country retreat en route to Bath. In 1729–30, Chandos employed John Wood the Elder to rebuild and modernize four houses (Chandos House) backing on to Chapel Court at Bath, with the idea of providing superior lodgings for himself and others visiting the spa. The original workmanship, however, was poor and tenants complained of thin partitions, loose tiles and smelly drains.

Chandos died at Cannons in 1744 and was buried in a tomb with his first two wives. Cannons was sold and pulled down in 1747–48 and most of his building projects have decayed or been changed. Chandos House in Bath retains his name.

Source: *Oxford DNB* (2004), vol. 8, pp. 421–3.

of paymaster-general during the wars of Spanish Succession and from the South Sea Bubble affair. His interest in property development in Bath was inspired by dissatisfaction with his lodgings, and with the general standard of provision for visitors, when he stayed at St John's Hospital in the spring of 1726. Over the summer he negotiated through an agent, the Quaker banker Richard Marchant, for the site of St John's Hospital which was owned by the corporation. By October, he had acquired life-hold leases, at a cost of £3,250. In January 1727 he contracted with John Wood to undertake the first stage of development, and this was financed largely by merchants, bankers and discount houses in London. An estimated 66 per cent of traceable investment came from the capital city.[5] Money was raised by means of bills of exchange, promissory notes and annuities, but the entire project was underpinned by the personal wealth of Chandos, and a network of provincial, national and international credit.

Credit was also essential to John Wood's career as an architect-developer on his own account. For the development of Queen Square, Wood acquired a five-acre site on the Barton Farm estate owned by Dr Gay and his descendants. Having negotiated a ninety-nine year lease at an annual rent of £137, Wood then granted seventy-five under-leases (worth over £350 in total annual ground rent) to masons, carpenters and others who used their leases as security to raise mortgages and finance the building of houses to John Wood's designs.

According to Neale, John Wood was not merely an architect who worked only with 'perfect harmony and the most delightful proportion', but one who believed that classical architecture came from God's command. Whether his vision of Bath was inspired by the Britannic myth which identified the ancient city as the metropolitan seat of the Druids, or by the idea of a new Rome, his buildings were designed to be uplifting to the onlooker, and so arranged as to provide the space and setting for civilised urban living.

For instance, the north side of Queen Square (1728–35) was built in the Corinthian order; symbolising Nature in all her spring-like glory, it commands the enclosed space with all the 'grandeur of a palace'. By contrast, the Parades (1740–48) provided open spaces on the outside of the buildings for promenading and social intercourse, seen as a distinguishing feature of urban society. John Wood designed, and his son completed, the King's Circus (1754–69) as two perfect circles, with the outer circle divided into three segments, representing the idea of the Trinity, and the three orders of columns placed above each other,

John Wood the Elder might well be dismayed to find his masterpiece, the north side of Queen Square, being choked by ivy, dominated and shaded from the south by too large trees, crowded by traffic, and its view cluttered by insensitive street furniture.

PHOTOGRAPH: CARNEGIE, 2004

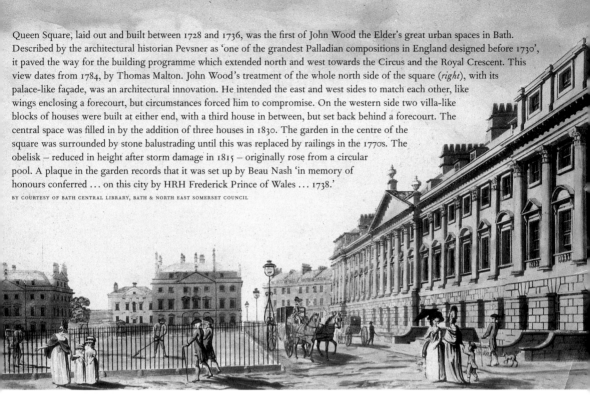

Queen Square, laid out and built between 1728 and 1736, was the first of John Wood the Elder's great urban spaces in Bath. Described by the architectural historian Pevsner as 'one of the grandest Palladian compositions in England designed before 1730', it paved the way for the building programme which extended north and west towards the Circus and the Royal Crescent. This view dates from 1784, by Thomas Malton. John Wood's treatment of the whole north side of the square (*right*), with its palace-like façade, was an architectural innovation. He intended the east and west sides to match each other, like wings enclosing a forecourt, but circumstances forced him to compromise. On the western side two villa-like blocks of houses were built at either end, with a third house in between, but set back behind a forecourt. The central space was filled in by the addition of three houses in 1830. The garden in the centre of the square was surrounded by stone balustrading until this was replaced by railings in the 1770s. The obelisk – reduced in height after storm damage in 1815 – originally rose from a circular pool. A plaque in the garden records that it was set up by Beau Nash 'in memory of honours conferred ... on this city by HRH Frederick Prince of Wales ... 1738.'
BY COURTESY OF BATH CENTRAL LIBRARY, BATH & NORTH EAST SOMERSET COUNCIL

symbolising 'virginal beauty, elegance, and attitude'.[6] If inspiration was Wood's intention in designing the King's Circus, he failed to convince the critics at the time. Tobias Smollett has his character, Matthew Bramble, discuss it as 'a pretty bauble, contrived for shew',[7] while an anonymous writer in 1779 described it, cruelly, as 'a handsome Wedgwood plate', a vulgar symbol of conspicuous consumption.[8]

The King's Circus led, via Brock Street, to the Royal Crescent, built by John Wood the Younger between 1767 and 1775, and this provided a grand climax to the series of Palladian buildings designed by the Woods, father and son. The triumphal sweep of the Royal Crescent, with its 114 Ionic columns, broad, flag-stoned promenade and gently sloping foreground, commanded a magnificent site. It signalled a move away from the formal garden design that marked John Wood the Elder's work in Queen Square and was probably influenced by the taming of nature inherent in the work of the landscape gardener, 'Capability' Brown, who was at the time working at Kelston and Newton St Loe near Bath.

William Johnstone Pulteney, the key figure in the development of Bath in the 1780s and early 1790s, was in somewhat different circumstances from those of either Chandos or Wood. The second son of a Scottish landowner, he was an Edinburgh lawyer and a partner in a Dumfries bank. He took the name Pulteney on marrying into that family. Like Chandos, Pulteney was an immensely wealthy man, but he was constrained by the fact that the Bathwick estate, inherited by his wife in 1767, was entailed. The estate had not been fully exploited because of the lack of a bridge between Bathwick and Walcot. If it was to be developed,

John Wood, architect and town planner, was born in Bath and baptized at St James's Church on 26 August 1704. He was the son of a local builder, George Wood, of whom little is known. John Wood was educated at the Blue Coat School and probably received training in building work from his father before becoming a joiner in London in 1721. There he worked with other craftsmen and became a principal builder on the Cavendish-Harley estate, then being developed north of Oxford Street. He took out building leases for the construction of about ten houses in the new streets and acted as surveyor of the large house being built by James Brydges, the Duke of Chandos, in Cavendish Square. It was Chandos who hired Wood to return to Bath in 1727 to build superior lodging houses as a speculative investment on the site of St John's almshouse.

It was also in 1727 that Wood married Jane Chivers, the daughter of one of

John Wood the Elder (1704–54). The architect John Wood and the Duke of Chandos were the key entrepreneurs in the crucial first phase of Bath's eighteenth-century development.
BATH CENTRAL LIBRARY, LOOSE PICTURES COLLECTION

Chandos's housekeepers. They had three sons and three daughters. The eldest son, John the younger, followed his father's profession helping to complete his architectural vision of Bath, most notably the Circus and the Royal Crescent. Wood convinced himself that Bath was founded for the 'capital Seat of a famous King' and his grandiose plans, along Roman lines, included a royal forum, a grand circus, and an imperial gymnasium. The corporation dismissed his plans for rebuilding the old town, whereupon Wood leased land from Robert Gay on the edge of the city to create Queen Square as a speculative venture on his own. Wood's magnificent elevations showed how a range of ordinary town houses could be united so as to have the outside 'appearance of one magnificent Structure'. Wood himself lived at no. 9. The completion of Queen Square in 1736 with the building of a chapel proved a pivotal development in the physical expansion of Bath.

North and South Parade were built as two long terraces of lodgings, surviving as the remnants of Wood's scheme for a vast 'forum' on the site of the abbey orchard. Wood's patron, Ralph Allen, commissioned the building of a large Palladian mansion, to advertise the virtues of the Bath stone from his Combe Down quarries. Prior Park proved to be one of the finest examples of English Palladianism, situated in an elevated position overlooking the city, and enriched by Thomas Paty's superb carving. The splendid Circus, at the top of the steep climb of Gay Street from Queen Square was begun before Wood's death and completed by his son. The linked geometry of Queen Square and the Royal Crescent, began by the younger Wood in 1767, makes up the most dramatically impressive piece of picturesque townscape in Georgian England.

Wood died in Bath on 23 May 1754 and was buried in the parish church of St Mary at Swainswick, just outside the city.

Source: *Oxford DNB* (2004), vol. 60, pp. 112–14.

above 'An exact prospect of the summer house, walks and gardens with a fine view of the River Avon and fields adjacent'. George Speren's fan-shaped view, 1737, of the Summer House and walks in one of the riverside pleasure gardens. Speren (1711–96) was a Welshman who moved from Gloucester to Bath, where he opened a shop in the Orange Grove. Clearly the polite company at Bath were fond of fishing and boating on the Avon, as well as promenading along its banks. The common problem of flooding along the river, together with the muddiness of the banks, would have provided a powerful incentive for the creation of safe, clean and proper facilities for parading during the season. The Parades were the result.

below South Parade was the first to be built. This engraving by John Hill from an aquatint by J. C. Nattes (*c*.1765–1822) was published in 'Bath Illustrated by a Series of Views', 1804. The sloping land to the river made this an expensive site to develop: massive foundations were needed to create the level terrace, but the slope was used to advantage as the houses nearest the river have two storeys below street level. At the time of this engraving the bridge from the end of North Parade had not yet been built, although development of the Bathwick estate on the east bank had begun.

The Orange Grove, with gentry on the walks in one of George Speren's drawings dating from 1737. The Orange Grove was laid out in the late seventeenth century and re-landscaped in the 1730s, with gravel walks and formal planting. In a typical gesture designed to promote Bath to a genteel clientele, Beau Nash erected the obelisk after the visit of the Prince of Orange to take the waters in 1734.

'WHEN ALL THESE WORKS ARE COMPLETED ... THIS CITY, ALREADY THE MOST SPLENDID IN ENGLAND, WILL BE AS NOBLE AS CAN BE CONCEIVED.'

FANNY BURNEY, 1788

right The obelisk in what is now known as the Alkmaar Garden at the Orange Grove. The Alkmaar Garden was founded upon the liberation of the Netherlands from Nazi occupation in May 1945 and is maintained by the Bath–Alkmaar Twinning Association.

Two students are having their graduation photographs taken by the obelisk.

PHOTOGRAPH: CARNEGIE, 2005

Pulteney needed to convince the trustees that this was a sound investment. He evidently did so, for by 1769 a scheme for a bridge over the Avon had gained the approval of the trustees and also the support of the corporation. Under the necessary Act of Parliament (1769), the trustees were given collective powers to grant building leases and water rights to the corporation, to allow it to build a reservoir in Bathwick, and to extend the powers of the Bath magistrates to the area. They were also empowered to raise a £3,000 mortgage on the estate to pay for the bridge, but Pulteney used his own resources to provide short-term funds to speed up its construction. The building of Bathwick new town was financed in much the same way as that of Queen Square, described above, but Pulteney also drew on his private wealth to supply some mortgage money at the outset of development.

The emergence of new financial institutions in the eighteenth century made a significant contribution to the building boom of 1785–92. By this time easy credit was available in Bath as well as from London banks. The first bank in the city was founded in 1768, but five more were established between 1775 and 1790. They were a popular amenity with visitors, who could now draw up in their carriages in Milsom Street to cash a bank draft, rather than travelling to the resort carrying large sums of money over roads frequented by highwaymen. The banks also provided investment for the regional cloth industry and for the local coal mines, and they played a crucial part in the success of small developers with little capital, such as the architect John Eveleigh. When he developed Grosvenor Place (1791–92) most of the investment came from mortgages raised at Bath banks.

This short cul-de-sac opposite Sally Lunn's is North Parade Buildings, known originally as Galloway's Buildings. Completed in 1750, they are attributed to Thomas Jelly but perhaps designed to the plans of the apothecary William Galloway, who was involved in speculative development. The project did not fulfil expectations, as wealthy visitors increasingly preferred to stay in the upper town, and the houses soon became tenement dwellings for the labouring classes.

PHOTOGRAPH: CARNEGIE, 2004

George Speren's fan design showing South Parade around 1757 was confusingly entitled 'Parade Gardens before North Parade was constructed'. In fact this view shows South Parade from the south, bisected by Duke Street, with Pierrepoint Street on the far left of the picture. North Parade lies beyond this view, parallel to South Parade. The river Avon runs at the right of the picture. The costly foundations, incorporating up to two storeys of cellars, which were needed to create level terraces on the Abbey Orchard site can be clearly seen beneath the Parade, with gardens laid out in the foreground. The chinoiserie of the border was a fashionable design at the time.

BY COURTESY OF BATH CENTRAL LIBRARY, BATH & NORTH EAST SOMERSET COUNCIL

The corporation was cautious about involving itself in speculation and borrowing before the 1750s, but it acquired powers of compulsory purchase in 1711 in connection with the Avon Navigation scheme, and these powers were extended in 1766 to facilitate the redevelopment of the markets. As a result, the civic body remained a major landowner, and by the 1750s revenue from property rents was being augmented by the sale of leases. Eventually, the authorities found the confidence to undertake their own development. In 1755 Bladud's Buildings were begun and the success of this venture in raising revenue brought about a change of attitude. The corporation was arguably over-cautious before 1750, after which it did too little, too late. It was frequently castigated for its caution and lack of imagination ('Narrow minds will ever have narrow views' as Smollett wrote of it in 1752) towards developing and improving the city, but in its defence, Sylvia McIntyre has pointed out that it was not obvious in the first part of the century that Bath's popularity would last.[9] Outright opposition to all improvements would have been against the interests of most members of the corporation, but the costs involved deterred them from undertaking major

The elegant Duke Street is typical of Palladian Bath architecture, with the widest pavement in the city. It was built in 1740–48, together with the North and South Parades and Pierrepoint Street, as part of John Wood's uncompleted Royal Forum.

PHOTOGRAPH: CARNEGIE, 2004

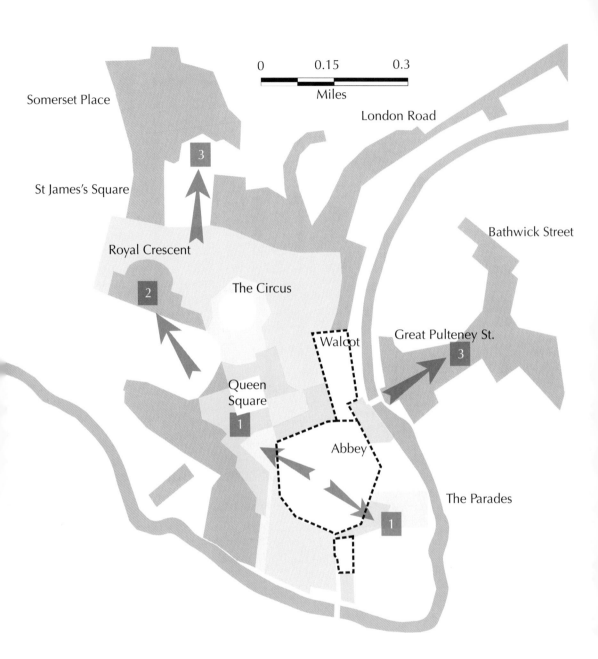

Somerset Place

St James's Square

Royal Crescent

The Circus

Walcot

Great Pulteney St.

Queen Square

Abbey

The Parades

London Road

Bathwick Street

Phases of development

	1700–1737
	1738–1758
	1759–1774
	1775–1796

City and suburbs before 1700

The grey arrows indicate principal development trends

1. First significant building outside the medieval core

2. From Queen Square north to The Circus
   and Royal Crescent

3. Across Pulteney Bridge to establish a Georgian
   'new city' on the Bathwick estate, and north of
   St James's Square to Somerset Place

top Numbers 7–10 The (King's) Circus. Such is the size of the tree at the centre of the space that only in high summer or deep winter can the architecture be admired without long shadows intruding on the scene.

PHOTOGRAPH: CARNEGIE, 2004

above The Circus, 1773, an aquatint by John Robert Cozens (1752–99). Originally called the King's Circus and designed by John Wood the Elder in 1754, this was the first Circus to be built in England. Wood died shortly after the foundation stone was laid, but the work was completed over the next two years by his son, John Wood the Younger. The three segments of the Circus consist of thirty-three houses in all: ten in the northern segment; eleven in the south-western; and twelve in the south-eastern. Three of the properties have side entrances and so the Circus is numbered 1–30, and the symmetry of the façade disguises individual frontages consisting of different numbers of bays. The Doric frieze on the ground floor features carved emblems representing the arts, sciences and occupations, and includes masonic devices. Female masks and garlands decorate the top of each range of columns. The rows of acorns on the roofline are an explicit allusion to the Druidic mythology of the Bladud tradition of Bath's origin. As can be seen here, the central space of the Circus was designed as an empty cobbled space with no central feature. Planting and a lawn were introduced in 1829.

© VICTORIA ART GALLERY, BATH AND NORTH EAST SOMERSET COUNCIL

projects. The corporate revenue was not large – an average of £375 per annum in the 1690s and £531 in the 1700s. It rose to £965 in the 1720s and £1,565 in the 1740s, but evidence from the chamberlain's accounts shows that expenses rose equally, or more rapidly. Moreover, income from the spa itself was not substantial. The pumps and baths brought in a maximum of £230 per annum up to 1750, but most of that sum was absorbed by the costs of maintenance and repairs.[10] Yet, between 1755 and the early 1790s, the corporation's enthusiasm for development matched that of private entrepreneurs. During that period, sites were cleared for a new town hall and markets, corporation land outside the walls was given over to speculative building, and part of the city walls was demolished to assist this development. Improvements were made to the Pump Room and the

'The Completion of
the Royal Crescent',
by Thomas Malton
junior (1748–1804).
Malton's watercolour
is dated c.1769, but
the Crescent begun
by John Wood the
Younger in 1767 was
not actually completed
until 1775. The main
structure appears
complete and, judging
by the smoke from
several chimneys, some
houses are occupied,
but several masons are
still working on large
blocks of stone in the
foreground. Perhaps
Malton visualised what
the completed Crescent
would look like when
complete?

baths, and the decayed city centre was redeveloped to give better access between corporation-owned facilities in the lower town and the rapidly growing upper town. All these activities were financed by borrowing. Interest charges accounted for a growing proportion of municipal expenditure, rising from an average of 5 per cent over the years from 1700 to 1771 to 24 per cent of total expenditure by the late 1790s.[11]

Relationships and connections between aristocrats, entrepreneurs and the local political elite involved in building clearly existed. John Wood had worked for the Duke of Chandos before returning to Bath in 1726. Wood had an uneasy relationship with the corporation, which never employed him as an architect, but his first employment in the city as a sub-contractor on the Avon Navigation is

PRIVATE LAWN
SUBSCRIBING
RESIDENTS ONLY

The Royal Crescent was built on meadow and pasture land with clear views down to the river and well beyond the urban centre of Bath. The ha-ha served a practical purpose in the late eighteenth century, when cattle and sheep were still grazed on the green hillside. The lawns, stretching down to Victoria Park, remain undeveloped and provide a spectacular setting for open-air concerts and other events.

PHOTOGRAPH: CARNEGIE, 2004

said to have resulted from the influence of Ralph Allen. Allen arrived in Bath at the age of nineteen in 1712, where he made a fortune from his career in the postal service and subsequently purchased the stone quarries as well as investing in many local enterprises. He quickly established himself as one of the most prominent businessmen in Bath, and was soon absorbed into the political elite. In March 1725 he was made an honorary freeman. Four months later the council elected him as a member and he went on to be mayor of Bath several times.[12]

Many members of the corporation, including physicians, surgeons, clothiers, plumbers and glaziers, were also private developers. So too, however, were many skilled tradesmen who had no role in the governing body. It was 'craftsmen undertakers' who built most of Bath's new housing in the period from 1730 through to 1800. Of the 37 houses erected in Milsom Street in about 1764, and of the 60 or so built in St James Parade after 1767, 20 and 46 respectively were put up by craftsmen in the building trade. The necessary capital was supplied, it seems, by long-term loans, and it is likely that craftsmen of different trades took adjoining plots in order to pool their skills. This may have been the case in the construction of Bennett Street around 1774: the identifiable builders included six carpenters, four masons, two plasterers and a tiler, who between them supplied all the necessary skills, except those of plumber, glazier and painter. Moreover, craftsmen-builders usually retained newly built houses for letting either to seasonal visitors or leisured residents (who were disinclined to buy and thus tie up their capital) or to Bath's less well-off inhabitants. This provided opportunities for the accumulation of capital and for further entrepreneurial activities, as the career of John Hensley indicates. Hensley, a carpenter in the late 1760s, operated as a timber merchant and coachbuilder, and one of the more prominent 'undertakers' or developers until his death in 1802. His estate (auctioned in 1803)

Walking northwards
out of Bath, the left
side of Walcot Street
is dominated by the
backs of the houses to
the west – Bladud's
Buildings and the
Paragon – perched
on high retaining
walls which now
house workshops and
garages.

PHOTOGRAPH: CARNEGIE, 2004

included thirty-seven dwellings, of which eleven were in fashionable terraces
and twenty were court tenements. Of these properties, thirty-four were sold for
£11,010 and the remainder were valued at about £750 in total.[13]

In comparison with other provincial towns, building developments in Bath
were commonly planned on a grander scale and at greater expense. A significant
part of the land was dedicated for open space, ornate squares and gardens. Stone
terraced houses had frontages of 10–14 feet and commanded prices of between
£500 and £1,500. These were several times more expensive than houses built in
industrial towns. Rents were also high in Bath. In Milsom Street, built in 1763
on 99-year leases, rents were between 4*d.* and 5*d.* per square yard, about three
times the cost of 11*s.* 2*d.* in streets on the edge of Birmingham in the 1760s.[14]

Development costs were high in Bath. The levelling of the hillsides, where
necessary, the amenities provided, and sometimes the provision of credit to
builders, all contributed to the costs. An example of the size of the loans

Robert Adam did not design many of Bath's buildings, but he was responsible for one of the city's most readily recognisable landmarks. Pulteney Bridge (1769–74), with its shops on both sides, is unique in Britain. As the only bridge towards the east of the city, it was crucial to the development of the Bathwick estate and it opened up an extensive new town to the east. Although much altered over the centuries, the southern, downstream side remains close to the original design.

PHOTOGRAPH: CARNEGIE, 2004

incurred on major promotions is found with the Younger Wood owing £8,000 in 1771 to two men in Bath and Bristol, with the loan secured on the ground rents of his developments since the death of his father in 1754. In another case, Charles Spackman, a coachbuilder and the developer of the Lansdown Crescent, borrowed £14,317 from a Bath banker between 1790 and 1792.[15]

The northern side of Pulteney Bridge is mean and shabby by contrast with the picture-postcard southern elevation, yet this is the view from the Podium and the Riverside Walk which are now prime tourist sites in Bath. It is also the view from the Hilton Hotel dining room.

PHOTOGRAPH: CARNEGIE, 2004

Great Pulteney Street by Thomas Baldwin, 1788–93, is one of Britain's finest formal streets. This view is from Laura Place, with the Holburne Museum at the far end. The museum was built as Sydney House in 1796–97, which provided coffee, tea and card rooms for people using the Sydney Gardens; there was a ballroom on the first floor as well as, intriguingly, a public house in the basement for the use of the chairmen, coachmen and other servants who were not allowed in the pleasure gardens themselves.

PHOTOGRAPH: CARNEGIE, 2004

Edward Street, one of several short streets running southwards off Great Pulteney Street in the neo-classical style, designed by Thomas Baldwin as part of the development of the Bathwick estate between 1780 and *c*.1820.

PHOTOGRAPH: CARNEGIE, 2004

Bath's Georgian architecture is striking for the uniformity of the façades in its terraces and crescents. This was achieved by the developers' insistence on a careful regulation of the builders through covenants in the conveyances of the plots, a practice that is evident in the development of Westgate Buildings in the 1760s. The developers – a tailor and a hosier's widow in Bath – expected the builders to erect a substantial stone and timber house 22 feet wide in a line with the rest of the houses in the block, but to erect the whole front and particularly the windows and doors, 'of such height and with such ornaments and in such manner agreeable to a design and plan drawn of the elevation of the whole pile of building'.[16] Both developers and builders signed to show their agreement.

The apparent unity of Georgian Bath is achieved through the common use of building in Bath stone and the classical uniformity of its architecture. It was not planned as a unity but rather grew piecemeal in several phases throughout the century. Building land was divided among a number of owners on the north and west of the city, so preventing the working out of a homogeneous plan. Typically, developers worked on a few acres at a time and prepared schemes unrelated to neighbouring projects. While Queen Square, the King's Circus and Royal Crescent were all planned separately, the Woods linked them together. St James Square, planned in 1790 on the same estate by different developers, had no relation to the Wood schemes. The principal exception, the Bathwick district on the east of the city, was promoted by a single owner, William Pulteney, and took place at the height of Bath's building boom in the later 1780s.

Thomas Warr Attwood designed the twenty-one houses which make up The Paragon between 1768 and 1775. They were built on land leased from the corporation, with the standard elevation for buildings on civic property.
PHOTOGRAPH: CARNEGIE, 2004

above A view of Lansdown Crescent, with
chairmen awaiting customers.

below A view of the Paragon, right, and Axford Buildings beyond, with the
Vineyards on the left, by J.C. Nattes, 1804.

Table 1 *The occupations of members of the Corporation of Bath at twenty-year
intervals through the eighteenth century*

1700 (26 members)

1 tailor	2 saddlers
1 mercer	2 vintners
1? clothier	1 attorney
14 unidentified	13 of the 26 owned or had owned lodgings or inns

1720 (28 members)

1 clothier	2 saddlers
4 vintners	2 maltsters
1 barber	1 milliner
1 baker	1 glazier
1 distiller	1 shopkeeper
4 apothecaries	1 mercer and quarry owner
1 linen draper and mercer	7 unidentified
3 of the 28 may have owned lodgings or inns	

1740 (30 members)

1 linen draper	1 woollen draper
1 saddler	6 vintners
2 maltsters	1 baker
1 shopkeeper	1 upholder
1? attorney	1 'gent'
1 ironmonger or tallow chandler	3 plumbers and glaziers
6 apothecaries (1 also 'gent')	1 postal contractor and quarry owner
3 unidentified	

1760 (30 members)

1 saddler	1 vintner
1? baker	2 attorneys
3 surgeons	1 silk weaver
1 ironmonger	1 postmaster
1 carrier	1 bookseller
1 tallow chandler	1 'esq.'
1 linen and woollen draper and wholesaler	2 plumbers and glaziers (also builders)
8 apothecaries (1 'gent', 1 'esq'.)	1 carpenter and joiner
1 wine cooper and land developer	1 postal contractor and quarry owner
1 unidentified	

1780 (30 members)

2 linen drapers	1 silk weaver
1 hosier and hatter	1 laceman
1 bookseller	1 saddler
1 carrier	2 physicians
6 surgeons	3 attorneys
5 apothecaries (2 'gents')	2 bankers (both originally apothecaries)
1 mailcoach contractor, theatre owner, etc.	3 unidentified

As Table 1 shows, the corporation included many men of apparently humble occupational backgrounds. There was a relative lack of participation in civic government by the resident social elite. However, towards the end of the century there is a discernible increase in the proportion of professionals – for example surgeons, physicians and attorneys.

1800 (30 members)

1 linen draper	1 saddler
1 brewer	1 wine merchant
7 apothecaries	5 surgeons
2 bankers	3 esquires
1 theatre owner	4 doctors of physick (1 knight)
1 surgeon and/or physician	1 chemist and druggist
2 unidentified (possibly apothecaries)	

Source: Sylvia McIntyre, 'Bath: the rise of a resort town 1660–1800', p. 224, in Peter Clark (ed.), *Country Towns in Pre-industrial England* (Leicester University Press: Leicester, 1981).

The Circulating Library and Reading Room, 43 Milsom Street, which also served as the state lottery office.

Political power in Bath was in the hands of businessmen, shopkeepers, tradesmen and commercial interests. A distinctive feature of local administration in Bath during the eighteenth century, and beyond, was the relative lack of participation by the resident social elite in the political life of the city. As Table 1 illustrates, the corporation included many men of apparently humble occupational backgrounds. Participation in the governance of Bath was, however, determined by those who already held power, since the city was run by a self-perpetuating oligarchy. The corporation elected its officers from its own members. Aldermen (a minimum of four and a maximum of ten) and common councillors held office for life. Vacancies were filled by nominations from the council, which usually selected men who had purchased the freedom of the city. The corporation (which also sent two Members to Parliament) controlled the freemen, who had rights to practise trades and to share in the income from the commons. Freedom could be achieved by servitude (which entailed serving an apprenticeship within the city limits) or by purchase, the price of which was increased from just over £10 in 1733 to £75 in 1801. The mayor, nine aldermen and twenty councillors formed the governing group, which kept tight control of business within the city.

The advantages to an ambitious man of being a member of this group are exemplified by the career of Thomas Warr Attwood, who clearly used his position for self-advancement. He was a partner in the Bladud Bank, and served on the council committee set up to supervise the building of the new

CIRCULATING LIBRARY AND READING ROOM

BOOKSELLER
BINDER
STATE
LOTTERY
STATIONER
OFFICE

THE FIELD

Guildhall in the 1760s. Although described as a plumber and glazier by trade, he managed to secure for himself the position of city architect. He then succeeded, despite some opposition to his plans and estimates, to win the contract for building the Guildhall. The pursuit of vested interests and the practice of nepotism were marked features of local government in eighteenth-century Bath, as in many other places. The resident social elite, largely excluded from the political life of Bath, played only a minor part in the city's development. The leisured and professional classes were mainly confined to the role of lessees, but even in this role they were out-numbered by tradesmen, and their significance declined over time. These classes accounted for 36 per cent of lessees for the Parades (1740–49) but at most only 20 per cent of those for corporation developments in 1761 and 1781; a similar picture can be seen in Bathwick between 1788 and 1792.[17]

Conflicts of interest arose between various parties within the city during the building of Bath. The corporation clashed with William Johnstone Pulteney over his belated decision to build shops on Pulteney Bridge. His influence and power were sufficient to allow him to override the objections of the corporation, but local interest groups defeated him on another part of his plan for the Bathwick estate. Before Pulteney Bridge was completed, he proposed a second one across the Avon at Bathford. He intended to put in a new turnpike which would have diverted London traffic from the turnpike through Walcot, across the Bathwick

A late eighteenth-century view of Pulteney Bridge and beyond, with ferry boats carrying passengers across the river to the Spring Gardens, Bathwick. The original drawing, by T. Hearn, was exhibited at the Royal Academy in 1792.

estate and into the city over Pulteney Bridge. This would have raised land values in Bathwick to the benefit of the Pulteney estate, but it was strongly opposed by the corporation and by the trustees of the existing Bath Turnpike (established in 1707), who included several council members and some developers. Pulteney's scheme came to nothing, for his opponents triumphed when it was first raised in 1771 and did so again in 1774. The structure of investment in the Bath turnpike reveals only limited involvement by its trustees, whereas the role of the small urban saver became increasingly important.[18] Investments of £500 or less, and in the range of over £500 but less than £1,000, made up a significant portion of the value of total holdings in the company in the period between 1785 and 1805. Much of this investment was local, and from the later eighteenth century tradesmen and artisans appear occasionally as contributors. Women were particularly important in the 1770s, when they provided 46 per cent of the capital then raised, and they were drawn from all classes. Among the gentlewomen and the widows and daughters of professional men, lodging-house keepers and even a few servants also featured as investors. When the turnpike trustees themselves were in conflict with the corporation in the 1780s they were therefore defending the interests of a group far broader than any local elite. News

Walcot Parade, *c.*1770. Above the London Road, Walcot Parade has the highest raised pavements in Bath. When first built, these fashionable houses faced open countryside. Many are now converted into flats.

PHOTOGRAPH: CARNEGIE, 2004

'A PRETTY BAUBLE, CONTRIVED FOR SHEW.'

'... A HANDSOME WEDGWOOD PLATE.'

CONTEMPORARY COMMENTS ON THE CIRCUS, BATH

109

spread that one of the powers being sought under the proposed Improvement Act in 1789 would allow the corporation to raise money by imposing an extra half-toll on the Bath turnpike, to be used as security for borrowing £25,000. Local landowners, colliery owners, coal hauliers and citizens joined the trustees in opposition to the proposal. The corporation gained the powers it sought, but the Act embodied exemptions and provisos designed to ensure that visitors to the city – rather than residents or tradesmen – would pay the toll, and thereby finance the development of facilities for their benefit and that of Bath's economy.

As a result of the 'rage for building', lodgings for visitors became cheaper, and improved in quality and comfort. The weekly cost of hiring a room fell from 10 shillings in 1700 to half that price by the 1740s, when John Wood estimated that the city could accommodate 12,000 visitors. Physical expansion was closely associated with social segregation in eighteenth-century Bath, and what was a 'good address' changed over time. The northern half of Avon Street (built in the 1730s as part of the first phase of development outside the city walls) was designed to provide fashionable lodgings, but within a generation Avon Street

left The Saracen's Head, one of the city's oldest public houses, dates from 1713 and stands at the back of St Michael's Church, with entrances both to Walcot Street and Broad Street. The Broad Street frontage retains its overhanging gables and is typical of how much of early half-timbered Bath would have looked before the great rebuilding of the eighteenth century. Charles Dickens stayed at the Saracen's Head in 1835 while he was a parliamentary reporter.

PHOTOGRAPH: CARNEGIE, 2004

right St Michael's church in Broad Street, *c*.1833. This lithograph shows the classical church built 1734–42 by the local stonemason John Harvey. It replaced the medieval church but was rebuilt again a century later, in 1834–37. Reflecting the religious enthusiasm of the period, the pew accommodation was then increased from 500 to 1,200.

BY COURTESY OF BATH CENTRAL LIBRARY, BATH & NORTH EAST SOMERSET COUNCIL

had lost its wealthy clientele to the new developments north of Queen Square. The area between the abbey and the river Avon, in a low-lying part of the city frequently inundated by flood water, gradually came to be one of small-scale industry and working-class housing.

Visitors endured considerable inconvenience as the city was developed. It was less of a problem in the outlying areas – Camden and Lansdown Crescents or the building of Pulteney Street on Bathwick meadows – but with the Pump Room and Bath Street, in the heart of the city, discomfort was unavoidable. Fanny Burney, who admired Bath's impressive beauty – 'it looks like a city of palaces' – was nevertheless moved to write in 1788 to her sister, Hetty:

> This city is so filled with workmen, dust & lime, that you really want two pairs of eyes to walk about in it – one for being put out, & the other to see with afterwards ... Even the streets round the Pump-room are pulling down for new edifices, & you can only drink from their choice stream, by wading through their chosen mud ...
>
> Certainly, unless you are advised to come hither for health, I should advise you not to see this place these two years, at least, for pleasure; as the avenue to the Pump rooms will not be sooner finished, & walking here in winter must be next to impracticable. However, when all these works are completed, & the completers, with the usual gratitude of the world, are driven aloof, this city, already the most splendid in England, will be as noble as can be conceived.[19]

Topography mirrored the differences between social classes. As Lady Nelson observed when writing to her husband from New King Street in the spring of 1797, in Bath it was the case that 'the higher you go, the dearer'.[20] By this time it had become fashionable to rent a house for the season, rather than lodgings, but while annual rents were £90 in New King Street they were £160 in Gay Street.

The increased numbers of visitors brought valuable income to the city. The historian Neale has estimated that the earnings of innkeepers from the letting of 324 rooms and providing stabling for 451 horses brought in just over £9,000 per annum, while expenditure on other items added a further £18,000. This was roughly equivalent to the income derived from lettings in lodging houses.[21]

The standard rate for a room in the 1720s was 10s. per week and 5s. for a kitchen or garret. A substantial lodging house, such as that owned by the Duke of Chandos and worked by Mrs Phillips, consisted of forty rooms, seventeen garrets and seven kitchens. Weekly earnings of up to £26 for the twenty weeks of the season, plus a further £100 from out-of-season income, yielded a profit of around £500 per annum. If the twenty-nine lodging houses in Bath generated,

The rear views of some of Bath's architectural gems often reveal piecemeal construction and many odd accretions behind the uniform façade. This first-floor extension was probably built to provide a water closet.

PHOTOGRAPH: CARNEGIE, 2004

on average, the more modest figure of £300 each per annum, a total income into the city amounted to almost £10,000 from the renting of rooms alone. Add to that a further £20,000 paid for other services and visitors brought something of the order of £60,000 to the city in the early part of the century.

Such calculations also reveal the importance of a middling sort of people – innkeepers, lodging-house keepers, shopkeepers, and tradesmen of all kinds – who were needed to sustain the pleasures of the fashionable company.

The fashionable company

The number of visitors that actually went to Bath in any one year is difficult to establish. Estimates range from 8,000 at a season in the early eighteenth century to Wood's claim of accommodation for some 12,000 by the 1740s. The visiting company listed in the *Bath Journal* from its origins in 1744 gives some indication of the numbers who were deemed to be of sufficient 'quality' to merit inclusion. These rose from 510 in 1746 to 2,525 in 1760, 3,091 in 1780 and 5,341 in 1801. This growth in numbers was encouraged by Bath becoming more accessible between the late seventeenth century and 1800, as transport facilities and roads improved. The number of weekly services from London to Bath (a distance of some 107 miles) was between 32 and 46 from 1740 to 1777, but had increased to 147 by 1800. Moreover, the

Gentle satire at the expense of the company on North Parade. Originally Grand Parade, it was intended as a summer promenade where visitors could enjoy a shaded aspect.

BY COURTESY OF BATH CENTRAL LIBRARY, BATH & NORTH EAST SOMERSET COUNCIL

One of George Speren's fan designs, 1737, showing the interior of Mrs Lovelace's Rooms – named after the retired opera singer who ran the second Assembly Rooms, in the lower town, at that time. Built in 1729, they were known variously as Lindsey's, Wiltshire's and Gydes' Rooms. They were demolished when York Street was built in the early nineteenth century.

journey time from London by road (which was over 60 hours before 1680) fell from 36 hours in 1750 to little more than ten hours by the late 1790s. The summer season gradually evolved into two short seasons in autumn and spring, but in 1762 the master of ceremonies estimated that it had extended to six full months. Evidence from the *Bath Guides* indicates that, from 1780, the expensive season for lodgings lasted nine months, from September to May. Improvements to lodgings and public facilities, in addition to Bath's growing popularity, probably account for this change. Indeed, as early as 1739 the poet Alexander Pope 'drank Bristol Hotwell water in Bath, because he wanted the comforts available there in winter'.[22]

The season at Bath became an integral part of the annual social round of the nation's aristocracy and lesser nobility, but as the premier resort in England, the city attracted an increasingly extensive range of visitors. The cultural elite of the Georgian period, for example, was also attracted to

Garrick's Head public house occupies part of the ground floor of the Theatre Royal building. The bust over the entrance, by Lucius Gahagan, dates from 1831.

Bath. Among the litany of famous names associated with the city are those of the novelists Fielding, Smollett and Jane Austen, the painter Gainsborough, and the actors Garrick and Sarah Siddons. And, as the city grew in size and prestige, the social composition of its visitors broadened to include many modest clients from the middling gentry and the rising professional and commercial middle classes. Among these less distinguished visitors was a boat-owner from Langport, Somerset, who stayed for three months from September 1796. His wife tried the

Prior Park, 1752, by Anthony Walker. Ralph Allen opened his house and gardens to visitors on one day a week. The stone tramway was a tourist attraction in its own right, here being viewed by some of the fashionable company. The tramway, one of the earliest rail systems in the country, carried stone from Allen's Combe Down quarry to the wharf on the river Avon at Widcombe.

waters at the Hot Bath once and the couple went to prayers at the abbey several times, as well as making one attendance at Lady Huntingdon's propriety chapel. They made no visits to the Pump Room or to any functions at the Assembly Rooms.[23]

The entertainments and pleasures on offer in Bath were vital to its success as a spa. In general, it was the lure of fashionable frivolity that brought in the visitors, even though some, like the Langport boat-owner and his wife, did not participate

fully in the social round. By the 1720s, according to Defoe, bathing was 'made more a sport and diversion, than a physical prescription for health'.[24] Simply to be in Bath for the season, 'Where gaming and grace, Each other embrace, Dissipation and piety meet,'[25] to see and be seen as part of 'the company', was the underlying motive for most visits whatever the ostensible reason. At least two-thirds of those who came to take the waters did so, in the opinion of one commentator in 1776, 'entirely from the influence of fashion and to alleviate an insurmountable itch for pleasure'.[26]

Bath's appeal to all kinds and conditions of men and women, in the relentless pursuit of pleasure and escapist fantasy, was captured in a contemporary satire, *Amenities of Bath*, by Thomas Haynes Baily:

Proposed alterations
to the Cross Bath,
dated 22 July 1797.
The reconstruction,
by John Palmer, was
completed in 1798.
BY COURTESY OF BATH CENTRAL
LIBRARY, BATH & NORTH EAST
SOMERSET COUNCIL

left John Wood's
design for the Hot
Bath, to replace the
medieval bath on the
site.

right The Hot Bath in
1829, as it was rebuilt
by John Wood the
younger in 1775–77.
BY COURTESY OF BATH CENTRAL
LIBRARY, BATH & NORTH EAST
SOMERSET COUNCIL

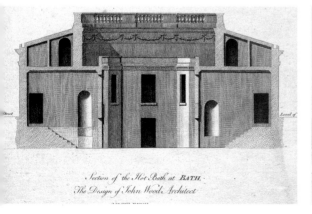

In this auspicious region all mankind
(whate'er their taste) congenial joys may find;
Here monied men pass for men of worth,
And wealthy cits may hide plebeian birth;
Here men devoid of cash may live with ease;
Appear genteel, and pass for what they please;
Here single men their better half may claim
And flirting spinsters lose that doleful name;
Here husbands weary of domestic strife
May please themselves, and live a single life;
And married ladies, in their husband's view,
May freely flirt, and boast their conquests too;
Here boys and girls may marry in their teens,
And live on visionary ways and means;
Here fortune-hunting beaux delude the fair
With large estates and castles in the air;
Here lovely belles so sensitive appear,
They fall in love at least four times a year;
Here busy Scandal's ever-ready tongue
Will interfere to regulate the young,
Brings every hidden mystery to light,
Corrects the weak, and sets the erring right,
Declares what actions they should choose or shun,
What they may do and what may be done.
Here doctors conscientiously contrive,
By daily calls, to keep their friends alive;
Whilst daily calls produce a daily fee![27]

Yet the social tone had changed considerably by the mid-eighteenth century. The city had been transformed from a riotous, brawling place into one that was at least superficially decorous, where social life was governed by rigid conventions. This transformation is commonly ascribed to Richard 'Beau' Nash (1676–1761), who imposed a strict code of behaviour on 'the quality' who thronged the spa. Nash came to Bath in 1705. An educated man who had, however, already failed in more than one career, he had a passion for gambling and a reputation as a talented organiser of social events. His known connection with court life and the social scene in London were, no doubt, useful assets when he came to Bath as little more than a penniless adventurer. Contemporaries and some historians credit Nash with enormous influence on the development of Bath and even portray him as the primary instigator of most of the improvements made to the spa, but his role has been greatly exaggerated. Even his 'appointment' as master of ceremonies in 1705, a part of the Beau Nash legend, is not documented in the corporation records, and he was probably chosen informally by the company to fulfil this function.[28] Nonetheless, as 'King of Bath' Beau Nash set the social

tone of the spa by imposing – through sheer force of personality – his rule of conduct on the visitors. Duelling and the carrying of swords in the city were discountenanced, men in riding boots and women wearing white aprons (the emblem of prostitution) were banned from assemblies. Nash's code of manners was published and posted up in various public places. It also appeared in the *Bath Guides*, until long after his death in 1761.

Diversions and entertainments abounded in Bath. Visitors of distinction were

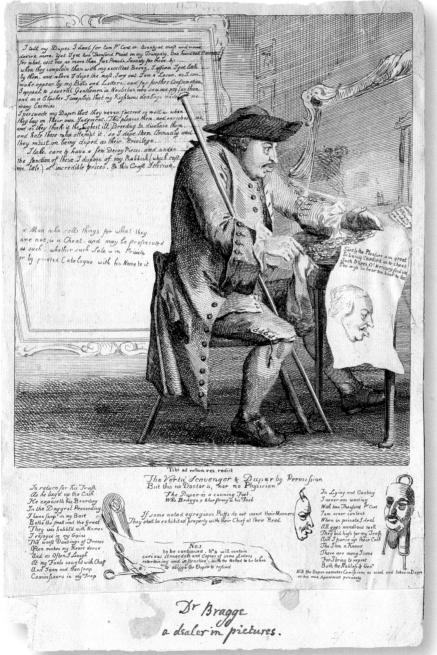

'Dr Bragge – a dealer in pictures', but 'no Doctor, nor no Physician'. Bragge evidently duped many of his customers into paying a great deal more for his treasures than they were really worth: 'I persuade my Dupes that they never succeed so well as when they buy on their own judgement. This pleases them and enriches me … I take care to have a few Decoy pieces and under the sanction of these I dispose of my Rubbish (which cost me little) at incredible prices. By this Craft I thrive.'

Richard Nash, self-styled 'master of ceremonies' and social celebrity, was born on 18 October 1674 in Swansea, the son of Richard Nash, glassmaker, and his wife, the niece of the royalist army officer, Col. John Poyer. Nash was educated at Camarthen grammar school and in 1692 he matriculated from Jesus College Oxford. His father wished him to embark on a legal career, but Richard was more attracted to the social life at Oxford, and at the age of seventeen he became involved with a local woman to whom he proposed. Nash was dismissed from his college and began a brief period as a womanizer.

His father purchased him a commission in the army, but he soon escaped the unwelcome regimentation to enrol as a student at the Inner Temple and began to find his true vocation as a man about town. He endured private hardship to present a continuously elegant and refined public image. Extravagance and his self-promotion through amusing and much recycled anecdotes became Nash's defining characteristics. His many acts of generosity also formed part of his lifelong personality trait. In 1695, he supervised a pageant held at the inns of court in honour of William III, and this success led him within a decade to offer his services as assistant to the master of ceremonies, Captain Webster, at Bath.

Nash was probably drawn to Bath in 1705 for the same reasons as many other gamblers and philanderers, but his talent for showmanship, for capturing the public mood, and for understanding the economic realities facing the town's corporation, set him on his transformed career. Following Webster's death in a duel in late 1705, Nash was elected to the post of master of ceremonies in Bath.

His biographers claim for him a vital role in the transformation of the city from a place of convalescence to one dedicated to fashionable entertainment. In truth, his arrival coincided with a period of change as the corporation sought to respond to the demands of an increasingly prosperous set of visitors. Nevertheless, he played his part in the improvement of civic amenities in Bath, introduced a band of London musicians paid for by subscription, and improved communications around and within the city. Weekly subscriptions and the profits from gambling also

An oil painting of Richard 'Beau' Nash (1674–1761), c.1761, by the Bath artist William Hoare (1707–92). The portrait was presented to the corporation by the artist after Nash's death in 1761.

Popjoy's restaurant, next to the Theatre Royal in the Sawclose. Beau Nash and his mistress, Juliana Popjoy, moved to this house in the late 1750s, and it was here that Nash died, aged 86, in February 1761.

PHOTOGRAPH: CARNEGIE, 2004

financed Harrison's new assembly rooms for dancing, refreshments and card games.

Nash's central aim was the creation of a community in which rank and background were respected but were also attuned to his principles of accommodation and assimilation. Social conduct was governed by politeness and an affable sociability. His famous 'Rules to be observ'd at Bath' laid down the procedures for the fashionable company under the strict guidance of the self-styled 'King of Bath'. He rebuked not merely a gauche tradesman or country squire, but famously criticized the duchess of Queensberry for wearing an apron and forbade Princess Amelia to continue dancing after 11 p.m. In 1716 Nash was granted honorary freedom of the city for the cultural and commercial benefits he had brought. The next twenty years saw Nash at the height of his powers and from 1735 he spent July and August at Tunbridge Wells where he introduced new facilities and entertainments. His presence in both places was supported by his take from the gambling tables, and when this was revealed in court in the 1750s, after Nash claimed he had been cheated out of 2,000 guineas, his public stock began to fall. Further disputes arose over Nash's alleged profiteering from public subscriptions. These scandals undermined his standing and authority. By the late 1750s, he was severely in debt and had to sell many of his effects and moved to more modest lodgings on the Saw Close. The corporation granted him a monthly pension of £10. He died in 1761, aged 86, and was survived by his former mistress, Juliana Popjoy, who had left Bath after their separation, resolving 'never more to lie in a bed', spent the next thirty years living in a hollow tree near Warminster until her death in March 1777.

Source: *Oxford DNB* (2004) vol. 40, pp. 225–32.

This handsome memorial in Bath abbey pays poetic tribute to Beau Nash, who died in relative poverty in 1761, by then a figure of fun in high society but still held in affection by some:

If social Virtue make remembrance clear,
Of Manners pure, on decent rule depend;
To His Remains consign One Gratefull Tear,
Of Youth the Guardian, and of All the Friend ...

PHOTOGRAPH: CARNEGIE, 2004

listed in the local papers and greeted on arrival by the master of ceremonies. Bell-ringing and music from the town band were part of the welcome, despite complaints from the sick, but like everything in Bath they had their price, from half a guinea (52p) upwards according to social rank. A visit to the Pump Room and baths was part of the daily round, if not to bathe then to enjoy the spectacle of the 'quality' and trade folk 'jostling each other without ceremony'.[29] The Lower Rooms (originally Harrison's, opened in 1708) and Upper Rooms (1778) included card rooms, tea rooms, and ballrooms for the twice-weekly balls which were funded by subscription tickets. These were formal events in the early evening, followed, after a tea break, by country dancing with no distinction of social rank. Nash's code decreed that balls ended promptly at eleven o'clock. Theatrical performances and musical events provided alternative evening entertainments. Days were whiled away by strolling along the streets or in the pleasure gardens, shopping or merely window shopping, browsing in the libraries or dropping into a coffee house. But, despite the best efforts of Nash, every taste was catered for; beneath the veneer of elegant refinement and strict codes of public behaviour there lay a sordid world of gambling, pornography and vice.[30]

Gamblers and card sharpers flocked to Bath in the early eighteenth century. Even Beau Nash's income derived from his luck at the tables, for he received no salary as master of ceremonies. Public concern about the nationwide craze for gambling led to various Acts of Parliament to suppress private lotteries and games of chance. New games were invented to evade the Act of 1739 and, as they in their turn were made illegal, the prohibition on games involving numbers was circumvented by substituting letters for figures as, for example, in the game 'Even or Odd'. Nash promptly bought up all rights in the game, after taking professional advice as to its legality. E and O, as it was known, was introduced at Bath and Tunbridge Wells, with Nash taking a share of the profits from both spas. He was cheated of some of his share – or so he believed – and sued his partners for £20,000. Nash lost the case, and his reputation: his vested interest in organised gambling had not previously been common knowledge, and his amateur status was destroyed by the revelation. Beau Nash lived on until 1761 in relative poverty, no longer the darling of 'the quality' but the butt of jokes among the visitors. Meanwhile, E and O, and all games of chance, were prohibited by Act of Parliament in 1745. As a result, gaming

The western gable wall of the terrace on the south side of the Orange Grove. The terrace was built as a plain row in 1705–8, but was given a new façade (visible on the left) by Major Davis (see page 174) in 1897. Davis added the ground-floor shop fronts and shell hoods to the upper windows, as well as the corner feature at the far end of the terrace.

PHOTOGRAPH: CARNEGIE, 2004

was banned from the assembly rooms, and keepers of illegal gaming houses in the city were prosecuted. Inevitably, this simply drove gambling underground. As late as 1790 a visitor commented that there was virtually no other place in the world where gaming was carried on to such a pitch as it was at Bath.

Part of the proliferation of obscene writing in the first half of the eighteenth century was made up of the pornography that was available in Bath. The most notable example is Thomas Stretzers' *A New Description of Merryland*. Merryland, a 'Paradise of Pleasure, and Garden of Delight' was the female body, its physical form and sexual attractions described in the manner of a serious work of topography. It was brought out in 1740 by James Leake, Bath's leading printer and bookseller. Within two years it had gone into a tenth edition and become the book of the season, gleefully discussed by mixed company over the coffee cups and card tables. It is highly likely that similar books were available from some of the ten bookshops and libraries in the city at the end of the century. Indeed, Georgian Bath, according to R. S. Neale, was 'suffused with sex'. It certainly provided opportunities for romantic flirtations and illicit sexual encounters as well as functioning as a marriage market. Brothels and bawdy houses, street walkers and casual prostitutes were commonplace, long before Smollett's reference in 1771 to 'the nymphs of Avon Street', a pointer to the infamous 'red-light' district that Avon Street became.

So many of the visitors to Bath left some record of their impressions that innumerable perspectives compete for attention. Alexander Pope enjoyed the amusements of the place in 1714, whereas Horace Walpole disliked the company at Bath in the 1760s. The artist William Landor loved the city, but Jane Austen, who visited and lived there at times (and who is closely associated with Bath in her novels *Northanger Abbey* and *Persuasion*), is said to have hated the place. Many writers, however,

The Grand Pump Room (1790–95) is by Thomas Baldwin, but the work was completed by John Palmer after Baldwin's dismissal in 1793. The building replaced the first Pump Room which had been built in the style of an orangery and opened to the public in 1705. It provided a place to drink the waters and to view the bathers in the King's Bath. It soon became a popular place to meet in the mornings. As visitor numbers increased more space was needed, and the Pump Room was extended in the 1750s and then completely rebuilt as seen here towards the end of the century. An opening ceremony was performed by the Duchess of York in 1795. Following the rediscovery of the Roman baths in 1878–80, the Concert Room extension was opened in 1897.

PHOTOGRAPH: CARNEGIE, 2004

The 640 or so monuments in Bath abbey record some of those who, like Anne Finch of Essex, came to take the waters but found no cure. After 'a tedious and severe illness', she died in August 1738, 'in the flower of her age and Bless'd with a plentiful Fortune ... the first real occasion of Greif [sic] she gave her Sorrowful Mother was her DEATH.'

shared an urge to mock Bath's pretensions by poking fun at its image and satirizing its proclaimed fashionability and elegance. One of the most caustic literary representations of Bath is in Smollett's *The Expedition of Humphry Clinker* (1771). Smollett's landowner from Wales, Matthew Bramble, found nothing but disappointment in Bath. His naive young niece Lydia saw the corrupting city as 'an earthly paradise', but Bramble was critical of the architecture, horrified at the sight of ulcerated bodies in the baths, and uncertain whether 'the patients in the Pump-room don't swallow the scourings of the bathers'. As for the company, Bramble declared Bath a place where 'a very inconsiderable proportion of genteel people are lost in a mob of impudent plebians'. To his horror, one of the 'distinguished' visitors welcomed by bell-ringing was 'Mr Bullock, an eminent cow-keeper of Tottenham'. Bramble's nephew described the social mix at Bath to a friend in the following terms:

The Penitentiary Chapel to Ladymead House in Walcot Street. Ladymead House became a female penitentiary in 1805 for the purpose of rescuing 'fallen women' in Bath. The chapel, built in 1845, replaced houses used until 1824 as an isolation hospital to treat venereal diseases. It is a surviving monument to the practice of prostitution in the city as well as to the charitable endeavours of those who tried to combat 'the great social evil'.

No. 20 The Vineyards, a Palladian villa dating to *c.*1765, opposite Axford Buildings. The Vineyards, so called from the vines that were grown on the slope until around 1730, are unusual for Bath in the variety of styles and scale of buildings.

PHOTOGRAPH: CARNEGIE, 2005

Yesterday morning, at the Pump-room, I saw a broken-winded Wapping landlady squeeze through a circle of peers, to salute her brandy-merchant, who stood by the window, propped upon crutches; and a paralytic attorney of Shoe-lane, in shuffling up to the bar, kicked the shins of the chancellor of England, while his lordship, in a cut bob, drank a glass of water at the pump.[31]

By the 1770s, such chaos of the social orders in Bath deterred many of the quality from visiting. Over the second half of the eighteenth century Bath slowly ceased to be a centre for elite fashionable groups, although it continued to attract growing numbers of middling-gentry visitors, and those of the professional and commercial middle classes, whose presence somewhat lowered the social tone. Those of the nobility and upper classes who did visit became more status-conscious and showed a preference for select private parties rather than the vulgar throng of evening assemblies. The miseries of public places in Bath were further deplored by satirists Samuel Sensitive and Timothy Testy, who captured the expectation of sensual delight, but also the social disdain of the period:

In the pit, at the opera – turning briskly round, on hearing a box-door open close by you, in hopes of feasting your eyes on some young angel whom you expect to appear, and beholding, instead of her, that sort of hideous old-crabbed looking crone of fashion, whose face is as full of wrinkles as her head is of diamonds.[32]

The growth of the city and the rise in its popularity had increased social segregation and altered the forms of social life. The master of ceremonies could no longer meet all the visiting company, and public entertainments were being replaced by private events among various 'sets' or cliques. Other spas – smaller, more exclusive and often cheaper – were now competing with Bath. Leamington Spa and Tunbridge Wells were attracting visitors, and Cheltenham (where the population rose from 3,076 in 1801 to 13,396 in 1821) was a well-established rival. Moreover, a change in medical opinion in favour of sea-bathing encouraged the development of seaside resorts.

Lansdown Road: late eighteenth-century houses. Here, as elsewhere in Bath, advantage has been taken of the slope to provide ground-level storage space. Conversion to use as a garage, as above, would add considerably to the value of the property.

PHOTOGRAPH: CARNEGIE, 2004

Royal patronage is often seen as crucial to the growth of Brighton, visited
by the Prince of Wales from 1783, and of Weymouth, where the King was a
visitor from 1789. Their visits (as in the case of royal patronage of Bath in the
late seventeenth and early eighteenth centuries) were not actually a cause of
the development of these resorts, but an indication of the powerful influence of
medical fashion. Just as Bath benefited earlier from the medical enthusiasm for
inland spa waters, so Brighton and other coastal resorts gained economically

from the new enthusiasm for sea-bathing. By 1801 Brighton was the largest resort in Britain, with a population of 7,339. The number of recorded visitors to Brighton in 1760 was 400, but over 4,300 visited the resort in 1794. Smaller resorts closer to Bath were also developing. As early as 1788 Ilfracombe, for example, was reported to be 'remarkably full of genteel company . . . from most parts of the country'.[33] Furthermore, the influence of the Romantic movement developed the fashion of visiting mountains and moorland, while after the end of the Napoleonic wars, in 1815, European tours also competed with the attractions of Bath. Yet it was the sheer size of Bath that effectively destroyed its reputation as an exclusive resort of the quality.

The number of houses in the city increased by 45 per cent between 1780 and 1793. Market forces had earlier led to the speculative building boom of 1710–20, in response to the demand for lodgings, but an even more active period of construction took place from 1780 to 1793, after Bath had passed its social peak as a fashionable resort. By 1793, war with France had broken out and the last phase of development ended abruptly. The resulting economic uncertainty led to a general loss of confidence that culminated in a financial crash. Two of Bath's banks went broke, several entrepreneurs and members of the corporation were made bankrupt, and buildings stood unfinished as funds ran out. Receipts for the half-toll on visitors using the turnpike roads into the city reached their highest level in 1792, then dropped sharply between mid-1793 and mid-1795. There was no sustained recovery until the early 1820s, although the building industry recovered somewhat around 1805, and for a lucky few, individual fortunes revived. The builder John Pinch, made bankrupt in 1800, was active as an architect-developer by 1807. A new theatre was built at Beauford Square in 1804–5, and housing was put up at New Sydney Place (1807–8), Park Street (1808), Cavendish Place (1808–17) and Sion Hill Place (1817–20). Several churches were also built, including St Mary's at Bathwick (1814–20), which was designed by John Pinch.

The opening decades of the nineteenth century, then, foreshadowed Bath's developing status as a highly desirable place to live. What attracted people to Bath was no longer the social glamour of its heyday but more mundane things, such as the cost of living. This was what brought the Eliot family of Jane Austen's *Persuasion* (1818) to Bath in 1814. When Sir Walter Eliot's spendthrift ways forced him to retrench by letting his country residence, Bath was chosen as the most appropriate place for a prolonged visit because 'he might there be important at comparatively little expense'.[34] The period from 1700 to 1820 had therefore witnessed Bath's rise to become the most fashionable resort, followed by its decline into staid respectability. It was 'discovered' and enjoyed by a

Marshall Wade's house at 14 Abbey Churchyard, built c.1720. The Bible Society had its depot here in the early twentieth century. The house is now occupied by the National Trust gift shop.

BY COURTESY OF BATH CENTRAL LIBRARY, BATH & NORTH EAST SOMERSET COUNCIL

wealthy elite who tired of it as their presence, and the development stimulated by their demand, increased its popularity and size so much that it lost its defining exclusivity as a destination for the 'quality'.

The enduring image of Bath, promoted even in many modern guide books, offers a celebratory and heroic perspective on the Georgian city. It is seen as the embodiment of the highest aspirations of its age for an ordered and gracious society, and its creation is often ascribed to the individual talents of Ralph Allen, Beau Nash and John Wood. In reality it was the product of market forces and the fashions of the time, and what it became was open to harsh critical and satirical commentaries from writers such as Smollett and Austen. Our understanding of its image needs to be informed not only by the gracious world portrayed by Gainsborough and Reynolds, but also by the savage caricatures of Rowlandson and Gilray. Bath was, as Neale says, a 'valley of pleasure' for some, a 'sink of iniquity' for others.[35]

St Mary the Virgin, Bathwick. The finest of Bath's Gothic Revival churches, designed by John Pinch the Elder in 1810, and built in 1817–20. The building costs of over £14,000 were met largely by private loans.

PHOTOGRAPH: CARNEGIE, 2004

Raby Place, Bathwick Hill, designed by John Pinch the Elder, 1818–25. Originally called Church Street, Raby Place exhibits many typical nineteenth-century external features such as the ironwork balconies with tented canopies seen to the left. The development of Bathwick Hill reflected the flight of the middle classes from urban living to the new suburbs. Architectural styles also shifted from the classical terraces characteristic of Bath to picturesque Regency villas. On the upper slopes of Bathwick Hill Henry E. Goodridge (Pinch's successor as surveyor to the Bathwick estate) built a series of Italianate villas in the 1830s and 1840s.

PHOTOGRAPH: CARNEGIE, 2004

Although the spa was indeed the pre-eminent resort of frivolity and fashion for most of the period from 1700 to 1820, the emphasis often given to its appeal for 'the quality' and the cultural elite obscures other important aspects of its history. There is, for example, no place in the present-day image of 'Georgian Bath' for the other extreme of the social order – the thieves, prostitutes, pickpockets and beggars, whose presence constantly threatened to undermine the notion of Bath as a centre of elegant refinement. Moreover, the importance of its leisure function can easily be over-emphasised, thereby distorting our understanding of its increasingly varied economy and social mix. As we shall see in the next chapter, the lower orders of society and the labouring classes also played their full part in the life of Britain's premier resort, and Bath's prosperity was certainly not dependent solely on the income derived from its wealthy visitors.

'... THE FIRST OBJECT THAT SALUTED MY EYE, WAS A CHILD FULL OF SCROPHULOUS ULCERS, CARRIED IN THE ARMS OF ONE OF THE GUIDES, UNDER THE VERY NOSES OF THE BATHERS ... GOOD HEAVEN, THE VERY THOUGHT MAKES MY BLOOD RUN COLD!'

THE EXPEDITION OF HUMPHRY CLINKER, 1771

CHAPTER 4

The lower orders, 1700—1820

THE LABOURING POOR were the least visible element of Bath's contemporary image.[1] Well into the nineteenth century and indeed beyond, Bath was perceived predominantly as a place without significant industry or extensive trade. Far more conspicuous was the undesirable 'company' whose arrival in the city was invariably heralded by the annual influx of wealthy visitors. An assortment of rogues, vagabonds and petty criminals also came for the season, and for specific events such as the Bath races. Their presence could not be ignored, for Bath was notorious for its beggars. The nursery rhyme 'Hark, hark, the dogs do bark, the Beggars are coming to town', dated about 1790, records the response to their arrival, and they were a subject of common complaint when it was customary to pen a few lines in celebration of a visit to the city:

'HARK, HARK, THE DOGS DO BARK,/THE BEGGARS ARE COMING TO TOWN'

NURSERY RHYME, *c.*1790

> I always have heard that the provident major
> Had a terrific rod to make beggars beware;
> But I find to my cost, they infest ev'ry street –
> First a boy with one eye, – then a man without feet,
> Who cleverly stumps upon two pattern rings, –
> One bellows, one whimpers, one snuffles, one sings;
> From Holloway's garrets and cellars they swarm;
> But I pause, – on this subject I'm growing too warm.[2]

Beggars, rogues and vagabonds

The old Elizabethan Act of 1572 that had been intended to regulate the presence of the sick and poor was never more than partially effective, and after it lapsed in 1714 they came to Bath in ever growing numbers, in search of a cure for their ailments or alms from the city's charities and visitors. Charitable benevolence was a part of Bath's self-image, but the authorities were always uneasy about the threat to social order posed by the underclass. They were also continuously concerned about the possibly damaging effect the notorious beggars of Bath might have on the city's trade and reputation. Their attitudes and policies were based on the perceived need 'to discriminate real objects of charity from vagrants and other imposters who crowd both the church and the town to the annoyance of the gentry residing here and who ought to be, by the care of the magistracy, expelled and punished'.[3]

A mixture of humanitarianism and enlightened self-interest therefore inspired the charitable activities of Bath's wealthy residents. Beau Nash, Ralph Allen, John Wood, numerous apothecaries and physicians, and many other members of the local elite became involved with a project to build a hospital for 'poor lepers, cripples and other indigent persons resorting to Bath for cure, well recommended and not otherwise provided for'.[4] The city became 'the hospital of the nation' and managed thereby to impose some control on the poor sick while also contributing significantly to maintaining the health of the national workforce. Founded in 1738 as the Bath General Hospital (now the Royal National Hospital for Rheumatic Diseases), it was unique at the time in admitting patients from all parts of the country. Its specialism in the treatment of rheumatism and arthritis grew out of the proven effectiveness of hydrotherapy in cases of paralysis. Admission to Bath General Hospital was tightly controlled. Only those deemed likely to benefit from the waters, and who had been recommended by a 'responsible person' as

Holloway in the early twentieth century. Much of Holloway to the south of the Avon was swept away in the late 1960s, when nearly 400 houses (most of which dated from before 1875) were demolished to make way for Calton Gardens, the housing development known to its detractors as the 'hen coops' of Holloway.

BY COURTESY OF BATH CENTRAL LIBRARY, BATH & NORTH EAST SOMERSET COUNCIL

being worthy of charity, were allowed entry. This policy went some way towards ensuring a suitably deferential attitude on the part of the patients, and it also benefited the reputation of the hospital. A careful selection of suitable cases for treatment guaranteed a satisfactory level of 'cures', providing evidence of the efficacy of the Bath waters.

Between 1790 and 1811 fourteen new charitable organisations were founded in the city. These included the Stranger's Friend Society (1790) and the Society for the Relief of Lying-in Women (1792). In 1805 the most important charity for the poor in Bath was founded. It was the creation of the social elite of Bath and became financed by the same group. Its original, and revealing, title was 'The Society for the Suppression of Common Vagrants and Imposters, the relief of Occasional Distress, and the Encouragement of the Industrious Poor'.

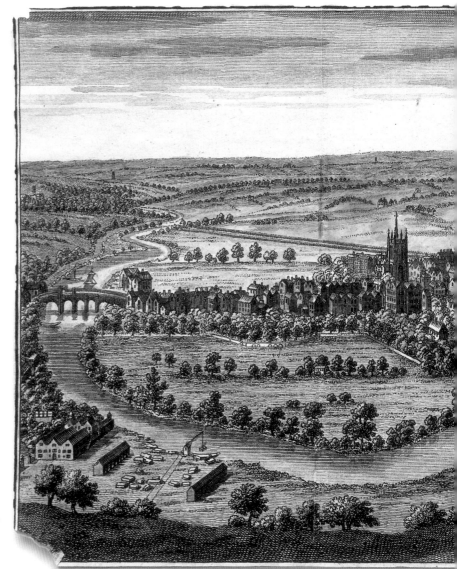

South East View of Bath, 1764. This copper engraving by J. Ryland shows the city still set in open fields and quite compact, although development was already under way outside the city walls. The tramway from Ralph Allen's Combe Down quarry terminates at the wharf on the south bank of the river, left foreground, where stone is being loaded by crane onto a vessel. Down river is the Old Bridge, with Broad Quay beyond it on the north bank.

Later in the nineteenth century its title was changed to the Monmouth Street Mendicity Society. It was a forerunner, in its policy of discriminating charity and case-study approach, of the famous Charity Organisation Society, which was founded nationally some 60 years later.

Contemporaries did not fully understand the economic basis of mendicity, but their fear of 'imposters' reflected their outrage at the threat to the social hierarchy that profitable begging posed. The Monmouth Street Society employed anecdotal evidence in its annual reports to support the claim that beggars represented a mass of trickery posing as genuine poverty. The case of a black beggar was cited in the 1812 report. When the man was arrested for assaulting a woman during a quarrel over sharing their takings,

THE LOWER
ORDERS,
1700–1820

he was found to have collected 8s. (40p) from passers-by in only a few hours. The underlying question was who would work for the employing classes if a man could get as much from a day's begging as he could from a week of honest work. Yet the belief that most of the vagrants and beggars in Bath were imposters was not actually borne out by the Society's own figures. Only about a third of the cases investigated could be classed as fraudulent. Those who applied to the Society for relief included the resident poor, but also men on the tramp looking for work, the wives of soldiers on active service, and the continual flow of emigrants from Ireland *en route* to London from Bristol. The numbers helped by the Society probably account for a large proportion of the total passing through Bath, but by no means all. In 1817, a year of acute economic depression, 5,062 travellers were aided by the Monmouth Street Society.

'THIS PIECE OF GROUND WAS IN THE YEAR 1736 SET APART FOR THE BURIAL OF THE PATIENTS DYING IN THE BATH GENERAL HOSPITAL, AND AFTER RECEIVING 238 BODIES WAS CLOSED BY THE GOVERNORS OF THAT CHARITY IN THE YEAR 1849, FROM REGARD TO THE HEALTH OF THE LIVING.'

PLAQUE BY BOROUGH WALLS

The labouring poor

The city attracted numerous immigrants from its rural hinterland and beyond. An analysis of the places of origin of over 350 applicants for poor relief in the years between 1763 and 1824 shows that only a minority, less than 20 per cent in fact, had been born in Bath.[5] The counties of Somerset, Wiltshire and Gloucestershire accounted for 56 per cent of the total, the remainder coming from more distant parts of England, from Wales, Scotland and Ireland, or from overseas. There is further evidence of long-distance migration from Ireland in the records of the Catholic community in Bath. By 1785 there were over 400 adult Catholics in Bath, more than a quarter of whom were Irish. The social and occupational structure of the Bath Catholic-Irish community is, however, likely to have been as diverse as that of the small Jewish community.

Jewish settlers in Bath came from various parts of Britain, and from continental Europe. They included professional men and tradesmen as well as men like Joseph Moses, who earned his living as a street trader in 1764.[6]

There were also African, Afro-Caribbean and Asian people living in Bath in 1700–1820, although little is known of their numbers or experience. Personal service was their most probable occupation, although there are scattered references to 'black' paupers and casual labourers. The first definite evidence of the presence of Asian servants occurs in 1812, by which time Bath was established as a favourite place of retirement for military officers and former employees of the Indian Civil Service and East India Company merchants. The economy of Bath was linked with the slave trade, which may explain the presence of some ethnic minorities in the city. Investment in Bath from Bristol, which owed much of its prosperity to the trade, was one aspect of this involvement. Moreover, the Duke of Chandos was implicated by his role in the Royal Africa Company, while the Pulteneys owned large American plantations, and in addition, many of Bath's wealthy residents and visitors derived their income from overseas estates. It was fashionable in the eighteenth century to have a black boy among the household servants, and in 1759 the *Bath Journal* offered a thirteen-year-old for sale, advertised as 'quite black, well-built, intelligent, musical, trained as a footboy and skilled in waiting at table'. Humanitarian sentiments co-existed with complacency about slavery, however, and Bath was caught up in the national anti-slavery campaign of the late 1780s and early 1790s. Two of the local papers supported abolition, but the political elite was unsympathetic to the cause. The corporation held aloof, and a petition against slavery (signed by over 1,000 people in Bath) was presented to Parliament by Somerset MPs, because the city's representatives declined to do so.[7]

Information about the occupations of Bath's inhabitants during the eighteenth century is extremely sparse. The sources of evidence are few, and they relate

'QUITE BLACK, WELL-BUILT, INTELLIGENT, MUSICAL, TRAINED AS A FOOTBOY AND SKILLED AT WAITING AT TABLE.'

ADVERTISEMENT, BATH JOURNAL, 1759

A POOR CARPENTER

Thomas Roberts was born in Monmouthshire and apprenticed in 1781 to an iron-foundry at Lydney, in Gloucestershire. He qualified as an iron-founder after five years' service, but in 1792, when he was aged twenty-six, he went to Bath. There he agreed with Richard Hewlett, a carpenter and speculative builder, to work for him for three years in order to learn the trade of carpenter without formal apprenticeship.

Thomas was grossly exploited as cheap labour during his early years in the city. He was paid only 4s. to 5s. a week while learning his new trade, at a time when unskilled labourers in Bath were earning around 9s., and agricultural labourers in Somerset and Wiltshire could earn 7s. to 8s. a week. At the age of fifty, Thomas Roberts was an applicant for poor-relief on behalf of himself, his wife, and their four children. He faced an impoverished old age.

Source: R. S. Neale, *Bath*, pp. 76–7.

The Poor House, Walcot.

Walcot Street today accommodates a number of small retail businesses. In the nineteenth-century city directories listed a broader range of trades and enterprises: in 1854, for example, there was a thriving manufacturing sector including a basket maker, a bookbinder, boot and shoe makers, brush maker, cutler, gun maker, hatter, locksmith, tailor, milliners and dressmakers, straw-bonnet makers, stonemason, sign-writer, printers, wheelwright and umbrella maker. In the service sector there were several regular markets as well as grocers, tea dealers, butchers, poulterers, bakers, a chemist and druggist, one corn factor, a salt merchant and a tripe dealer. On the street also were listed two 'Eating and Chop House Keepers', and one pawnbroker.

chiefly to the skilled trades and the professions. For the period from 1706 to 1769 the enrolments of apprentices to freemen provide some indication of the most popular trades, while by 1773 the *Bath Guides* list members of certain professions. Directories of trade and commerce, newspapers, and visitors' accounts of the city also yield some evidence but there is insufficient data to support anything more than generalisations.[8]

Accommodating the visitors and meeting their needs employed a substantial proportion of the labour force but, nonetheless, Bath was not without trade and industry. Two fairs a year were still held, albeit of dwindling importance and partly superseded by a larger fair at Lansdown during the month of August. The regular food market grew in size and economic importance as Bath developed. Guides to Bath and other watering places usually contained comments about the availability, quality and price of provisions, which made the markets a particular concern of the corporation. The shambles area was improved around 1745 and in the 1760s stalls for market gardeners selling produce were laid out. In the following decade, associated with the building of a new Guildhall, a permanent market place was built. Markets were held on two or three days each week, and they were regulated by the corporation through a system of inspection and the licensing of traders. The

An aquatint of the west front of the abbey and Abbey Churchyard, 1788, by Thomas Malton. Wade's Passage runs between the houses abutting the north wall of the Abbey and Marshall Wade's house.

Bath market became something of a feature and it was said to surpass anything in London in 'its excellent order and abundance'.[9]

Although there was no large-scale industry, crafts and retail trades flourished in Bath. Manufacturing on a small scale in craft workshops was characteristic of the city in the eighteenth century, and continued to be so in the nineteenth century. What relatively large-scale industry there was often went unnoticed by visitors, and was conveniently ignored by many contemporary commentators on Bath, because it was located in peripheral areas beyond the old centre or in the newly built parts of the city. There were two cloth mills at work in the parish of Walcot in 1730, and industrial villages grew up beyond the city limits. The manufacture of wool cloth continued in the parish of Lyncombe and Widcombe, and at Twerton, long after it had ceased in the city itself. By the end of the century, other industries were established in Bath but their presence was not intrusive. Brewing, glass manufacture, soap-making, and iron-making were of increasing significance in the local economy. However, these were relatively small enterprises and they were located in the unfashionable area of Bath along the riverside. Consequently, they did not impinge on the dominant perception of Bath as the resort of quality.

Bath, despite its specialisation, clearly had a mixed economic base in the

A DOMESTIC SERVANT

Martha Abraham was the daughter of a substantial tenant farmer at Chew Magna, in north-east Somerset. Unlike many girls of her generation (who were likely to start their working lives at the age of eight or nine as domestic servants at between £2 and £5 a year), Martha, who was born c.1746, lived at home with her parents until she was about twenty years old.

She then went to Whitchurch, near Bristol, as servant to a gentleman for an annual wage of £5. Almost a year later, 'being in poor health', she moved to Bath and stayed – perhaps supported by her family – until she was recovered, when she returned to Chew Magna and took work for a Mr Doyling at £6 a year. Two years later Martha moved on again, to the Hotwells at Clifton, where she stayed for three years as an unwaged housemaid in a lodging house. It was not unusual for servants in lodging houses and hotels to work for only their board and lodging, relying on the generosity of guests for 'tips', but on moving back to Bath Martha chose a steady wage of £5 yearly and her keep in the household of Mr Nightingale of St James's parish.

Nine months later, she quit this job and went into service for James Mullaway, a wine merchant in the same parish. Mullaway paid Martha a good wage of £8 a year, in addition to her keep, and she 'lived under that hiring' for some fifteen months until October 1773, when she 'quitted that service and went into the country to her friends at Chew Magna for a week only'.

Back in Bath, she hired herself as servant to Mr John Bryant, a soap-boiler in Walcot Street, in the parish of St Michael's. A few months later, in early 1774, Martha Abraham – now aged twenty-eight, unemployed and pregnant – was examined for poor relief. Martha deposed that the father of the child she was carrying was her former employer, the wine merchant James Mullaway.

Some two-thirds of the applicants for poor relief in Bath and Walcot between 1763 and 1674, were women, and about half of these were unmarried, pregnant women or abandoned wives with one or more child. It is likely that Martha Abraham was dismissed by Mr Bryant as soon as her pregnancy became visibly apparent.

Source: R. S. Neale, *Bath*, pp. 72–4.

Table 2 *The occupations of Bath inhabitants during the eighteenth century*

A *Evidence from the enrolment of apprentices analysed by the occupations of masters*

| | Numbers of apprentices enrolled | | |
Occupations of masters	1706–27	1728–49	1750–69
Clothiers and weavers	1	3	–
Tailors	73	55	61
Cordwainers	96	70	47
Drapers, milliners, mercers and haberdashers	17	13	22
Other textiles/dress	13	22	21
Building	81	91	129
Other crafts	47	39	67
Victualling	97	67	71
Medical	33	27	34
Other professional services	1	–	–
Transport and entertainment	46	49	62
Miscellaneous	3	–	–
Total number of apprentices	508	436	514

B *Percentage of apprentices enrolled in occupational groups*

	1706–27	1728–49	1750–69
Clothing and shoemaking	39.4	37.4	29.4
Building	15.7	20.9	25.1
Crafts	9.3	8.9	13.0
Victualling	19.1	13.1	13.8
Professional	6.7	6.2	6.6
Services	9.1	11.2	12.1
Miscellaneous	0.6	–	–

Source: Adapted from Table 18(A), p.215, S. McIntyre, 'Bath: the rise of a resort town 1660–1800' in Peter Clark (ed.), *Country Towns in Pre-industrial England* (Leicester University Press, Leicester: 1981).

eighteenth century. Its occupational structure (as far as it can be reconstructed) is set out in Tables 2 and 3, but this quantifiable evidence tells us little of the occupations of the unskilled or the semi-skilled. These workers are subsumed within the unhelpful categories 'other' or 'miscellaneous'. Yet Bath obviously offered opportunities to rural immigrants.

John Silverthorn, residing in the parish of St Michael, was examined on 7 September 1764. He was about 39 years of age, born in Trowbridge, Wiltshire, where his father grew up. Both his father and mother died when he was very young. Soon after, he was apprenticed by his uncle, the overseer, to James Mowly of Bathford, Somerset, tiler and plasterer, with whom he lived and served for the term of five years, and completed his apprenticeship when his master moved to Batheaston. He had done no other act to gain a settlement, except nine years

Ralph Allen's cottages. These cottages on Prior Park Road south of the river are a rare survival from the early eighteenth century. These workers' cottages were built by John Wood the Elder around 1737 to house some of Ralph Allen's stone miners.

PHOTOGRAPH: CARNEGIE, 2004

before, he married Ann Pritchard. They had three children, aged 6, 5 and 1½, all residing in the parish of St Michael. John Silverthorn made his mark in the presence of Mayor Samuel Bush and Frances Hales.[10]

The building trades prospered as the town expanded, and this was a labour-intensive industry. Especially so in Bath where steep, uneven sites had to be levelled, and much of the work involved in building the squares and crescents required little more than muscular strength. Strength was also the prime requisite for those who worked as 'chairmen', carrying the wealthy visitors about the town. The numbers of chairmen (licensed by the corporation, which published a tariff or list of charges according to distance and steepness of the road) rose in the period 1744 to 1799 from 120 to 340.[11] Some men would have found work in delivering coal from door to door in Bath, or in loading and unloading cargo at the riverside. Others may have worked in the capacity of mere 'hands' in the inns, lodging houses, coffee rooms, workshops and small factories of the city. Men and women (though comparatively few) worked as 'bath guides' – supervising the clientele at the spa,

below The broad categories of employment listed in Table 3 reflect the general concentration of trade and manufacturing in the central parishes of SS Peter and Paul (the abbey parish) and St Michael, as well as in Lyncombe and Widcombe.

Table 3 *Occupations of Bath inhabitants, by parish, according to the 1801 Census*

	Agriculture	Trade, manufacturing and handicrafts	% of population in agriculture or trade	Other occupations
Bath city				
St James	2	372	9.4	3,588
St Michael	1	933	25.2	2,766
SS Peter and Paul	1	2,305	93.6	159
Walcot	253	1,935	12.4	15,371
Bathwick	34	104	3.8	2,582
Lyncombe and Widcombe	93	575	20.6	2,122

Source: Table 18(E), p.217 Sylvia McIntyre, 'Bath: the rise of a resort town 1600–1800', in Peter Clark (ed.) *Country Towns in Pre-industrial England* (Leicester University Press, Leicester: 1981).

providing the bathing costumes and generally being at the beck and call of the visiting company as they took the waters. Both men and women survived by working as costermongers or street sellers, selling a range of goods from fruit and vegetables, to haberdashery, ballads and pamphlets. A willingness to carry provisions about the town for retailers or to act as 'porter' to overburdened visitors laden down with purchases from Bath's tempting shops made it quite easy for those immigrants without skills to earn money – but the proliferation of poor strangers seeking a livelihood as 'basket carriers' provoked the corporation into establishing a licensing system in 1767, which curtailed such activities. Domestic service was an important sector of employment, particularly for women. Indeed, Bath seems to have offered more labour opportunities for women than for men, and this is one reason for the greater number of females recorded in the census returns from 1801. Servants were needed by Bath's permanent residents, as well as its visitors, not only as footmen, ladies' maids, or general domestics, but also as gardeners and laundresses. Those who worked for 'the company' were sometimes employed directly, but they could be supplied by the lodging house or inn-keeper. When Louis Simond stayed at the White Hart in 1810 he noted that 'the servants have no wages – but, depending on the generosity of travellers they find it their interest to please them', and he went on to say that the servants cost him about 5s. (25p) a day.[12]

The Poor Law settlement examinations which were held to determine entitlement to poor relief in Bath, or preferably elsewhere, provide examples of migrants who were attracted to Bath in search of better employment prospects. Large numbers of female servants found work in the city, but there was little security of employment in domestic service:

Elizabeth Shoare was examined on 21 May 1763 before Mayor Frances Hales and John Chapman. She was living in the parish of Walcot but was born in the parish of Frome Selwood in Somerset. About four years previously she was hired as a servant to the late Dr Chittick in Chapel Row, in Walcot, living in his house for about two years. Then about a year and a quarter since, she became the servant of Mr Coe in Bradley's Buildings in St James's parish at a rate of £5 per year. This lasted nine months when she left her master for about five weeks, returning on his request for a further seventeen weeks. Elizabeth

A monument in the abbey erected in 1764 'to the memory of the best of Parents, Leonard Coward of this city, Lace-Merchant, and Elizabeth his wife'. The dutiful and loving son died in 1795. Coward probably traded in lace supplied from Devon and the south Midlands, which were both centres of lace-making until machine production of the fabric began in Nottingham in the late eighteenth century.

PHOTOGRAPH: CARNEGIE, 2005

141

signed her name with a mark. On the basis of her testimony, she was entitled to relief in Walcot, Bath, as well as in her home parish of Frome Selwood, having been hired for a year living in with her master.[13]

Skilled migrant workers coming to Bath faced the power of the citizens or freemen who, under the control of the corporation, determined who had the right to practise trades within the city. The corporation increasingly encouraged the purchase of 'freedom', as a means of raising revenue, although whether they were legally entitled to do so is uncertain. However, by 1810, the purchase price was over £250. The most powerful company was that of the Merchant Taylors, reflecting the role in the local economy of the wool and cloth industry. Membership of a company and freedom of the city gave a man considerable influence and scope for ambition, even if he did not practise a trade. The Quaker Richard Marchant served an apprenticeship to his father and became a Merchant Taylor, but his career was that of land speculator, building developer, and agent for men engaged in urban development, such as the Duke of Chandos.

Freeman heads of families in Bath apprenticed their sons, and the sons of near relatives, to a wide range of occupations, numbering 68, for much of the eighteenth century. Between 1724 and 1769 the most numerous apprenticeships were as shoemaker (137), carpenter (122), tailor (81), barber and wig maker (77), apothecary (65), mason (51) and baker (50). These occupations were all related to the demands of the visitors, but the general growth of population in Bath inevitably increased the market for the services of tradesmen such as bakers,

'The fish market', from Thomas Rowlandson's Comforts of Bath. The high quality of provisions on sale at the market was emphasised in the *Bath Guides*, although here the gouty visitor seems rather unimpressed by what he sees.

grocers and chandlers. Moreover, a growing diversification of employment as the city expanded is suggested by the fact that the proportion of apprentices entering the manufacturing sector (other than building) rose in this period from 11 to 25 per cent. However, citizen control of trades in Bath was eroded as the result of a dispute between the Company of Merchant Taylors and William Glazeby, who traded in the city as a tailor from 1756 but whose right to do so was challenged in 1759 by the Company. Legal wrangles dragged on until 1765. The final decision went against the Merchant Taylors and laid down that the power of regulating and fining non-freemen lay with the corporation. This effectively destroyed the power of the companies who thereafter never paraded their privileges through the streets of Bath. Only one apprentice tailor was enrolled in the following three years, and by 1774 the total number of enrolled apprentices in any trade in Bath had fallen to two. The skilled sector of the labour market was thus opened up to those who had the money to purchase freedom, which became the only means of attaining citizenship, but increased competition from incomers led to violence and intimidation by tailors trying to protect their interests. Several of them were involved in attempts to compel cut-price journeymen to leave the city in 1784.

The immigrant and Bath-born labouring classes lived somewhat apart from the upper classes, unless they were resident servants, but class segregation in the social organisation of space was less marked in Bath before 1820 than it became later, when the process of suburbanisation speeded up. Overcrowding was a common experience as pressure on the housing stock arose from the influx of labour required to build the Georgian city, or attracted to it as a general labour market. Consequently, once-fashionable lodgings became tenement buildings let out by the room. Gardens and stable yards in the Avon Street area, developed for lodgings in the early eighteenth century, became filled in with courts and workshops. New artisan housing for skilled workers was, however, built in the eighteenth and early nineteenth centuries, in Morford Street, Ballance Street, and Lampards Buildings. All of these were in close proximity to the King's Circus and the Royal Crescent. To sustain the comfortable life styles of wealthy residents and visitors it was necessary to have laundresses and dressmakers, chimney sweeps and gardeners living nearby.

Little is known of the living standards of the labouring classes in Bath during this period, or of levels of unemployment at any time, although seasonal unemployment was probably commonplace. The building industry (which would have employed substantial numbers of unskilled workers, who were likely to be laid off in the winter months) remained depressed for ten years or so after the crash of 1793. R. S. Neale has suggested that living standards fell for most of Bath's workers in the late eighteenth century, by at least

THE LOWER
ORDERS,
1700–1820

The view from Guinea Lane, 1833, looking towards London Road. The church spire is that of St Swithin's (1777–80) on the Paragon, Bath's only surviving classical-style parish church.

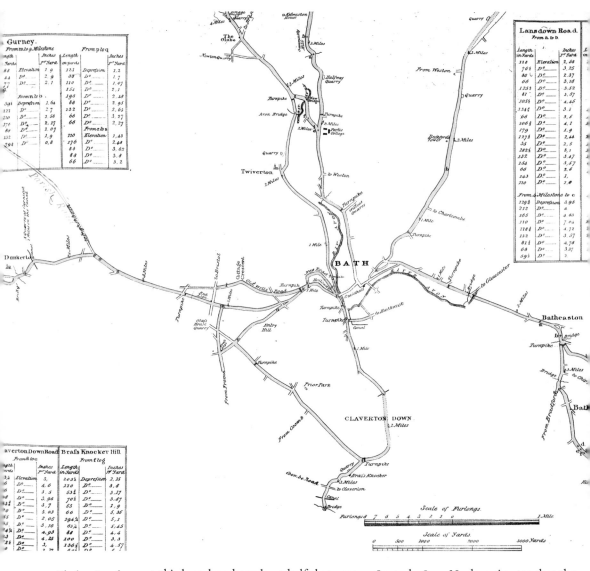

The location of turnpikes in and around Bath, 1827. The Old Wells Road, centre left, is now the suburban Bloomfield Road. Cottage Crescent, built c.1801, has become Bloomfield Crescent. Note the numerous small quarries which were a feature of the entire Bath and north-east Somerset district.

BY COURTESY OF BATH RECORD OFFICE

a third, and perhaps by a half, between 1780 and 1801. Neale estimates that the average weekly earnings of unskilled labourers rose by 20 per cent between 1779 and 1800, but that purchasing power – the 'real' wage – fell sharply. A penny loaf purchased in 1800 weighed only half what it had in 1780.

A good insight into the lives of the labouring poor can be found, paradoxically, in the coroners' inquests that identified the causes of unusual deaths. Common patterns can be discerned in lives blighted by poverty, drink, violence and despair. However, R. S. Neale's condemnation of the lives of savages without any saving graces can be firmly rejected. Research by Jan Chivers shows that amidst all the hardships borne, the poor still exhibited concern and kindness for their neighbours, and even cooperation with local watchmen and officials.[14] Two examples from several hundred cases suffice to show the plight of poor women, commonly resorting to infanticide, suicide or running the occupational hazards

Banner Down Road		
From Turnpike to ½		
Length in Yards		Inches p.r Yard
99	Elevation	2.94
132	Dº	2.62
66	Dº	4.25
66	Dº	3.9
402	Dº	3.54
66	Dº	2.23
66	Dº	2.65
366	Dº	1.32
66	Dº	1.43
66	Dº	2.56
66	Dº	2.32
176	Dº	3.05
154	Dº	4.3
110	Dº	3.26
66	Dº	3.
110	Dº	2.43
110	Dº	3.3
110	Dº	2.56
96½	Dº	2.17
198	Dº	2.74

GLOUCESTERSHIRE.

SOMERSET

WILTSHIRE

MILES

BANNER
DOWN
To ¼ Mile

of prostitution. An inquest was held before the Coroner on 14 April 1783 into the death of a new-born female child found lying dead in the King's Circus on the property of Sir Neal O'Donnell, baronet. Four servant witnesses and the surgeon testified that the body of the child was found in the 'necessary house' belonging to the dwelling. It was only discovered when the servants went in search of a black cat last seen in the vault of the privy. On holding a candle and looking down the vault, a servant called Beaton discovered the face of a child. He threw water on it to wash away some of the filth from it, and found it to be a female infant which from the appearance of it had been in the vault some considerable time. The servants all claimed they had no suspicion of any female in the house being with child and that the mother was unknown to them. It was also clear that there was a high turnover of servants in the house. The verdict of the inquest was that the child had been born alive to a mother not yet known, but who was considered guilty of murder: '… not having the fear of God before her eyes but being moved and seduced by the instigation of the Devil, feloniously, wilfully and of her malice aforethought did violently cast and throw down the new-born child in the soil or filth then and there contained in the said privy or necessary house and was then and there suffocated and smothered the child who died instantly'.[15]

Unfortunately, it was common for servant girls who became pregnant to rid themselves of unwanted infants in order to retain employment. When out of work, a regular feature of Bath's seasonal labour market, some had recourse to prostitution which was a flourishing industry in the city.[16]

On 6 March 1815, Mary Brown, a labourer's wife, was found lying dead at the Full Moon Public House at the bottom of Horse Street (later Southgate Street). Her last hours were recalled by several witnesses. Ann Reeves, who lodged in the same house in Attwood's Passage, testified that Mary Brown was drunk 2 or 3 times a day. The previous Saturday she had been seen leaving the Spreadeagle in Horse Street much the worse for liquor. She returned there from her lodgings with a young Wiltshire militia man, had 3 quarts of beer together, remaining till 8.30, and then went back with him to her lodgings. They then went off to the Plume of Feathers around 10 o'clock,

LOOKING DOWN THE VAULT … ONE OF THE SERVANTS DISCOVERED THE FACE OF A [DEAD] CHILD … HE FOUND IT TO BE A FEMALE INFANT WHICH FROM THE APPEARANCE OF IT HAD BEEN IN THE VAULT SOME CONSIDERABLE TIME.

where publican John Bradley testified that they had drunk a pint of beer and 2 glasses of gin and water. By 10.30 Mary Brown had become very abusive, using improper language, and the landlord asked her to leave, which she refused to do. At about 11.30, all the men left together, with Mary Brown – by now highly intoxicated – following them down the street. Around 8 the next morning she was fished out of the river Avon and taken to the Full Moon. No marks of violence were found; the verdict was death by drowning.[17]

Poverty and protest

Throughout the eighteenth century poverty and hardship fostered the recurrent threat of social upheaval. Sporadic outbreaks of violence and class hatred reflected a smouldering popular resentment of wealth and privilege. Across the country, the old order sought to protect its power and influence at times of turbulence at home and revolution abroad by resisting all reforms, retaining control of the political sphere, and maintaining the status quo. The aristocracy and gentry developed charitable activities in towns where they were influential, such as Bath, as an extension of their rural tradition of creating dependency among the tenantry on landed estates. The lower orders were expected to render due deference, loyalty and gratitude in return for largess from the elite.

Applications for relief inevitably went up during economic depressions but the numbers of poor relieved, and the timing of the foundation of charities, were related less directly to economic circumstances than to the level of anxiety among the wealthy classes about the threat to socio-political stability from the labouring poor. Charitable activity increased at times of political unrest and decreased when the relationship between rich and poor became more harmonious. The ideology that inspired much 'do-gooding' is exemplified by the evangelical pamphleteer Hannah More who was based at Bath in the 1790s, conducting her mission to quarry workers and miners on Mendip from Great Pulteney Street. More's numerous *Cheap Repository Tracts* were published by Samuel Hazard of Cheap Street, and they were widely circulated in the city. Nearly every bookshop in Bath stocked them, and street hawkers queued at Hazards to buy discounted bundles. The dominant theme of these moralistic tracts was that the social hierarchy was ordained by the Almighty, and that any challenge to the prevailing order invited divine retribution.[18]

'PEACE AND A LARGE BREAD, OR A KING WITHOUT A HEAD.'

Despite the attempts by the upper classes to impose social control on the lower orders, popular protest erupted in mob violence and riot in Bath during the late eighteenth and early nineteenth centuries. The writer Philip Thicknesse was hanged in effigy by a mob from Batheaston in 1780, ostensibly for having offended local patriots by intervening on behalf of a man taken by a press gang for naval service. Thicknesse himself believed the incident was provoked by 'the Gambling and trading part of the town', who had been offended by his mockery of the pretensions of Bath in his recently published *Valetudinarian's Bath Guide*.

In June 1780 Bath saw its share of violence during the nationwide Gordon riots, which demonstrated anti-Catholic feeling in support of 'Church and King'. A Catholic priest was attacked, the city's Catholic chapel was burned to the ground and nearby Catholic-owned property was looted. The Bath Volunteers failed to control events on the Friday and withdrew after one rioter was shot. Violence continued overnight, until troops from Wells and Devizes reached the city on Saturday. The leader, a footman named John Butler, was executed for his part in the riot. The loyalism of the mob was no consolation to the traders and authorities in Bath, for damage to the city's economy and image was immediate. Many wealthy visitors departed hurriedly, and the linen-draper and magistrate Francis Bennett urged the corporation to do all it could to restore the 'former lustre' of Bath's name as a peaceful place of safety.

Between 1792 and 1804 the elite in Bath responded to the rhetoric of revolutionary France, and growing radicalism among the labouring classes, by campaigning so vigorously against 'sedition' that the period was dubbed Bath's 'Reign of Terror'.[19] The campaign was co-ordinated by the Bath Association for Preserving Liberty, Property and the Constitution of Great Britain against Republicans and Levellers. The city's branch of this national organisation was chaired by the mayor, its committee drawn from magistrates, members of the corporation and principal property owners. Its activities created a tense, repressive atmosphere. French visitors were regarded with suspicion, allegedly seditious meetings were banned, and informers were encouraged to betray radical sympathisers. Several tradesmen were boycotted as suspected Jacobins. The Association took part in the national public bonfire ceremonies in the winter of 1792–93, to burn effigies of Tom Paine, whose egalitarian tract *The Rights of Man* had been declared seditious and its author tried *in absentia* for treason. It was a criminal offence to publish, circulate or possess a copy of this polemic. A journeyman tailor, Benjamin Bull, was arrested in August 1794 on the orders of the mayor after an informer reported Bull to the authorities. At his family lodgings in Wine Street, 38 copies of the pamphlet were found. Bull was imprisoned, but his destitute family was supported by public subscription, on the condition that he publicly renounced his sedition. Here again charity was used as a means of coercion. The tailor duly declared himself 'truly penitent' in the *Bath Herald*, a month before his release.

Radical organisations included a Bath branch of the London Corresponding Society, according to an informer, and the United Britons (a secret organisation which sought to promote co-operation with the United Irishmen) may have had contacts in the city. The Bath Irish came under suspicion in May 1798 when rumours circulated that, after the failed republican rising in Ireland that year, they were harbouring and arming United Irishmen, although the *Bath Chronicle* dismissed the rumours as unlikely. Numerous individual radicals were prosecuted for 'sedition', chiefly tailors and shoemakers who were 'much addicted to inflame and promote sedition' in the authorities' opinion.[20] Only a minority of prosecutions was successful, but nonetheless the threat of the force of law was a weapon of intimidation. Coercion in the work place also occurred. Benjamin Bull had been sacked for his political opinions a week before his arrest, and the Bath and West Society (a powerful employers organisation) actively sought declarations of loyalty from employees. In these circumstances it is hardly surprising that several thousand workers signed the Bath Association's membership book at the Guildhall.

Although political radicalism was effectively suppressed by the turn of the century, when popular protest in Bath was prompted by food shortages some protestors adopted political slogans. Leaflets circulating in the city included one headed 'Peace and a large Bread, or a King without a Head'. In March 1800, anonymous letters to the mayor and several employers threatened attacks on their property if prices were not lowered. An attempt to fire Stotherts' Ironworks followed, and a brewery on the quay was burned down. Garden robberies, poaching and violent robberies from millers and butter sellers, became increasingly commonplace. The 'moral economy', or sense of natural justice, that inspired many food riots prompted 200 women to mob dealers in the market in May 1800, forcing them to sell their produce cheaply. The angry women then rampaged out to Larkhall, where they set upon a gardener and carried off supplies of potatoes. They were eventually dispersed by the yeomanry.

In response to social disorder, the wealthy residents of Bath followed the example of other cities and set up a Provision Committee in December 1799. Over the following year it raised £3,000 by donations, which was used to buy food and coal for resale at low prices, to avoid the stigma of charity. The corporation took action in February 1801 by offering free stalls in the market to bakers from the rural areas around the city. Poor relief rates rose, but high prices absorbed much of the increase, and ratepayers, themselves adversely affected by inflation, became vociferous in their complaints about the standard of relief, which was lowered in some poorhouses after investigations of accounts and expenditure. In the years 1800 and 1801, £14,000 was distributed

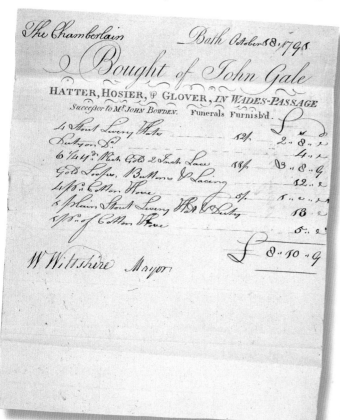

A bill dating from 1798 which has survived in the city chamberlain's accounts for items including rich gold lace, gold loops, buttons and lacing – probably for the mayor's ceremonial robes. The items were purchased from John Gale, 'HATTER, HOSIER & GLOVER, IN WADES-PASSAGE'.
BY COURTESY OF BATH RECORD OFFICE

in charitable relief but not all those in need were allowed to make purchases from the Provision Committee. This privilege was reserved for applicants with a written recommendation from a subscriber to the fund, who provided details of the applicant's name, address and family size. During 1801 a third of the city's population, some 10,000 people, were subsisting on a weekly distribution of rice. Local newspapers offered recipes for making rice bread and other dishes, but they lost no opportunity to remind the poor that they owed the rich 'respect, gratitude and obedience', and emphasised that 'idleness, discontent and riot, will make things worse'.

With its extremes of wealth and poverty, and a substantial labouring class, Bath was clearly a complex city in its heyday as a fashionable resort. It retained its dominant image in the opening decades of the nineteenth century, but that singular image did not reflect the occupational diversity of the city or the changes that had resulted from its expansion.

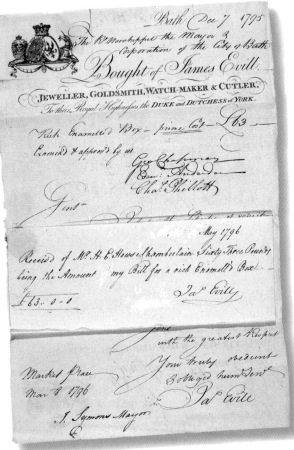

At the height of the Revolutionary Terror in France, James Evill, 'JEWELLER, GOLDSMITH, WATCH-MAKER AND CUTLER to their Royal Highnesses the Duke and Dutchess [sic] of York', is supplying the mayor and corporation of Bath with a 'Rich Enamel Box', costing the substantial sum of £63.

BY COURTESY OF BATH RECORD OFFICE

Bath was becoming a favoured place for permanent residence of the wealthy upper and middle classes, who chose to settle there in growing numbers rather than merely visit for a season's entertainment. This foreshadowed the altered image of Bath that emerged later in the Victorian period. Whereas the spa had been widely perceived as a temple of frivolity and fashion in its Georgian heyday, its dominant image in the nineteenth century was that of a sedate, unfashionable and conservative backwater, inhabited largely by maiden aunts and retired colonels. Bath then became the butt of satirists as a place where

> It sounds rather strange, but I tell you no lie,
> There's many good people that come here to die
> ... These folk, like Sir Lucius, find comfort in dying,
> Because in the Abbey there's very snug lying.[21]

This image, like the earlier one, emphasised only one aspect of the diverse realities of Bath's history. In the turbulent decades from 1820 and on into the early twentieth century, Bath was much more than a haven for old age and not all of its inhabitants were 'genteel residents'.

The Grand Ballroom at the Assembly Rooms, 1840, showing the orchestra gallery on the right and some of the ceiling panels decorated with elaborate plaster work.

The Queen's Levy in the Pump Room, 1817. Queen Charlotte, wife of George III, visited Bath in November and December of 1817, accompanied by the Princess Elizabeth and the Duke of Clarence. The royal party stayed in Sydney Place, and the Queen took the waters at the Pump Room each morning.

Genteel residence, 1820—1914 CHAPTER 5

T HE NEED for Bath to develop a new image was created by the economic consequences of its decline as the resort of fashion. Whereas in the eighteenth century Bath had courted 'the quality' for the season, in the nineteenth century it increasingly sought to tempt them to take up permanent residence in the city. The refined image it developed, in a bid to replace the loss of upper-class visitors with middle-class incomers, was also influenced by the general change over time in social values and attitudes.

The corporation's decision not to rebuild the Lower Assembly Rooms when they were destroyed by fire in 1820, but to erect a Scientific and Literary Institution on the site, reflected a move away from the frivolity of the eighteenth century to the more high-minded interests characteristic of the nineteenth century. The mood of the moment was caught in 1834 by Captain Roland Mainwaring, who proclaimed that by this decision 'Bath stands redeemed from the imputation of being a city devoted to pleasure and dissipation'.[1] Another change from the decadence of the Georgian age was reflected in the religiosity of Bath in the early Victorian period. The spate of church and chapel building and the growth of charitable societies expressed a new moral earnestness that dominated what in 1864 was claimed to be 'probably one of the most religious cities in the kingdom, at least externally'.[2] Indeed, religious enthusiasm threatened to destroy the public amusements of the city:

> The clergy of this town by their preaching and exhortations have endeavoured to suppress the various amusements of the place, and indeed so comprehensive have been their denunciations, that scarcely an entertainment of a publick character has escaped; concerts, balls, races, theatrical exhibitions, and even horticultural shows, have each of them been the subjects of clerical vengeance.[3]

The city was therefore undergoing another transformation. From being primarily the mecca of the rich in search of seasonal amusement it was to become much more a permanent retreat for pensioners and annuitants. This process had begun before 1820 but it gathered pace thereafter. What remained constant between 1820 and 1914, embodied in the language of the *Bath Guides* and in the utterances of local dignitaries, was a sense of the city's uniqueness, informed by the legacy of history. The ancient legend of Bladud, the link with

WILLIAM THOMAS BECKFORD
(1760–1844)

William Thomas Beckford, writer and art collector, was the only legitimate son of William Beckford, sugar planter and politician in Jamaica and London, and his wife Maria, née Hamilton, granddaughter of the sixth earl of Abercorn. The family owned twenty estates in the West Indies and, from c.1756, a 4–5,000 acre estate in Wiltshire, when an earlier house was replaced in 1768 with a lavishly furnished Palladian mansion, Fonthill. After the death of his father in 1770, the young Beckford was educated by a private tutor and later in Europe. Despite lengthy absences from England, he was MP for Wells (1784–90) and for Hindon, Wiltshire (1790–94 and again from 1806 until 1820). His writings include one of the earliest Gothic novels, *Vathek*.

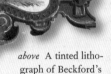

above A tinted lithograph of Beckford's Tower, 1844.

below The memorial on Beckford's tomb.

From 1796, he settled at Fonthill Gifford and (with the architect James Wyatt) began the transformation of the family mansion into the neo-Gothic Fonthill Abbey. Described by Byron as 'England's wealthiest son', Beckford had dwindled away his fortune until, by the early 1820s, his debts amounted to £145,000. When he arrived in Bath in 1822, Fonthill and two-thirds of his art collection had been sold.

Lansdown Tower was designed by Henry Goodridge as a study retreat for Beckford, and to house his library and the remnants of his collection. The 120 foot tower (completed in 1827) was sold after Beckford's death in 1844. It passed to the Rector of Walcot parish and became a funerary chapel. The garden became a cemetery where Beckford's tomb (above) can be found. The Tower is now owned by the Bath Preservation Trust and administered by the Beckford Tower Trust.

Sources: *Oxford DNB* (2004) pp.731–7; Philippa Bishop, 'Beckford in Bath', *Bath History*, ii (1988), pp.85–112.

classical antiquity through the Roman baths, and the architectural heritage of the Georgian masterpieces, were repeatedly publicised as enduring reminders of past glories. The past was also drawn upon to advertise the city's cultural traditions, through frequent references in the official guides to the famous artistic and literary figures associated with Bath in the eighteenth century.

A new image for Bath

In promoting Bath primarily as a place of 'genteel residence', its more immediate attractions were emphasised; any hint of the industrial or commercial character of the city was largely ignored or camouflaged. Naturally Bath continued to advertise the qualities of its hot springs in curing rheumatic disorders. It also drew attention to its mild winters and (after 1841) good railway communications with all parts of the kingdom. Particular prominence was given to the agreeable combination of high-quality shops and the availability of cheap food, coal and lodgings. Another virtue that Bath proclaimed repeatedly in its attempt to attract new residents was the very low level of its municipal, poor and water rates. For the modest contributions required, the city was able to offer fine buildings and parks, an increasing range of private schools, and amenities such as municipal supplies of water, gas and – by the 1890s – electricity. Diversions and amusements were still plentiful, at the Assembly rooms, the theatre and concert halls. Particular prominence was given to the city's growing reputation as a desirable place to live, since being among the 'right sort of people' was perhaps the most compelling reason of all for deciding to settle in Bath.

The refined and respectable image projected in the official guides was reinforced by commentators and journalists, who largely accepted it without question and

Royal Crescent, 1828, by Robert Woodroffe.

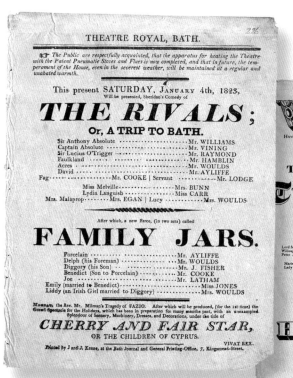

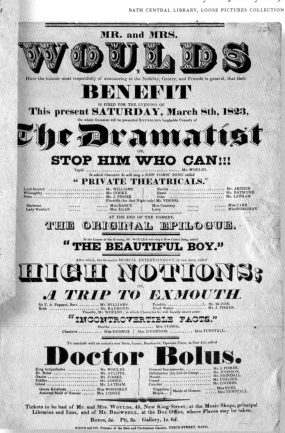

above A playbill for the Theatre Royal, appealing to a variety of tastes with a comedy, a farce and a tragedy on the bill for 4 January 1823, Sheridan's *The Rivals or a Trip to Bath* draws on his knowledge of the social scene in the city and perhaps on an unfinished play of his mother's, in which her 'Mrs Tryfort' anticipated Sheridan's 'Mrs Malaprop'.

echoed it in their own writings. The author of a magazine article in 1844, for example, informed his readers that:

> The visitant is well aware that Bath is not a city of trade. No manufacture worthy of note is carried on within its limits, nor is it the resort of commerce ... Of all places in the Kingdom, Bath is best fitted for the retirement of individuals with independent incomes, whether small or large. For those past the meridian in life, its quietness, beautiful neighbourhood, and warmth of climate particularly recommend it ... Trade in Bath consists principally in the sale of articles connected with the refinements rather than the necessities of life.[4]

Marketing Bath's new image proved so successful that the city became closely identified with its social elite. By the end of the nineteenth century its name was virtually synonymous with staid maiden aunts and retired military men:

> It is indeed a wonderful place of resort for very old people, of whom you see scores creeping placidly in the sunshine, or doddering about in corners

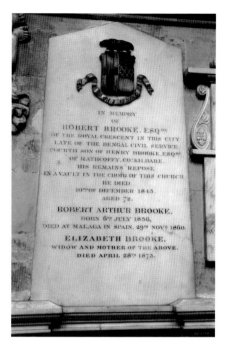

The memorial in Bath abbey to Robert Brooke of the Royal Crescent, 'late of the Bengal Civil Service', who died in 1843. Bath was a favoured place of retirement for employees of the colonial administration and former Indian army officers.

PHOTOGRAPH: CARNEGIE, 2005

sheltered from the wind ... Of these veterans, the large majority are composed of the retired military, among whom still linger the black stock with its satin 'fall', the pipe clayed buckskin gloves, the bamboo cane.[5]

Further evidence of congenial living for the military and respectable females is found in a piece entitled, *A Fortnight in Bath*, written in 1905 by William Dean Howell:

A large contingent of retired army and navy officers and their families contribute to keep society good there, and it is a proverb that the brains which have once governed India are afterwards largely employed in cheapening Bath ... I heard it said that the wheels of fortune were uncommonly well oiled for ladies who had to direct them unaided, and it seemed to me that the widowed or the unwedded could not be more easily placed in circumstances of refinement, which might be almost indefinitely simplified without ceasing to be refined ... Such is their control in matters which touch their comfort that it is said the consensus of feminine feeling has availed with the imperial government to prevent the placing of a garrison in Bath, on the ground that the presence of the soldiers distracted the maids, and enhanced the difficulties of the domestic situation.

The proclaimed old-world air of the place, the courtesy of its suitably deferential shopkeepers, and 'the uncommon civility of attendants at the Baths',[6] were especially appealing to a class of people anxious to preserve the traditions of a paternalistic society at a time of rapid socio-economic and political change. All the attractions and advantages of the city that managed to combine both high class and economical living were summarised in

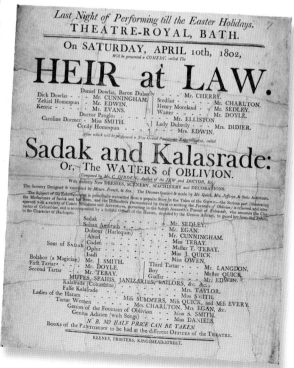

A playbill for the Theatre Royal, offering a comedy followed by a pantomime in April 1802. The theatre sank into provincial mediocrity during the early nineteenth century.

BY COURTESY OF BATH RECORD OFFICE

a letter quoted in the *Guide Through and Round Bath* of 1900. Signing himself 'A Contented Man', the writer declared that the city provided him with:

> refined society, where elegance and taste are the rule, vulgar show the exception, public amusement, delightful scenery within 10 minutes walk, house rent lower than anywhere else in a place offering the advantages of Bath, my table is *cheaply* supplied, and of the best, traders uniformly civil, obliging and fair ...[7]

Partly as a result of this marketing exercise, Bath continued to grow and develop as it adjusted to its changing role as a residential city. The physical expansion of the city incorporated middle-class suburbs that extended the spectacular developments of the eighteenth century. Bath remained one of the great cities of England until 1851, with a population of over 50,000. Thereafter its rate of growth lagged behind the general level of urban expansion. Yet, even when the aggregate population remained static during the second half of the century, suburban numbers grew apace.

'A WONDERFUL PLACE OF RESORT FOR VERY OLD PEOPLE, OF WHOM YOU SEE SCORES CREEPING PLACIDLY IN THE SUNSHINE, OR DODDERING ABOUT IN CORNERS SHELTERING FROM THE WIND.'

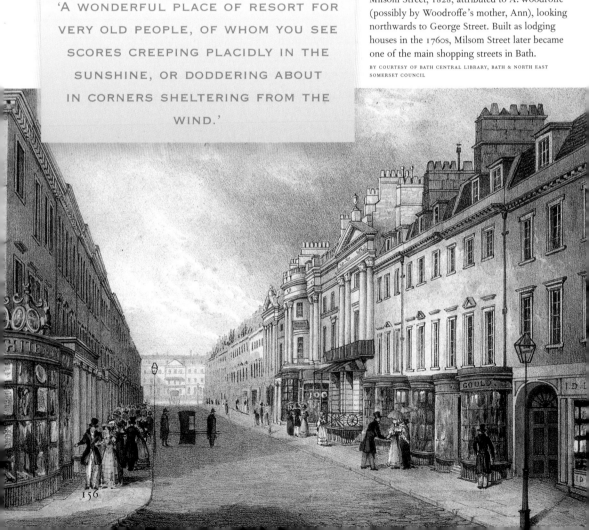

Milsom Street, 1828, attributed to A. Woodroffe (possibly by Woodroffe's mother, Ann), looking northwards to George Street. Built as lodging houses in the 1760s, Milsom Street later became one of the main shopping streets in Bath.

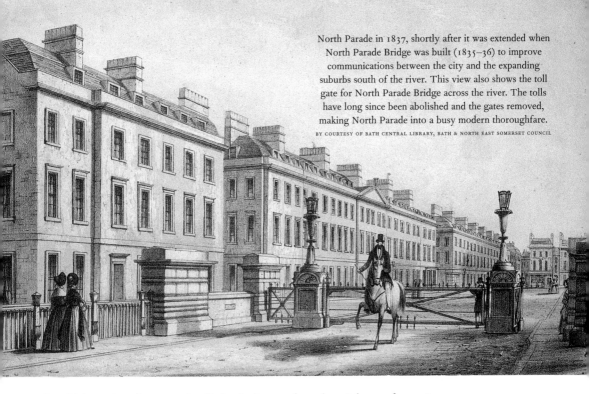

North Parade in 1837, shortly after it was extended when North Parade Bridge was built (1835–36) to improve communications between the city and the expanding suburbs south of the river. This view also shows the toll gate for North Parade Bridge across the river. The tolls have long since been abolished and the gates removed, making North Parade into a busy modern thoroughfare.

It is within such a framework of physical growth and social transformation into a residential city that we now turn to other developments, beginning with communications. Communications in and around the city were improved by the activities of the Bath Turnpike Trust in the 1820s and 1830s, and later by the arrival of the railway age. The corporation undertook some municipal improvements during the 1820s, and in the following decade laid out the Victoria Park, but new building in Bath from 1820 to the 1860s was almost entirely ecclesiastical, industrial or commercial. At this time only a few suburban villa residences stretched up Bathwick Hill, Lansdown Hill and on the southern slopes of Lyncombe and Widcombe. However, the city expanded in size in the late nineteenth and early twentieth centuries as a consequence of major housing development and of changes to its administrative boundaries. During the thirty years before the First World War, Bath acquired a great suburban skirt that incorporated neighbouring rural parishes.

'REFINED SOCIETY, WHERE ELEGANCE AND TASTE ARE THE RULE, VULGAR SHOW THE EXCEPTION...'

The appointment of John Loudon McAdam as surveyor to Bath Turnpike Trust in 1826 marked the beginning of ten years or so of changes to the city's infrastructure, notably an increase in the number of vehicular bridges over the river Avon. Cleveland Bridge, between Bathwick and Walcot, was constructed in 1827, and housing development in Cleveland Place soon followed. New Bridge, on the Bristol Road, was widened and refashioned during the 1830s, and North Parade ceased to be a *cul de sac* in 1835 when work began on North Parade Bridge. Further down the Avon, in the increasingly industrial part of the city, the Victoria Suspension Bridge was erected in 1836.[8] The Great Western Railway line from Bristol to London opened along its entire length when the Box tunnel (a major feat of engineering for its time) was completed in 1841, but the twelve-mile section between Bristol and Bath came into operation a year earlier. The Midland Railway Company constructed a spur to Bath from its Birmingham–Bristol line in the late 1860s, and in 1874 this was linked to the Somerset and Dorset line serving the south coast.

Numerous churches, chapels and cemetery chapels were built between the 1840s and 1890s, including the Swedenborgian church (1844) off Manvers Street, a Moravian chapel (1845) in Charlotte Street, and St Mary's Roman Catholic church (1880s) in Julian Road. Domestic building was more varied in both style and materials than in the Georgian period. Housing along the Upper Bristol Road

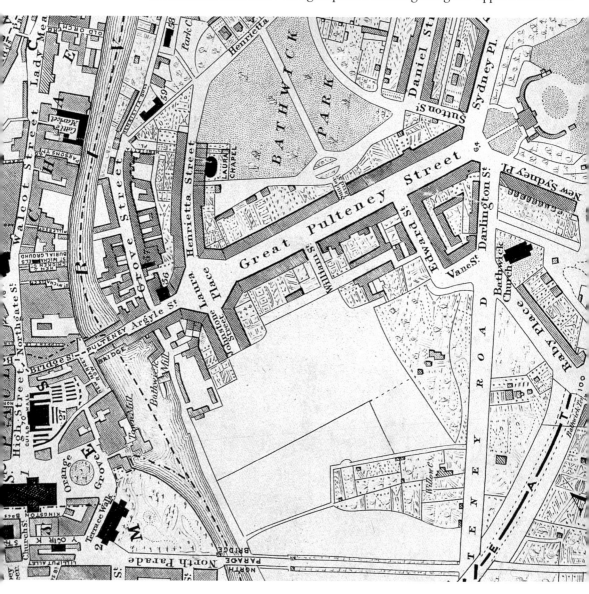

was constructed mainly of Bristol pennant rather than Bath stone or, in some instances, of pennant stone at the front and cheaper red brick at the back.[9]

In the late nineteenth century there was another building boom in Bath. The council was then involved in improving civic amenities, and private investment in speculative building financed extensive suburban housing developments. Desirable detached and semi-detached villa residences on the outskirts of the city were widely advertised in the 1880s and 1890s, and in the Oldfield Park area there was a large development of terraced artisan dwellings. This was a popular residential location with Bath's railway and post office clerks.

Official figures show that Bath's population increased at a modest rate, to reach 54,240 by 1851. It then remained virtually static until the last decade of the century, falling by 8 per cent to 49,839 between 1851 and 1901, but over the next ten years it increased by almost 2 per cent to reach 50,721 in 1911. What these figures conceal is the redistribution of the city's population away from the inner-city districts and toward the suburban areas. Furthermore, the administrative boundaries of Bath became progressively outdated in the later nineteenth century. As a consequence of suburban growth, the two satellite parishes of Twerton and Weston functioned increasingly as part of the city. They were officially incorporated within its boundaries in the early twentieth century, but this was a long-overdue recognition of their function. The aggregate population of Twerton and Weston grew from 6,046 in 1851 to 17,025 by 1901. If these numbers are added to Bath's population, as part of the operative area of the city, then the decline in population between 1851 and 1901 of 8 per cent becomes an increase of the order of 10.9 per cent in the same period.

The expansion of the suburban parishes was a long-term trend in Bath, discernible from the early nineteenth century, but the effects of the process were not fully understood by some of its leading citizens. The Reverend George Tugwell (Rector of Bath from 1870) confidently declared in a speech at the mayor's banquet of 1890 that 'The city grows in all directions'. He went on to suggest that the population of the suburban parish of Bathwick, a mere 250 in 1791, would

GENTEEL RESIDENCE, 1820–1914

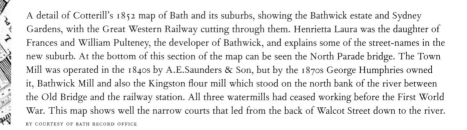

A detail of Cotterill's 1852 map of Bath and its suburbs, showing the Bathwick estate and Sydney Gardens, with the Great Western Railway cutting through them. Henrietta Laura was the daughter of Frances and William Pulteney, the developer of Bathwick, and explains some of the street-names in the new suburb. At the bottom of this section of the map can be seen the North Parade bridge. The Town Mill was operated in the 1840s by A.E.Saunders & Son, but by the 1870s George Humphries owned it, Bathwick Mill and also the Kingston flour mill which stood on the north bank of the river between the Old Bridge and the railway station. All three watermills had ceased working before the First World War. This map shows well the narrow courts that led from the back of Walcot Street down to the river.

BY COURTESY OF BATH RECORD OFFICE

159

probably be returned as between 5,000 and 6,000 in 1891.[10] His optimism about the growth of the city, at a time when its population was officially in decline, reflects a local tendency to identify Bath with its suburban population while ignoring the state of the inner-city parishes. It is true that the migration of wealthy citizens to suburban areas initially increased the population density of inner-city parishes, as the poorer classes crowded into the premises left vacant in the centre. This, however, was a short-lived phase. Employment opportunities in the city itself were, in all probability, reduced with the decline of the Bath season, but alternative work was available in the textile trade in the suburban parish of Lyncombe and Widcombe, and just outside the boundary at Twerton. Even so, from 1801 to 1851, the trend was for the aggregate population growth of the inner-city parishes to be substantially smaller than the increase for the city as a whole. Moreover, by the 1830s some of the poor, in their turn, had removed themselves to tenements on the outskirts of Bath.

Underlying the overall decline of 8 per cent in the city's population between 1851 and 1901 there was a marked differential in the fall and rise of populations in inner-city and suburban parishes. This was not simply a reflection of the flight from the city of the prosperous commercial and professional classes, retreating to

their gothic villas. Artisans and labourers were also moving to the suburbs. In the last quarter of the nineteenth century the process of suburbanisation was greatly accelerated. Only 18 per cent (twenty out of 111) of the new houses built in Bath during the twelve months from October 1899 to October 1900 were located in the three central parishes of the city. Those who were left behind in the inner-city areas were often the poorest sector of the population, compelled to live near their place of work. On the other hand, needlewomen, charwomen and laundresses may well have lost valuable contacts and custom as gentry families and the middle classes drifted to the suburbs.

Suburban growth tended to increase the geographical segregation of different social classes. Speculative housing developments were aimed at specific classes, so the suburbs quickly became identified with the social status of their inhabitants. The shopkeepers and humble tradesmen who moved out to new villas found themselves among neighbours of a similar socio-economic background. Moreover, as the process of suburbanisation accelerated, so the physical distance from the poor became a barrier to understanding the condition of inner-city slums. The reputation of the

The hills encircling Bath provide a picturesque backdrop, as seen here from Beechen Cliff. They have also constrained the patterns of suburban development over the last 200 years so that the city has retained its relatively compact townscape.
PHOTOGRAPH: CARNEGIE, 2005

urban poor assumed alarming proportions to those who rarely came into contact with them, but who, in the comfort of a drawing room behind shuttered windows, read lurid newspaper accounts of the 'animal' behaviour of the under class. As the drift to the suburbs began to encompass the lower-middle classes and the socially aspiring working classes, it also increased the gulf between the 'respectable' and the 'rough' among the lower ranks of Bath society.

The social structure of the city was always more complex than many contemporaries and some historians, influenced by the prevailing image of Bath, have assumed. The opinion of the Revd Warner, that 'the higher classes of people and their dependants constitute the chief part of the population, and the number of lower classes is small',[11] was representative of the erroneous views of people of his class and time. Yet this paternalistic analysis of the social structure, based essentially on two classes, persisted long after Warner wrote in 1801. A modern analysis would separate the groups identified by Warner as 'dependants' into occupations, according to their economic function. The large numbers of shop assistants, craftsmen and domestic servants working in Bath in the nineteenth and early twentieth century were, nonetheless, widely regarded as 'dependants' rather than 'workers'. It fitted the projected image of Bath, as a city of 'little trade and no manufacture', to minimise the working-class presence by camouflaging all those sectors which earned their livings by providing goods and services for the upper classes, or being directly employed by them.

In reality, the working classes formed the great majority of the population in Bath, and the broad trend over time was for the size of the working population to increase. The male labour force grew by 35.3 per cent (from 9,409 to 12,734) between 1851 and 1901, while in the same period the female labour force

GENTEEL
RESIDENCE,
1820–1914

The London to Bristol and Bath stagecoach by Charles C. Cooper (1803–77). The number of weekly services from London to Bath rose from under fifty in the later 1770s to 147 by 1800, at which time the journey took some ten hours.

PRIVATE COLLECTION,
© CHRISTIE'S IMAGES

expanded by 23 per cent (from 8,712 to 10,713). The combined numbers of males and females living on independent means also rose, from 2,875 to 3,155, but this was a slight increase compared with the growth in the commercial and industrial labour force.

Throughout the years between 1820 and 1914 Bath's population was subject to a process of gentle ageing. It consistently had a larger proportion of elderly people than most other cities of comparable size. Nevertheless, it would be a mistake to accept the view that Bath was a geriatric community, the 'cradle of old age', as one contemporary described it in 1900.[12] The attraction of Bath as a place of retirement raised the proportion of its population over 60, but there was also a continuous migration of young women into the city in search of work. The comparative lack of male employment opportunities was responsible for an out-migration of young men, which created a large disparity between females and males of marriageable age.

The variation in population growth between different parishes and wards in the

A section of Cotterill's 1852 map showing the river Avon below the old Bath Bridge. The Royal Crescent is at top right, together with its 'windbreak', Marlborough Buildings. An extensive open area of land provides an important buffer between these refined boulevards and the burgeoning commercial and industrial district along the river. The large buildings to the left next to St John's church are the gas works, established in the early nineteenth century and expanded over the years. Councillors began discussing the desirability of introducing gas lighting to the city's streets as early as 1814 and the first gas lamps were lit in Bath five years later.

BY COURTESY OF BATH RECORD OFFICE

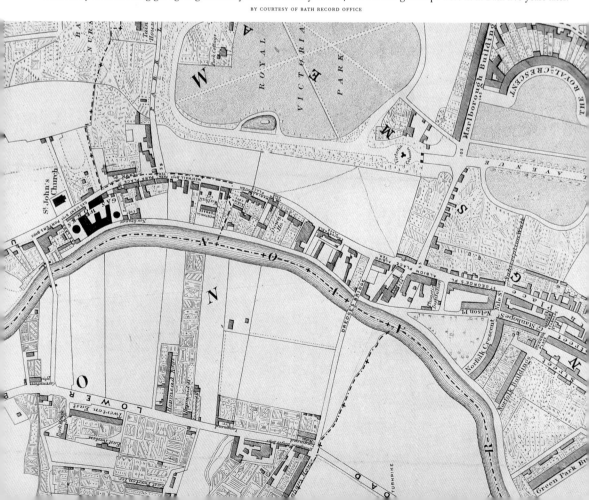

city was echoed by important differences in the age structure and gender ratios of the populations of inner-city and suburban parishes. A comparison between the age structure of Bath as a whole and the suburban parish of Bathwick in 1841 reveals that there was little difference between the two in the age distribution of the male population, but the ratio of females to males in Bathwick in 1841 was 229:100.

Women outnumbered men in the total population of the United Kingdom throughout the period from 1820 to 1914, but Bath shared with Cheltenham a severe imbalance between the sexes, which reflected the popularity of spa towns as places of genteel residence for wealthy unmarried and widowed women, and also the demand for female domestic servants. The disparity between females and males in Bath remained in the region of 140 to 150 women per 100 men from 1841 to 1901, a demographic feature that varied between parishes and changed over time. The highest ratio of females to males in 1891 among the inner-city parishes was 148:100, in St Michael's parish. The ratio in the suburban parish of Bathwick in the same year was almost two to one at 196:100. In the poorest areas of the city, in the wards of Lyncombe and Widcombe and St James's, the respective ratios in 1901 were 121:100 and 138:100. The superabundance of females was particularly marked in the two most socially exclusive wards of the city. The ratio of women to men was 210:100 in Bathwick and 251:100 in Lansdown.

The persistent imbalance in the gender ratios of Bath's population is of particular significance in the context of the city's reputation as a marriage market. This had been one of its traditional functions for visitors since the height of its fashionable appeal in the Georgian age. Yet in terms of its demographic structure Bath was the least likely location for the arrangement of marriages. Even with the annual influx of visitors for the season, there was a universal lament about the shortage of men at public functions. It was reported in *London Society* in August 1870 that 'It is the misfortune of Bath society that at most parties there is a scarcity of gentlemen', and this complaint reverberated down the decades to 1914. In the marriageable age group between 21 and 40 men were greatly outnumbered, most particularly in the parishes that would be represented in a 'respectable' marriage market. Yet ambitious mothers still held to the belief that Bath society was the ideal setting for displaying a daughter to attract a suitable marriage partner. The numbers of foreign language teachers, music tutors, and drawing masters listed in city directories from 1820 to 1914

Victoria Park, *c.*1840, showing the triangular obelisk known as the Victoria Column, commemorating Victoria's accession in June 1837.
BY COURTESY OF BATH CENTRAL LIBRARY, BATH & NORTH EAST SOMERSET COUNCIL

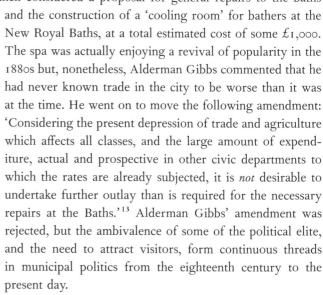

A 'Registered Albert Shape Bath Chair' by James Heath & Co., Patent Bath Wheel Chair Manufacturers of 4 Broad Street. The invention of the bath chair – a wheeled invalid carriage which replaced the sedan chair as a means of conveying patients to and from the baths – has indeed been attributed to Heaths of Bath, around 1750. The term later became a generic name.

suggest that many hopeful young ladies were busily engaged in acquiring the superficial accomplishments deemed necessary for making a 'good match'.

As Bath adjusted to its changing fortunes in becoming a residential city, the corporation faced a dilemma over the need to provide attractive features for the visitors, without losing potential new residents by putting additional burdens on the rates. Opinion was evidently divided as to the best option for the local economy. Vested interests relying primarily on the tourist trade were supported in their desire to promote Bath as a health resort by those members of the political elite who looked back nostalgically to the city's past role and function. They were opposed by those who did well economically from the influx of new wealthy residents, and by new residents themselves, who were encouraged to settle in the city because of its low rates and generally cheap living costs. The debate over spending ratepayers' money on amenities for visitors is illustrated by events in August 1882, when the council considered a proposal for general repairs to the baths and the construction of a 'cooling room' for bathers at the New Royal Baths, at a total estimated cost of some £1,000. The spa was actually enjoying a revival of popularity in the 1880s but, nonetheless, Alderman Gibbs commented that he had never known trade in the city to be worse than it was at the time. He went on to move the following amendment: 'Considering the present depression of trade and agriculture which affects all classes, and the large amount of expenditure, actual and prospective in other civic departments to which the rates are already subjected, it is *not* desirable to undertake further outlay than is required for the necessary repairs at the Baths.'[13] Alderman Gibbs' amendment was rejected, but the ambivalence of some of the political elite, and the need to attract visitors, form continuous threads in municipal politics from the eighteenth century to the present day.

Promoting the image of Bath was nonetheless good for

Monumental inscription in Bath Abbey to Venanzio Rauzzini (1747–1810), conductor of music in Bath for thirty years. A Roman by birth, Rauzzini was a renowned castrato who became one of the most successful teachers of vocal techniques in England. Mozart wrote his famous *Exultate Jubilate* for Rauzzini in 1774. A portrait of Rauzzini by Joseph Hutchison (1747–1830) hangs in the sun lounge of the Pump Room.

PHOTOGRAPH: CARNEGIE, 2004

business in general. Indeed, the civic leaders' efforts to guard jealously the reputation of the city could have a profound influence on policy decisions affecting the lives of all the residents of Bath. The city, like many others, was a victim of the first major epidemic of Asiatic cholera in Britain during 1832. The first incidence of the disease in Bath appeared in July of that year. Energetic measures to restrict its spread were undertaken, but the recently established Board of Health was faced with an awkward dilemma. If it were to release the daily total of cholera victims to the central board in London, as it was duty bound to do, there was a substantial risk of very damaging publicity appearing in the London press just at the start of the Bath winter season, when visitors would normally arrive. A majority of the city's Board of Health decided against the release of the figures. No information on the epidemic was given to local newspapers and a prayerful silence was maintained in the hope that the cholera outbreak would soon die out. It did not.

To finance the necessary measures against the epidemic, money had to be raised from each of the city's six parishes, according to the size of their populations. Most of them bluntly refused to provide the required sums from the rates, because the cholera was largely confined to the poorest area of the city in the Avon Street district. The Board of Health was therefore forced to apply to London for the authority to compel the parishes to pay up. The reply was frankly mystified. Why should Bath need to raise so much money to combat the cholera, when there was no evidence of disease in the city? In order for the Board of Health in Bath to be empowered to implement its preventative measures, evidence had to be submitted to the Central Board. It was provided only after assurances were received that the returns of cholera victims would remain confidential and out of the press. The need to protect the city's reputation as a health resort, and to avoid frightening off prospective visitors for the season, very nearly prevented the authorities from protecting the bulk of the city's residents from disease in 1832.[14]

Another example of the conflict of interest between residents and visitors occurred in the late nineteenth century, when the city council was involved in developing civic amenities. Extensions to the Guildhall, plans for the Empire Hotel, and a new art gallery were all part of the improvements. The clash of interests was sharply brought out in a piece of satirical verse provoked by proposals for the art gallery:

ONE QUARTER OF THE 74 CASES OF CHOLERA IN BATH OCCURRED IN AVON STREET.

GENTEEL RESIDENCE, 1820–1914

An impressive memorial in Bath abbey to William Bingham, 'a native and senator of the United States of America', who died in Bath, aged 49, in February 1804.
PHOTOGRAPH: CARNEGIE, 2004

The latest fad that folly can devise
To squander money, falling from the skies;
'A Gallery of Art', the biggest boon,
For still the parrot cry is, 'Room, more Room'.
Not for the labourer, or the artisan;
Let such men herd in slums as best they can.[15]

In this instance the needs of the poor were felt to have less claim on the civic purse than those of other, more powerful interests. Yet the writer's attack on the council's wasteful expenditure was, in reality, a defence of the interests of the wealthier ratepayers rather than the largely unenfranchised poor. Slum clearance and subsidised municipal housing, as an alternative to the art gallery, would have required the council to borrow money from the local government board, and to have levied substantially more from the rates.

Nonetheless, although there were conflicts of interest over spending from the rates, the general perception persisted from 1820 to 1914 that Bath's economic prosperity depended on its ability to attract outsiders. Wealthy new residents were welcome, but the need to attract visitors was also widely held to be crucial to the city's success.

Taking the waters: visitors and the Bath season

While Bath was becoming more of a residential city, it still retained an interest in attracting visitors, not least because of a reluctance to abandon its former glory, but also because there were many vested interests dependent upon passing trade. Bath was no longer the leading fashionable resort by the 1820s, but it still had a unique feature in its hot springs. Marketing its appeal as a spa treatment centre continued to be a matter of importance to the authorities and others. More visitors meant improved business for doctors and shopkeepers, better custom for hotpliers and lodging-house keepers, and more employment for dressmakers, laundresses and bath chairmen and, later, cab drivers. There were, indeed, many vested interests concerned to promote the image of Bath as a health resort for visitors between 1820 and 1914. However, the gradual realisation that the city's principal role was changing brought about a crisis of confidence that was reflected in the ambivalent attitudes of the council to the spa facilities, and in the perennial debate over whether or not to raise the rates paid by residents in order to provide amenities for visitors. The response to Bath's social decline as a resort encompassed both a determined optimism and a sense of loss at the city's fading reputation. The *Bath Guide* for 1830 listed numerous diversions for the visitors, and proclaimed: 'From a perusal of the foregoing scenes of amusement and recreation, it will be readily conceived that in a full season, no place in England affords a more brilliant circle of polite company than Bath'.[16]

An enduring attraction for visitors and residents were the city's shopping facilities, which were regularly advertised in contemporary accounts. The

Sydney Gardens Hotel in the 1840s, now the Holbourne Museum.

GENTEEL RESIDENCE, 1820–1914

following example, dating from 1887, serves for others of similar description in the period between 1820 and 1914:

> The shops of Bath are a revelation to the stranger, and give token of the fact that Bath is still the centre of fashion and luxury not only to the fashionable visitors, but to the whole of the West of England. Kings of Milsom Street would do credit to the Rue de Rivoli or Regent Street, for sustained splendour and gorgeous raiment.[17]

Yet by 1832 it was widely recognised – if not yet officially acknowledged – that, 'Bath was deserted by fashion, after having served as its Temple', and in the same year the *Bath Chronicle* gave expression to the prevailing ambivalence. In January 1832 it reported that, 'we have every reason to believe that the present season will be one of the gayest which Bath has witnessed for some time'. However, later in the same month, it informed its readers that the master of ceremonies was striving unsuccessfully to encourage more patrons to 'this once-favoured city'. The fall in numbers of visitors made an impact on local

Sydney Gardens, c.1840. Established in 1795, Sydney Gardens is the only surviving example of several pleasure gardens that were a feature of the entertainments provided for visitors in the eighteenth century.

Great Pulteney Street in the 1830s, one of Robert Woodroffe's series of views in the city. Woodroffe was the son of a boot and shoe maker in Milsom Street; he practised as an artist and drawing master from 1826 to the end of the 1860s.

events, leading, for instance, to the curtailment of Bath races from three to two days in 1833. Similarly, a Sydney Gardens gala in 1838 seems to have lost money for its organiser. It was reported that 'the attendance was not commensurate with the exertions of the proprietor'.[18]

Visitors who came to Bath for the season, which lasted from November to around Easter, were in general less wealthy and more solidly middle class than their counterparts during the city's Georgian heyday. Improved communications, first by road and then by rail, were vital in making Bath more accessible to visitors from all over the country, but they were accompanied by unexpected hazards and disappointments. At the beginning of this period, travelling to Bath still entailed arduous journeys by coach. Road improvements made such journeys somewhat more comfortable than in the past, but local newspapers' accounts of many incidents of petty highway robbery on roads leading into the city throughout the 1830s suggest that they could still be dangerous expeditions. The advent of the railway age raised hopes of an influx of visitors to Bath. Yet it was Bristol-based entrepreneurs rather than Bathonians who dominated the group that promoted the Great Western Railway (GWR), and there was some local resistance to railway development. The company's plans were approved by Parliament in 1835, but were opposed by the Kennet and Avon Canal Company and by the Bath Turnpike Trust, which administered and maintained fifty-one miles of road, collected the tolls from fifty-one gates and operated five weighbridges in the city. Loudon McAdam, surveyor to the Turnpike Trust, spoke out publicly against the 'Calamity of Railways', but it was not only those who were directly threatened by competition who doubted whether the railway would benefit Bath in its attempts to attract visitors. A correspondent to the *Bath Chronicle* in May 1835 put forward the view that Isambard Kingdom Brunel's scheme was 'a plan to reduce the population of your fair City', by luring potential visitors to London.[19]

The corporation, nonetheless, assisted the GWR company over the purchase of land for the line, the station and goods yards, in the expectation of a boost to the number of visitors, although it also imposed certain restrictions. These chiefly concerned bridges and tunnels, and the protection of the water supply in the parishes of Lyncombe and Widcombe and Bathwick. The area around the GWR station (later known as Bath Spa) was designed to make an impressive entrance to the city. Two new roads were laid out: Dorchester Street (running westward to join Southgate Street at the city bridge) and Manvers Street (running northward to join Pierrepoint Street) were planned as terraces of substantial houses, with the Royal Hotel and the Manvers Arms (renamed the Argyll Hotel) standing on the corners facing the station. The GWR line from Bristol to London opened along the entire route in 1841, but when the twelve-mile section from Bristol to Bath went into service (August 1840) huge crowds attended the inaugural ceremony, and such was the interest in the new form of travel that twenty trips each way were made between Bath and Bristol on the opening day. The regular

'BATH WAS DESERTED BY FASHION, AFTER HAVING SERVED AS ITS TEMPLE.'

GENTEEL RESIDENCE, 1820–1914

A trade card for James Heath & Co. of 4 Broad Street, opposite St Michael's church, 1880–81. Bath was a centre for furniture- and carriage-making but Heath specialised as a manufacturer of Bath Wheel Chairs. Royal patronage ensured sales at home and in overseas markets.

BY COURTESY OF BATH CENTRAL LIBRARY, BATH & NORTH EAST SOMERSET COUNCIL

service thereafter was ten trains each way on Mondays to Saturdays, with four on Sundays, at a single fare of 2*s*. 6*d*. (12½p) first class and 1*s*. 6*d*. (7½p) second class.[20]

However, the main impact of the railway was not on the tourist trade but on speeding up the process whereby the industrial area of the city became concentrated in the southern part of Bath along the Lower Bristol Road, where transport networks converged. The two new hotels facing the railway station (built in Georgian style) were symbols of the commercial hopes invested in the coming of the railway and the expected revival in the numbers of visitors, but the Royal Hotel and the Manvers Arms stood in isolation for some time. The economic climate did not encourage speculative building, and Manvers Street and Dorchester Street remained undeveloped until later in the century.[21]

Despondency about the city's prospects as a health resort deepened with the realisation that the GWR had not boosted visitor numbers. Official interest in the spa diminished to such an extent that the corporation let the baths to a private individual in the early 1860s. After a trial period the lessee terminated the agreement

A panoramic view of Bath from Beechen Cliff in 1846, one in the series published by Everitt, it shows what a visual impact the Great Western Railway made on the southern part of the city. Bath Spa station appears as it was originally built, completely roofed over and with an entrance to the south side. Vacant land on either side of Manvers Street (running north from the station) awaits development. Note the densely packed working-class housing in the Dolemeads, right foreground.

BY COURTESY OF BATH CENTRAL LIBRARY, BATH & NORTH EAST SOMERSET COUNCIL

in 1864, and no other entrepreneur could be persuaded to take up a new lease. In the same year, the post of master of ceremonies became redundant. The lack of visitors was beginning to affect the city's hotel trade seriously. York House had already been turned into a post office and numerous smaller hotels had gone out of business. The famous White Hart, opposite the Pump Room, closed down permanently in 1864. The severity of the situation prompted renewed activity, heralded in an address by the mayor to the corporation: 'Having thought much lately of the change that Bath has undergone, I have come to the conclusion that we ought to make a vigorous effort to revive its prosperity and that we cannot do better than follow the old lines'.[22] In response to the mayor's address a committee was set up. It proposed replacing the White Hart with a prestigious new hotel, equipped at basement level with the most modern bathing facilities, and fitted with lifts to take patients from their suites to the baths. The baths were re-opened in 1867, and the Grand Pump Room Hotel was itself completed two years later in 1869, the year traditionally seen as marking a revival in Bath's prosperity. The new baths, built entirely with corporation money, were widely approved:

Monuments to the misplaced optimism of the 1840s, these two hotels stand on either side of the end of Manvers Street, opposite the railway station. The Manvers Arms (later the Argyll Hotel) and the Royal Hotel were both built in the 'Bath Georgian' style, attributed to H. E. Goodridge, *c*.1840.

PHOTOGRAPHS: CARNEGIE, 2004

Everyone who sees the beautiful suite of baths adjoining the hotel ... sees also what the city has gained in this respect. Conveyed by a lift from bedroom floors, the patient is not subject to hazardous and comfortless exposure, while the variety of baths, suited to various forms of complaint, is a great advantage.[23]

The Grand Pump Room Hotel was not, however, an instant success. It only slowly began to attract an increasing number of visitors, although some recovery in the local economy was apparent from the late 1860s. Another large hotel of 'good repute' opened shortly afterwards, and it was reported that private family hotels had multiplied and that houses and lodgings had been better let than for many years.

'Heath's Newly invented Close[d] Clarence Chair', from the company's marketing material.

BY COURTESY OF BATH CENTRAL LIBRARY, BATH & NORTH EAST SOMERSET COUNCIL

At the same time, more railway developments improved national communications with Bath and brought renewed hope of visitors from the Midlands, the North and, via Liverpool, from even further afield. During 1869–70 Queen Square station (more recently known as Green Park station) was built as the terminus of a spur from the Midland Railway's Birmingham to Bristol line. When, a few years later (1874), the station was linked with the Somerset and Dorset line, access to Bath from neighbouring counties and the south coast was improved. More visitors may have journeyed to Bath on day trips, but the line raised the worrying possibility of more competition from seaside resorts.

In the year 1881–82, 60,000 bathers passed through the four city baths. The revival of the spa was well under way. Moreover, the council agreed at its March meeting in 1882 to further promotion by spending £300 annually, 'in

GENTEEL RESIDENCE, 1820–1914

advertising the advantages of the hot mineral springs. W. H. Smith & Son, advertising contractors, have undertaken to provide large show boards and display at 100 principal stations for five years at £200 per year'.[24] These advertisements featured Minerva leaning on a shield in the upper part, with details of the yield and temperature of the springs and with a selection of photographs of the city. The virtues of the springs were extolled and compared advantageously to continental spas. A version of the poster, in the form of a circular, was sent to every medical practitioner in the United Kingdom. Expenditure on advertising was strongly supported by Alderman Wilkinson, Chairman of the Baths and Pump

The Grand Pump Room Hotel (1866–69) in Stall Street. It was demolished in 1959, replaced by the present Arlington House.

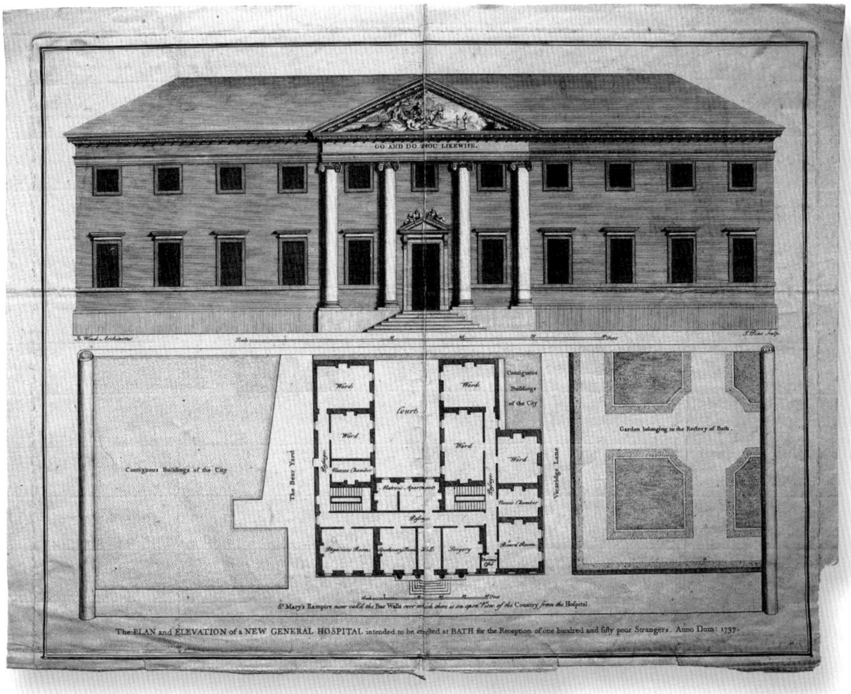

Plans for the New General Hospital, 1737, later known as the Mineral Water Hospital and now the Royal National Hospital for Rheumatic Diseases. The yard of the Bear Inn is shown to the left of the plan.

BY COURTESY OF BATH CENTRAL LIBRARY, BATH & NORTH EAST SOMERSET COUNCIL

Room Committee, who reckoned that 'for every pound spent on ... advertising there would be a £10 return to the citizens of Bath'. The numbers of visitors certainly rose once the spa was being vigorously promoted. The number of bathers using the city baths more than doubled in the decade after 1876, to reach 86,223 in 1886. During 1888 this figure rose to 94,835. The renewed interest in the Bath waters benefited the corporation, the medical profession, the hoteliers and tradesmen such as the enterprising Mr Cater, who secured the monopoly of

'MAJOR DAVIS'

Charles Edward Davis (1827–1902) was born near Bath, the son of Edward Davis, an architect, and his wife Dorothy, who was the widow of a Captain Johnston. Known as 'Major Davis' to distinguish him from his father, the rank derived from his commission in the Worcestershire militia; he had also been a member of the Bath volunteer rifles.

He began his career as his father's pupil. His early works included the restoration of Prior Birde's chapel in Bath Abbey and several houses, among them Twerton House. It was Major Davis who laid out Victoria Park, and he also designed the cemetery buildings on the Lower Bristol Road.

He was architect and surveyor to the corporation of Bath for nearly forty years and is noted particularly for his work on the baths and as the architect of the Empire Hotel. His extensive private practice was responsible for the design of several local churches, and for the schools at Twerton.

Major Davis married Selina Anne Howarth in 1858 but had no children. He was elected a fellow of the Society of Antiquarians in 1854, and published various pamphlets on the bath waters. He died at his home, 18 Bathwick Hill, on 10 May 1902.

Sources: *Oxford DNB* (2004), vol. 15, pp. 432–3.

bottling the spring water. It was claimed to be therapeutic to the gouty and the rheumatic and it proved highly profitable to Mr Cater, who devised a process for aerating it to preserve the carbonate of iron content.

The authorities, now firmly committed to the spa and the need to encourage visitors, were determined not to be left behind by advances in medical science. During the 1880s the city surveyor, Major Davis, and Dr Henry Freeman, surgeon to the Royal United Hospital and later a mayor of Bath, were sent on an extended tour of European spas to study new treatments. On the basis of their report, the council built a complete new suite of douche and massage baths at the corner of York Street and Stall Street. When they were opened in 1889 they were an immediate success. 'Continental' treatments were very much in vogue and it was claimed that visitor revenue doubled 'almost overnight'.[25]

The mineral water hospital itself played an integral part in the image and function of the city as a health resort. Lists of patients discharged were printed every month in local newspapers. Some patients were discharged because of misconduct, others discharged themselves before treatment was completed, and some were classified as 'improper', meaning that they were unsuitable for treatment. For the remainder, medical staff employed a simple classification in the published lists, as 'cured', 'much better', 'better', 'no better' or 'dead'.[26] Because the outcome of all cases was published, it was obviously in the interests of the hospital to demonstrate a high rate of cures or substantial improvements. This added to its prestige and encouraged donors and subscribers to give generously to its funds. It is likely that at least some of those 'cured' by the waters had, in reality, spontaneously recovered from their ailments.

Meanwhile, the redevelopment of the spa from the 1860s had led to the excavation of the Roman Baths.[27] These were to become one of the city's enduring tourist attractions. Part of the pediment of the temple of Sulis Minerva had been discovered when the Pump Room was built in 1790, but there were no attempts to uncover

The Royal Mineral Water Hospital, designed by John Wood the Elder (1738–46), Upper Borough Walls. Founded in 1716 as the General Hospital for 'the deserving poor', the hospital was built on the site of the old theatre. It had a capacity of 108 bed spaces in the seven wards, but was enlarged in 1793 by the addition of an attic storey designed by John Palmer.

PHOTOGRAPH: CARNEGIE, 2004

A drawing of the Bath United Hospital in Beau Street, built in 1825 with a new wing added in 1867 as a memorial to Prince Albert.

BY COURTESY OF BATH CENTRAL LIBRARY, BATH & NORTH EAST SOMERSET COUNCIL

more remains until after the White Hart Hotel closed down in 1864. At that time, an enthusiastic antiquarian, James Irvine, was employed as clerk to the works by the architect Sir Gilbert Scott, who was carrying out restoration work on the abbey. Irvine knew of the discoveries of 1790 and, deducing that the body of the Sulis Minerva temple lay under the White Hart opposite the Pump Room, he began exploratory excavations as soon as the hotel closed. When demolition and rebuilding on the site was under way (1867–69) he carefully recorded all the

The demolition of the eighteenth-century Kingston Baths, c.1920s. one of the council's improvements that modified the Georgian city. This site south of the abbey was paved over the form the present courtyard by the Tourist Information Centre.

BY COURTESY OF BATH AND NORTH EAST SOMERSET COUNCIL, ROMAN BATHS MUSEUM

SITE of LARGE ROMAN BATH & HYPOCAUSTS DISCOVERED 1754

Excavations in progress beneath the partially destroyed Queen's Bath, c.1880s.

GENTEEL RESIDENCE, 1820–1914

below A remarkable photograph of the exposed Great Bath, *c.*1895, on what was evidently a grand civic occasion, possibly the Mayor and Antiquities Committee with invited guests at some event publicising the decision to incorporate the Roman baths into the Pump Room complex. In any event, at least half a dozen of the finely dressed Victorian gentlemen are wearing chains of office, and the focus of their attention seems to be the small group under the makeshift canopy.

findings unearthed. The authorities took no official interest in the Roman remains at this stage, but over the next decade Irvine successfully engaged the interest of Major Davis, the city surveyor, in his discoveries. Davis instigated excavations that revealed the Roman reservoir built around the original spring beneath the King's Bath. Once this project was completed (1878–79), he went on to carry out further excavations in the following year, which led to the uncovering of the Great Bath. This provoked considerable local excitement and the council, somewhat belatedly, recognised the potential of the site as a visitor attraction. An Antiquities Committee of the council was soon set up, and funds were raised to complete the excavation.

The project was bedevilled by conflicts of interest and personality clashes. Some local tradesmen, concerned about the effect on their businesses of the disruption around the site, took the council to court for causing a nuisance. Extra funds had to be raised to purchase the Poor Law offices, which stood on part of the Roman site. Major Davis became involved in an acrimonious public debate about who had actually discovered the baths. As an antiquarian himself but also city surveyor, Davis found himself facing a dilemma in 1886 when the douche and massage baths were being built: he was naturally in sympathy with those who wanted to preserve the archaeological remains discovered on site but, as an employee of the city council, it was his duty to build the baths as quickly and cheaply as possible. Such

Excavations of Roman remains in progress, c.1880.

was the antipathy to Davis, who was the focus of considerable hostility in the late 1880s and 1890s, that his conduct as city surveyor was the subject of a committee of enquiry. He was exonerated, albeit guardedly, from accusations of misconduct, but he remained a controversial figure in Bath.

By 1889 visitors could view the Roman antiquities, although no immediate attempt was made to tidy up the site, and the Great Bath was left uncovered. For some nine years it remained exposed to the elements, and it suffered considerable

The gutted interior of the Theatre Royal after a disastrous fire in 1862.

erosion from the weathering process. It was not until 1892 that a scheme was proposed to extend the Pump Room and thereby incorporate the Roman antiquities into the complex. The project included a new concert hall to relieve the overcrowding in the existing Pump Room, which was a cause of complaint now that visitor numbers had increased. Plans were put out to competition, which was won by the London architect J. M. Brydon who had planned the Guildhall enlargement of 1891. Major Davis was effectively excluded from this competition by the manoeuverings of a faction on the council that managed to get the brief rewritten at a late stage, ostensibly on the grounds of cutting costs. This, however, was not the end of Davis's career. The discovery of the Roman baths and the general upturn in Bath's appeal as a spa in the closing decades of the nineteenth century gave a boost to civic pride. The Pump Room extension, completed in 1897, was followed by the commissioning of Major Davis in 1899

The former Empire Hotel and Parade Gardens. The confident exuberance of the Empire, designed by Major C. E. Davis, endears it to some while offending others. Threatened with demolition following the departure of the Ministry of Defence, the upper storeys have been converted into luxury retirement apartments, with bars and restaurants on the ground floor.

PHOTOGRAPH: CARNEGIE, 2004

to design a new purpose-built hotel as another prestigious amenity for visitors. The building of the Empire Hotel (completed in 1901) and of the parade in front of it reflected the optimism generated by Bath's late Victorian prosperity but, in reality, this had petered out before the Empire opened its doors.

The social tone and character of Bath changed over time, as it developed its genteel image after 1820. It became more solidly middle class, and its visitors also changed. Conferences began to be of increasing importance by 1900. The Society of Architects, among many other similar bodies, held their annual conference in the city between 1906 and 1910, as did the British Medical Association and the Institute of Mechanical Engineers. In January 1913 the city entertained 400 doctors from London, who were taken on a motor tour of the area before being received by the mayor and the chairman of the Baths' Committee for tea at the Pump Room. Other items on the itinerary were demonstrations of methods of treatment, a description of the Roman antiquities, and an address on the radio-active waters of Bath.[28]

Meanwhile the social scene during the Bath season remained outwardly vibrant, but patterns of leisure were altering throughout the country during this period. The entertainments and amusements offered to visitors changed with national

The Theatre Royal, Sawclose, was designed by George Dance and built between 1802 and 1806 with a frontage facing Beauford Square. The entrance was moved to the Sawclose in 1863 when a major redesign of the interior was undertaken by C.J.Phipps, following a fire. What had been Beau Nash's first home in Bath was then requisitioned and a single-storey extension was added to its front to accommodate the new box office.

trends, but also in response to the increased number of middle-class permanent residents. Newspaper accounts of theatrical performances, concerts, balls and gala celebrations give a somewhat misleading impression of the gaiety of social life in Bath. These traditional attractions were still on offer, but the city could make no claim to high culture in the period from 1820 to 1914, and private entertainments by and for residents increasingly replaced the public social life of earlier times. The Theatre Royal sank to a level of provincial mediocrity in the early nineteenth century, no longer the nursery for the London stage, as formerly it had been in the career, for example, of Sarah Siddons. Theatrical decline reflected the structural shift from a high-class resort to a middle-class residential city. It was not regularly well-patronised, and even Amateur Night, one of the most popular features of the later nineteenth century, was not always well supported. Similarly, musical concerts were less frequent than they had been in the late eighteenth century, although the private *soirée* became an important event in the social calendar. People's Concerts twice a week at the Guildhall often lost money for the promoters. The ball remained the supreme social event, attended by the elite and the socially aspiring, in order to see and be seen in the 'right' company. Yet even these events changed over time. Public subscription balls, a unique feature of Bath's entertainment in the 1700s, became much less significant. Increasingly between 1820 and 1914 balls were annual events organised by clubs or societies for their members (predominantly residents); or they were celebration or inaugural balls held to mark national and local events. Bath races, reinstated as a biennial event in spring and summer after mid-century, were always the excuse for a week of carnivals, fêtes and balls. Card-playing assemblies flourished in the season, and the Assembly Rooms also provided billiard tables by the later nineteenth century.

Exclusiveness was practised in public entertainment, to preserve the right social tone. In the 1860s a guinea (£1.05) paid for a season of Subscription Balls, with 5s. (25p) extra for the card assembly, while 6d. (2½p) was the charge for tea. These were indeed 'moderate prices for admittance to one of the most polite assemblies in the kingdom', but it was not only the cost that excluded those of low social status from these gatherings: 'Certain rules are drawn up, by which all retail traders, articled clerks of the city, theatrical and other public performers are excluded from its saloons'.[29] Similarly, uniformed attendants were employed in the Victoria Park and other pleasure gardens to chase away the rough and 'undesirable'.

The growing numbers of wealthy permanent residents offset to some extent the depression which Bath, in common with other English spas, experienced in the early part of the period from 1820. Throughout the year from October 1835 to October 1836 the Assembly Rooms attracted sufficient patronage to remain open between Easter and November, i.e. out of season. Similarly, the customary practice of shops selling high-quality goods closing down during the summer months became eroded in the 1830s and 1840s, by which time all-year-round demand made this unnecessary. The growth of clubs and societies listed in the city directories from the 1820s onward also reflects the increase in the permanently resident population, as well as the general development of leisure activities. Some organisations, such as the Athenaeum and the Bath and County Club, had a membership beyond the city limits and provided a meeting point for visitors and residents. Others, like the Floral and Horticultural Society (formed in 1834), were likely to have a distinctly local membership. The national interest in sport, in new forms of activities, and in 'rational recreation' was shared by the residents of Bath, who in the later nineteenth century formed boating and rowing clubs, athletics societies, football and bicycling clubs. Organisations for the serious-minded also flourished. Old established ones, the Natural History and Antiquarian Society for example, were joined by new ones, including the Bath Ladies Microscopical Society which was formed around 1887–88 and was still in existence in 1910–11.

Many of the occasional entertainments in Bath would have attracted both visitors and residents, according to taste and class. Madame Tussaud's travelling exhibition which visited Bath in November 1831 is one example, while Wombwell's Menagerie (which came to the city regularly over a period from the late nineteenth century) is another. Hanoverian bands, which enjoyed great popularity in Britain around the turn of the century, could be heard frequently in Bath at promenade concerts held in Sydney Gardens and elsewhere. These concerts were held in the summer months, organised by the Band and Fête Committee. No doubt the promenade concerts were enjoyed by people living in the city, although their addition to the attractions of Bath also reflected efforts made in the 1890s and early twentieth century to expand visitor numbers outside the traditional 'season'. Drinking the waters in the open air had always been recognised as one of the enjoyable features of many continental spas, but English health resorts were slow to adopt the idea. The authorities in Bath did so in 1910 when, as 'a great movement forward in the direction of the city's future as a summer resort', the Hot Water Mineral Fountain was opened under the Colonnade in the Institution gardens. By the time of the First World War the corporation's success at turning 'the routine of water-sipping into an alluring out-of-door amusement' had made the gardens at the Colonnade one of the most popular rendezvous for visitors during the spring and summer.[30]

As the city became predominantly a place of genteel residence, long-established bodies, such as the Literary and Scientific Institute, were supplemented by numerous clubs and societies catering for a variety of tastes. Temporary membership was offered to visitors by some of these organisations in the early 1900s, including the Chess Society and the Bath Lawn Tennis Club. The city's respectable image was firmly based on the social status and values of its new middle-class inhabitants, but visitors to Bath were also likely to be 'the right sort of people' who could be admitted to one's club albeit only on 'certain conditions', as some organisations stipulated. Those who settled permanently in the city shared on a long-term basis the short-term experience of the visitors, who were integrated only to varying degrees into the life of polite society in Bath.

Residents and residential life

The new residents who moved to Bath in this period were mostly middle class but they were not a homogeneous group. The social status of some families and individuals was undoubtedly less secure than that of others. Furthermore, differences in age, gender, occupation and financial circumstances would have shaped their aspirations and perhaps limited the degree of their integration into the social and political life of Bath. Personal tastes and preferences would also, to some extent, have determined the level of participation of the newcomers.

The growth of Bath, and particularly the process of suburbanisation, contributed to the erosion of the cohesiveness that had typified social life in the city when it was dominated by a small, wealthy elite. Cliques or 'sets' emerged as the city grew, and all-embracing public entertainments declined in significance. These different social groups overlapped or merged at times and within some organisations but retained a clear distinctiveness. This fragmentation of the social elite was commented upon by a writer in *The World* of 1876, who noted that society at Bath 'ramifies into four distinct classes – with great assiduity and skill a native may continue to belong to three of them; but even this would require some amount of ingenuity. There is a High Church set, a Low Church set, a literary set and a fashionable set'.[31]

'BATH RAMIFIES INTO FOUR DISTINCT CLASSES ... THERE IS A HIGH CHURCH SET, A LOW CHURCH SET, A LITERARY SET AND A FASHIONABLE SET.'

There is some evidence to suggest that the outsiders who were attracted to the city's suburbs were increasingly drawn from the less wealthy sections of the respectable classes, many of them living on fixed incomes and limited means. It is revealing that the increase in the number of these genteel residents, which accounted for most of the suburban growth in the later nineteenth and early twentieth centuries, did not create a corresponding demand for domestic servants. Between 1871 and 1901, a period of rapid suburban housing development and of an apparent increase in middle-class settlers, the numbers of resident domestic servants employed actually declined while the aggregate number of charwomen and washerwomen rose steadily to reach 1,061 by 1901.[32] These women could be employed on a daily basis or have work put out to them, thereby saving the cost of maintaining them in the household. The 'paraphernalia of gentility' was perhaps increasingly beyond the means of some of Bath's new residents, who could not afford the level of servant-keeping that obtained in the mid-Victorian period, and who were forced to make economies in their household management. Dinner parties, *soirées* or musical evenings, 'at homes' and other private entertainments became more fashionable throughout the nineteenth century, encouraged partly by the Victorian enthusiasm for the family as the focal point of life, but the decline in support for the theatre and other public amusements in Bath may also reflect the financial circumstances of some incomers to the city.

Women, even those of the right social status and sufficient wealth to participate fully in the social life of Bath, would have been further constrained by the conventions of the times. For many of them it seems that the church and charitable activities formed the hub of their social life, and were deemed as especially suitable for unmarried or widowed women of the middle and upper classes. Mrs Arabella Roxburgh, granddaughter of a baronet from Yorkshire, is representative of many wealthy widows who retired to Bath in the later nineteenth century. She lived unostentatiously, devoting much of her time and income to works of piety and charity. During her lifetime she presented a number of pictures to the city, in the hope that they might form the nucleus of an art gallery. Many local charities benefited from her will after her death in November 1897: she left £12,000 as a fund for providing annuities for unmarried women or widows, and a quarter of the residue of her estate was designated for the provision of scholarships to the Bath Technical School and other educational establishments. The remainder of her fortune, some £8,000, was left to the city for the purpose of founding the art gallery.[33]

It was over the question of improving amenities for the city, financed wholly or in part from the rates, that the new residents of Bath were most likely to form a distinct interest group. In such instances, however, they often found themselves in alliance with other ratepayers, and it was as such that they acted in concerted opposition. Low rates were one of Bath's persistently advertised features and every suggestion for improvements that might lead to their increase was resisted.

The Ladymead fountain, Walcot Street, dates from 1860. Located near the late eighteenth-century steps which ascend to Bladud's Buildings and the Paragon, this Victorian watering and resting place for horses at market time is largely redundant today, except for the floral contribution it provides to Bath's many Britain in Bloom competition entries.

PHOTOGRAPH: CARNEGIE, 2004

The strength of feeling that existed was demonstrated at an uproarious meeting in the Guildhall on 8 November 1869, when the question of a free public library in Bath was raised in the context of general improvements, including the extension and development of the water supply.[34] Other factors, as well as the likely impact on rates, influenced the vote against the motion in support of the library. The venture was particularly strongly opposed by working-class ratepayers, who believed it would be used mainly by the middle classes.

The wealthy incomers to Bath seem to have been more favourably disposed to contributing to civic amenities voluntarily rather than through the rates. Plans for an art gallery in the city had been mooted for many years before it was eventually built at the turn of the century. Sir Jerom Murch (many times Mayor of Bath) had constantly advocated such an institution and he left a legacy for that purpose when he died in 1895. Mrs Roxburgh, as described above, had followed his example in 1896, but had taken the precaution of attaching a time limit of five years to her bequest. Unless the art gallery was built within that period, the city would lose her legacy of £8,000. Subscriptions were invited for the double purpose of an art gallery and a free library, but determined opposition to the inclusion of a library led to a compromise, whereby the gallery was built in conjunction with a reference library to house the Guildhall collection of books of local interest. The provision of a public library was again deferred, but subscriptions, many from prominent citizens, were sufficient for the gallery and Guildhall library to be commissioned as a memorial to Queen Victoria's Diamond Jubilee in 1897, although it was not completed until several years later.

For a glimpse at the social calendar in Bath during the closing years of the nineteenth century there is no better guide than the regular column – 'Penelope's Diary' – in the *Bath and County Graphic*. It covered a wide range of activities, from the sporting fixtures of Bath High School for girls to religious lectures and the private parties given by the social elite. In reporting such events as a garden party given by Mrs Yorke-Fausset in the grounds of Bath College, in aid of the Royal Victorian Home for Women, 'Penelope's Diary' illustrates the Victorian practice of making a social event out of a moral obligation:

> The weather was perfect, and tea under the spreading branches of a huge old cedar was very refreshing. Tables were dotted about the grounds bearing basket work made by the inmates of the Home, which is for the reception of inebriates and other cases. It is actively supported by the Duke and Duchess of Beaufort, the Duchess of Bedford, the Countess of Dudley, Lady Battersea, and many other ladies.[35]

The roll-call of illustrious patrons or guests was an integral part of the 'Diary' and Penelope also took a keen interest in the decorations at social events, which were invariably described as 'charming'. She also lovingly recorded details of the glamorous dresses on display, as in the following extract from an account of an evening reception and ball held by the 'Prince of Mayors', George Woodiwiss, in 1897:

Miss E. Marshall was gowned in white moiré, with silk trimmings ... Miss Spender wore a soft blue silk with very long train and long sleeves, a style which suited her slight figure; then the Misses Cary looked exceedingly well in a rich white satin, relieved by very little trimming, well adapted to their height and figures ...[36]

No doubt those singled out for a mention of their appearance enjoyed a warm glow of satisfaction, but the intimate tone of this and other pieces, and the full descriptions given of decor and dresses, suggest that Penelope was writing for a wider audience than the social elite. Bath, with its cheap living and 'right sort of people', provided a sanctuary for many middle-class women who were never invited to the glittering occasions that they took pleasure in reading about. Keeping up to date with 'Penelope's Diary' was perhaps some compensation for their own reduced circumstances, making them feel that they too participated in the social scene, if only vicariously.

The new image of Bath was so firmly established by the turn of the century that accounts of the city often focused almost exclusively on its residents rather than its visitors. In the *Shilling Guide Book* series, brought out by the Ward Lock publishing company of London during the First World War, the volume on Bath informed its readers that life there had 'become more vigorous and prosperous than of old' because:

while thousands still flock to Bath for the sake of the healing waters, the city has become the permanent abode of a dignified and well-to-do community, attracted thither by interesting associations and a beautiful neighbourhood, by stately streets and crescents and enchanting parks and gardens, that have won for the place the proud and well deserved title of 'Queen of the West'.[37]

By 1914 Bath was so closely identified with its social elite and its firmly established genteel image that the complexities of its functions were largely overlooked. In reality, although it was characterised by extremes of social structure, Bath was predominantly a small-scale industrial city during the period between 1820 and 1914. It was home to a substantial labouring population as well as to its new middle-class residents. In the next chapter, we examine the growth of industry and changing occupational distribution as well as exploring some important aspects of working-class society in Bath.

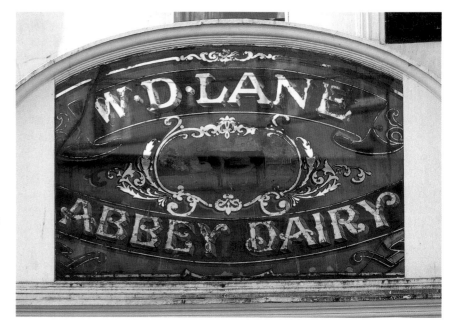

A shop sign on Lower Borough Walls advertises the Abbey Dairy of W. D. Lane, who supplied 'finest dairy produce' to Bath's residents and visitors.

PHOTOGRAPH: CARNEGIE, 2004

A city at work, 1820–1914 CHAPTER 6

T HE CITY of Bath has traditionally been seen as outside the main trends of industrial and commercial development in the eighteenth and nineteenth centuries. Contemporary understanding of its economy was somewhat distorted by the belief that the prosperity of Bath was dependent on the wealth it could attract from outsiders. Moreover, historians have arguably been too ready to accept the dominant, genteel image of Bath and to ignore much of the evidence which challenges or contradicts that prevailing image.

The entrepreneurial activity, and considerable investment, associated with the construction of Georgian Bath stimulated not only the building industry itself, but also the development of extensive stone quarries, the growth of industrial villages, the formation of the Turnpike Trust, the construction of tramways and the canalisation of the river Avon, all before the mid-eighteenth century. Thereafter, continued building and rebuilding and high levels of expenditure on quality consumer goods attracted numerous tradesmen, general labourers, and craftsmen to the city.[1] The development of the surrounding complex of industrial villages owed more to national trends in economic development than to the city's function as a spa resort or fashionable place of residence. Incipient industrialisation was under way between 1800 and 1830, with the establishment of steam-powered manufactories in brewing, soap-making and glass-making. Stotherts' ironmongery developed into a foundry, while woollen mills were erected on the river Avon at Twerton, and coal mining was attempted at Batheaston.[2] Further substantial changes were to alter the character of the city over the rest of the century.

Changing occupations amid the growth of industry

Trade and small-scale industry (which were frequently represented in the same business) formed the major sector of male employment in the city, and, where defined by occupation, approximately three-quarters of the population enumerated in nineteenth-century census returns were of the working classes (see Table 4). Between 1841 and 1891 Bath's occupational structure differed from the national average only between various categories of employment, but not substantially in terms of social class structure. Lower than average proportions engaged in manufacturing (1841: Bath, 25.78 per cent; England and Wales, 30.77 per cent. 1891: Bath 22.26 per cent; England and Wales, 32.72 per cent) were balanced out by higher than average male employment in building, transport and dealing. The

left Bath from Bathampton in the 1840s by T. F. Dicksee (1819–95). A horse-drawn canal boat on the Kennet and Avon is juxtaposed with a goods train on the GWR Bristol to London line, opened in 1841. The canal company could not withstand the competition from the railway and in 1852 it was taken over by the GWR.

size of the working population increased throughout the period 1851 to 1901, even though the aggregate size of the population remained fairly static. Over those fifty years, the male labour force increased by 35 per cent and the female labour force rose by 23 per cent.

These structural realities have received too little recognition. Although the prevailing character of economic activity in Bath was relatively small-scale compared with factories in the great industrial towns, Bath should, nevertheless, be recognised as a city with a strong industrial sector. It ranked with many medium-sized industrial towns, and its nineteenth-century population was too large to be sustained by merely seasonal trade associated with its role as a place of entertainment. Evidence of the complexities of the city's industrial and commercial past lingers on in street names, such as Midland Wharf and Brassmill Lane, and in the remnants of industrial buildings along the river. Far from being a place without trade, industry, or commerce, it was essentially – and increasingly so, from at least 1851 – a working city whose prosperity depended primarily on mass demand from all of its residents, and on its success in meeting needs in a market much wider than Bath itself. By the turn of the century, as a local historian reminds us, Bath:

> generated its own electricity, produced its own gas, possessed two busy railway yards and was served by three railway companies, exported giant dockland cranes and shorthand primers to every corner of the world, brewed its own beer, milled its own flour and wove its own cloth, modelled the world in 'Plasticine', fitted out the Queen Mary with furniture and panelled rooms, produced its own building materials and even its own cars.[3]

Table 4 *Male occupations in Bath, 1831*	
Occupation	*Number of males over 20 years*
Capitalists, bankers and other educated men	1,196
Building trades	1,074
Labouring (non-agricultural)	1,480
Retail (including some craftsmen)	2,797
Domestic service	670
Shoe-making	529
Furniture and coach-making	351
Tailoring	349
Labouring	110
Total	8,556

Source: 1831 Census; R. S. Neale, 'The Standard of Living 1780–1844: a regional and class study', *Economic History Review*, 19 (1966), p. 593.

The Dundas Aqueduct, designed by John Rennie and constructed in 1804, carries the Kennet and Avon over the upper reaches of the river Avon. It was named after Charles Dundas, chairman of the canal company. In this view two horses are driven by a single canal worker, and draw what appears to be a passenger barge. Between 16 July and 21 September 1833 a total of 2,272 passengers from Bath were carried to Bradford-on-Avon, and 2,313 on the return service. Each journey took less than an hour and ran twice daily from c.1837, by which time there were first- and second-class cabins, and a string band which entertained the passengers.

Canal cottages at Widcombe, photographed in the early twentieth century. In 1823 the company owned six wharves in Bath and had agents stationed both at Avon Quay and at Sydney Gardens wharf.

Throughout the nineteenth century, the city was experiencing significant economic changes, reflected in the changing structure of industrial and commercial occupations. Despite the difficulties of occupational definitions varying in the decennial census, the broad trends that can be identified show an increasing proportion of all occupied males employed in the building industry, rising to over 16 per cent by 1901, when this sector was particularly buoyant, because of the suburban building boom of the last decades of the nineteenth century. Cabinet-making and coach-making (both representative of the traditional small-scale enterprises characteristic of Bath's industry) expanded, and new industries – such as printing and bookbinding, and engineering – were established. Retailing and commerce were both subject to major expansion. Allied to industrial growth, there was an increase of employment in various forms of transport, which occupied 1,134 male workers (including 247 railway workers) in 1901. By 1900–10, bus companies, the trams, and several taxi firms were also an integral part of the transport sector. Local industries in

The river Avon to the south of the city formed one major nucleus of trade, commerce and communications. Water-borne trade via the Kennet and Avon as well as the river led to the development of quays and warehouses, while the route chosen for the new railway contributed to the area becoming more heavily industrialised over time.

relative decline from around the mid-nineteenth century included brewing, soap boiling, and steam dyeing, and Bath shared the national experience of falling numbers in certain trades where new technology reduced the demand for labour. Industrial production for a mass market increasingly replaced handwork in tailoring and shoe-making, for example, both of which sectors had employed substantial numbers in Bath. The 453 tailors of 1841 fell to 308 by 1901, and their numbers were further reduced over the next decade to 261 in 1911. In the same period the fall in the numbers of shoemakers was even greater, from 605 to 202 between 1841 and 1901, to 167 by 1911. However, the numbers of males employed as cabinet-makers, French polishers and upholsterers rose from 228 in 1841 to 342 in 1901. Those engaged in coach-making increased from 111 to 204 over the same period. Many of Bath's small-scale enterprises were featured at the Great Exhibition in 1851, and achieved a national and even international recognition.[4] The quality products of Knight & Son, upholsterers to the Prince of Wales, were shipped all over Europe, while there was a large demand from London for the 'Victoria carriages' built by the Bath coach-making firm of Fullers. Moreover, new industries grew up alongside the traditional crafts. Between 1841 and 1901 the number of men employed in printing more than trebled, rising from 58 to 199. By 1911, 212 male workers in Bath were printers or lithographers. Sir Isaac Pitman's printing business, founded at Nelson Place in 1845, was a part of the general expansion of printing and publishing in Bath. Pitman (born at Trowbridge, Wiltshire, in 1813) wrote several books on spelling reform, commercial practice and educational matters, and published his own *Phonetic Journal*. He is remembered chiefly as the pioneer of shorthand. In 1859 new premises were built on the Lower Bristol Road and these were enlarged in 1913. Pitman's served markets far beyond Bath, as a major printing and publishing company and one that was internationally known for its shorthand primers and instruction books.[5]

Engineering and machine-making was another expanding sector. This category accounted for only 37 occupied males in 1841, but those numbers rose to 410 by 1901. The engineering firm of Stothert & Pitt, a particularly successful business, originated as an ironmongery and developed into an iron foundry at its Newark Street works before moving to a larger factory on the Lower Bristol Road.[6] In 1851 metals and engineering industries generally employed 540 'hands'.[7] The name of Stothert & Pitt became virtually synonymous with dockside cranes from around the 1860s, but, before this specialisation, the company manufactured a diverse range of items such as treadmills, pumping engines, garden rollers, leather-tanning machines and apparatus for heating, cooking, and washing in hospitals or other large institutions. The company exhibited, and won prizes, at the Great Exhibition of 1851, the Paris Universal Exhibition (1867) and the London International Inventors' Exhibition (1889). Its products could be found in towns and cities throughout the United Kingdom, the Channel Islands, continental Europe, Canada, Australia, South America, and the subcontinent of India.[8] In 1911 the metal and associated industries (which included the manufacture of electrical appliances, cars and motor cycles, as well as engineering and machine-making) employed 961 of Bath's male workers.

One new industry, located at Bathampton but almost

In the city directory of 1852 this house at no. 35 Milsom Street was occupied by one John Strawbridge, brush manufacturer. It was quite common in the nineteenth century for small-scale commercial operations such as this to be located right in the heart of the city.

PHOTOGRAPH: CARNEGIE, 2004

certainly drawing some labour from the city itself, was the manufacture of Plasticine. This modelling material was invented by William Harbutt, who came to Bath in 1874 as head of the Art School but later ran his own Paragon Art Studio in Bladud's Buildings. Plasticine was developed in 1897 for use in his art classes but Harbutt also sold it in small quantities to local shops. Advertising soon led to a growth in demand, and in 1900 production on a commercial scale began in an old steam flour mill on the Kennet and Avon canal at Bathampton, where a gas engine was installed to power the mixing and blending machines. Plasticine also had industrial uses, and it remained one of the chief products of the company for most of its 83 years' existence, although Harbutts diversified over time into a broader range of artists' materials and related items.[9]

SIR ISAAC PITMAN

Sir Isaac Pitman (1813–1897) was born at Trowbridge, Wiltshire, the third of eleven children of Samuel Palmer, manager of a weaving mill, and his wife Maria, née Davis. After a limited education, Pitman worked as a clerk in Edgell's cloth mill and, from 1829, in a mill set up by his father. In 1831, he spent five months in London at the Training College of the British and Foreign School Society, after which (aged 19) he took up a teaching post in Lincolnshire. In 1835, he married a well-to-do widow, Mrs Mary Holgate (d. 1857) and shortly after took charge of a newly founded elementary school at Wootton-under-Edge, in Gloucestershire. By then Pitman

Sir Isaac Pitman & Sons Shorthand and Publishing Works, Twerton-on-Avon. Est. 1888
Removed from Bath to Twerton 1888

The premises of Isaac Pitman's 'shorthand and publishing works, Twerton-on-Avon'. The business occupied premises in various parts of the city but, as the hand-written caption states, it 'removed from Bath to Twerton, 1888'.
BY COURTESY OF BATH CENTRAL LIBRARY, BATH & NORTH EAST SOMERSET COUNCIL

had become devoted to the teachings of the New or Swedenborgian Church, and this brought him into conflict with the school committee. He was consequently dismissed, and for the next two and half years he ran a competing school. In 1839 he moved to Bath and set up a small school at his residence, 5 Nelson Place. His work in preparing and publishing his system of phonetic shorthand had so expanded that, in January 1846, he 'suspended' the school and turned the classrooms over to printing and binding his publications. He moved to various other premises as the business grew and, by the end of 1874, he was established as an editor, printer, and publisher on an industrial scale. In 1886 he took his sons into partnership, founding the firm known as Isaac Pitman & Sons. He remained devoted to the New Church from his mid-twenties. He was fiercely committed to vegetarianism and very hostile to smoking and drinking. He was knighted in 1894, and after fifty-eight years of residence in Bath, he died there at his home, 17 Royal Crescent, in January 1897.

Source: Oxford DNB (2004), pp. 429–31; see also Owen Ward, 'Isaac Pitman and the Fourth Phonetic Institution', Bath History, vii (1998), pp. 139–45.

Female industrial workers in Bath, as in the country generally, were concentrated in particular trades. Clothing was the outstanding one and, overall, it was a growth area for the employment of women and girls in the city. In 1831 some 10 per cent of the female labour force was engaged in the manufacture of cloth or clothing, but this rose to 16.8 per cent by 1901. Stay-makers increased their numbers substantially between 1841 and 1901, from 75 to 233, rising to 255 in 1911. Production became mechanised from the 1870s with the establishment of Bayers' corset factory in the south of the city, beside the river, and the founding of Drew, Son & Company as a corset manufacturer and wholesaler, with premises at Gascoyne Place and in Trim Street. The fact that the change to mechanised, factory production did not displace stay-makers, but actually increased their

St James's Bridge, which carries the Great Western railway line across the river Avon east from Bath Spa station. The station can be seen, right, in this 1846 print. The same bridge can be seen from the opposite side in the illustration on page 171.

The Lotor soap works in Morford Street, c.1920s. Employment opportunities for women began to increase as the economy matured and diversified.

numbers, suggests that the Bath corset-makers were serving the needs of an extensive and growing market. Indeed, Drew, Son & Company advertised its speciality corset as obtainable from all drapers and ladies outfitters 'throughout the Kingdom and Colonies'. Moreover, the company claimed its product had larger world-wide sales than any comparable undergarment.

Within the commercial sector of employment, wider opportunities existed for both men and women by 1900. Commercial occupations accounted for just under 12 per cent of male employment in 1871, rising to over 19 per cent by 1901. The numbers of clerks, merchants, agents and accountants, porters and messengers, all rose substantially over a thirty-year period. No female clerks were recorded in Bath before 1871. It seems likely that the primary cause of the growth in numbers of female clerks employed in the city, from 8 in 1871 to 111 by 1901, was the rapid expansion of the commercial sector, rather than the introduction of the typewriter. Later in the twentieth century the female typist became the archetypal woman at work, and women largely replaced male clerks and office workers, but new opportunities for women working in the commercial sector in Bath were accompanied by an increase in male employment in commerce in the late nineteenth century.

The corn market building on Walcot Street, by Manners & Gill, 1855.
PHOTOGRAPH: CARNEGIE, 2004

The relationships between Bath's occupational structure and its residential and tourist functions are complex, but it seems clear that the most important economic developments which took place from the 1820s to the early twentieth century were directly related neither to the city's visitors nor to the influx of new middle-class residents. In 1841 Bath had twelve hotels. Together with the lodging houses in the city they employed 130 female workers. The number of hotels increased, over a fifty-year period, to 24. Female employment also increased, as the numbers working in this sector rose to 438 by 1871, and to 542 by 1901. Yet the fastest growth in this sector (over 200 per cent in 30 years) occurred between 1841 and 1871 (rising from 130 to 438) when, by all accounts, the numbers of visitors coming to take the waters were relatively few. The moderate expansion over the following thirty years (just under 24 per cent) reflects Bath's resurgence as a health resort from the 1870s to 1900, but the occupational distribution of females, aged ten years and over, in Bath in 1901 suggests that the spa function of the city was not a leading sector of its economy. Between 1901 and 1911, the total number of women employed in hotels and lodging houses actually fell by almost 50, to 494.

Moreover, although indoor domestic service (excluding hotels) was (at just over 17 per cent) the largest single category of employment for women in 1901, the numbers had not risen significantly since 1871 despite the influx of new middle-class residents to the growing suburbs. No full-scale study of servant-keeping in Bath has yet been undertaken by any historian, but an analysis of households in Northampton Street and Rivers Street over the period from 1851 to 1881 revealed that the lower-middle class and professional middle-class households in those streets employed on average only one resident female servant.[10] These findings support the view that the 'paraphernalia of gentility' was beyond the means of many of Bath's genteel residents, who seem to have made economies by reducing the numbers of servants they employed. Furthermore, the numbers of male servants declined substantially from 860 in 1841 to 340 in 1901, and thereafter fell dramatically to a mere 79 by 1911. This also suggests that the servant-keeping classes in Bath were, in general, less well off by the beginning of the twentieth century. Keeping a man servant was the first sign of affluence (their wages were persistently higher than those of women), but even in the mid-nineteenth century Mrs Beeton, in her definitive *Book of Household Management* (1861), concluded that the expense could not be justified on an annual income of less than £1,000.[11]

The trends within professional occupations, for both men and women, seem related more directly to wider changes in society than to the growing popularity of Bath as a place of genteel residence. Male professional occupations fell from 13.4 per cent of all male occupations in 1851 to 10.9 per cent by 1901. Within this broad category, clergymen and teachers increased, but both occupations were having to expand their services to meet the needs of a mass society. The numbers of clergy rose most rapidly before 1871, in line with the pace of church building. The growth in numbers of teachers was more evenly spread, reflecting the expansion of educational provision in Bath before the Act of 1870, which established state education. This was clearly related to middle-class demand, although charity schools and private establishments catered for some children of lower social classes before the 1870s. The city directory of 1902 listed 17 boys' schools, 34 girls' schools, 7 language teachers, 81 music teachers, and 1 military and naval tutor. Male teachers rose from 59 in 1841 to 155 in 1901, while over the same period the number of female teachers increased from 182 to 397. Women in Bath, as throughout the country, gained entry in significant numbers only in the lower-paid professional jobs, such as teaching and nursing. Nurses and midwives numbered 106 in 1841 and 325 in 1901, but in that year there was only one female doctor in Bath and there were no female lawyers in the city. By 1911 the numbers of nurses and midwives had risen to 387 but women had made no inroads to the higher professions in Bath.

Male professions likely to be serving chiefly the needs of the comfortable classes experienced a reduction in their numbers. There were 52 lawyers

This former bank on the east corner at the top of Milsom Street is matched by another typically Victorian bank chambers on the opposite corner. Both were built by W. J. Wilcox in 1865 and 1875 respectively.

PHOTOGRAPH: CARNEGIE, 2004

197

(including barristers and solicitors) in Bath in 1841; these had increased to 87 by 1871 but fell back to 61 by 1901 and thereafter rose to 70 in 1911. A sharper reduction took place in the number of physicians, falling from 105 in 1841 to only 81 in 1901. There appears to be little connection between Bath's resurgence as a health resort in the late nineteenth century and the demand for medical practitioners, although by the early twentieth century it is possible that some of these professional classes were living outside the city and 'commuting' to places of work within Bath.

The city directories, however, give some indication of a growth in demand for services and trades associated with permanent residence in Bath. From the 1880s into the early twentieth century new entries or increased numbers can be found of house agents, furniture removers, domestic agencies, painters and decorators, specialist paper-hangers, and sellers, tuners, and repairers of pianofortes. There is also some indication that companies diversified to meet new demands. The City Metalworks, for example, directed its advertisement in the 1909 directory to the market for its products and services for heating private houses, greenhouses and conservatories.

Nonetheless, dependence on local consumers and visitors to Bath lessened as the base of the city's economy broadened. Population growth certainly expanded local demand for a wide range of goods and services, but throughout the nineteenth century Bath became more and more of an industrial and commercial city, dependent for its economic success on meeting national demands. The expansion of some traditional craft industries and the growth of new enterprises were responses to the growing wealth of the nation, but developments in transport and communication were also crucial to the growth of national markets.

At the beginning of the nineteenth century the Avon Navigation was of particular economic significance. Local products, such as Bath stone and beer, were shipped by barge to Bristol docks for distribution to other parts of the United Kingdom. (The beer trade was chiefly to Swansea and Cardiff, to supply the South Wales coalfields.)[12] Then, in 1810, after fifteen years of construction work at the cost of around £900,000, the Kennet and Avon canal opened.[13] Thereafter it was possible to

Bowler's shop on the corner of Corn Street and the Amebury, 1933. J. B. Bowler & Sons Ltd were brass founders and engineers, and manufacturers of aerated waters. The company was founded in 1872 and continued in existence until the late 1960s. The Bowler collection, including engineering works and a 'fizzy pop' factory, is the main exhibit at the Museum of Bath at Work.
BY COURTESY OF BATH CENTRAL LIBRARY, BATH & NORTH EAST SOMERSET COUNCIL

below A detail of Cotterill's map of 1852 (with south at the top), showing Brunel's Great Western Railway at Bath and the suburbs south of the river. Bath's location in the valley bottom meant that the great engineer had to survey the route carefully: two river crossings were required within a short distance as well as extensive embankments. Despite these difficulties Brunel cleverly managed to locate the city's station just within the city, taking advantage of the undeveloped floodplain near the river. Typically, he designed some of the features with medieval battlements and gothic arches (*right*). Widcombe remained semi-rural in the mid-nineteenth century, with suburban growth concentrated south-east of the railway and in the Holloway district. The Widcombe Nursery occupied a large area of land left of Prior Park Road. North of the river note the courts off Southgate Street and the working-class Avon Street district, where numerous small industries flourished behind Broad Quay and New Quay.

BY COURTESY OF BATH RECORD OFFICE

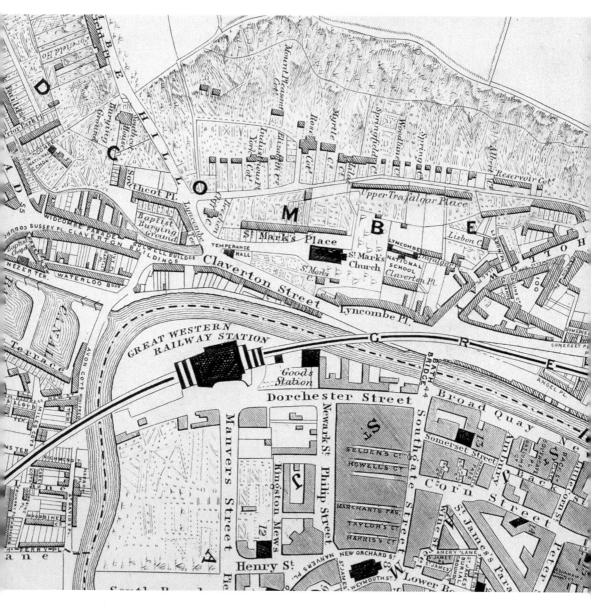

transport goods from Bristol to London in four days, despite extensive locking systems on the canal at Widcombe, in Bath, and at Devizes, in Wiltshire. In the months of March and April 1830, 9,415 tons of goods were carried on the canal from Bath to destinations in the southern counties or London, whereas in the same period comparable tonnage on the Avon Navigation from Bath to Bristol docks was only 1,655.[14] The canal, in its turn, was superseded by the railway. The Kennet and Avon Canal Company was one of the main opponents of the Great Western Railway Bills of 1834 and 1835, and once the second Bill was passed the Company attempted to cut costs and increase revenue by various means. From 1837 traffic was allowed to operate by night as well as by day, and in 1841, fly-boats of up to fifteen tons (giving a larger capacity than before) were permitted on the Bath to Reading section of the canal, and economies were made in manpower and wages. The company could not, however, withstand the competition from the railways. Once the GWR line from Bristol to London was operating, goods could be transported in hours over distances that took days by canal. Canal company receipts fell from over £51,000 in 1840–41 to less than £40,000 in the following year,[15] and in 1852 the Kennet and Avon was taken

An aerial photograph
of the river Avon
to the west of Bath
Bridge (bottom right),
*c.*1930s.

over by the GWR.[16] The railway network expanded further when the Midland Railway spur-line to Bath (1869) linked the city with the manufacturing areas of the Midlands and the North. This stimulated the growth and specialisation of some local industries, but it also increased competition by bringing in products from outside the locality. In this respect, it made a particular impact not on the economy of Bath, but on the long-term decline of the nearby Somerset coalfield, as cheaper coal raised in the developing Midlands coalfield eroded the traditional markets for Somerset coal. The location of industry in Bath remained much the same while these developments in transport progressed, but from the 1840s onwards the focus of activity was the railway lines and associated goods yards, rather than the quays and wharfs along the waterways.

As its economy diversified, Bath continued to attract labour from far beyond the city limits, particularly female labour. Domestic service continued to be an important sector of employment for women. Although we have shown that the level of servant-keeping declined over time, there is evidence to suggest that domestic work was readily available for those who did not share the growing working-class antipathy to service, as alternative opportunities grew. Moreover, as late as 1911 the largest single occupational group of women in Bath was the domestic service category. 3,824 women were employed as 'domestic indoor servants', a further 424 worked as 'washers, ironers, manglers, etc.' and another 301 earned their wages as 'charwomen'. Out of a total 10,446 females aged ten and upwards engaged in occupations, the number employed in 'domestic offices and services' of all kinds was 5,388 – over half of all Bath's female working population. Domestic agencies advertising in Bath frequently aimed their publicity at prospective employees as much as employers: 'Good servants of every description wanted immediately' recurs in advertisements from the 1870s onward. Similarly, the expanding industrial and commercial sectors also attracted female labour into Bath, some for work and training in the clothing trades. Much of the high quality women's clothing sold by Jolly's of Milsom Street (as with other similar companies) was made up in the firm's workrooms. Jolly's employed 17 women in 1861, including draper's assistants, milliners and mantle makers, as well as domestic servants. Of these, 7 were born in distant counties beyond the west country region.[17] In 1911 the textiles and dress trade employed over 2,000 women in Bath. In addition to the 255 corset makers, there were 859 dressmakers, 232 milliners, 223 tailoresses and 117 shirt-makers or seamstresses. Over 100 women were occupied as dealers in articles of dress, and another 264 were miscellaneous 'other workers'.

By the 1890s several strictly-run church hostels and other similar organisations existed for the purpose of helping young workers who migrated to the city. Most of them were concerned with women, although there was a branch of the Young Men's Christian Association (YMCA) with premises in Broad Street. Without reference to class or occupation, the YMCA promoted itself as a body concerned for 'the spiritual, intellectual, social and physical welfare of young men', to which ends it offered Bible classes and evangelical lectures, a library of 'selected works', newspapers and periodicals, draughts, chess, bagatelle, and a gymnasium. The Young Women's Christian Association (YWCA), in contrast, had more specific interests and provided fewer general facilities. Its aim was 'to promote the welfare of young women in the various workrooms and houses of business in the city'. Bible and other classes, and religious lectures, were organised for young women but the only other diversions on offer were a reading room (supplied with 'suitable

The malthouse at the London Street brewery in the early twentieth century.

The Jolly family were drapers who formed one of the best-known drapery and later department stores in the West of England – Jolly & Sons of Milsom Street, Bath. James Jolly (b. 1775) was born in Norfolk and followed his father into the linen drapery trade. After moving to Deal, Kent, in the 1810s, he went on to open a branch shop in fashionable Margate which, by 1826, was managed by his son Thomas Jolly (1801–89). A seasonal branch was opened in Bath in 1823 and this quickly developed into a 'Parisian Depot' in New Bond Street. In 1831, a new shop, managed by Thomas Jolly, opened in Milsom Street, trading as Jolly & Sons. This was extended in 1834 with an imposing plate glass frontage.

The shopfront of Jollys department store in Milsom Street. The hats in the window displays suggest that the photograph was taken sometime around the 1920s or 1930s.

BATH CENTRAL LIBRARY, LOOSE PICTURES COLLECTION

Thomas Jolly was a Liberal, elected to the town council in 1839, and serving as mayor in 1861 and again in 1868. He was a staunch ally of the reforming mayor of Bath, Jerom Murch, in his campaign for a Corporation water supply in the 1860s. Jolly retired from the council in 1883, only to be re-elected again in 1885. By the time of his death in October 1889, at his home, Parkview Lodge, Oldfield Road, he was by far the longest-standing member of the council. He had also been a Poor Law guardian, and been active in many local organisations.

His eldest son, William Cracknell Jolly (1828–1904), took over the business and also followed his father into public life. The shop was enlarged in 1879 and extensively refurbished in 1888. Quarterly price lists were distributed throughout the south of England as part of a growing mail-order trade. In 1881, an agency was opened in Bombay 'for ladies who have commissions from friends in India'.

The family assiduously promoted its royal connections and held a number of warrants for supplying the royal household. W. C. Jolly joined his father on the council in 1874 where he became a tireless promoter of civic improvement. He served as mayor in 1894, retiring to Hampstead in 1899, and died at Eastbourne in 1904.

The Jolly family continued to have a major interest in the business in the first half of the twentieth century. The firm, acquired by Dingles of Plymouth in 1965, is now part of the House of Fraser, but retains the well-known name of Jolly's in Milsom Street, Bath.

William Cracknell Jolly (1828–1904), shopkeeper and town councillor, and Mayor of Bath in 1894.

BATH CENTRAL LIBRARY, LOOSE PICTURES COLLECTION

periodicals' and one weekly newspaper) and a library stocked with 'a selection of religious and instructive works'. The YWCA also provided accommodation, in Stall Street, to 30 young women 'coming to Bath as strangers'. It ran a separate Servants Home and Registry, to provide shelter for servants 'of a respectable character' when out of work. Such subtleties of discrimination, between women engaged in trade or commerce and those who worked as domestic servants, was further refined by the Young Women's Friendly Society (YWFS) (affiliated to the national Girls' Friendly Society), which operated from premises in Russell Street. The YWFS dealt with a 'better class' of client than did the YWCA, aiming to provide 'pleasant and domestic evenings for young women engaged in business or tuition'. It, too, provided some accommodation and, despite its title, seems to have imposed no upper age limit: the organisation's entry in the city directory for 1893 stated that 'Ladies are also boarded at a moderate rate'.[18]

The 'typical' resident of Bath in the period 1820 to 1914, if such a mythical creature existed, was neither a destitute beggar nor an upper-class pensioner. The typical resident was female, in that women outnumbered men, and she was more likely to be a domestic servant or a dressmaker than either a street hawker or prostitute or a woman (whether widowed or single) of independent means. Among the adult male population of the city, engineers and cabinet-makers were more representative than either upper-class pensioners or unskilled labourers. This large section of the population, encompassing a wide range of occupations and social status, was often overlooked by contemporary commentators and has been somewhat neglected by historians, other than R. S. Neale, who has been credited with 'discovering' Bath's working classes. Even Neale was rather more interested in the skilled artisans than in the standard of living of the unskilled and common labourers, who were dismissed as 'the lumpen proletariat', lacking a 'true' Marxist class-consciousness.

As we have seen, Bath changed significantly over the period from 1820 to 1914, and it did so in more complex ways than its dominant image suggests. It was not merely that its role as the resort of fashion was eroded and replaced over time, by becoming a favoured place of genteel residence. Simultaneously, it was becoming more industrial and commercial, and supporting a larger working class. Some old craft industries experienced a revival; new industries became firmly established; and retailing and commerce were both subject to major expansion. The labour force in Bath increased, primarily as a result of developments that were nationwide, rather than in response to the influx of new middle-class residents or to the brief resurgence of the spa after the 1870s. Changes in the occupational structure of the city, from the earlier decades of the nineteenth century to 1911, owed much more to new forms of transport, technological advances in industry, structural changes in retailing, and the general growth of government and commercial activity. The city continued to attract migrants from the rural hinterland and beyond, as an expanding labour market, and in the late nineteenth century its numerous charities still drew vagrants and tramps to Bath: numbers conveyed by the police to the casual ward of the workhouse, in the period 1885 to 1894, indicate a rising trend. Over that period, with some fluctuation in 1891–92, numbers rose from 4,675 to 6,577.[19] The genteel image had nonetheless been firmly established by 1900. It reflected the realities of Bath's admittedly declining appeal as a fashionable resort and of the process of suburbanisation that was attracting many new, middle-class residents to the city. What the dominant image obscured was the significant change under way in the occupational structure of the city, which reflected another, but equally valid reality: from at least the mid-nineteenth century, Bath was a predominantly working-class, small-scale industrial city.

Working-class society, social control and living standards

The splendour of Bath's Georgian architecture and the comfortable solidity of its large Victorian and Edwardian villas often evoke images of gracious living and a degree of affluence that are quite at odds with the realities experienced by the majority of the city's residents. Only a fortunate minority lived at such desirable addresses as the Royal Crescent or Newbridge Hill. Moreover, the process of suburbanisation increased residential segregation of the social classes in Bath throughout the nineteenth century, and particularly so from the 1880s into the earlier twentieth century.

In the early nineteenth century the inner-city parishes were the main centres of manufacturing and housed most of the working classes. For example, skilled craftsmen predominated in the parish of St James in 1831, when it was home to 12 per cent of the male population of Bath, but accounted for a much higher proportion of the city's artisans. The proportion of adult males in St James's employed in building, furniture making, coach-making, shoe-making and tailoring was twice that of Bath as a whole.[20] On the other hand, Lyncombe and Widcombe, lying outside the city boundaries until the mid-1830s, was a suburban industrial parish and one of the poorer ones up to 1840. The textile industry was located there, as was much of Bath's growing industrial sector of the later nineteenth century. Small shopkeepers predominated among the inhabitants of the inner-city parish of SS Peter and St Paul, while larger shopkeepers were particularly numerous in the central parish of St Michael (which included the fashionable shops of Milsom Street). Walcot was a very large parish, housing over half of Bath's total population in the mid-nineteenth century, and many of the poorest parts of the north and west of the city lay within its boundaries, although the Lansdown district of Walcot was a comparatively wealthy residential area.[21]

'URBAN DECAY IN THE SOUTHERN PARTS OF THE CITY HAD CREATED BATH'S MOST NOTORIOUS SLUM ... THE AVON STREET DISTRICT.'

By the 1830s, urban decay in the southern parts of the city had created Bath's most notorious slum, in what was known as the Avon Street district. Natural and physical barriers defined this area, rather than administrative ones. Most of it was in St James's parish but some parts extended into the parishes of Walcot, of St Michael's, and of SS Peter and Paul. The commercial thoroughfares of Southgate Street, Lower Borough Walls, and Westgate Buildings marked its eastern limits. The open spaces of Saw Close and Kingsmead Square lay to the north, with wasteland to the west, and the river Avon was its southern boundary. Some 10,000 people, or about one-fifth of the population of Bath, lived within the Avon Street district in the mid-nineteenth century. This was by no means a constant figure, but one that changed over time and fluctuated with the seasons, as migrant workers and other itinerants moved in and out of the city. Avon Street itself was described in the 1820s as the home of 'at least 300 people who obtain a living by begging, thieving, or on the miserable wages of prostitution'.[22] Shops were open on Sundays, public houses for almost the whole of every day, and street-corner gambling and obscene language were frequently complained of by Bath's respectable residents. Newspaper reports often highlighted the association of Avon Street with criminal activity, as in July 1820 when six inhabitants of the street were imprisoned for brothel-keeping, and in September of the following year, when seven juveniles aged 17 to 19 were sentenced to death at the Somerset Assizes for various offences of assault, robbery, and highway robbery.[23] From the 1830s, the Avon Street district succeeded Holloway as the main area for the reception of travellers; by the end of the nineteenth century the 'nymphs of Avon Street' were no longer in evidence, although prostitution still flourished in other parts of this southern district. From the late 1840s, an increasing presence of poor Irish living in over-crowded lodgings attracted negative reporting which gave Avon Street an enhanced reputation for violence and disorder:

MON — AN AVON STREET RIOT —

Richard Barret, an Irishman, was charged with being drunk and disorderly in Avon St., on Saturday night.

It appeared that a crowd of people were assembled before the door of the Fountain public-house, in consequence of some outrage committed by the prisoner, while he was at a window upstairs, threatening the mob outside. Presently afterwards some woman connected with him, hurled a lump of coal upon their heads. Some of the crowd, in retaliation, smashed the window, when the prisoner rushed out of the house, furiously wielding a poker, and followed the people down the street, attempting to strike indiscriminately, as he proceeded.[24]

The notoriety of Avon Street persisted into the early twentieth century, even though conditions improved in terms of population density, overcrowded and insanitary housing, inadequate water supply, and the incidence of epidemic disease. Within the southern slum district as a whole, however, the changing character of Avon Street was perceived more clearly than it was by outsiders. The 'locals' who lived there around 1900 regarded Little Corn Street, the haunt of itinerant tinkers, as the roughest of the streets, dubbing it 'Little 'Ell' because of the frequent outbursts of violence among its inhabitants. Avon Street, in contrast, had risen in comparative social status to become recognised as a relatively wealthy street, inhabited by respectable tradesmen and lodging-house keepers, many of whom owned their own property. Even the travellers who lodged there were 'well off', for they could afford to pay 3*d.* (1¼p) for a bed while their poorer counterparts went to cheaper, unregistered lodgings elsewhere, or resorted to the casual ward of the workhouse.

Similarly, Holloway became a somewhat more respectable working-class district, as the southern slums across the river became the chief lodging house area of the city, and new artisan cottages were built at Calton Road and in other parts of Holloway. The changing status of streets or districts within particular parishes has not been studied extensively, but a further example of the process can be found in Northampton Street, in the parish of Walcot. Northampton Street (together with Morford Street, Ballance Street and Lampards Buildings) was one of the sites developed as artisan dwellings in the late eighteenth and early nineteenth centuries, despite its close proximity to King's Circus and the Royal Crescent, which housed the professional and the upper middle classes. By 1851, however, Northampton Street's 39 houses were occupied by 82 chiefly lower middle-class households (defined by rateable value of the houses, and the occupation of head of household). 'Gentrification' was clearly under way in nineteenth-century Bath. Between 1851 and 1881 the number of houses in this street remained constant, but the number of households fell to 65. Tradesmen predominated among male heads of household in Northampton Street in 1851; thirty years later residents included more annuitants and fundholders and representatives of the lower professional classes, such as school teachers.[25]

Differing levels of income, occupations, and social values, all contributed to the formation of subtle social hierarchies, even within outwardly homogeneous residential districts. The gulf between the 'rough' and the 'respectable' among the labouring classes was particularly marked, although it was perhaps never as great as the contemporary middle classes perceived it to be. There is evidence to suggest that working people gave their own meanings to such key words as 'respectability' and, moreover, that some elements of 'rough' behaviour (notably heavy drinking) were quite commonplace among working men as a whole until the later nineteenth century.[26] Nonetheless, an extreme example of the violent disorder that could be caused by Bath's slum dwellers was recalled by the travelling showman, 'Lord' George Sanger, in his description of an incident at the Lansdown Fair in the 1820s. A mob of savage roughs from the city's slums arrived at the fair towards evening, bent on destruction. They were led by a gigantic, red-haired virago called 'Carotty Kate', a notorious figure 'as strong as a navvy' and much feared in Bath, where she lived at a place called Bull Paunch Alley:

> Half-stripped, with her red hair flying wildly behind her, she incited the gang of ruffians with her to wreck the fair. The drinking booths were the first to suffer. The mob took possession of them, half killed some of the unfortunate owners, and set to work to drink themselves into a state of frenzy more acute

than before. The scenes that followed are almost indescribable. Not content with drinking all they could, the ruffians turned on the taps, stoved in barrels, smashed up bottles, and let the liquor run to waste. Then they started to wreck the booths. Canvas was torn to shreds, platforms were smashed and made bonfires of, wagons were battered to fragments. Everywhere was riot, ruin and destruction.[27]

Carotty Kate and company were eventually rounded up by the stallholders, and they took revenge for the damage to their property by resorting to physical violence themselves. The men were dragged on a rope through a deep pool at the bottom of Lansdown Hill. Then, after being allowed to recover and 'drain' on dry ground, they were dragged uphill to the wagons where they were tied, two at a time, to wheels and thrashed with whalebone whips. Kate herself was spared a ducking, but was fastened to a cart-wheel to witness the flogging of the men. Then she was seized by six stout women and caned by two more until their fury was spent. The police, equipped with heavy staves, intercepted the returning mob and a bloody battle ensued. Many arrests were made, after numerous injuries had been inflicted and one officer was crippled for life.

THE MOB WAS LED BY CAROTTY KATE ... A NOTORIOUS FIGURE, 'AS STRONG AS A NAVVY' AND MUCH FEARED IN BATH.

This is a particularly vivid example of the 'roughs' of Bath on the rampage, but street disorder and violence were commonplace in the poorer districts and the provision of extra police on occasions such as the annual fair, the races, or at election times, was not always sufficient to ensure the maintenance of public order in the supposedly quiet and civilised city of Bath.[28] In the early nineteenth century, the city's streets were plagued by juvenile gangs, as well as by notorious beggars, hawkers and street traders of every description. Bath was reputedly one of the major centres of crime outside London, and it was said in 1828 to have a distinct criminal class, comprising some 60 per cent of the 'boys of the town', who survived by crime alone, chiefly stealing from shops and picking pockets.[29] The general level of street noise and disorder was quite out of keeping with Bath's reputation as a quiet resort for the invalid and the elderly.

George Cox was a tradesman who 'felt a great desire to speak to poor sinners' in the most deprived parts of the city. 'Once seeing a man strike a woman down into the gutter, he remonstrated, but was soon stopped by the question; "Poll, thee dost not mean to let him take I to the station, dost?" And the reply of the woman who jumped up and looked fierce was, "No I don't"; and turning to Mr Cox she said, "He's a right to knock I down as often as he's a mind, for all anybody". "O very well," said Mr Cox "then I wish you both good night"; and he left them.'[30] The incident not only reveals the casual violence common to poor districts but the limited success of missions to the poor. It also points to the working-class sense of solidarity that resented outside interference.

Even among the 'respectable' working classes, resorting to violence was a means of enforcing community values, which persisted into the early twentieth century. Respectability included a powerful moral stigma against illegitimacy, as Louie Stride (born in 1907), the bastard child of a prostitute, recalled in her memoirs. After numerous 'moonlight flits' from one slum district of Bath to another, mother and child made another move, around 1910, from a tenement in Walcot to a small, hovel type of cottage at the back of a sweet shop in Holloway. Next morning all the women in the neighbouring cottages 'attacked my mother verbally and in person called her a "Scarlet Woman", and they threw her goods out in the yard, "coming to live amongst a lot of decent people with a Bastard", they weren't going to tolerate that and they didn't'.[31] For Louie and her mother this meant another 'handcart ride', to a part of the lower town where prostitutes and their bastards were less of an affront to respectable inhabitants. Yet Holloway, viewed from without and from the perspective of the dominant middle-class culture, was seen as a homogeneous district in terms of socio-economic structure and cultural values. Together with other areas of working-class residence, such as Snow Hill, the Dolemeads, and the Avon Street district, it was perceived as 'poor' and 'rough'.

What outsiders overlooked, or found difficult to comprehend, was the degree of social stratification that existed within working-class communities. Not even at the height of its notoriety as Bath's worst slum was Avon Street inhabited only by the very poor. It was a 'poor' area in comparison with more select parts of Bath: four out of five of the 182 houses in the streets, courts and alleys connected with Avon Street and Milk Street, had a rateable value of less than

Louie Stride (Mrs Ross), 1907–90.

Walcot Infants' School, c.1912. Louie Stride is the shaven-headed child sitting left of the teacher.

Pratt's Hotel in South Parade, where Louie Stride worked as a chambermaid in the 1930s.

£15 per annum in 1839, compared with the King's Circus where three out of every five houses were worth over £150 per annum and none was rated at under £110.[32] In Avon Street itself, the majority (69 per cent) of the 90 houses were within a rateable value of £5 to £6 in 1862. Just over 12 per cent were rated at less than £5 per annum, but almost a fifth (18.5 per cent) were valued at over £10 per annum.[33] Moreover, 35 houses, or 38.9 per cent of the total, appear to have been owner-occupied, and the pattern of ownership of property in Avon Street indicates that some of its residents were petty capitalists. Fifteen people owned two properties in the street in 1862, and a further eight people owned between three and six houses. The publicans, shopkeepers, lodging-house keepers and master craftsmen who lived in Avon Street and the surrounding district formed the upper socio-economic strata of the area's working classes. From 1832 onward (when the Reform Act introduced the £10 property qualification for the franchise), some of them also provided political leadership to a populous working-class part of the city.

Because inadequate recognition was given to the hierarchy of status within the working classes (and to differing, class-based perceptions of 'respectable' or acceptable behaviour), the process of suburbanisation, which increasingly took the better-off away from the inner-city parishes, reinforced the fears of the authorities and the middle classes that social segregation had left the urban poor bereft of moral leadership. What then followed was legislation to reform or improve aspects of urban working-class living, but this was invariably framed within the parameters of middle-class culture, and often infringed on traditional freedoms. Throughout the nineteenth century and beyond, the working classes were subjected to increasing interference and regulation in the workplace, in the public streets, in their leisure pursuits, and even within the family. Differing sets of values between legislators and those most affected by new regulations made some degree of conflict inevitable.

Both the rough and the respectable among Bath's poorer residents were affected by the reorganisation and extension of the forces of law and order. Until 1836 Bath had three autonomous police forces, each with different powers, and police authority did not extend to the Holloway district south of the river, in the parish of Lyncombe and Widcombe. A new borough police force was established in 1836, under the central direction of the Watch Committee and the Chief Constable. Thereafter, the whole city was policed by a single authority, and the instigation of regular day and night patrolling of the streets led to more acceptable standards of public order. Closer regulation of street activity was an important function of the borough police, and no doubt the relative success of the force made the streets of Bath safer and more pleasant for all of its residents, particularly in the last quarter of the century. However, the 'move on' policy of police in the central commercial streets threatened the livelihood of the urban poor who made their living as hawkers and costermongers. Emma Rose, for example, was charged in 1863 with causing an obstruction in Southgate Street, by placing a basket of fish near the footway. She was fined 1s. (5p) and costs, or three days' imprisonment. In passing sentence, the Mayor observed that 'the Bench were determined to repress the use of obscene language that now prevailed in some parts of the city'.[34] Conflict between the police and the street traders continued, and the strict supervision by a full-time professional police force (supported by wide powers under local by-laws) created new areas of conflict. The uniformed authority focused its attention on working-class districts, where closer regulation of lodging-houses, pubs and popular forms of recreation (such as gambling) was met with widespread suspicion. Hostility showed itself in sullen resentment, verbal abuse of the police, and occasionally in physical assault. Following the arrests of people discharging fireworks in London Street on 6 November 1876, it was recorded in the Watch Committee Minutes that 'the mob consisting of 4 or 5 hundred persons resisted the Police with such effect that the prisoners had to be conveyed to the Police Station by way of Cleveland Bridge when bottles, stones and other missiles were freely thrown at the police whose helmets and clothing were damaged'.[35]

The respectable classes of Bath evidently shared with the police force a concern about the proliferation of pubs in the poorest parts of the city. A memorial presented to the annual licensing meeting in 1867 pointed out that there were 74 bakers' shops and 51 butchers' shops in the city and borough of Bath, but that within the same area there were '300 places for the sale of intoxicating drinks'. Experience showed, the memorialists claimed, 'that poverty, immorality, and crime are in proportion to the facilities afforded for the sale of spirituous liquors'.[36] Heavy drinking – 'the curse of the working classes' to many respectable Victorians – undoubtedly caused poverty in many families, and some public houses and beer shops were closely associated with criminal activity: a police return sent to the Watch Committee in 1869 referred to fifteen that were known to the force as the resort of thieves and prostitutes. Nonetheless, most public houses had a wider function that was rarely recognised, as meeting places and venues for various clubs, and as an informal source of news about jobs or lodgings. Their landlords were summoned most frequently for serving drinks after hours, or allowing gaming on their premises – 'offences' in the eyes of the law, but such prosecutions were often perceived by landlords and their customers as an infringement of traditional personal freedoms.

From the 1870s, legislation created new categories of offences, which brought some parents into conflict with the law. Compulsory vaccination of children against smallpox and enforced attendance at school for all between the ages of five and thirteen were two improving measures that led to some previously blameless characters appearing before the Bath magistrates. Vaccination was neglected by many parents, who did not understand its implications, but it was also resisted on principle by some who either resented what they saw as undue interference in family life by the authorities, or who had genuine fears about the process. It was, however, only a minority of parents who did not comply with the law, and preventative measures were increasingly successful in reducing the incidence of smallpox epidemics. This success, it seems, led to some degree of complacency among parents and the authorities themselves. Of all children born in Bath in 1905, 1906, and from January to June in 1907, the percentage vaccinated was 82.6 per cent, 72.1 per cent, and 67.9 per cent respectively. Prosecutions declined as the level of vaccinations declined.[37]

Non-compliance with the law on this issue was, perhaps, more likely to be due to negligence or to ignorance rather than to principle or to rational fears, but parental resistance in the poorer parts of the city to compulsory schooling was inextricably bound up with working-class culture, the family economy, and the survival strategies with which the urban poor coped with daily life. Compulsory schooling struck a severe financial blow to the household economy of many poor families, who not only lost the crucial earnings of children, but found an extra expense imposed on their limited budgets by the fees required for schooling. Yet, both before and after compulsory attendance at school was introduced, it was only a small minority of parents in the poorer working-class districts of Bath who did not avail themselves of the opportunities for their children to gain some education. Charges brought against parents by the School Board reveal a predictable pattern of summonses to addresses in the Avon Street district, the Dolemeads, Holloway, Snow Hill and Larkhall, – all those areas of the city which were distinctively working-class and also housed the poorest of Bath's residents. The abolition of school fees in the late nineteenth century no doubt contributed to the rise in average school attendance in Bath, which reached 86.8 per cent between 1899 and 1901.[38] But as late as 1901, the census report estimated that 209 boys and 80 girls aged ten and under fourteen (or 11.5 per cent and 4.4 per cent respectively) were engaged in occupations.[39] A local government inspector of schools commented in 1902 that 'ambition to improve themselves either mentally or financially seems to be dormant among the class that form the bulk of the population'.[40] For the small but severely deprived under class, who lived their lives in the culture of poverty, education beyond that of the streets had no value. A contribution to the family economy was of more immediate concern than a formal education, and it is not surprising that about half of the total of 55 child workers identified in Bath in 1910 were registered as pupils of St Paul's School in Avon Street.[41]

Little can be said with confidence about the standard of living of 'ordinary' residents of Bath, because of the lack of evidence on wage-rates, earnings and prices. Neale has drawn some broad conclusions, for the period from 1780 to 1850, from his analysis of wage-accounts kept by the Overseer of Highways in

'[THE] AMBITION TO IMPROVE THEMSELVES EITHER MENTALLY OR FINANCIALLY SEEMS TO BE DORMANT AMONG THE CLASS THAT FORM THE BULK OF THE POPULATION.'

LOCAL GOVERNMENT INSPECTOR, 1902

Walcot parish, in relation to the weekly publication in local papers of a selection of retail prices in Bath market, but it should be borne in mind that his sources were very few and that the data on earnings was confined to labourers working on the highways. However, Neale considered it 'probable' that the movement of wages for this group of highway labourers indicated the direction and magnitude of wage movements for the whole group of non-agricultural labourers who, in 1831, numbered 1,480 and constituted approximately 20 per cent of the adult male work force in the city. His general conclusion was that living standards fell in the early nineteenth century but that by 1832 'real wages' (that is, the purchasing power of earnings in relation to prices) were at a level comparable to those of 1780. In 1835 they reached a level 22 per cent higher than the base year of 1780 but declined thereafter, and it was not until 1841 that real wages showed a definite and sustained improvement. Neale estimates that during the mid-1840s the standard of living of labourers, if fully employed, was about 50 per cent higher than it had been in the late eighteenth century.[42]

No detailed study exists on wage levels in Bath in the period between 1850 and 1914, but there are two indicators that suggest that a gradual improvement took place in the standard of living for at least some sections of the working classes. Firstly, the changes in the occupational structure of the city – including the growth of employment in regular, if not always better paid jobs in commerce and new industries such as printing and engineering and a decline in traditional, often low-paid and casual labouring jobs and in the craft industries of tailoring and shoe-making – must have had a beneficial effect on the overall standard of living of the working classes in Bath. Also, the wages of domestic servants increased at an above average rate and this affected many female workers in Bath, even at the expense of fewer jobs being available. Secondly, it is generally agreed that real wages (taking into account the level of prices) at a national level improved by 60 per cent or more for the average urban worker between 1850 and 1900.[43] This improvement was effected more by a fall in prices than a rise in actual wage levels but the purchasing power of the working classes increased as a result. It is most likely that on the whole the working people of Bath shared in the nation's experience of growing prosperity, although the poorest among them, the labourers, hawkers and casual workers, were the least likely to have benefited.

Class differences in public health remained a constant, even after important gains were made by 1914. The life chances of the working classes were bleak compared to those of the higher social classes. In 1842 the average age of death

The Eastern Dispensary, Cleveland Place East, built in 1845 as a Goodridge charitable institution where the sick poor could get medical advice and medicines. Other dispensaries existed in Bath: the South-West (1837) at No.1 Albion Place on the Upper Bristol Road; and the Southern (1849), in Claverton Street, now demolished.

PHOTOGRAPH: CARNEGIE, 2004

among gentlemen and professional persons living in Bath was 55; among the families of labourers and artisans in general it was 24 and 25 respectively, but the families of shoemakers died at the average age of only 14.[44] These startling figures have not been satisfactorily accounted for, but probably reflect the high levels of infant and child mortality rates in the marked variations in life expectancy among Bath's residents. This was influenced by place of residence as well as by income and occupation, for the incidence of disease was naturally greatest in the poorest areas of the city. In the cholera epidemic of 1832, a quarter of the 74 cases in Bath occurred in Avon Street. Seven years later, it was also the chief centre of a smallpox epidemic that affected a total of 300 people. When cholera broke out again, in 1848, the Avon Street district as a whole (which housed one in five of the total population) was once more among the areas of the city where the disease was particularly prevalent, although other locations of low quality housing (such as Snow Hill and the Dolemeads) were equally conspicuous.[45]

In general Bath shared in the reduction of mortality rates that took place throughout England and Wales. Between 1841 and 1880, the annual average general mortality rate for Bath City fluctuated between 22 and 24 per 1,000, which was close to the national average for England and Wales for the same period. From 1881 to 1900, both rates declined in tandem. Bath's mortality went down from 18.5 (1881–90) to 17.1 (1891–1900) compared with 18.6 and 17.5 nationally. Incorporated within a decline in the city's mortality rate was a less marked disparity in those of different districts. In the 1840s Lyncombe and Widcombe recorded the highest mortality rate at 30.5 per 1,000 population, whilst the lowest figure came from Bathwick, at 19.8 per 1,000 population. Even within a single district, as in Lansdown in 1843, the rate was roughly twice as high in the poor districts such as Avon Street and Milk Street compared with the wealthy areas like the Royal Crescent and Marlborough Buildings.

By the last two decades of the century there was a narrowing of the gap between the highest and lowest district mortality rates. While the annual rate for Bath was 15.1 per 1,000 for the period 1897–99, Walcot had the highest district rate (16.5), followed by Lyncombe and Widcombe (12.1), and Bathwick recorded the lowest rate (11.2). Clearly assisting the downward trend of mortality in all districts was the movement of population away from the unhealthy central and low-lying districts to the less crowded and better-housed suburbs.

Overcrowding in the central parishes had been reduced during the second half of the century by the gradual migration of the population to the suburbs. In 1851 a total of 11,647 persons lived in 1,349 houses in the inner-city parishes, whereas in 1901, in the same parishes, 7,577 individuals were living in 1,342 houses.[46] This represented a significant improvement in living space: fewer one-roomed households and more people living in two and three rooms. Nonetheless, poor housing was one of the social problems common to all urban centres in the nineteenth and early twentieth century, which Bath's working classes as a whole shared. The Dolemeads, developed as a working-class district in the mid-nineteenth-century, quickly degenerated into a slum. A few decades later a large part of this district was an 'insanitary area' as defined by the Housing of the Working Classes Act (1890). The houses, on a low-lying site, were damp and the whole area (known to its inhabitants as 'Mud Island') was frequently flooded. Particularly severe flooding there in 1882 and again in 1894 eventually prompted the council to undertake improvements involving, unusually in Britain at this time, council house-building. A scheme for building small houses was approved in September 1898, but final sanction from the Local Government Board (to raise a loan of £10,500) was not given until December 1899. Redevelopment entailed raising the site above its pre-existing level, by as much as thirteen feet in some places, and it was not until the summer of 1901 that the first seven houses (in Archway Street) were declared 'fit for human habitation', in a public ceremony. By the end of 1902 Excelsior Street had been completed. A total of 42 new houses were erected in the Dolemeads by 1907. The majority were let at rents of 5s. (25p) a week, compared to a rent of about 3s. 6d. (17½p) for the substandard housing they replaced. Dolemeads' tenants had once been notorious for not paying their rent, but the Medical Officer of Health was gratified to report, at the end of six years of improvements, that there was neither a bad debt nor any arrears among the council's tenants in the new houses. The MOH accepted the opinion of 'a gentleman who knows the locality', who explained this exemplary behaviour by suggesting that 'Whereas a man used to spend 3/6 a week in "drink" and 3/6 a week for rent, he now spends 5/– a week for rent and 2/– for "drink". Formerly the wretched houses drove the men and women to public houses, now they live at home'.[47]

Nonetheless, the MOH did not fully accept the argument of those housing reformers who believed that 'in order to elevate the slum dweller, we must first do away with the slum'. On the contrary, he shared the views of the civic representatives of Birmingham (with whom he had visited several European cities, under the auspices of the National Housing Reform Association) who asserted that 'the Housing Problem can only partially be solved by attending to the neglect of the house owners; the poorer classes of this country primarily need educating to the value of cleanliness, neatness and general house pride, to enable the advantages of the English system of housing to be enjoyed to the full'.[48]

The council itself carried out redevelopment schemes in several parts of the city in the late nineteenth and early twentieth centuries, not only in the Dolemeads but also in the James Street, Avon Street and Milk Street areas, and at Lampards Buildings. It also experimented in housing reform by adopting a scheme first used in Nottingham, whereby subsidies were offered to property owners as an inducement to improve sub-standard housing. A small district in Bath known as the Amebury, bounded on the north by Corn Street and on the south by Somerset Street and Back Street, was redeveloped in 1909–10 by the owner, who accepted £150 from the authorities in return for demolishing several houses and erecting in their place wash houses and sanitary accommodation to serve the needs of tenants in the remaining houses.[49]

Bath's housing problem was not on the same scale as that of the large industrial cities, but the need for adequate housing at affordable rents was proportionally much the same. In spite of the council's efforts, not all of Bath's residents were adequately housed on the eve of the First World War. The total number of houses in the city found unfit for human habitation (under various Housing Acts and regulations) was 39 in 1911, 22 in 1912, and 22 in 1913. These numbers are not large but, during the same period, a further 162 houses were found to be 'seriously defective from the point of view of danger to health or structural faults'. Moreover, the MOH acknowledged that an unspecified number of small houses were 'unsuited for family life', even though they could not be represented as unfit for habitation. Such houses were a constant source of trouble to the authorities. Let at low rentals, they tended to become overcrowded and the subject of 'notices', requiring clearance or improvements under the Public Health Acts. By 1914, the council had built 98 new houses and improved many more. Of the new properties, 7 were 'double tenements' (divided into two one-bedroomed flats), and the remainder were self-contained houses. These dwellings were let at rents from 3s. to 3s. 6d. for tenements, and from 4s. to 6s. 6d. for houses. The MOH was confident that there was sufficient accommodation for the better-paid artisan class in Bath, but in his report for the year 1914 he emphasised that there remained a need for two and three-bedroom houses at rentals of from 3s. to 5s. weekly. The poorest section of the working class, especially those with large families, were still disadvantaged in the housing market.

Overall, the material conditions of life had improved for every social class in the city by the end of the nineteenth century as a result of better systems of sanitation and of water supply. But suburbanisation and housing reform benefited chiefly the better-off among the working classes, who could afford the artisan dwellings built in Oldfield Park and elsewhere, or the relatively high rents of the new council houses and of properties improved by private landlords. Nonetheless, even the very poor lived in less overcrowded conditions, as more of the population moved out to the suburbs, and public health regulations gradually improved many aspects of life. Standards of living rose for most people, partly as a result of cheaper food (much of it imported), and the nationwide social reforms of the Liberal Government of 1905–14 introduced old age pensions, school medical inspections, health and unemployment insurance and the provision of school meals. Yet, in terms of relative deprivation, little had changed. Extremes of wealth and considerable variations in life-chances, according to social class, persisted. It is probable that in Bath, as elsewhere at the turn of the century, about 30 per cent of the population lived in poverty. This level of deprivation was indicated by the pioneering social investigations of Charles Booth in London (1880s) and B. S. Rowntree in York (1899). Furthermore, on the eve of the First World War, a 'respectable' working-class family with a head of household in full time employment, at an average wage of 'round about a pound a week' found it a constant struggle to make ends meet.

opposite An Election Ball, 1835, by George Cruickshank. The grotesque figures and outrageous head-dresses are a visual echo of Christopher Anstey's earlier illustrated poem of the same title. Anstey's *An Election Ball*, published in 1776, is a humorous satire on taste and manners in Bath society at that time.

Voice of the people, 1820–1914

T HE CONTRAST between image and reality which has informed much of this book so far is extended in this chapter to the political behaviour of the Bath electorate, to social class relations in the city, and the class consciousness of its working people. The history of modern Britain reveals that in the radical politics of the early decades of the nineteenth century some sections of the middle and working classes campaigned in alliance for parliamentary reform, but that the 1830s also witnessed the emergence of distinctly working-class politics. Disappointment over the limitations of the 1832 Reform Act weakened the class

AN ELECTION BALL

London, Published by McLean, 26 How

alliance and contributed to the development of Chartism, the first working-class mass movement in British history. The challenge of Chartism, defeated by a combination of force, paternal welfarism, and internal dissensions, had petered out by 1850, but some of the ideas that informed the movement were carried forward to later decades. In the third quarter of the century, however, there was a fundamental change of political atmosphere, as the working classes became essentially reformist. Rather than challenging the system, they sought to make progress through incorporation within the existing framework. This was further extended with the revival of socialism during the last two decades of the century, which was integral to the development of independent working-class politics and the formation of the modern Labour Party – as a social-democratic rather than a revolutionary body – in 1906.

In Bath, social harmony was an integral part of the city's genteel image during the period 1820 to 1914 and, indeed, there were several factors that made it an

unlikely setting for violent class conflict and independent working-class movements. The dominant contemporary view of the city as a place without trade or industry, inhabited by substantial numbers of wealthy upper-class and professional middle-class residents, embodied the assumption that its social structure made class relationships more harmonious here than in the manufacturing centres. A wide variety of benevolent charities, administered and supported by wealthy citizens in Bath, reinforced dependency and social subordination. Moreover, social historians have found that class conflict was, in general, less marked in places like Bath, with a mixed economy, than it was in single industry towns. The scale of production also had some influence on class tensions. These were lessened where there were greater opportunities for upward mobility, as in the small units of production typical of Bath's craft and industrial sector.

The dominant image of Bath has influenced many historical studies of the city during the Georgian period and has been largely repeated by those that have focused on selected aspects of life in the city during the nineteenth century. R. S. Neale challenged that view in his comprehensive social history of Bath from 1680 to 1850. He identified a class consciousness among some of Bath's tradesmen and artisans in the 1830s, but concluded that by 1850 middle-class interests and upper-class hegemony had combined to block the aspirations of an emerging working-class politics. Thereafter, Neale argues, Bath became a conservative backwater epitomised by its genteel image, bereft of radical politics and characterised by social class harmony which was sustained by paternal benevolence from above and due deference from the working class. This image is echoed in some studies of Bath during the nineteenth century. The local historian John Wroughton, in contrast to Neale, has identified stability as the key word in understanding Bath during the tumultuous 1830s, the Age of Reform.[1] Roy Hope, writing on education in the city from 1830 to 1902, found 'attitudes of acceptance, resignation and social conformity tended to prevail among its comparatively contented working

left Bath from Beacon Hill, 1848. One of a series of views published by William Everitt and sold at his City Repository of Arts on Pulteney Bridge.

BY COURTESY OF BATH CENTRAL LIBRARY, BATH & NORTH EAST SOMERSET COUNCIL

219

population'.[2] Yet the political behaviour of Bath's population did not always reflect its genteel image, particularly in the earlier nineteenth century. Moreover, in spite of its high social classification as a spa and a place of middle-class residence, far from being a wholly conservative city it was, rather, a centre of liberal strength. The Conservatives always remained a political force, but mostly in a minority position from 1850 to the First World War. Beneath the much-vaunted social harmony of the mid-nineteenth century, politics continued to be permeated by conflicts of class interest.

In this chapter we explore the contrast between the image of Bath and the realities of its people's politics, between outward social harmony and the persistence of class conflicts. First, the participation of the working class in some popular movements of the nineteenth century is considered. Some aspects of the electoral behaviour of the population in relation to parliamentary politics up to 1914 are discussed, before moving on to comment on organised labour at the turn of the century. Thereafter, the focus shifts to municipal politics, and other local agencies in which the conflict of class interests was most apparent in Bath.

Popular movements and parliamentary politics

Bath shared in the revival of radicalism from around 1812 on into the 1840s, which reflected the national mood for parliamentary reform.[3] Radical opinion demanded an end to rotten boroughs and extensions to the franchise. Until the Reform Bill was passed in 1832, political activists in Bath were preoccupied

largely with the national campaign for reform. They also organised local meetings and petitions, and became increasingly active in parish vestries, which they used as public platforms from which to protest over issues such as tithes and assessed taxes. The basis of the campaign was an alliance of the unenfranchised. It involved numerous tradesmen and artisans, some labourers, and middle-class Radicals and Whigs sympathetic to reform. The leadership was middle-class, but in the 1830s several working-class initiatives threatened to destroy the existing co-operation. Independent working-class politics posed a challenge to middle-class supporters, who tended to withdraw when it seemed that they might lose control of the aspiring lower classes.

Bath returned two MPs to Parliament, but before the Reform Act of 1832 only the thirty members of the corporation had the right to vote. Nonetheless, many of the unenfranchised took a lively interest in elections and particularly as the campaign for radical reform gained in popularity. In 1820 the city was represented by Lord John Thynne, the Tory brother of the Marquis of Bath,

The central section of the Guildhall, High Street, was built by Thomas Baldwin in 1766. The dome and the flanking wings of the building are late nineteenth-century additions by J. M. Brydon, who also designed the former library and art gallery (1898) in Bridge Street, now the Victoria Art Gallery. The Guildhall was the seat of local government until 1996, when the city council was incorporated into the newly formed district council of Bath and North East Somerset. Bath and North East Somerset Council continues to use the Guildhall as part of its council offices.

PHOTOGRAPH: CARNEGIE, 2004

who was himself the recorder of the city, and the Whig General Palmer who had been first elected at Bath in 1808, as a nominee of the Marquis of Camden, the Lord Lieutenant of Somerset.

Palmer, no radical but sympathetic to reform, had fallen out with the Marquis of Camden by 1820, and there were rumours of a plot to oust him from his seat by getting the lawyer Sir William Scott elected in his place. Scott, it seems, was expected to step down when the Marquis of Camden's son, Lord Brecknock, became of age to stand for Parliament. This was widely regarded as an attempt at Tory gerrymandering, aimed at strengthening the grip of aristocracy and thus blocking reform. Local radical opinion was outraged at the prospect 'that Bath will have the honour of being represented by two relatives of two Marquises, and thus draw closer the bonds of union betwixt our Body Corporate, our Noble Recorder, and our Noble Lord Lieutenant'.[4] Palmer declared he would contest such an election as illegal, on the grounds of interference by a peer in an election to the Commons. In the face of public opinion the plan was abandoned, and both Palmer and Lord Thynne were re-elected in 1820.

However, once Lord Brecknock was of age he stood for election, in 1826, at which point Bath did indeed become represented by Lords Brecknock and Thynne. Elections in 1828 and 1829 produced the same result, provoking the radical *Bath Journal* to comment in 1829 that 'Never were the citizens of Bath made more sensible of their degraded condition, for never were members returned more completely in opposition to the well known wish and judgement of the people in county, city or borough'.[5] Palmer lost to Lord Brecknock by only one vote on that occasion, and thereafter he became the hero of local radicals as the representative of liberty and freedom.

'BATH WILL HAVE THE HONOUR OF BEING REPRESENTED BY TWO RELATIVES OF TWO MARQUISES, AND THUS DRAW CLOSER THE BONDS BETWIXT OUR BODY CORPORATE, OUR NOBLE RECORDER, AND OUR NOBLE LORD LIEUTENANT.'

He became even more the focus of enthusiasm when, at the election of 1830, the corporation proved more responsive to public opinion and Palmer regained his seat with a majority of two votes. Large and jubilant crowds were on the streets to greet the result, and Palmer and Lord Thynne were 'chaired' in procession through central Bath. Both MPs sought the goodwill of the unenfranchised, by distributing, as they passed, silver coins and 'tickets' for some 600 gallons of beer. The rejection of the Whig's first Reform Bill forced another election in May 1831, by which time the public mood was even stronger for reform. Lord Thynne and Palmer were again elected. Palmer's victory was greeted with much enthusiasm and with cries of 'The Bill, The Whole Bill, Nothing But the Bill'. He was duly chaired through the crowded streets, but Lord John Thynne, the Tory, suffered the indignity of being pelted with so much rotten fruit that he was driven to take refuge in the White Hart.[6]

There was widespread indignation in Bath when the Lords rejected a second Reform Bill, after it had been passed by the Commons in early October 1831. The immediate response was a display of mourning. Many shops closed and a muffled peal was rung from the parish church of St James. Some days later a large but peaceful demonstration of protest took place, attended by an estimated 20,000 people. The main assembly was in Queen Square, but the contingent from the radical working-class parish of St James set out independently to meet up with the main body in front of Sydney Gardens Hotel, at the end of Great Pulteney Street. The enfranchised and unenfranchised, the respectable classes and the organised workers of Bath, all came together in this grand procession, which was accompanied by numerous bands. The crowd carried many banners, inscribed with such slogans as 'The United Trades', 'We Are All Agreed' and 'The Bill or Nothing Else'. Speaking from the hustings, the middle-class leadership enthused over the strength of support for reform and urged the necessity of avoiding violence. There was much rhetoric spoken about 'the wonderful and unparalleled unanimity' that existed between 'the lowest classes and those immediately above them', but the voice of the working people was heard only faintly. One representative of the journeyman hatters of nearby Oldland Common addressed the crowd, to speak in praise of the King and his ministers 'in their endeavours to obtain for us a just and equal representation'.[7]

In nearby Bristol, news of the Lords' rejection of the Bill sparked off mass riots. The Bath troop of the North Somerset Yeomanry was called out to assist the authorities in Bristol, but the commander was prevented from mustering his troops. An organised crowd of about 1,000 people set upon Captain Wilkins, forcing him to take refuge in the White Hart, which they then attacked. Wilkins escaped, but a section of the crowd then set off to occupy the Guildhall, in an attempt to prevent police interference. Order was restored by the early hours of the morning, after 300 constables had been called out and six arrests made. The event suggests the existence of an organisation with knowledge of the authorities' intentions, and the ability to raise a strong force to thwart their objectives.

Another working-class initiative was taken the following month, when some 3,000 people attended a meeting at the Tennis Court, Morford Street, to form a political union. The meeting was chaired by Mr Keene, editor of the *Bath Journal*, but no other leading middle-class radicals attended. They declined the invitation to do so with a variety of trivial excuses, although J. Hawksey Ackersley wrote expressing his qualified support on condition that the proposed Union should follow the pattern of the Birmingham Political Union (1830), which was an organisation firmly under middle-class control. In the absence of middle-class reformers the main influence on the artisans and petty tradesmen who met at the tennis court were delegates from the militant, working-class Bristol Political Union (1831). One of them spoke regretfully of the absence of middle-class leaders, but in terms which implied a continuing commitment to the notion of class co-operation:

> They leave us to do as well as we can without them. The time may come when they will want us, and our presence will be valuable to them; should that time

arrive, we will not leave them as they now leave us, to do as well as they can, we will not retaliate.[8]

The Bath Political Union was formed with a majority of artisans on its council. James Crisp, a Baptist master hatter and long-time radical, was elected as its president. Within six months the Bath Political Union claimed a membership of 1,500.

The formation of the Bath Political Union was an outward sign of the tensions emerging in the class alliance on which the reform campaign was originally based. Such strains became even more apparent after the Reform Act became law in June 1832. The provisions of the Reform Act brought into the franchise adult males who occupied houses of an annual rateable value of £10 or over. The effect was to increase the Bath electorate from 30 to 3,000, many of the new voters being artisans and petty tradesmen who had been pressing for reform. The event was celebrated in Bath with a Grand Reform Gala in Sydney Gardens,[9] but the Reform Act fell far short of meeting the aspirations of working-class radicals. It had, nonetheless, created a substantial working-class electorate in Bath. Their votes, about a quarter of the total, were proportionally rather more significant than those of their counterparts in many medium-sized industrial towns like Rochdale and Oldham. Poll-book evidence suggests that the newly-enfranchised tradesmen and artisans formed the bedrock of support for the radical MP, J. A. Roebuck, in his electioneering in Bath between 1832 and 1847.[10]

At the first election under the new franchise, in December 1832, there was no Tory candidate. Both the Earl of Brecknock and Lord Thynne had withdrawn. Such was the strength of anti-aristocratic and anti-Tory feeling that local Tories did not put forward a nominee, although R. B. Foster of Lansdown had offered to stand so that 'the rank, wealth and worth of Bath should not be totally unrepresented'.[11] Palmer stood again, with a second Whig or Liberal, H. W. Hobhouse. Radicals apparently regarded Hobhouse as a Tory in Liberal disguise, and concern about his lukewarm attitude to further reform prompted a search for a third candidate. J. A. Roebuck, a young man of 25 who had been recommended by radicals in London, was put forward as a candidate, albeit an unlikely one: he was a political democrat, probably a republican and certainly an atheist.[12]

Roebuck offered the electorate a radical programme including support for shortened parliaments, further extensions to the franchise and the secret ballot, the abolition of slavery, religious liberty and the abolition of tithes, repeal of assessed taxes and a general reduction in government expenditure. He appealed to a broad constituency of the new electorate, and was popular with many of those still excluded from the political system. A crowd of 7,000 assembled at the Orange Grove to observe the official nomination of candidates, and a similar crowd turned out for the declaration of the poll. To the delight of the crowd Palmer and Roebuck were elected.

Even at this triumphant moment the class alliance was under strain. Many working-class radicals regarded the Reform Act as the beginning of a wider

Born in Madras in 1802, the fifth of six sons of Ebenezer Roebuck, an employee of the East India Company, J.A.Roebuck (1802–79) spent his youth in Britain from 1807 and in Canada when the family emigrated in 1815. Frail and suffering from ill-health and lameness, he was educated mainly at home, where he read widely while working on the family farm. His self-education convinced him that working men could acquire knowledge and live a civilized life. He returned to Britain in 1824, entered the Inner Temple, was called to the bar in 1831, and became a QC in 1843. His legal practice was small and he supported himself with occasional writing in legal, literary and political journals.

He became a close friend of John Stuart Mill and was introduced to the ideas of Jeremy Bentham. His coterie of friends, members of the London Debating Society, were known as 'philosophic radicals'. He also worked with Francis Place in the National Political Union in pressing for a peaceful, constitutional resolution of the Reform Bill crisis in 1831–32. In December 1832, he was elected as one of the two MPs for Bath, and in January 1834 married Henrietta, daughter of Thomas Falconer, a Bath clergyman. In the reformed parliament, Roebuck was one of the most active and doctrinaire radicals. His speeches and writings railed against the privileges of the aristocracy and the church, and he advocated an extension of the franchise as the basis of good government. However, he was adamant that the people needed to be educated to be capable of governing themselves and develop habits of industry and forethought. In 1833, he moved, unsuccessfully, a Commons resolution for a system of national compulsory education for children aged six to twelve, anticipating the 1870 Education Act. He campaigned for an unstamped press and published a series of thirty-six unstamped weekly *Pamphlets for the People* in 1835–36.

Roebuck lost his seat in Bath in 1837, opposed by religious dissenters, but he enjoyed a high reputation amongst radicals and local Chartists. He defended Henry Vincent and other Chartists at their trials, but abhorred the violence associated with the Chartist movement. He was re-elected for Bath in 1841, but through ill-health, was less active than before. He supported Peel's Tory government on some issues, but in accordance with his belief in laissez-faire economics, opposed aid to Ireland and protective factory legislation (except in the case of children). In supporting the Maynooth grant, he antagonized dissenters and in 1847 lost his seat in Bath to Lord Ashley.

In 1849, he was returned unopposed as MP for Sheffield, and although he antagonized his constituents over union malpractices in the wake of the Sheffield outrages, and provoked opposition from temperance associations and for his views on church-state relations, held his seat until 1868 and again from 1874 until his death in 1879. He crossed over to the Conservatives in 1859, although he retained a reputation for independence of mind. He supported the union between Britain and Ireland and saw Britain as the guardian of international morality. In 1878, he backed the Conservatives' Balkan policy in supporting the Turks against the Russians, and Disraeli recommended him as a privy councillor. The fiery radical of his youth, who relished the nickname of 'Tear 'em Roebuck', had become closer to the Conservatives than his fellow Liberals. He died in London on 30 November 1879 and was buried at Bushey, Hampshire.

Source: http://www.oxforddnb.com/articles/23/23945-article.html

process of reform, whereas some middle-class supporters were content to regard it as an end in itself and had no wish to support demands for a full democracy. By 1837 disunity was a feature of radicalism in Bath. Roebuck was losing some voters partly because of his belief in religious toleration, exemplified in his support for a government grant to the Roman Catholic seminary at Maynooth in Ireland. Working-class supporters of Roebuck were also dismayed at his advocacy of 'inhumane' treatment of the poor under the Poor Law Amendment

Act of 1834, discussed more fully below. At the same time, the local economy was depressed, which enabled the Tories to put this down to the notion that five years of radicalism had been bad for business.

In the general election of 1837 both Palmer and Roebuck lost their seats to Tory candidates. Roebuck claimed that his defeat was due to 'Tory gold, Tory intimidation and Whig duplicity', in what was known locally as 'The Drunken Election'. Large-scale 'treating' and the possibilities of coercive influence with an open voting system certainly influenced electoral choices in the late 1830s, but the newly-enfranchised electorate was a volatile mass not tied to any party by traditional allegiances. The people were likely to vote on the particular issues at specific times, and it seems that the result reflected a rejection of some parts of Roebuck's politics.

Meanwhile, in the autumn of 1837 a Bath Working Men's Association (BWMA) was formed. The BWMA held its first public meeting in October 1837, presided over by a shoemaker, Thomas Bolwell, and chaired by the president of the Bath Political Union, James Crisp. The guest of honour was Henry Vincent, from the East London Democratic Association, a 24 year old compositor who became a prominent Chartist leader. The meeting adopted a programme demanding universal suffrage, no property qualification for MPs, annual parliaments, and the secret ballot. What was significant about this event was that it was a meeting of working-class people, organised and addressed by working men. The class divide was growing between middle- and working-class radicals, reflected in the priority each class gave respectively to the secret ballot and to universal suffrage. Middle-class radicals who were also tradesmen in Whig- or Tory-dominated wards were particularly concerned about the conflict of interest set up by open voting: 'Get the Ballot. If possible with an extension of the Suffrage, but if we can obtain no more, by all means let us get the Ballot', said Mr Jolly, the up-and-coming radical Liberal draper of Milsom Street.

Disappointment over the limits of the Reform Act turned politically-aspiring labouring men away from co-operation and attracted many to Chartism. Chartism was a nationwide umbrella movement centred on demands for political reform, set out in the Charter published in London on 8 May 1838, but gathering together local grievances given expression through nationwide agitation.[13] The Charter was introduced to an enthusiastic Bath audience in June 1838 by Thomas Bolwell (chairman of the BWMA), with Henry Vincent and several local working men as speakers. One of these, George Bartlett, a Chartist shoemaker and supporter of Feargus O'Connor, said of the middle class, that they 'left us to fight our own battle. Thus they acted as they ever do act ... they obtained power for themselves'.[14] Here was evidence of the suspicion and distrust, following the limited achievement of the extension of the franchise in 1832, that caused a rift between radical middle-class leaders and resentful working-class allies. Bartlett was later arrested and found guilty of sedition, and imprisoned for nine months. Whilst advocating the violent overthrow of a corrupt political system, at his trial, he nevertheless forgave the magistrates as equal victims of circumstance.[15]

The experience of Chartism in Bath was similar to that in many regional capitals and in cities where political radicalism had established itself long before the drafting of the Charter. The city had substantial numbers of Chartists, but was less militant than nearby industrial centres, such as Trowbridge and Bradford-on-Avon (Wiltshire) or Frome (Somerset), and there were attempts in Bath to reach a political accommodation between Chartists and other reforming groups.

The Bath Chartists, numbering some 1,800 to 2,200, held regular meetings in the city. They were involved in activities in Wiltshire and Somerset, supported the National Petition to Parliament, sent a representative to the National Convention of 1839, and also agreed to support the idea of a 'Sacred Month' or general strike, if the Petition was rejected. A demonstration planned for Whit Monday 1839 was banned from the city, where 130 police, 600 special constables, 80 parish constables, a troop of Hussars, and six troops of Yeomanry were mustered by the authorities. The Chartists held their meeting nonetheless, but in a field at Midford (three miles south of the city), and barely a tenth of the anticipated crowd of 15–20,000 turned up. Local leaders, Henry Vincent and W. P. Roberts, had been arrested and the show of force was an effective deterrent. The largest contingents at Midford came from Trowbridge and Bradford-on-Avon, with 250 from Bristol and only about 100 from Bath, with smaller groups from Frome, Westbury and elsewhere. The meeting was a set-back for local Chartists. The county magistrates, declaring it to have been a total failure, predicted that no similar gathering would recur. Nonetheless, further repressive measures were taken against Bath Chartists in the ensuing autumn, when spies infiltrated private meetings and arrests were made on charges of sedition.[16]

Despite all this, the movement retained a considerable following. By 1841 there were weekly Chartist meetings in the city. A poster for one of them appealed to the poor of Bath and alerted the working classes against being bought off by charitable handouts from wealthy citizens. It exhibited the language of class antagonism. The poor were heavily taxed to keep members of the royal family living in luxury, the rights of the people could only be restored by an extension of the franchise:

SUFFERERS – You are oppressed, but have no power to rid yourselves of oppression. The power has been wrested and withheld from you – you have been robbed of your rights, which is THE CAUSE of your destitution … It is time, however, THE SYSTEM SHOULD be changed and Honest Popular Government be established, which alone can permanently benefit the Working Classes … IF JUSTICE WERE DONE YOU, THERE WOULD BE NO NECESSITY FOR CHARITY.[17]

At the same time, by emphasising moderation and good order, the leadership was attempting to rebuild links in support for Chartism, with middle-class radicals from the Anti-Corn Law League.[18] This body had been founded in 1839 to fight for repeal of the Corn Laws (1815), which restricted the entry of foreign grain to this country. The League attracted support from middle-class Liberals in Bath,

'IF JUSTICE WERE DONE YOU, THERE WOULD BE NO NEED FOR CHARITY.'

A HISTORY
OF BATH

who blamed the Corn Laws for urban distress caused by food shortages and the rising price of bread. This argument was rejected by the Bath Tories in a series of posters and through the editorial columns of the *Bath Chronicle*, where the opinion was put forward that repeal would lead to unemployment on the land and a general lowering of wages. The Anti-Corn Law League tried to prove that all classes stood to gain from repeal but, in the country as a whole, attempts at an accommodation between the League and the Chartists were not successful, because of the latters' suspicions that the economic interests of employers and workers were hostile to each other. In places like Bath, where political radicalism based on class alliance had been the norm for some twenty years, attempts at co-operation were more appealing to the working-class Chartists and more likely to succeed. Moreover, the demands for repeal of the Corn Laws and for constitutional reform had been frequently associated in radical politics since 1815. An alliance was formed in Bath between the League and the Chartists at a meeting in the Guildhall held in December 1841, for the purpose of drawing up a petition to Parliament calling for repeal of the Corn Laws and the implementation of the Charter.[19]

By 1841 the mood in the country as a whole had turned against the reforming tendencies of the Whig government. Moreover, although with hindsight it is apparent that militant Chartism had failed by the early 1840s, the threat the movement posed to the established order evoked a conservative response. There was a strong swing to the Tories nationwide in the election of 1841, which brought Peel's Ministry into power. However, 'genteel' Bath went against the national trend and J. A. Roebuck regained his seat. He and the radical Lord Duncan decisively beat the Tories. It is significant that it was in this same year that the Bath Chartists made an accommodation with the Anti-Corn Law League. The realisation that independent, extra-parliamentary politics as represented by Chartism was unlikely to succeed disposed Bath's working-class radicals to renew class co-operation at local level, and persuaded those with a vote to support the parliamentary party whose policies accorded most closely, albeit imperfectly, with their aspirations.

Not all of the people of Bath rejoiced at the 1841 demonstration of renewed radicalism. The *Bath Chronicle* declared:

> Bath is a dark blot on the present general election. At a time when other places are, to their high honour, throwing off the trammels of modern Liberalism, Bath has put them on in their worst shape. It has returned not merely radicals or ultra-radicals, but persons who are 'something else'. We are taunted throughout the country with having sent to Parliament two disciples of revolution ... 'Hotbed of all that is wild, reckless, and revolutionary in politics' is the phrase which is abundantly used in speaking or writing of Bath.[20]

Bath as a hotbed of revolutionary politics in the early nineteenth century was not easily accommodated within the image of a genteel city. Its radical politics of the 1820s and 1830s subsided, however, after the 1841 election. Chartist activities continued but on a diminishing scale, culminating in the last recorded Chartist meeting in Bath, in March 1848, the year of European revolutions and the Communist Manifesto. Thomas Bolwell presided at this final meeting of potential revolutionaries to be addressed by a long-standing radical, the master hatter Cox, the 'veteran general' who had been associated with Chartism in the city since 1841.

The election of 1847, Neale argues, marked the historical moment at which radical consciousness died in Bath and paternal welfarism triumphed. The prospect of cheaper bread (the Corn Laws were repealed in 1846) appeared to be more attractive than universal suffrage. Moreover, the Bath Whigs and Tories co-operated in choosing Lord Ashley (later Lord Shaftesbury) to stand against J. A. Roebuck. Ashley was presented to the electorate as a social reformer dedicated to the welfare of working men, as his work in the Ten Hour Movement was said to demonstrate. (The factory reform movement led to legislation in 1847, reducing the hours of labour of textile workers). Ashley took the seat, on a swing of about 5 per cent against Roebuck.

'HOTBED OF ALL THAT IS WILD, RECKLESS, AND REVOLUTIONARY IN POLITICS.'

The election marked the end of Bath as a hotbed of radicalism but did the city become thereafter, as Neale claims, a conservative backwater? Certainly the political behaviour of its population changed over time. Between 1820 and 1832, many working people without the vote co-operated with the middle classes in the radical campaign for parliamentary reform. The lively politics of those years was not in keeping with Bath's image. In the second stage, from 1831 to 1850, the class alliance came under strain as working people developed their own aspirations and attempted to act politically for themselves through the Bath Political Union, the Working Men's Association and the Chartist movement. The 1832 Reform Act gave the vote to the middle classes, but, although the £10 property qualification enfranchised a substantial number of manual workers, it fell far short of their demand for universal suffrage. Their middle-class allies were widely seen as having abandoned the workers. Moreover, the working classes were threatened by the 1834 Poor Law Amendment Act, which took away parish administration of poor relief and created larger Poor Law Unions, presided over by elected Boards of Guardians. Each Union was to erect a workhouse, nicknamed 'bastilles' by anti-Poor Law campaigners, and no relief was to be given to the able-bodied poor outside the workhouse. The workhouse test, whereby an able-bodied person was deemed to be in need of relief only if he or she went into the workhouse, was particularly repellent to the labouring classes. Here again, the support of Roebuck and others of the middle class for the New Poor Law was perceived as a betrayal of the class alliance. The weakness and eventual failure of Chartism prompted the working class, it seems, to turn back to co-operation with middle-class allies in the Anti-Corn Law League, and in returning Roebuck to Parliament again in the 1841 election. By the later

1840s, however, a less radical and more reformist working-class politics may be suggested by Lord Ashley's success at the polls.

The repeal of the Corn Laws in 1847 and the Ten Hour Act of 1848 undoubtedly helped to renew popular confidence in the integrity of the existing system of government. The apparently new frame of mind in the third quarter of the nineteenth century also owed something to the economic background. The period roughly from 1850 to 1875 was, in general, prosperous, and the working classes shared to some extent in the increase in national income. Working-class radicalism was expressed during these years in support for the Liberal Party. This was the party of nonconformity, espousing the cause of disestablishment of the Anglican Church and of temperance, and on these grounds they enjoyed considerable working-class support. The party was committed to social reform, opposed to coercion in Ireland, and it challenged privilege wherever it existed.

The size of Bath's electorate was more than doubled by the second Reform Act of 1867, which enfranchised all male heads of households in the city and thus gave the vote to just under 7,000 men. Both the Liberal and Conservative parties courted the working-class vote, but in the country as a whole the majority of working men voted Liberal, particularly skilled workers. Bath tended to return one Liberal and one Tory to Parliament, with intermittent exceptions, and the Liberal vote was particularly solid in most working-class wards.

From the mid-1880s into the early twentieth century national trends were reflected in local voting, with the Conservatives gaining ground up to the election of 1906 when the Liberals were returned to power. The Reform Act of 1884 (which gave the vote to many male rural workers, not enfranchised in 1867) brought increased competition for the working-class vote. What is noticeable about the political behaviour of the people of Bath is the continuing underlying strength of Liberalism. Analysis of Parliamentary election results in the city shows that between 1830 and 1900 the Liberals retained a slight edge over their political rivals during most of the period. Between 1830 and 1850, Liberal candidates, including radicals, won 5 seats to the Conservatives 3; in the 1850s, they won 7 seats to the 2 won by the Conservatives, and achieved the highest poll in all five contests; in the 1860s and 1870s, Liberals won 6 to the Conservatives 5 seats and topped the poll in four out of six elections. In fact, it was only in the 1890s that the Conservative Party emerged the stronger, taking advantage of the Liberal split over Home Rule for Ireland. Between 1880 and 1900, the Liberals in Bath still won 7 seats to the Conservatives 5, but the Conservatives topped the poll on 4 occasions, 3 of them in the period 1892 to 1900.[21]

The later nineteenth and early twentieth centuries were notable for a revival of independent working-class consciousness and movements. This was reflected in the growth of trade unions in the 1880s – especially the 'new unionism' that organised the unskilled and some women workers – and in the spread of socialist ideas. In 1893 the Independent Labour Party was formed, to secure the election of working-class MPs independent of the Liberal Party, and in 1900 an alliance of trade unions with various socialist bodies established the Labour Representation

Committee. Arising out of these developments, the modern Labour Party came into being in 1906. Nevertheless, working men in Bath were content to be represented in Parliament by middle-class Liberal MPs. The Trades and Labour Council, established in 1891, seems to have taken few if any political initiatives beyond supporting Liberal candidates at Parliamentary and local elections. The city directory for 1914 lists no socialist organisations, although there were Liberal Clubs and Associations in working-class Larkhall, in Lyncombe and Widcombe, and at Walcot, with both Liberal and Conservative Clubs in Twerton. The electorate had no opportunity to vote for a Labour candidate until after the First World War, at the general election of 1918. Yet there is evidence of some socialist activity in the city. Scattered references in the local press record occasional events such as an 'instructive' talk on socialism given to the St James's Men's Friendly Society in January 1902.[22]

There were clearly contrasts between the image of Bath and the realities of working-class political behaviour in the period 1820 to 1914, especially in the first half of the nineteenth century. We now turn to the persistence of class conflict in relation to changes in the administration of the borough and some aspects of municipal politics, to the administration of the Poor Law, and to the structure and policies of the School Board.

Consensus and conflict: urban politics in Bath

Ever since the late sixteenth century, Bath Council had held responsibilities with regard to municipal property and corporation interests in the spa facilities. The charter of 1590, which formally incorporated the city, formed the basis of borough administration in Bath until the early nineteenth century. Following the reform of municipal corporations in 1835, Bath extended the size of its electorate, experienced a shift in the balance of power between the Conservatives and Liberals, and acquired new authority to establish a municipal police force. However, as we shall see, the reform rhetoric that accompanied the introduction of the 1835 act was subverted by the commitment of the reformed council to a policy of retrenchment and to the reduction of the debt incurred by the former unelected corporation.

Pressure for municipal reform had gathered momentum as part of the radical campaign for greater democracy and the removal of corrupt practices. It was a logical extension of the 1832 Reform Act. The Royal Commission on Municipal Corporations was highly critical of the old corporations in its report (1835). The men of property who governed Bath recognised the inevitability of some concessions to democracy at local level after 1832, but they made a small gesture in defence of the rights of property during the summer of 1835. At a meeting in July the corporation passed a unanimous resolution to forward to the House of Lords, which stated its objection to the prospect of 'placing the Corporation Estates under the Control of persons without the property Qualification and giving such persons the power of levying Rates on the Inhabitants'. In the same month a public meeting in support of the Bill attracted about 1,000 people.[23] This was a mere handful in comparison to the huge crowds that had attended earlier reform meetings. Local Tories and Whigs, who feared a radical triumph under the new system, had formed an alliance in the Bath Liberal and Constitutional Association, to act as a united front against 'flaming Radicals', but, as described above, many individuals who had been active in the movement for reform pre-1832 regarded the Reform Act as an end in itself, and were unsympathetic to further change.

The changes embodied in the Municipal Corporations Act (1835) created new councils that were accountable to a greatly increased electorate. Council debates and accounts were to be open to the public. Male household suffrage was established for local elections, with three-year residency and rate-paying qualifications. The Act also changed significantly the structure of municipal government in Bath; thereafter, the council was composed of 42 councillors, 6 for each of the 7 municipal wards: Bathwick, St James, St Michael's, Kingsmead, Lansdown, Lyncombe and Widcombe, and Walcot. These wards were created by a redrawing of parish boundaries, which split the radical parish of SS Peter and Paul in two. Part of it was incorporated into St James, and the rest (with some addition from the southern part of Walcot) became Kingsmead ward. The remainder of Walcot parish was also divided, the eastern, more working-class area becoming Walcot ward, while the wealthier part of the parish became Lansdown ward.[24] As a result, social class segregation and the potential for conflicts between different districts became more evident. There were also some curious companions within wards that encompassed diverse areas, and nowhere more so than in Kingsmead ward. This contained the notorious slum of the Avon Street district, but also wealthy Queen Square, the Circus, the Royal Crescent, and Marlborough Buildings. The electors of Avon Street and its environs were of insufficient standing to be considered eligible for municipal office, but their votes were crucial to the electoral success of the tradesmen who sat on the council for Kingsmead ward. Those electors who lived in the Circus and its adjoining streets felt that they were not properly represented by mere tradesmen, and preferred one of their own kind.

The Act of 1835 was less radical than it might at first appear. It did not sweep away the old custom of oligarchic control in Bath. One-third of the new council was to be elected annually; a third of the elected councillors became aldermen for six years, by nomination from among themselves; and the mayor was to be elected annually as before. The fourteen aldermanic posts were used from the outset of the new system as an extension of the power obtained by the majority party. Consequently, the Bath Liberals, who did comparatively well in 1835, were able to retain overall control at times when later local elections returned a majority of Conservative councillors. Throughout most of the mid-nineteenth century the mayor and the chairmen of important committees were appointed on the basis of Liberal patronage. By such means, the dominance of the Liberal Party in Bath was preserved.

Although the reformed body was described in a series of satirical letters, published in 1836, as a 'braggart mob of saddle-makers, old clothes men, hatters, undertakers',[25] it was still men of property who governed Bath. Candidates for election had to own property worth £1,000, or occupy property of the value of £30 per annum. The first election under the new system, in December 1835, brought large Whig-Liberal gains in Bath as throughout the country, although at least six members of the old corporation were elected to the new council. Its composition reflected the success of the challenge to the old elite posed by the new propertied middle classes, who had been excluded from the political system before the 1830s. The ironmonger John Stothert and the coachmaker Thomas Fuller were two of Bath's wealthy manufacturers elected in 1835. Only three of the new men did not own property in the city. The most significant structural change was the increase in commercial representation over time, rising to almost half (49.6 per cent) by 1861. Moreover, despite Bath's image as a place of genteel residence, it was not shopkeepers who dominated the commercial sector on the council. Men engaged in manufacturing, as opposed to retail trade, accounted for a substantial proportion of the commercial interest during the period from 1836 to 1870. Municipal reform ushered in a period of Whig-Liberal hegemony, but the Tories retained a sufficient presence on the council to remain a threat, especially as some members felt able to change party allegiance in response to public opinion. As early as 1836 complaints were being published about some councillors elected in the Liberal interest who had already 'turned their coats'. Nonetheless, in 1835 the balance of power swung from the Tories to the Whig Party, which was able to dominate the council-chamber for more than a generation, whilst the Tories always retained sufficient strength to remain in contention for power. Also, by exercising considerable influence in agencies and institutions beyond the Guildhall, the Tories were able to sustain pressure on public opinion and in the council-chamber.

'A BRAGGART MOB OF SADDLE-MAKERS, OLD CLOTHES MEN, HATTERS [AND] UNDERTAKERS ...'

In the reform era of the 1830s and 1840s, the party battles were intense. By the 1850s and 1860s, conflicts appeared to give way to a more consensus form of politics. The Tory approach of seeing the post of mayor as above politics, and investing it with due pomp and ceremony, was accepted by the Liberals. Moreover, a form of civic gospel was preached in the 1860s and 1870s, outlining a spirit of unity and common purpose for all the citizens of Bath. Yet this was partly a process of image-making and was never able to unite the disparate interest groups within the city. Beneath the rhetoric, class differences and sectional interests remained ever present in a fragmented and divided society.

The outward political consensus, that was a marked feature of Bath's municipal politics from 1848 to 1851, was a part of the realignment of social classes, which was evident in relation to parliamentary politics. The electorate returned a majority of Tories to the council in 1848, the year after Ashley had defeated the radical J. A. Roebuck at the general election. The following year, the Bath

Conservative and Liberal Associations agreed not to contest the local elections, an agreement that was broken only in the Kingsmead ward, where class politics were most apparent, ranging from the poorest voters of the Avon Street district to the wealthy inhabitants of Royal Crescent and its environs. In 1850 it was agreed by the political parties that no electoral contest would take place, and in that year, retiring councillors in each ward were replaced by new men of the same political allegiance.[26] The Guildhall was popularly known at this time as 'Conciliation Hall'. Yet class and sectional interests remained significant in municipal politics. As a minority, the wealthy social elite living in the upper town or the affluent suburbs, mainly Tory voters and often Anglican in religion, had a shared interest in resisting the aspirations of the trading and labouring classes, but they were in no position to exercise power with any degree of consistent success. The strength of the Liberal group on the council was centred on the lower town, on councillors drawn mainly from the commercial middle class and supported not only by their kind, but also by working-class traders and artisans.

The men who came to greatest prominence as councillors during the nineteenth century were those who built up a network of contacts and influence through participation in local agencies outside the council. Two examples must suffice. The Conservative William Sutcliffe (1801–52) was at times a magistrate, a Poor Law Guardian, president of Bath General Hospital and honorary secretary of the Bath Ragged and Industrial School. He also founded the Sutcliffe School (a juvenile reformatory), served on the prestigious committees of the Royal Literary and Scientific Institute and of the Mineral Water Hospital. In addition, he was a member of the Bath branch of the Health of Towns Association. Sutcliffe was mayor of Bath in 1848.[27]

Jerom Murch (1807–95) was an outstanding figure in Bath's history.[28] The municipal career of this radical Liberal developed somewhat later, after he had resigned his role as a Unitarian minister and recovered from a breakdown in his health. Before becoming a councillor in 1862 he had built up support within all the key elite groups in Bath. He was descended from a Huguenot family that settled in England, in retreat from religious persecution, during the seventeenth century. Educated at University College, London, he devoted the early part of his career to the Unitarian Ministry. Murch settled in Bath in 1833, where he was appointed minister of Trim Street Chapel. He later acquired a fortune of some £80,000 by marrying an heiress, Ann Meadows. A radical reformer in his outlook, Murch was politically active in Bath for over sixty years, even though he was not directly involved in municipal politics until the 1860s. He was vice-chairman of the board of guardians for nearly twenty years, and president of the Literary and Philosophical Society for over thirty years. He also served at times as president of the board of governors of the Mineral Water Hospital, chairman of the Theatre Royal Company and chairman of the Grand Pump Room Hotel Company. He was also a member of the Bath branch of the Health of Towns Association, and took a great interest in several philanthropic organisations, in addition to being a stalwart member of the school board from the 1870s.

Murch met Conservative councillors in several supposedly politically neutral bodies. Despite his nonconformist background, he was able to penetrate the Anglican strongholds of the Bath and County Club and the Abbey Restoration Fund. His long involvement in a wide variety of bodies in Bath, before standing for election as a Liberal, enabled him to build up considerable personal support. Within a year of being elected to the council he was chosen as mayor, in 1863, and again in 1864. In fact, he held the office seven times in all, and was regarded as the mayor *par excellence*. Murch used his personal influence as mayor to attempt to build a consensus behind the civic gospel of municipal improvement. The civic gospel was founded on belief in a common moral purpose that incorporated the responsibilities of the social elites with the needs of the poorest in society, to be reconciled through the agency of municipal government. Yet in Bath, a city seen as a place where social harmony characterised class relationships, the civic gospel failed to override the fragmented and dysfunctional social structure that so often thwarted the implementation of improvement measures in the 1860s and 1870s.

One of the obstacles to achieving support for the implementation of improvement schemes, such as in the city's water supply, was the continuation of old powers that differed between the city parishes.[29] This state of affairs perpetuated a narrow, parochial mentality at the expense of schemes for improvement for the whole city. A fear of adding a burden to the rates limited the progress in public health provision. The city's response to the 1848 Public Health Act also promised more than was delivered in the passing of the Bath City Act in 1851. The corporation became the local Board of Health, establishing its own powerful subcommittee, the City Act Committee, but most of the powers such as the appointment of a Medical Officer of Health (MOH), and the registration and regulation of slaughter houses, were not acted upon immediately. It was not until 1864, under the leadership of Murch, that the city began a civic programme of improvement that was to assist not only in the revival of the city's prosperity but also provided a comprehensive corporation water supply, the appointment of a qualified MOH, extensive street improvements and the acquisition of the Royal Victoria Park. Over the next fifteen years the civic gospel was increasingly in evidence in Bath, the corporation endeavoured to provide a unity of purpose by investing in greater amenities as a means of achieving prosperity for all its citizens. But, beneath the lofty tone of moral improvement, sectional, class and parochial interests continued to set limits to what the corporation could achieve. The projected image of government by consensus and with a common purpose could not always disguise the conflicts that so often circumscribed improvement measures.

A few dry seasons highlighted the scarcity of water, and the council obtained additional powers in the passing of the 1851 Bath City Act. Theoretically, this was an important step forward in sanitary provision as the local enactment of the powers authorised by the 1848 Public Health Act. The corporation now had the power to borrow extensively to promote a wide range of sanitary improvements, but successful implementation was another matter. Despite plans for a comprehensive scheme of waterworks envisaged for Batheaston, only a very small reservoir, containing a mere 114,000 gallons, was constructed. Instead of the estimated £30,000 loan required, the council borrowed only £6,000 and spent a total of £10,000, drawing on the difference from the surplus revenue from the corporation waterworks.

During the 1850s and 1860s, there was an increased demand for water but, again, an inadequate response to improving the supply. In 1835, consumption had been approximately at the level of 6 gallons per head per day to 2,381 water

tenants. By 1861, the number of water tenants had risen to 4,073, with an average supply of 13 gallons per head per day, although a sufficiency was reckoned to be more like 25 gallons. Total supply had increased from 94,000 gallons to 348,000 gallons, but additional sources of supply were needed to meet the ever-growing demand for water. Amidst widespread dissatisfaction at the shortage of water, compounded by the exceptionally dry summers of 1864 and 1865, the council prepared a major scheme to improve the sanitary condition of the city and to extend the municipal water supply. The issue provoked the sharpest conflicts of interest over council policy during the second half of the nineteenth century. In 1864 a new sense of urgency was given to the condition of Bath with the visit of the British Association to the city. This provided an opportunity to gain national publicity for the spa, and the authorities were clearly anxious that nothing should spoil the impressions of delegates to the conference, or impair Bath's reputation as a health resort for residents and for visitors. These anxieties were touched upon by 'Civis', in a letter to the *Bath Chronicle*:

> It is quite delightful to see the state of trepidation into which our complacent Corporation has been thrown by the thoughts of the approaching visit of the British Association. It reminds one strongly of boys at school who have been idle, and are at last frightened at the near prospect of a sound whipping ... Let us look at the Bath Railway Station, the public flys and carriages, the pavements, the botched Market, and many other things, and ask ourselves how these will look in the eyes of travelled men – whether they are as they ought to be in 1864. Let us then no longer live upon a reputation made for us 60 or 80 years ago, and almost if not quite worn out, but let us set about in right earnest to earn one for ourselves worthy of the present day.[30]

'IT REMINDS ONE STRONGLY OF BOYS AT SCHOOL WHO HAVE BEEN IDLE AND ARE AT LAST FRIGHTENED AT THE NEAR PROSPECT OF A SOUND WHIPPING ...'

As pressure for public health improvements grew, investigations revealed new evidence of inadequate sanitary provisions and water supply. An improvement scheme was duly prepared by the council, but this was rejected by the ratepayers at a stormy meeting in April 1866. The central objection was the estimated cost (£85,000), which alarmed a powerful lobby of wealthy residents of suburban parishes. Most of these residents took their water supply from private companies, and felt that the cost of the scheme would fall most heavily on them, while the immediate benefits would go to the poor inhabitants of the central parishes. This was a perennial conflict. It was invariably difficult to command support from all sections and interest groups for any improvement that was perceived as benefiting only one district or group, but would have to be financed by everyone. In part, this reflected the persistence of a parochial mentality into the age of municipal government, but underlying class conflict was a contributory factor.

At the defeat of the 1866 water bill, Murch acknowledged the strength of opposition and the clash of interests involved, yet still proclaimed his faith in a civic gospel of improvement:

> With all my heart, sir, I trust that future efforts may be made, and that in every respect they may succeed. For I do not abate one jot of the principle with which I started – that no greater duty devolves on those in power than that of seeing the city well supplied with water. And of this who can doubt, that, although Bath may, for reasons seeming good to her, delay the great work, she will ere long do it? She will not let heathen cities in ancient times put her to shame; she will remember what her neighbour Bristol is doing, how Glasgow has gone to Loch Katrine for water, and how London will probably go to the mountains of Wales; she will grumble a little more, and then trusting that her debts will be diminished, and her coffers replenished, she will enable some future Mayor to boast that every house in the beautiful city over which he reigns – every house even the poorest – has its stream of pure and healthy water.[31]

'NO GREATER DUTY DEVOLVES ON THOSE IN POWER THAN THAT IN SEEING THE CITY WELL SUPPLIED WITH WATER.'

The impetus to progress remained intact despite the ratepayers' initial rejection of the scheme. A series of official reports set out the defects, which were seized upon by Samuel Sneade Brown (the self-styled scourge of the council on the sanitary question) for use in his campaign to raise public awareness about the matter. It was given added force with the appointment in 1866 of Bath's first MOH, Dr C. S. Barter, who investigated and reported on the sanitary condition of the city in 1867 and 1868. His findings were published in pamphlet form in 1869, and were a comprehensive indictment of the past neglect of public health. He naturally supported the campaign to increase the water supply, and made the telling point that every individual in Manchester had 'more than ten times the quantity of water which every individual in Bath has'.[32] By 1870, after a decade of discussions, a fairly comprehensive municipal water supply was established in Bath. At the outset, it was recognised that competing interests were involved. The parochial interest was reinforced by differential rating systems, which set district against district. The private water companies, in which some councillors and salaried officials held shares, formed another interest group. The council was sensitive to pressure over the rates from the wealthy burgesses of Lansdown, and to the needs of poorer ratepayers in Larkhall and elsewhere. One councillor urged equal justice for both parties,[33] a worthy sentiment that did not acknowledge the political reality that with a Liberal-dominated council, the interests of Conservative Lansdown would have to take second place to those of Liberal Larkhall.

The key point about the events and debates from the 1860s to 1870 is the unpredictability of the situation. Council policy was not frustrated by the permanent opposition of a few vested interests. Events were influenced by chance happenings, by individual personalities, and by the volatility of the public mood. It was the shifting alliances among the elected councillors, and the changing perception of the voters in Bath that dictated the rejection of the council water scheme in 1866 and the passing of the Bath Waterworks Act in 1870. The latter was, in effect, a compromise, resulting from the conflicts of the 1860s. The landowner Mr Gore Langton, of Newton St Loe, had employed delaying tactics in 1866 to push up the £7,000 compensation he was offered, but in 1870 he was forced to settle for only £2,500. The wealthy Lansdown lobby had successfully opposed the 1866 plans but later found to its horror that the purity of supplies from the Charlcombe Water Company were suspect. They then campaigned, even more vociferously, in favour of a municipal water supply. However, the Act of 1870 preserved the vested interests of the private companies (albeit temporarily) and, ironically, suburban Lansdown was the least well served part of the city for some time to come. Developments that took place following the 1870 Act enabled virtually all the citizens of Bath to enjoy the benefits of a good water supply. By 1878, 7,712 houses and 50,128 inhabitants were supplied with a

daily average approaching 30 gallons per head.[34] The system was still only intermittent, with supplies only available at set times, but a major advance had been accomplished in both the quantity and quality of water.

The last political achievement of Jerom Murch was to steer through council the project for extensions to the Guildhall in the late nineteenth century. At the end of his distinguished career he received a knighthood. Obituary tributes in the local press following his death in 1895 commented on his influence over the city as a whole and in council, where it was said to have been only rarely resisted, while in the *Bath Year Book* of 1896 it was observed that 'almost every local institution which could claim to exist for the public good had to place on record its grateful recognition of services which he had rendered'.[35] The characteristic language of Victorian civic eulogy should not be allowed to conceal the fact that Murch's enormous contribution to the city could only be

Jerom Murch (1807–95), wearing the robe and chain of office of Mayor of Bath. He served as mayor no fewer than seven times during his long career in local politics.

piecemeal. It was a heroic failure that fell short of his great municipal vision – the corporation as an engine of social progress.

Murch left a legacy to the city for the purpose of building an art gallery – a venture that he had advocated for many years prior to his death. Proposals for an art gallery revived an ongoing debate over the question of a municipal lending library. The acquisition of cultural civic amenities such as libraries and art galleries gave expression to civic pride in many Victorian cities, but in Bath the matter also encompassed the wider issue of the city's general economic prosperity, with some councillors and others arguing that civic amenities would be a sound investment, adding to the attractions of the city for potential visitors and new residents, while others believed that any rise in the rates would not only antagonise existing rate payers but also deter prospective incomers. The art gallery was eventually commissioned as a memorial to Queen Victoria's Diamond Jubilee (1897), in conjunction with a reference library to house the Guildhall collection of books of local interest. The total cost was met by the legacies of Murch and Mrs Roxburgh,[36] with additional subscriptions from residents. Many prominent citizens contributed to this form of 'municipal charity', which saved on the rates and gave the wealthy an opportunity to demonstrate their commitment to the civic good by their publicly-acknowledged donations.

The spirit of civic union was popularised by leading citizens and clergymen such as the Rector of Bath, who asserted in a speech of 1890: 'We are learning to set aside our differences, to throw away the scum of religious dislike, and partizan jealousy and hatred ... valuing our fellow citizens only as they live together, in amity and peace, and are fellow labourers in the cause of civic good'.[37] The concept of the civic good was the 1890s successor to the aspirations for a form of political consensus in the 1850s and the civic gospel of the 1860s. The endurance of this kind of political discourse was testimony to the need to overcome the protracted wrangles in the council chamber and to attempt to reconcile the conflicting interests of all sections of the population beyond the Guildhall.

Thus, as we have seen, beneath the veneer of social harmony in genteel Bath, class and sectional interests remained an enduring feature of municipal politics. Moreover, the contest for power was not confined solely to the hustings or the council chamber: it was conducted over a wider arena that encompassed other agencies of government such as boards of guardians and the school board, and to these we now turn.

In the administration of poor relief in Bath during the 1830s Tories and Whigs competed for political influence, with both parties trying to outbid the other as champions of the poor. Conservatives frequently promoted themselves as protectors of the 'deserving' poor, thus appealing to deferential working-class voters and no doubt to many independently-minded others, who feared that, in reduced circumstances, their fate would be the workhouse. Liberals were more likely than their opponents to make much of the plight of the 'poor ratepayers', and so justify economies to keep the poor rate low and thus maintain the loyalty of their property-owning working-class constituency. The truly poor, without a vote determined by a property qualification, were merely the pawns in a political game.

The Bath Poor Law Union was established in 1836, with the radical utilitarian Revd Thomas Spencer (curate of the nearby parish of Hinton Charterhouse) as its first chairman. Given the nation-wide furore over the implementation of the Poor Law Amendment Act of 1834,[38] it is not surprising that the Bath guardians were subject to some animosity or that as the election of a new Board approached, in the spring of 1837, they sought to defend themselves against accusations of incompetence and harsh administration. Spencer particularly castigated the Tory city magistrates for 'mischievous meddling':

> There have been perpetual messages from them to the Relieving Officer, requesting him to relieve able-bodied men; women with illegitimate children; or to give orders for medical relief or for coffins, and in cases where the very contrary had been decided by the Board after careful enquiry.[39]

The magistrates responded in another pamphlet, which specifically condemned the 'inhumanity' of the guardians. The acrimonious debate continued, and attention focused on a test case for control of Poor Law administration in Bath. This concerned an old woman named Ann Perry, who was housed and fed by a Mary Price, in return for help in the house and with Mrs Price's laundry business

THOMAS SPENCER

Clergyman, writer, and Poor Law reformer, Thomas Spencer (1796–1853), the son of Matthew Spencer (died in 1831) and Catherine Taylor (died 1843) was born at Derby, where his father kept a large school. After teaching for a time at Quorn School, Derby, he entered St John's College, Cambridge in 1816, and graduated in 1820. At Cambridge he fell under the influence of Charles Simeon, the evangelical, and he became ordained as a deacon. After a few short-term curacies, he was elected to a fellowship at St John's in 1823 that he retained until his marriage in 1829 to Anna Maria Brooke.

In 1826, he was appointed to a perpetual curacy at Hinton Charterhouse, near Bath, on an income of £80. Spencer built a house, erected cottages, established a school, a clothing club, a village library and field gardens. He fought against intemperance and pauperism and reduced outdoor relief; the poor rates were then reduced from £700 to £200 a year. When Hinton was incorporated into the Bath Union, Spencer was elected as the first chairman of the Board of Guardians in 1836. An enthusiastic Poor Law reformer, he wrote several pamphlets on the subject for a national audience, but based largely on his own efforts in Hinton and his knowledge of the Bath Union. These brought him into conflict with local magistrates. He travelled around the country preaching and lecturing, chiefly as a temperance advocate, but also writing on church reform, education, and the corn laws. Some of his pamphlets had a large circulation. Spencer resigned his curacy in 1847, moved to London, and devoted himself to the pulpit and the platform.

He died at Notting Hill on 26 January 1853 and was buried at Hinton. Revd Tom Mozley, one of his former pupils, recalled that he was a 'decidedly fine-looking man, with a commanding figure, a good voice and a ready utterance'.

Source: *Oxford DNB* (2004) vol. 51, pp. 898–9.

in Avon Street. In October 1836, Mary Price applied to the guardians for out-relief on behalf of the increasingly infirm Ann Perry. The guardians offered only admission to the workhouse, but the magistrates subsequently overruled this decision and made an order for out-relief to be granted. The order remained a dead letter while the opposing groups became embroiled in a dispute that dragged on until January 1837. It involved the mayor, the magistrates, and an influential sector of Bath public opinion, in open conflict with Spencer and his supporters on the board of guardians. Eventually, the assistant commissioner was sent down from London to investigate the case. His findings supported the board, but the case culminated in the magistrates pursuing the matter in law, which found in their favour. On 13 January 1837, some three months after applying to the guardians, Ann Perry was awarded out-relief, but within three weeks she died, thus obliging the board by finding for herself an alternative permanent relief from old age, infirmity and poverty. Her case was debated as a matter of principle, clothed in rhetoric about humanity and justice, but it was fundamentally a struggle for control of the patronage and influence that could be exercised through the Poor Law.

The school board was another agency of local government for the contest of competing interests. In the field of elementary education it was religious divisions that superficially overlaid deeper divides. In the 1830s and 1840s religion had been an integral yet divisive factor in politics. Bath was broadly representative of

Unpretentious houses set on the raised pavement which continues on to the Vineyards. The rock-faced Gothic chapel is the Hay Hill Baptist Church, built by Wilson and Wilcox, 1869–70.

PHOTOGRAPH: CARNEGIE, 2004

the nation, in that the highest and the lowest social classes tended to be Anglican, with dissenters found chiefly among the middle classes and the upper strata of the working classes. Religious conflict often closely underlined political differences. The preservation of the Anglican established church was central to Conservative thinking, and nonconformists looked to the Liberal party to remove restrictions on their civil rights. These national rivalries were reflected in Bath, where the Established Church was dominant in terms of church provision and numbers of adherents. At the religious census of 1851, the Church of England claimed over 60 per cent of sittings and total attendance in the city, compared with around 33 per cent of sittings and attendance for Protestant dissenters. Overall, religious attendance in Bath was one of the highest in the country, second only to Hastings.[40] Organised religion in Bath was essentially divisive, between Church and dissent, in inter-denominational rivalry between various Protestant sects, and between Protestants and Roman Catholics.

The Anglicans in Bath organised themselves to defend their schools, prior to the council's application to Whitehall in December 1870 for permission to form a school board following the Education Act of 1870.[41] The setting up of school boards was seen as an attack on the voluntary provision of denominational education. An appeal was launched for funds to maintain Church of England elementary schools, and a committee appointed to meet with leading nonconformists to discuss the composition of the prospective board. It was agreed that a distribution of six Anglican and five nonconformist representatives would 'fairly represent the mind of the city'. A Protestant alliance of Anglicans and nonconformists thus attempted to prevent any Roman Catholic candidate standing for election, which would have denied direct representation to the Roman Catholic community of Bath, composed of some 1,700 to 2,000 in the 1870s. In the event, there were eighteen candidates for the eleven seats and an election was therefore inevitable. This took place in January 1871. All residents on the electoral roll were eligible to cast up to eleven votes, distributed in any number among the candidates, a cumulative voting system that was adopted nationally as a means of safeguarding minority interests.

The candidates were three Anglican clergymen, three Protestant nonconformist ministers, one Roman Catholic priest; a barrister and a solicitor; three 'gentlemen' and two 'gentlewomen'; a self-styled Professor of English Literature; a silk-mercer, one engineer and iron-founder, and a provision merchant. The Working Men's Reform Association backed two radical councillors, an independent gentleman and a provision merchant, one of whom was also supported by the Bath Temperance Society. The results gave the Church of England a majority on the school board, which meant that it was essentially a Conservative body. By January 1874, when the Board's three-year term of office concluded, it had introduced through a local by-law compulsory full-time school attendance for children between the ages of five and thirteen, and made enlargements to some church schools. Its activities had cost the ratepayer little more than 5d. (less than 2½p) in the pound per annum. At the election of 1874, only two

Liberal-sponsored candidates were successful, but both were nonconformists and, moreover, their election strengthened the representation of the trading and commercial classes. Thereafter, the board came increasingly under the influence of the Church Schools Managers' Union, formed at a meeting chaired by the Reverend Canon Bernard (chairman of Bath school board) at the Abbey Church rooms in March 1876. The Union was a coordinating body that aimed to protect Anglican education by promoting the return of supporters of church schools to serve on the school board.[42]

Anglicans dominated the board until its demise in 1902, when it was replaced with a Local Education Authority. There was, nevertheless, sustained Liberal and nonconformist hostility to the dominance of the 'Church Party'. Liberal-sponsored candidates did not do well in the election of 1886 (only two of the six were elected), although in that year general opposition to the Church seems apparent in the greater social diversity of nominators, who included more tradesmen and craftsmen than previously, and in the surprising success of the independent Roman Catholic candidate, who was not only re-elected but topped the poll. By the 1890s, the organised working classes were campaigning for better educational standards, through the co-ordinating body of Bath Trades Council that, at the 1892 school board election, supported middle-class Liberal candidates sympathetic to its aspirations. In that year the chairman of Bath's Liberals, W. C. Jolly, led a sustained attack on the retiring board, accusing it of complacency over truancy levels, castigating it for a negative attitude to higher-grade education for the most able working-class children, and challenging the right of the Church of England to command continually a majority on the strength of its role in elementary education. This opposition, however, was divided and lacked the coherence of the 'church party'. It had no organisation comparable to the Church Schools Managers' Union.

A public elementary school place was available for every child in Bath before the end of the nineteenth century. In addition, evening classes and a technical day-school had been established, and the curriculum, although restricted by later standards, had been expanded beyond the 'three Rs' and religious instruction. The board's policies had clearly served the interests of the establishment in maintaining the religious influence of the Church, and they did not fully meet the aspirations of nonconformist parents or the needs of all children. The Roman Catholic community (too small to threaten Anglican dominance, and itself concerned to uphold denominational education) managed to maintain and extend its elementary schools but, well before 1902, the Protestant nonconformist schools of Bath had all closed down. The nonconformists found it difficult to maintain their few schools because of limited financial resources, and hoped that the board would take over their premises. It only did so in a few instances, and it was reluctant to build new schools while places were available in church schools. Many nonconformist parents found themselves forced to send their children to Anglican schools. Moreover, in 1897 only 101 of the 274 pupils at St John's Roman Catholic School, in a poor part of the lower town, were actually

Catholics. Non-denominational teaching was available at Bathforum School but this establishment continued to charge fees and it educated chiefly the children of the upper working-class and lower-middle classes. The board's reluctance to build schools restricted parental choice and led to a shortage of places in some districts, notably in the growing industrial parish of Lyncombe and Widcombe. The conservative attitude of the board predisposed it towards minimal standards in terms of curriculum and length of schooling, which, according to the Roman Catholic solicitor Austen King, handicapped Bath children in the labour market. Chairman of the school board in 1897, King argued that 'a lot of clerks' places were taken by boys from a distance who had the advantage of a longer education than that which was given in the city'.[43] There were parents in Bath who sought non-denominational education for their children, and some who wanted higher standards at elementary level, as well as greater opportunities for secondary education. Their aspirations were not met by the school board, whose primary concerns were to uphold the interests of the Established Church and keep the rates down.

In conclusion, it may be seen that the contrast between image and reality, identified previously in relation to social and economic aspects of the nineteenth-century history of Bath, was also apparent in the broadly defined area of politics during the period 1820 to 1914. The contrast was at its sharpest from 1820 to the late 1840s, but the consensus view of Bath as a conservative backwater from mid-century onward is an over-simplification. Radical politics persisted in the electoral strength of Liberalism through to the end of the century. The notion of

A north-east view of
the Abbey in 1836, by
W. Millington, with
the Orange Grove on
the left.

BY COURTESY OF BATH CENTRAL
LIBRARY, BATH & NORTH EAST
SOMERSET COUNCIL

social harmony had some reality, but it was promoted as an ideal that served the genteel image of the city as a place apart, free from the blatant class antagonism of some industrial towns. Like the modern notion of Britain as a 'classless society', it was underlain by continuing conflicts of class interests. These were most obvious in terms of municipal politics and the clash of interest groups. Various socio-economic factors made Bath an unlikely place for the development of an aggressive class politics in the 1890s to 1914, but in this it was more representative of Britain as a whole than those few urban centres characterised by extreme radicalism.

left The fire at Prior Park in May 1836 destroyed most of the interior of the mansion which, from 1829, had been owned by the Roman Catholic church. Another major fire occurred in 1991; a second restoration of the building was completed in 1995. The house remains in use as a Roman Catholic school, but the garden now belongs to the National Trust.

BY COURTESY OF BATH CENTRAL LIBRARY, BATH & NORTH EAST SOMERSET COUNCIL

Twentieth-century Bath | CHAPTER 8

T HE PACE OF CHANGE in Bath was slow during the first half of the twentieth century. In terms of population and physical size the city grew only moderately, and the social scene remained largely as it had been around the turn of the century. The First World War made some short-term impact, but it was the Second World War that brought lasting change to the occupational structure and, moreover, was a watershed in the history of the city. Thereafter Bath was caught up in the process of rapid socio-economic change that was at work in the country as a whole. New industries were developed and the service sector expanded considerably, while increased leisure and rising living standards combined with improvements in transport to foster the emergence of an age of mass tourism. By the 1980s Bath was recognised as a centre of international culture, and the value of its architectural heritage was acknowledged by its inclusion in the UNESCO list of world heritage sites. This inevitably sharpened the continuing debate over conservation and development, which reflects the perennial problem of reconciling the needs of the majority of the city's residents with those of wealthy incomers and visitors. Bath continues to draw upon its past to attract the tourists of today, but it remains essentially a small, provincial city of greater complexity than is suggested in the official guides or travel brochures. As in previous centuries, the reality of Bath is both more complex and interesting than its popular image.

The emergence of modern Bath, 1914–1945

The citizens of Bath shared the major experiences of the nation in the years from 1914 onward, as mass society became increasingly homogeneous. As elsewhere, the outbreak of war in 1914 brought an influx of troops to the city and an outflow of recruits to the armed forces, and, as the economy moved on to a war footing, the participation of women in the workforce increased substantially. Following the armistice in 1918 and the return to normality, many women were forced back into the home or into traditional occupations such as domestic service. During the inter-war period national concern over high unemployment, poor housing and the standard of health of the mass of the people was reflected in Bath, although conditions in this provincial city were very different from those which characterised such symbols of the age as the depressed shipbuilding town of Jarrow.

The Great War of 1914–18 brought with it a level of state intervention that affected the lives of the mass of the people in unprecedented ways. The introduction

opposite Kingsmead Square in the late 1920s, showing the variety of traffic typical of the time. Modern modes of transport – the electric tram approaching from Westgate Street and the motor lorry straddling the tram lines – had not yet made the horse-drawn cart obsolete. Shops on the left include a stationers, then W. Paisey, cutler, at no. 18, with the premises of Frederick Wright Ltd, tobacconists, next door. The wall sign on no. 19 reads 'FREDk. WRIGHT CIGARS'. At the corner shops, nos 20 and 21, Tuck & Son, drapers, advertise MILLINERY on their shopfront awning.

BATH CENTRAL LIBRARY, LOOSE PICTURES COLLECTION

Southgate Street, photographed on 28 April 1925. Southgate Street, bordered on each side by working-class housing, was at the southern end of the commercial spine of the city that extended through Stall Street, Union Street and Milsom Street. The electric trams to Weston and Twerton carry advertisements for the Bath Coal Company and Borwicks Baking Powder. A shop sign for Boots the chemist – one of the earliest chain stores – can be seen top left.

of passports restricted freedom of movement, conditions of work were prescribed, and the publication of news was restricted; licensing laws were tightened and the strength of beer was reduced, the quality and supply of some foodstuffs was regulated; and – from 1916 – British Summer Time was enforced.[1] In Bath the marching bands and recruiting drives of the first months of war were soon succeeded by troop trains bringing the wounded to Bath Spa station for transfer to local reception centres and hospitals. Some five million men joined the armed forces in the First World War, of which 11,213 came from Bath (out of a population of some 70,000), at least 2,969 of them as volunteers.[2] Approximately 1,000 Bathonians died in the service of their country and an unknown number were

wounded. Even as local volunteers and recruits left the city, there was an influx of troops to Bath including some from Canada and Australia. Fights between 'British Tommies' and colonial troops were commonplace, especially after the pubs closed at night.[3] The casualties of war were nursed at Newton Park House (in Newton St Loe, some three miles from the city centre),[4] in sanatoriums, church halls or other requisitioned buildings, until May 1915, when the Bath War Hospital was opened. Ten 50-bed huts on a cricket pitch at Combe Park made up the hospital but, as casualty figures rose, its capacity was increased until, by 1918, it could accommodate 1,300 servicemen.[5]

The former Bath Electric Tramways depot, Walcot Street. Built in 1903, the building housed a boiler house, an electric generator and workshops, as well as the trams. Closed in 1939, it was converted in 2000–2 into a complex of apartments, offices, workshops and a restaurant.

PHOTOGRAPH: CARNEGIE, 2004

Production for the war effort involved eight local companies, which manufactured munitions, parts for aircraft and submarines, ammunition boxes, and an experimental 'super tank'. With the exception of Bath Aircraft Company, war production was located not in specialised establishments, but in the workshops of engineering firms such as Stothert & Pitt and the Horstmann Gear Company, and those of woodworking concerns like Bath Cabinet Makers. Stothert & Pitt was the largest employer of labour, with a workforce of 1,185 men and 225 women – the firm manufactured about 200,000 of the 205,000 high-explosive shells produced in Bath. The munitions industry as a whole employed 2,128 men and 1,044 women in the city.[6]

The need for female labour to replace men joining the forces gave women new opportunities for paid employment, and not only in the armament factories.

Bath women also worked as tram conductors, as clerks in recruiting offices and food control centres, as ambulance drivers and nurses.[7] Many others undertook voluntary work for the war effort, in the kitchens and wards of the War Hospital, at convalescent homes, and at the Red Cross 'comforts depôt' in Wood Street. The Needlework Guild ('consisting of ladies' working parties') also made a contribution by producing some 250 articles a day, such as socks, shirts and bandages.[8]

The circumstances of war impinged to some extent on the lives of women of all social classes in Bath, as Louie Stride recalled in her memoirs. Aged seven at the time war broke out, living in squalid poverty with her prostitute mother, Louie noted that by 1915 'we were living a bit better ... not quite such hunger'. Her mother 'got very bold and brought men back to the attic, and I would discreetly disappear. It would be soldiers, and of course no shortage of them as Bath had a lot of big houses and schools that were taken over as billets'. One Canadian soldier became a regular caller to the attic, often bringing food from his billet at Prior Park School, and he eventually married Louie's mother. This provided reliable income in the form of 'ring money', the army allowance of 19s. 6d. (97½p) for a wife and child, which enabled mother and daughter to move to somewhat better accommodation. By 1917 they were living in the Dolemeads

Walcot Street in the 1930s. James Thomas, cycle engineer, traded at number 82, next door to the laundry run by Lee Sing and Lee Quong.

TWENTIETH-CENTURY BATH

Walcot Street in the 1930s, looking north. The shop-fronts remain largely unchanged in this street of small specialist shops, in what is now promoted as the artisan quarter of Bath.

area, where many of the inhabitants were women bringing up children alone. Some, like Mrs Stride, had husbands in the forces, others were war widows, and a few had been 'left in the lurch'. But not all the women of the Dolemeads lived without men:

> [Some] took in soldiers who deserted, usually colonials, Australians were very much in evidence ... one young woman had a very smart Australian hidden there for quite a long time, but she was rounded on, and the military police came and took him one day. She was very upset ... somewhat after she had a baby girl.[9]

Following the Armistice in 1918, Bath began to readjust to peacetime conditions, although reminders of the conflict lingered on. For Louie Stride, 'things got worse again' in 1919 when her step-father was 'demobbed' and began to spend much of his weekly pension of £1 on drink. Women found the demand for their labour falling, as men came home from war, and the munitions factories closed down. Convalescent soldiers were still numerous in Bath as late as March 1920, when the Trades and Labour Council organised an entertainment for some 1,000 wounded troops. In that year Armistice Day was marked with ceremonies of commemoration for the dead, and dinners and dances to celebrate the peace.

By then, however, the post-war economic boom was faltering, unemployment was rising and labour unrest was becoming widespread in Britain. Indeed, the following decades are often perceived as years of unremitting depression, of high unemployment, associated with poverty and poor standards of health and housing, but this bleak image has masked the reality of the changes from which the affluent consumer society of post-Second World War Britain emerged. The history of Bath in the inter-war period is essentially that of a slowly changing city which shared in the general improvement in social conditions throughout the country.

THE 'QUEEN OF THE
WEST' BECAME 'A
GRIME-ENCRUSTED ...
DRAB PLACE OF LITTLE
CHARM.'

The city was the most populous urban area in Somerset in 1921, with a total population of 68,669, rising to 68,815 by 1931. The physical size of the city was increased by the construction of 4,242 houses between 1918 and 1938, the majority of which were built by the private sector. The lack of planning controls at the time resulted in some ribbon development on the approach roads to Bath of the type of semi-detached houses typical of 1930s Britain. The city council provided over 1,000 new homes for its working-class residents in the 1920s and 1930s.[10] During these decades many Georgian family houses were subdivided, either into flats (thereby adding to the housing stock) or offices for doctors, solicitors and other professionals. In addition to housing developments, the city acquired three cinemas, a large Co-operative store, a Woolworths, a new post-office, and modern electricity offices. Several secondary schools were built in the suburbs, and a new Royal United Hospital was erected at Combe Park on the site of the temporary War Hospital.[11]

Southgate Street in the 1930s.

BY COURTESY OF BATH CENTRAL LIBRARY, BATH & NORTH EAST SOMERSET COUNCIL

While these physical changes, benefiting the mass of Bath's residents, were under way, the city was still promoted as a health resort in the official guides of the 1920s and the 1930s, particularly as an ideal place to spend the winter. The list of treatments available at the baths ran to several pages in the guides, and some hoteliers advertised their willingness to provide special diets for guests coming to take the waters. Visitors' tickets, covering admission to the winter-season concerts in the Pump Room and charges for drinking the spa water, were available at 'moderate prices'. The wording of advertisements for hotels and guest houses suggests that comfort, exclusivity and economy were regarded as prime attractions to prospective customers. Miss Gittens, for example, the proprietor of the Westbourne and Grosvenor hotels, offered excellent cuisine served at 'separate tables', and a gas fire in every bedroom, all at a 'moderate tariff'. It seems, however, that the popularity of Bath was at a low ebb between the wars. Louie Stride, who worked as a chambermaid in Pratt's Hotel, in the 1930s, remembers:

> Visitors for treatment usually came for three weeks and in the winter we had our 'permanents'. These were people who came back every year at a reduced rate usually. Bath was not a tourist attraction like today. The first coach loads

of Americans came about 1934–35, I think, and the hotels felt it was humiliating to take such people as 'one nighters', and I remember at the posh Empire Hotel, the coaches had to go around the back at [the] Police Station where [the] Guildhall is now, as it was so demeaning. It soon got common enough, and hotels were glad to welcome them and are now.[12]

There was little by way of public entertainment for the visitor other than the Pump Room concerts, and these were followed by a summer season of band concerts in the city's parks and gardens. The Assembly Rooms were obsolete by 1921, when the ballroom became a cinema and the tearoom was used as a sale room, although in 1931 a Mr Cork purchased the premises and made a gift of them to the National Trust, which undertook a restoration programme, completed in 1938.[13]

Bath did not feature in the list of 148 places in which the population figures were inflated by more than 3 per cent by visitors on census night in June 1921. Nor did the other inland resorts, Cheltenham and Leamington Spa. The largest numbers of visitors recorded were in the popular seaside resorts (places such as Blackpool, Margate and Southend), but the 20 places in England and Wales in which visitors accounted for the highest percentages of resident populations in the 1921 census, included such small to medium-sized resorts as Barmouth, Walton-on-the-Naze and Broadstairs.[14] These seaside resorts, specialising in quiet holidays for middle-class families, were attracting more early season visitors than Bath or its rival spas. The 'Queen of the West' had become 'a grime-encrusted … drab place of little charm' by the 1930s,[15] and city directories for the last years of that decade carry few advertisements for hotels. It seems likely that semi-permanent guests had by then become more significant than seasonal visitors to this sector of the local economy. Moreover, a shrinking market was perhaps curtailing opportunities – particularly for entrepreneurial women – to run small enterprises catering largely for visitors. The numbers of men occupied as inn- or hotel-keepers, publicans or beersellers, boarding- or lodging-house keepers, declined only slightly, from 177 in the first category and 74 in the second in 1921, to 164 and 68 respectively in 1931. But the numbers of women thus occupied fell more sharply, from 100 to 58 (inn- or hotel-keepers, publicans and beer sellers) over the decade, and in the same period the number of female lodging- or boarding-house keepers dropped from 536 to 371. Hotels did provide employment for working-class women, and an opportunity to see how the other half lived. As Louie Stride wrote:

What a revelation it was to me, seeing well educated, and really nice, aristocratic people, and some of course, not so nice! I had some lovely rooms to look after, first floor south, one was the room (or supposed to be) which Sir Walter Scott was in when he lived in South Parade. My clients varied tremendously. Some were very difficult and cranky, so I always had to be very diplomatic, an art I soon learnt. You would soon be out of a job if you were reported for being rude, or maybe the slightest thing, some of them were very autocratic.

Several long stayers I remember well. Poor old Miss Hayter, nearly blind and no relatives, or ever any visitors ... when she died, the relatives were numerous, came from the ground, I think. Then, next door was Mrs Parry Jones, a very elderly lady ... she suffered dreadfully from asthma, and I had to light a saucer of incense, or some such stuff for inhalation every night. Mrs Parry Jones had a glass eye, and I had to poke it out very carefully every night with a hairpin, and put it in a small glass of fluid made special. I shall never forget the feeling almost of horror to see this glass eye in my hand looking at me, [but] one soon got used to it. Also, she used a commode, and always left a 1/- [5p] on top when [she] had been obliged to use it. I must emphasise the fact that none of the rooms had toilets or bathrooms, [there were only] two bathrooms and loos on each floor ... All the rooms had coal fires, and jugs and basins, so coal had to be carried, and cans of hot water.[16]

However, Bath was better placed than many other cities when the inter-war depression set in. It remained a largely residential city, albeit with something of a tourist trade, but it was also a local and regional shopping centre and had an industrial sector which included engineering, cabinet making, the manufacture of cloth and articles of dress, printing and bookbinding, and other small often craft-based industries. This sector employed in the aggregate about 10 per cent of the total population.[17] There was no abrupt change in the occupational structure of Bath between the wars, but the overall trend was one of moderate decline in

Table 5 *Selected occupations of men and women in Bath, 1921 and 1931*

	Men		Women	
	1921	*1931*	*1921*	*1931*
Total population	29,326	29,162	39,343	39,653
Numbers in employment *	19,292	20,125	12,141	12,280
Agriculture, mining and quarrying	1,253	1,050	27	27
Workers in metal	2,058	1,815	19	16
Textiles and dress	685	540	1,867	1,319
Food, drink and tobacco	529	427	134	59
Wood and furniture	1,403	1,221	74	45
Paper, printing, bookbinding and photography	518	622	277	342
Building and construction	906	1,225	–	2
Painters and decorators	665	774	4	20
Transport and communication	2,577	2,558	92	56
Commercial, finance and insurance	2,528	3,148	1,421	1,627
Professional	806	808	1,129	1,182
Entertainment and sport	137	172	50	51
Personal service	980	1,228	5,931	6,147
Clerks, draughtsmen and typists	966	1,226	767	985

* 1921: aged 12 years and over; 1931: aged 14 years and over.
Source: Census (England and Wales) County Reports, Somerset: 1921 and 1931.

the primary sector (agriculture, mining and quarrying) and also in the secondary manufacturing sector, although as Table 5 shows there was a slight growth of employment in printing and associated trades.

Within the category 'Textiles and Dress' the manufacture of cloth was insignificant in comparison to the production of clothing. Weavers and spinners, once commonplace in Bath, had dwindled to fewer than 80 by 1931. The single largest sub-groups of occupations for men, employed in textiles and dress, were the tailoring trades and boot and shoe manufacturing, although neither accounted for many more than 200 at either inter-war census. The majority of women textile workers were employed in tailoring, dress and blouse making, and as corset makers or machinists. Their numbers fell by more than 500 over the decade. Areas of expansion, offering employment to both men and women, were chiefly in the 'white-collar' service sector. Between 1921 and 1931 the numbers of men and women occupied in commerce, finance and insurance rose by 620 and 206 respectively. Within this broad category, the growth of retailing was significant. The number of salesmen and male shop assistants rose from 830 to 1,018 between 1921 and 1931, while the number of women in this occupational group went up from 1,058 to 1,207. There was also an overall increase in the numbers occupied as clerks, draughtsmen and typists but the figures set out in Table 5 mask some gender differences in employment. The number of male clerks rose between the census dates from 821 to 970, but the number of female clerks fell from 748 to 607. Among office workers, female typists (341) were far more numerous than their male counterparts (11) in 1931.

On the whole, the unemployment rate in Britain was lower for women than it was for men (although the labour force was predominantly male), not least because lower wage rates made women more attractive as employees during the depression. Yet, as unemployment mounted, some employers preferred to give work to married men rather than to single women or, particularly, to married women. Indeed, there was a 'marriage bar' in some areas of employment for women. Such choices may explain the fall in the numbers of female clerks in Bath. Women were certainly excluded rapidly from those male occupations in which they had participated during the First World War, perhaps as a consequence of opposition to their presence by male trade-unionists and the prevailing notion that a woman's place was in the home. By 1921, only six female machine tool workers and thirteen 'other workers' were employed in the metal industries, and only one woman worked as a tram or omnibus conductor. Within the professions women in Bath remained most numerous in those of lower status, such as nursing and teaching, although by 1931 there were nine women doctors in the city. However, for most of Bath's female labour force domestic service remained the chief occupation. Some part of the increase in total numbers between 1921 and 1931 can be explained by changes in occupational categories,[18] but nonetheless there was an identifiable increase in the numbers of female indoor domestic servants from 4,239 in 1921 to 4,587 in 1931. Over the same period the numbers of male indoor domestic servants rose from 195 to 235. Male labourers and unskilled workers also increased, from 1,205 in 1921 to 1,660 in 1931.

Occupational change in Bath between the wars was broadly similar to the national experience. As the primary sector and secondary manufacturing industries declined somewhat, there was a growth in white-collar occupations. The production of new consumer goods, which created many jobs in some parts of southern England, was not a feature of the local economy, but the numbers employed in building increased in the city, as they did in the country as a whole. The building industry was one with a high demand for unskilled labour, but it was subject to seasonal unemployment during the winter months. It may well be

opposite Broad Street in the 1930s. Jelf & Co., motor and cycle makers (with works in Newark Street and, until 1925, a retail outlet at 9 Southgate Street), are advertised above one of the shops. The gabled building is now number 80, occupied by the furnishing and home goods store Rossiters of Bath.

that some of Bath's working-class men were forced into this sector, as they were perhaps into domestic service, by the state of the labour market.

In the west country as a whole, unemployment was persistently lower than the national average although it was locally high in specific occupations, such as coal mining. In Bath itself the available figures suggest that the numbers out of work followed the national trend.

At the census taken in 1931, 2,076 men and 545 women (10.3 per cent of males and 4.4 per cent of females in the total occupied population) were out of work, and the number of unemployed rose to 3,000 in the following year. No figures for the later 1930s have been located, but job opportunities were by then increasing in the area covered by the Bath and District Local Employment Committee. In the mid-1930s the Mendip stone quarries were taking on labour to meet the growing demand for road stone, and in 1937 some 150 unemployed men were engaged to lay a gas main from Bath to Frome.[19]
Moreover, the threat of war led to the creation of new jobs at an arms factory established at Corsham (Wiltshire), and in several other 'government undertakings' set up within travelling distance of the city. From at least 1937, Bath was attracting labour from areas of high unemployment in northern England and South Wales.[20] The growth of motor traffic in the 1920s and 1930s was a contributory factor to unquantifiable but significant changes in employment patterns. The proliferation of private transport (bicycles, motor bikes and cars) and of public bus services and 'works' transport extended the geographical labour market, and thereby fostered the trend towards commuting to a work place often far removed from home. Bath was no 'dormitory town' but, nonetheless, the local historian Bryan Little has suggested, between the wars an increasing number of its residents found work in the new industries, offices and factories of Bristol, some thirteen miles away.[21]

Bath was clearly not an unemployment blackspot but, with more than 10 per cent of its male labour force out of work in the early 1930s, it has a place in the ongoing debate over the links between unemployment and ill-health. Moreover, as a provincial city in a period of economic transition, changes in the health standards of its population and the housing conditions of its working classes are integral to the wider debate about the quality of life in inter-war Britain. For those without work, living on the dole entailed relative deprivation if not absolute poverty, but the Medical Officer of Health (MOH) found no evidence of ill-health as a direct consequence of unemployment in Bath. In his report for 1934 he stated: 'I am not aware of any definite evidence that the health and physique of the unemployed and their families differ significantly from that of the community as a whole'.[22] Nonetheless, a declining trend in the incidence of pulmonary tuberculosis among the child population of Bath in the period 1920 to

Table 6 *Number of workers registered at Bath Employment Exchange*

Year	Numbers registered as unemployed
1925	1,061
1928	1,143
1929	2,199
1930	2,618
1932	3,000
1933	2,350

Source: *Bath Chronicle*, in Anne Part, 'The development of the school medical service: a case study of Bath 1913–39', unpublished BEd dissertation, Bath College of Higher Education (1980).

opposite Southgate Street in the 1930s. Mitchell's general drapery store, right, occupied numbers 48–53. Note Brunel's skew bridge providing an imposing focal point for this view across the Old Bridge, with Beechen Cliff beyond.

1939 was sharply disrupted by a steep rise in the years 1930 to 1934, when the number of cases notified to the authorities amounted to 13 per cent of the total school population of 7,500.[23] This disease is closely associated with poverty and overcrowding, and it seems unlikely that it was entirely coincidental that more children were affected by it in the very years when the economic depression was at its deepest.

Yet in most respects the health and condition of schoolchildren in Bath had improved significantly by the end of the 1930s. No single factor can account for rising standards, but better housing, higher average family earnings, changes in diet, the fall in average family size, and the wider role of both national and local government in caring for the nation's children, all made some contribution. The development of the school meals service is one example of the increasing role of the state, although in Bath it had its origins in a voluntary scheme set up in 1904. It was introduced nationally by legislation in 1906 and thereafter expanded under various Acts of Parliament. By 1939 the school medical and dental service was also well established in the city, and in addition there were special schools for handicapped children, a child guidance clinic, and a juvenile employment committee in the city. The average height and weight of Bath schoolchildren aged twelve, measured over a 30-year period from 1909 to

An unidentified woman in her so-called 'slum interior'. The official classification of sub-standard housing as 'slums' was often resented by residents, who felt themselves stigmatised by the label. Very often they managed to cope remarkably well despite the poor physical standard of the accommodation and facilities and relatively low incomes.

1939, showed increases similar to those identified in York by B. S. Rowntree.[24] This evidence of improved diet was accompanied by other changes for the better. Epidemic disease was still a life-threatening risk, but the general trend was one of decline in cases of scarlet fever, measles and diphtheria. The crippling disease of rickets (caused primarily by a lack of calcium in the diet) became less common, combated in part by the provision of cheap 'school milk'. The incidence of flea-bitten bodies, lice-infested heads, of scabies, ringworm and impetigo, all diminished as standards of cleanliness and children's ability to resist infection rose. Whereas the overwhelming majority of children inspected by the school medical service in 1907 were officially classified as 'dirty', in 1939 only 30 children in every 1,000 were thus designated.

The health standards of the total population of Bath also improved over time. The standard death rate in 1925 was 10.5 for Bath, when for England and Wales it was 12.2. This was virtually unchanged in 1939 at a rate of 10.7 for Bath and 12.1 for England and Wales. The main causes of death were heart disease and cancer, afflictions chiefly of middle life and old age. The birth rate in Bath, however, was also proportionally low, at 14.0 compared with 18.3 for England and Wales in 1925, falling to 13.8 and 15.0 respectively by 1939. The infant mortality rate in the city (ie the number of deaths under one year per 1,000 births) had been 126 in 1900 but by 1925 it had fallen to 51.[25] It continued to decline thereafter although in 1939 it rose to 57. The MOH could offer no explanation for this rise, but he suggested that one contributory factor might have been the state of health of incomers to Bath from the distressed areas. The success of the local medical authority in reducing the death rate of children aged one to five years was recognised by the *Daily News*, which, in 1925, awarded a prize of £25 to Bath. In 1928 the same newspaper gave the city £10, the second of several prizes awarded to local authorities showing the greatest reduction in infant mortality in 1927.[26] These monies were spent on maternity and infant welfare services.

> THE OVERWHELMING MAJORITY OF CHILDREN INSPECTED BY THE SCHOOL MEDICAL SERVICE IN 1907 WERE OFFICIALLY CLASSED AS 'DIRTY'.

The living room at 12 Waterloo Buildings, Widcombe, from an undated collection of photographs of 'slum interiors', taken probably in the 1930s or the immediate post-war period. The wireless, net curtains, photographs and china displayed on the dresser on the left suggest that this was a respectable working-class home, despite the poor quality of the housing conditions.

BATH CENTRAL LIBRARY, LOOSE PICTURES COLLECTION

In his report for 1939, the MOH commented that the standard of health of Bath's population had improved more than he would have thought possible when he first took up his appointment twenty years earlier. Writing some six years later, however, he stated that 'the most poignant of all the problems' that he had dealt with in his career were related to the housing of the working classes.[27] His belief that a shortage of suitable housing 'is by far the greatest of all the causes which tend to undermine the health of the people' was reiterated in his annual reports from 1919 to 1939. Yet, as Dr Blackett acknowledged, the local housing problem was not comparable to that of many other urban districts. Housing conditions

Cooking and washing facilities of a fairly primitive nature at 45 Oriel Grove, Southdown.

BATH CENTRAL LIBRARY, LOOSE PICTURES COLLECTION

in Bath were better than those in the country as a whole and, moreover, they improved during the inter-war period.[28] The percentage of the population of England and Wales living in overcrowded conditions at the census of 1911 was 9.1 (in Leeds it was 11 per cent, in Finsbury 39.8 per cent); in Bath, in 1919, 2,846 people or 4 per cent of the population, were housed in overcrowded dwellings.[29] During 1920 and 1921, some 250 houses in the city were classified as unfit for human habitation and a further 979 were considered 'seriously defective'. Between the wars, however, as noted earlier, the local authority provided over 1,000 new homes in council houses or flats.

The first inter-war council estate, at Englishcombe Park, was developed in 1920. Council estates were also built at Rudmore Park, Larkhall and Southdown during the 1920s. The largest housing project was undertaken at Odd Down, where the Fosseway estate was developed in 1930 and 1931.[30] Further council initiatives were blocked by the decision of the National Government in 1933

Washing day meant heavy work with primitive facilities such as these, at 2 Waterloo Buildings, Twerton. Buckets of water had to be carried to the 'copper' in the corner, and heated by means of a fire in the hearth at its base; more water had to be hauled in to fill the tin bath for rinsing the wash before it was put through the 'mangle' or wringer (on the left).
BATH CENTRAL LIBRARY, LOOSE PICTURES COLLECTION

Number 34 Beechen
Cliff Place. The
facilities shown here
– gas-fired washing
boiler and cooker and
gas lighting – were
somewhat better
than in many 'slum'
dwellings.

to abolish all subsidies on housing, with the exception of slum-clearance
programmes. Pockets of slum housing in the Avon Street district and in the
Dolemeads were thereafter cleared and redeveloped, with workers' flats being
erected at Kingsmead and some council houses being built in the Dolemeads.
The provision of adequate mass housing was crucial to improving the social
conditions of the bulk of the population in the inter-war period, but in Bath,
as elsewhere, the building of council houses in the 1920s and 1930s did not
completely eliminate the problem. Overcrowding in parts of the inner city was
still a major concern of the MOH in 1939, as it had been in 1919. Moreover, 'the
difficulties of the housing situation' in the city were exacerbated by the influx of
men (and their families, in many cases) attracted to nearby munitions factories
from 1937 onward. In the closing months of 1939, following the outbreak of the
Second World War, there was another and very rapid inflow of population to
Bath, which added to the existing problems.[31]

Council housing at Rudmore Park, 1927. Other estates were built in the 1920s at Englishcombe Park, Larkhall and Southdown.

BY COURTESY OF BATH RECORD OFFICE

Before moving on to consider the conflict of 1939–45, in relation to the city, we turn to the labour movement and the voting behaviour of the electorate in inter-war Bath. During that period the local experience was an integral part of national events, and of the process of political change that accompanied socio-economic change in the country as a whole.

The labour movement in Bath, as elsewhere, was in confident mood for a brief time when the First World War ended. There was some degree of organisation in all of the city's main trades and industries, and a Trades and Labour Council representing skilled and unskilled workers was formed locally in 1893.[32] In 1918, a Labour candidate stood for a parliamentary election in Bath for the first time. By then the Labour Party had become a truly national party, with a new constitution, which made provision for individual membership. Its electoral chances had been improved by further extensions to the franchise under the Representation of the People Act (1918), which gave the vote to all men over 21 and women over 30. (Women gained the franchise at age 21 under further legislation in 1928). At

Council housing at Old Fosse Road, 1931. The Fosseway estate at Odd Down was the largest council housing development of the inter-war years.

BY COURTESY OF BATH RECORD OFFICE

the 1918 election, the sitting Conservative-Coalition member was returned with a majority of over 10,000 in a total poll of 20,849, but A. J. Bethell gained for Labour just over a quarter (25.2 per cent) of votes cast.

The confidence of Labour in 1918, however, was soon eroded. The early 1920s were a time when working people in general were subject to rising unemployment, falling wage rates, and determined attempts by employers and governments to further reduce wages as a means of improving the competitiveness of British industry. It was within this context that the labour unrest of the 1920s took place, culminating in the General Strike of 1926. Locally, in 1920, a wages dispute at Bath Cabinet Works quickly developed into a lockout (lasting several weeks from late July), which culminated in a return to work on the employer's terms. The Sawclose was the setting for several labour demonstrations in 1920 including a mass rally on May Day and a public meeting in August of that year in support of the miners' demand for nationalisation of the coal industry. Contacts with the Somerset Miners Association (SMA) undoubtedly heightened awareness in the city of conditions in the mining districts, and the association was supported by trade unionists in Bath during a major industrial dispute in 1921 and again in 1926, when the conflict between coal-owners and miners engulfed the wider labour movement in the General Strike.

Between 3 and 12 May 1926, 2,300 Bath workers from nineteen unions (including two that were not affiliated to the Trades and Labour Council) participated in the national strike. It made relatively little impact on the city, however, and despite its revolutionary undertones (much exaggerated by right-wing politicians and commentators) it did not provoke blatant class hostility in Bath. Gas and electricity workers took no part in the action, and 1,000 volunteers enlisted at the Guildhall to offer their services to the authorities. Essential supplies were maintained, the *Bath Chronicle* published as usual (after bringing out an emergency one-page edition on 4 May), the railways continued to run a 'skeleton' timetable, and the press reported that the number of visitors to the city had been reduced by no more than 10 per cent of the average figure for early May. Allegations of violent intimidation against a volunteer bus driver, and two subsequent arrests, were made in a *Sunday Observer* report, but the incident was grossly exaggerated. There were no arrests during the dispute in Bath, where, as James Tarrant (secretary of the Council of Action and of the Trades and Labour Council) told the press, leaders and strikers had 'done everything to ensure that we should not cause trouble to our friends in blue'.[33] Moreover, mass meetings at the Sawclose were addressed by the Liberal alderman Cedric Chivers, mayor of Bath in 1926. The owner of a printing firm, Chivers was a major employer in the city and for many years the municipal representative of the working-class ward of Twerton. Yet conciliatory attitudes were not shared by all those involved. The Bath Electric Tramways company issued an ultimatum to its striking workers to return by noon on 8 May. The manager announced that volunteer labour would be used thereafter and that any man not reporting for work would no longer be guaranteed his job. In the aftermath of the dispute, the Tramways management

TWENTIETH-
CENTURY
BATH

insisted that employees returning to work, and new recruits, should sign a 'non-union' undertaking. As for the miners, they remained in dispute until the end of the year, during which time the Bath Trades Council organised numerous fund-raising events, the proceeds of which were divided 50:50 between the nationwide Miners' Distress Fund and a local relief committee set up by the SMA.[34]

In spite of the collapse of the General Strike, the labour movement in Bath retained its cohesiveness. The Co-operative societies were first established in Bath in 1888, at Twerton, and by 1894 in the central part of the city. After the First World War they continued to expand with several additional local shops, a city-centre department store, and the formation of branches of the Co-operative Women's Guild in Widcombe, Oldfield Park and other areas. Although there was a trend towards the amalgamation of small unions into larger organisations between the wars, the Trades Council was not affected by this in terms of the number of unions affiliated to it – which was 28 in 1918 and 29 by 1930.[35] There were also attempts to organise the unemployed, which came mainly from unofficial bodies, notably the National Unemployed Workers Movement (founded in 1921 and not disbanded until after the outbreak of the Second World War). Concern over the threat of 'entryism' from the Communist Party deterred the official labour movement from actively responding to the problems of the unemployed until the early 1930s, when the General Council of the TUC decided that some leadership should be provided for those out of work, and it recommended Trades Councils as the most appropriate bodies to undertake the task. The Bath Trades Council seems to have followed up this recommendation. By the mid-1930s, a Bath Unemployed Association (affiliated to the Council and on occasions castigated as 'extremist' in the local press) was in existence, although there is no evidence to show the size of its membership.[36]

The Trades Council and Bath Labour Party shared premises known as the 'Labour Rooms', in the Green Park district, but it seems that the two organisations functioned as distinctly 'industrial' and 'political' parts of the labour movement. The Trades Council minute books for the inter-war period indicate that it focused its attention on trade-union matters, but by 1932 Labour Party activists were concerned that 'the forces of the Labour Party and the Trades Council have not been put to the best uses'. In September of that year the party suggested a joint meeting of executive committees 'to discuss what methods may be adopted to further the interests of the Trade Unions and the Labour Party in Bath'.[37] The Labour Party subsequently became formally affiliated to the Trades Council. Labour was clearly an established presence in the city, although a lack of evidence precludes a detailed analysis of its growth.

General election results show that some degree of political change was under way in Bath. Such change was a significant feature of the history of inter-war Britain. The Conservatives (as such, or in the National Government after 1931) were in power for most of the period, but in the 1920s and early 1930s their strength was seriously challenged by Labour, as the Liberal Party went into decline. Following the general election of December 1923, Labour formed its first government (a minority one, supported by Liberal MPs) early in 1924, but less than ten months later it was out of office. The election of May 1929 returned Labour to power, but mounting economic problems following the Wall Street crash led to the collapse of the second Labour administration, and the formation of a National Government with Ramsay MacDonald as Prime Minister.

In Bath the electorate favoured the Conservatives, but the Liberal vote held up and Labour attracted only minority support. It came bottom of the poll at every election it contested after the contest between Lloyd George's Coalition forces and Labour in 1918. No Labour candidate stood for the 1923 election, perhaps as a tactic to avoid splitting the anti-Conservative vote. Given its social and occupational structure, Bath was never likely to be a stronghold for Labour, but its core support was not seriously eroded by the ignominious fall of the second Labour government and Ramsay MacDonald's 'betrayal' in joining the national government. The local consequence of these events was a substantial increase in electoral support for the Conservatives, but the Labour vote recovered to just under 20 per cent of the total in 1935 (see Table 7). The strength of Liberalism, however, had persisted longer in Bath than in Britain as a whole, and it was not until the post-Second World War years that Labour became the main challenger to Conservative dominance in parliamentary politics in the city. One local factor contributing to Labour's popularity in post-1935 elections may well have been the presence of men and women from South Wales and the north of England, those workers from the distressed areas who settled in Bath from 1937 onward. They arrived in sufficient numbers to 'make a significant modification in the general character of the working-class population of the city',[38] and originated from parts of the country with well-established traditions of working-class support for Labour. The newcomers to Bath were followed by a further substantial influx of population, which occurred over a short period at the beginning of September 1939, as war once again engulfed the nation. Bath was a designated 'receiving area' for evacuees and during the first four days of September over

Table 7 *General election results in Bath, 1918–1935*

Election	No. of electors	Turnout (%)	Candidate	Party	No. of votes	%
1918	31,512	66.2	C. J. Foxcroft	Coalition Conservative	15,605	74.8
			A. J. Bethell	Labour	5,244	25.2
1922	33,023	82.4	C. T. Foxcroft	Conservative	13,666	50.2
			E. H. Spender	Liberal	8,699	32.0
			H. H. Elvin	Labour	4,849	17.8
1923	33,520	79.1	F. W. Raffety	Liberal	13,694	51.6
			C. J. Foxcroft	Conservative	12,830	48.4
1924	43,042	84.5	C. J. Foxcroft	Conservative	16,067	55.8
			F. W. Raffety	Liberal	8,800	30.6
			W. B. Scobell	Labour	3,914	13.6
[Death] 1929 (By-election 21 March)	35,373	70.1	Hon. C. W. Baille-Hamilton	Conservative	11,171	45.0
			S. R. Daniels	Liberal	7,255	29.3
			G. G. Desmond	Labour	6,359	25.7
1929	46,877	81.3	Hon. C. W. Baille-Hamilton	Conservative	17,845	46.9
			S. R. Daniels	Liberal	11,486	30.1
			G. G. Desmond	Labour	8,769	23.0
1931	47,932	80.6	T. L. E. B. Guinness	Conservative	24,696	64.0
			S. R. Daniels	Liberal	8,241	21.3
			G. G. Desmond	Labour	5,680	14.7
1935	49,022	74.5	T. L. E. B. Guinness	Conservative	20,670	56.6
			S. R. Daniels	Liberal	8,650	23.7
			G. G. Desmond	Labour	7,185	19.7

Source: F. W. S. Craig, *British Parliamentary Election Results, 1918–1949* (Unwin Bros Ltd, Woking, 1969; 3rd edn, 1983).

'Try that for size!' Evacuees, 1940, at a clothing centre run by the Women's Voluntary Service. The WVS, founded in 1938, played a key role in the mass evacuations of 1939, and its members made a vital contribution to the war effort on the Home Front.

4,000 people of all ages arrived by special trains, most of them from London's East End working-class communities.[39] Some were sent on to nearby towns and villages, but 2,296 (including about 1,700 schoolchildren) were billeted in Bath.[40] It has been estimated that between the beginning of September and the end of December 1939, the resident population of Bath rose by some 10,000, and mid-year estimates during the war show that the civilian population of Bath reached a peak of 83,000 in 1942.[41] Official evacuees were, however, only a small part of those who came to the city as a direct result of the war. A large number of private individuals, who could afford to move to what was perceived to be a place of relative safety, also sought accommodation in Bath. Their presence made it a target for sustained criticism in some sections of the national press, as a 'city of old crocks' living out the war in complacent comfort.[42] Such attacks largely ignored the fact that several government departments and their staffs had been moved to south-west England, and that Bath had been virtually taken over by the Admiralty. The Pump Room, the Pulteney, the Spa and the Empire hotels were all requisitioned, together with many schools, colleges and other large buildings. Temporary accommodation was erected at Foxhill to house some personnel but the main offices of the Admiralty were in central locations.

The arrival of the Admiralty probably enlivened the social life of wartime Bath, for as one writer has commented 'uniformed naval officers paced her streets as they had not done since the days of Nelson'.[43] However, they numbered several thousands and added to the pressure on housing. Moreover, their presence was no protection to the city, and any idea that Bath was exempt from the impact of total war vanished in the Baedeker bombing raids of April 1942, which reduced the recently restored Assembly Rooms to a pile of rubble.[44] Churches, chapels, and Georgian buildings in Queen Square, the Royal Crescent and the Circus were flattened or structurally damaged. The working-class residential areas of Kingsmead, Twerton and Oldfield were also hit. At least 400 people were killed and as many more seriously injured. Some 19,147 buildings were damaged. Out of a total of fewer than 20,000 houses, 1,000 were virtually destroyed and nearly 4,000 more were badly damaged.[45]

An eyewitness described the second Luftwaffe raid on the first night of the Bath Blitz:

> I had not gone off to sleep when the sirens went again and then the second dose began, for some reason I had decided to take cover under the kitchen table. Hansell followed and it got hotter and hotter for us. The noise of the bombs screaming down was really frightening and I must confess I thought every

The bombing of the Francis Hotel in Queen Square during the Bath Blitz, April 1942.

BY COURTESY OF BATH CENTRAL LIBRARY, BATH & NORTH EAST SOMERSET COUNCIL

King Edward Road, Oldfield Park, after the first night of the Bath blitz in April 1942.

one was for us. It wasn't until 5.20 a.m., however, that we really caught it and then there was a terrific crash followed by falling debris and I remember Mrs M say almost stoically 'My house is gone'. It wasn't gone, but everything was a shamble – furniture in front room upset and smashed, windows and doors completely out with ribbons of blinds and curtains trailing across the room. All the ceilings came down and later when we was [sic] able to look most of the road was gone. This was the result of a direct hit on the church opposite which was completely demolished, as also were about a dozen houses further down as a result of another couple of bombs. God, it was really terrifying and how thankful we were when the day dawned there was a deathly silence and we knew they had gone. When we looked down KE [King Edward] road we could see that in addition to the completely destroyed, every house had been made uninhabitable. The early morning was cold, there was no water or gas and everything was covered with dust and grime. Fortunately, the electric current was still on so Mrs M contrived to make us a cup of tea and had that and shared a cake. After that we started to clear debris and salvage our belongings.[46]

> OUT OF A TOTAL OF FEWER THAN 20,000 HOUSES, 1,000 WERE VIRTUALLY DESTROYED AND NEARLY 4,000 WERE BADLY DAMAGED.

After the second night's raid, our witness surveyed the scene of devastation:

Bath's beautiful Assembly rooms were still smoking this am. Between the corner end of Manvers Street and Southgate Street the whole area is a smoking ruin. Lorritts Biscuit factory is a tottering ruin and four churches around there are gutted. The amazing Abbey still stands serene although bereft of some valuable stained glass. This last night's damage, Poor little Holloway had a packet on Saturday but worse still last night ... I hear the wonderful Circus has been badly knocked about. But Milsom Street and Union Street seem pretty intact except for smashed windows.[47]

Later in the war, American GIs arrived in Bath as part of the build-up for the D-Day landings in 1944. These conscript troops remained under American military law enforcement that appeared to allow racial discrimination against black GIs. More blacks than whites were prosecuted for rape, and if found guilty received longer sentences. Disquiet was expressed in Parliament over whether rape was a capital offence only when committed by black GIs. The issue assumed national prominence with the notorious case of Leroy Henry, a former black truck driver from Missouri, who was charged with the rape of a thirty-three-year-old woman from Combe Down, Bath.[48] This case was the most widely publicised incident during the American presence in Britain. Henry was arrested, confessed to the crime, was duly convicted by the presiding American colonel, and was sentenced to be hanged. In the dock, Henry claimed that his confession had been extracted under duress, that he had met and paid for sex (£1 each time) with the woman on two previous occasions. On the night in question,

Kingsmead Street in the aftermath of the Baedeker bombing raids, April 1942.

he had gone to her house by arrangement, but she demanded £2 which Henry refused to pay. The sentence of death led to a public outcry.

The Mayor of Bath and 33,000 citizens called for a reprieve because of a miscarriage of justice. Popular pressure led to the matter being referred to the commander-in-chief, Dwight Eisenhower. To his credit, he considered the verdict unsafe and Henry was sent back to his unit. Some credit is also due to the people of wartime Bath.

As before, war ushered in occupational change. In addition to the armaments factories established nearby in the late 1930s, some of Bath's industries were later converted to the production of war materials. The engineering firm of Stothert & Pitt (which chiefly manufactured components for tanks) was the key firm involved during the period from 1939 to 1945, as it had been in the First World War. Munitions workers from Corsham in Wiltshire were organised by the Amalgamated Engineering Union, and the branch was represented at the Trades and Labour Council by four delegates, which suggests a substantial labour force and a high rate of union membership. Similarly by the period 1941–42 the Fire Brigades' Union had eight representatives listed on the Trades Council delegates roll. The affiliation of the Association of Engineering and Shipbuilding Draughtsmen to the Council in September 1942 can be accounted for by the presence of the Admiralty.[49] This marked a lasting change in the occupational structure, for when the war ended in 1945 central government decided that the Admiralty department should stay on in Bath. Some forty years later the Ministry of Defence was the largest single employer in the city, with a workforce of just over 5,600.[50]

Change and continuity from 1945 to the 1980s

Bath was caught up in the rapid and extensive changes that affected all aspects of life in Britain in the decades after 1945, but continuity with some aspects of its past was also a feature of the recent history of the city.[51] National trends were reflected at local level in the structure of the population and in overall patterns of employment, for instance. Yet, viewed within an historical context, it is apparent that well-established traditional features of Bath in earlier times have had some influence on the processes of socio-economic change.

In Bath as elsewhere the 1950s and 1960s were decades of confidence in the future, based on the expectation of continuous economic growth and full employment. It was then anticipated that Bath would expand to a population of some 100,000 by the mid-1980s, and most local employers assumed that their workforces would also rise over the same period. By the 1970s, however, attitudes and economic circumstances were changing. Plans for the minimal growth of Bath were in place by the end of that decade, and the ideal of full employment seemed an increasingly unrealistic dream. The boom years of the 1980s witnessed considerable investment in retail and office property in the city, but the later recession brought with it a rise in unemployment. The tourist trade has remained

Council housing:
Eastfield Avenue,
Upper Weston, 1948.
The city council
undertook major house
building projects in the
immediate post-war
years.

BY COURTESY OF BATH RECORD
OFFICE

of importance to Bath's prosperity, but the vitality of this sector is dependent on factors other than the efforts of the council to maintain the character of the city and to capitalise on its assets. These efforts range from attention to such details as the sort of shop frontages and types of advertising that retailers may use, to imaginative ventures such as the Bath Film Office, which provides a range of media production services that have been used by many well-known companies over the years. Nonetheless, however effectively the city is promoted, the state of the national and international economy can affect the tourist trade in Bath.

The population of the city in mid-1945 was estimated at 76,000 and thereafter it rose over thirty years to reach more than 84,500 in 1971. However, in the following decade it fell to below the level of twenty years earlier. Most of the increase to 1971 can be accounted for by the in-migration of new residents, although boundary changes in the mid-1960s brought the whole of Combe Down within the city limits, as well as an area extending almost to the village of Batheaston. Falling numbers over the decade to 1981 were attributable mainly to a movement of population out of the city, which may have been caused in part by a sharp decline in house building within the borough from around the mid-1970s. With a minimal growth policy in place from 1978, it is likely that Bath will remain for the foreseeable future a small city, with a population in the 80–85,000 range.

Despite its sometime image as 'a city of old crocks', in the immediate post-war

Table 8 *The population of Bath,
1951–1981*

Census year	Total population
1951	79,294
1961	80,901
1971	84,670
1981	80,771

Source: Census, England and Wales, County Reports (Somerset), 1951 and 1961; The City Plan, Mid-Stage Report, Bath City Council, November 1982, p. 17.

Post-war council
housing: flats above
shops in Combe Down
in the 1950s.
BY COURTESY OF BATH CENTRAL
LIBRARY, BATH & NORTH EAST
SOMERSET COUNCIL

years Bath did not have an exceptionally high proportion of residents aged 65
and over. In census reports from 1951 the seaside resorts of Clevedon, Weston-
Super-Mare and Minehead were identified as the urban districts of Somerset with
the most elderly populations. The demographic profile of modern Bath does
not differ significantly from that of the total UK population: women outnumber
men because of their longer life expectancy, and a rising life expectancy for both
sexes (coupled with a falling birth rate) explains the fact that the population as
a whole is an ageing one. However, Bath's popularity as a place for retirement
seems to have persisted: in 1981 people aged 60-plus made up 22.6 per cent of
the population compared with 18.4 per cent and 17.7 per cent in that category
within the County of Avon and Great Britain respectively. The contemporary
function of the city as a medical centre, and a proliferation of private residential
nursing homes, have perhaps added to Bath's attraction for the elderly. Another
change, more clearly in line with national trends, is that as average family and
household sizes have fallen, the number of households has increased, because
more people are living on their own.

Structural changes in UK employment patterns since the war are also reflected
in Bath. The primary and secondary manufacturing sectors have declined, and
service industries have come to dominate the national economy. Employment
in the manufacturing industries of Bath was increasing by nearly 3 per cent
per annum during the late 1950s and 1960s, while post-war reconstruction and

development ensured that the local construction industry remained buoyant. The building of the University of Bath on a greenfield site at Claverton Down was one major project that provided many skilled and unskilled manual jobs for several years from the late 1960s into the early 1970s.

Growth in the manufacturing sector centred on the traditional industries of Bath. The Horstmann Gear Company and Bath Cabinet Makers were representative of established firms that expanded old premises or built new ones, and the shoemakers Clarks of Street opened a factory in Bath.[52] In the early 1970s engineering accounted for 5,000 jobs; 2,000 workers were employed in printing and publishing, and a further 800 were occupied in the manufacture of clothing. Mechanical engineering accounted for the largest number of workers in the manufacturing sector of the early 1980s (5.9 per cent of the total), most of them employed by Stothert & Pitt, a company whose origins could be traced back to an eighteenth-century iron foundry. The scale of industry in modern Bath remained relatively small: over half of the manufacturing firms employed fewer than ten people. During the 1980s some 'high tech' companies were attracted to the city's industrial estates, but the data set out in Table 9 is indicative of long-term trends in local employment. As early as 1965, service employment in the city predominated over manufacturing by a ratio of 3:1. At the beginning of the 1980s almost 78 per cent of employees worked in the service sector.

Table 9 *Patterns of employment in various industries during the 1970s*

Industry	Bath				Great Britain as a whole	
	1971	%	1978	%	1971 (%)	1978 (%)
Primary*	412	0.90	279	0.63	4.32	3.25
Manufacturing	7,745	18.60	7,245	16.42	34.12	31.98
Construction	2,780	6.70	2,516	5.17	7.12	5.50
Service	30,686	73.80	34,058	77.20	53.64	59.26

* agriculture, forestry and fishing, mining and quarrying.
Source: The City Plan, Mid-Stage Report, Bath City Council, November 1982.

Within the service category the two most important occupational orders were professional and scientific services, and public administration and defence. These subgroups accounted respectively for 22.7 per cent and 17 per cent of employment in services. Growth in these areas reflected both post-war change and some continuity with the past. Once the 'Hospital of the Nation', modern Bath had become a medical centre. The Royal United Hospital complex at Combe Park provided 2,400 jobs in 1980, while the District Health Authority employed 4,000 people in the city. In addition, there were several other NHS (later 'Trust') hospitals in Bath, as well as numerous private nursing homes and the Bath Clinic. The expansion of higher education, particularly since the 1960s, gave the city a new role as an education centre. The presence of the University of Bath and Bath College of Higher Education (now Bath Spa University) made some impact on the locality beyond the occupational structure. The influx of a student population of several thousands intensified the competition for scarce and increasingly expensive rented accommodation. It also created a demand for more 'youth orientated' entertainment.

As with higher education, public administration became a growth area as a result of central government policies, associated with the expanding role of the state in post-war Britain. However, from the late 1970s government endeavours were made to 'roll back' the public sector, and in a council report of the early 1980s, it was noted that privatisation policies might ultimately lead to a fall in local employment in public administration. The continued presence of the Ministry of Defence was also uncertain by the end of the 1980s. The MOD moved out of the Empire Hotel after almost fifty years, in 1988, but it remained the largest single employer in the city with a workforce of over 5,000. Relocation of some or all of the Bath labour force was under review thereafter. The likely consequences caused concern about direct job losses, and the possible knock-on effect on the hotel trade, the housing market, and the retail sector. Moreover, the MOD had made a vital contribution to Bath's prosperity by attracting defence-related companies to the city.

A persistently important strand in the economy has been retailing. This too was subject to radical change from the 1950s, when small shops owned by independent traders were commonplace and there were few department or chain stores in the city. The trend moved towards larger shops, staffed by fewer employees, as self-service or 'cash and wrap' replaced old-style selling and multiple chain stores increasingly replaced independent traders in many British towns. In Bath the distributive trades accounted for 13.4 per cent of all employment around 1980. The Southgate shopping area in the lower town was developed as part of the post-war reconstruction programme, but by the late 1980s, the northern part of the city centre was becoming the prime shopping area. There was considerable investment in the retail sector during that decade. Green Park station, which had stood empty and increasingly derelict for many years, was redeveloped by Sainsburys, in a scheme that incorporated meeting rooms, offices, small retail units and extensive car parking, as well as the superstore itself, which opened in 1983. The Colonnades shopping mall (on Bath Street) was completed in 1986, and the Podium (linking New Bond Street to Pulteney Bridge) was developed between 1987 and the early 1990s. Smaller developments were also undertaken, at Abbey Gate Street, Upper Borough Walls and elsewhere. Modern Bath had become a regional shopping centre for a population of over 300,000 in a catchment area extending to Stroud (Gloucestershire) in the north and including much of west Wiltshire. Visitors to the city, however, continued to make a significant contribution to the prosperity of retailers: it was estimated in 1986 that 50 per cent of the total annual influx into Bath of some 3 million tourists used the shopping facilities.[53]

Bath today has its share of familiar chain stores, such as Boots and Marks &

Spencer, W. H. Smith and McDonald's, and high-quality retailers like Habitat and Laura Ashley, but it did not become an 'anywhere town' of the 1980s. The central shopping area retained much of its character. Large out-of-town shopping centres were not developed, in part, because of the city and county authorities' policies aimed at maintaining the dominance of central Bath. Another factor was the lack of sites sufficiently large to be considered suitable, except on land designated for industrial purposes. Moreover, small traders remained relatively numerous in Bath. In among the premises of multiple stores, the wine bars and gift shops, there could be found greengrocers, newsagents, bakeries, and specialist booksellers, antique dealers, snuff and tobacco sellers. Some 50 per cent of those employed in retailing worked in small shop businesses. Independent traders, however, were under pressure from high rents and business rates during the recession of the later 1980s, and as trade declined many were forced out of business.

The recession also made a wider impact on the local level of unemployment, but modern Bath and the surrounding region remained one of the relatively prosperous areas of the country. The unemployment rate in Bath remained low until the mid-1970s, and, although a steady upward trend developed thereafter, the rise was at a slower rate than that in Avon county or Great Britain as a whole. The ratio of numbers registered as unemployed to job vacancies in 1981 (when 8.7 per cent of the occupied population was out of work) was particularly high for unskilled manual workers and for skilled men such as carpenters, electricians, bricklayers, and machine-tool setters. This was not unique to Bath. As the primary and secondary manufacturing sectors declined nationally, there was a falling demand for labour based on muscular strength and for the skills of craftsmen-artisans, trained in their work through traditional apprenticeships. Nonetheless, it was the policy of the local authorities to retain manufacturing and a varied economy although, as in the past, prosperity was regarded as inextricably linked to dependence on visitors to the city. It was argued by those who administered Bath that the tourist trade generated trade and employment in businesses other than those directly serving the needs of the visitors. The transport and service industries and the manufacturing sector were said to benefit indirectly from tourism. Moreover, the ability to maintain and develop services for the benefit of the city's resident population was also considered to be dependent on the tourist industry, and on the prosperity of the shops in the city.

It was pointed out in the City Plan report of 1982 that Bath was perhaps unique among local authorities in that less than 10 per cent of its gross rate expenditure was actually met from the rates. Bath ratepayers enjoyed almost the lowest district rate in the entire country. The city attracted a high level of rate support grant from central government at that time, but it also benefited from events in its past, and the policies of earlier custodians of its heritage. It will be recalled that after the dissolution of the monasteries in the sixteenth century, lands and property were transferred to the corporation. As owners of virtually all of the walled city, the eighteenth-century corporation shrewdly retained its chief assets and the freehold of land developed as Bath became the resort of fashion. Consequently, the city of the 1980s derived considerable income from council-owned tourist attractions such as the Pump Room and the Roman Baths, as well as from modern facilities such as car parks and leisure centres. The city's investment estate as a whole contributed the equivalent of a 9.45p rate to the council in 1982–83, about 60 per cent of which derived from commercial rents on shop property in the central area.

Tourism, widely regarded as the mainstay of Bath's prosperity, directly employed only an estimated 14 per cent of the working population in 1980. Nonetheless, successive councils in the post-war era placed great emphasis on the benefits of tourism in terms of trade and business. The Roman Baths, the Pump Room, and the delights of shopping in Bath were promoted as vigorously as they had been in guide books of the nineteenth century, but the spa function of the city, on which it built its reputation, had been – somewhat surprisingly – in abeyance for many years after temporary closure in the late 1970s. The council retained ownership of the spa after legislation in the late 1940s created the National Health Service, but it became little more than an outpatient department of the old Mineral Water Hospital. Interest in the hot springs as a unique asset revived over the years and a Development Plan issued in 1966 included proposals for improvements to the spa, with a more commercial approach to the waters. It seemed likely then that the spa might again became one of the major tourist attractions. But within ten years, Bath ceased to be a spa at all: the waters were turned off in December 1976 for an investigation into their purity and for repairs to a leaking conduit in Stall Street. Within months of the repairs being completed in 1978, an amoebic contamination was discovered in the waters. Bath without its spa was unthinkable to some people, and letters to the press and complaints to the council soon followed.[54] Following this, for more than fifteen years, while hydrotherapy treatments were carried on with heated tap water in place of that from Bladud's healing springs, the future of the spa was a recurring theme in local debate about the development of Bath. Research undertaken in that period led to a greater understanding of the hot spring and its waters, and long-term development plans envisaged the city becoming a spa resort of fame equal to its reputation in centuries past.

Whether or not the sick in search of cure will come to be a part of the modern tourist trade remains to be seen, but some visitors of the late twentieth century were attracted by other traditional features of Bath. A survey of the intentions of visitors to Bath in the winter of 1981–82 revealed that most of those interviewed were particularly interested in shopping. Over 50 per cent of participants intended to 'enjoy the shops', compared with just under 22 per cent who looked forward to enjoying the renowned architecture and general sightseeing. This suggests that the authorities were justified in emphasising the economic links between the tourist and retailing sectors. The modern visitor, however, was increasingly likely to be a 'day tripper' rather than a long-stay holiday-maker. Bath has become ever more accessible from London (107 miles to the east), the

Midlands and South Wales. Indeed, the city of today is easily reached from all parts of Britain: by inter-city rail service it is only 80 minutes' journey time from London, and it is located on the M4 corridor while also being within a relatively short distance of the M5. It was estimated that between August 1972 and July 1973 some 340,000 day trippers visited Bath, arriving chiefly by coach or train.[55] In addition, the demand for holiday accommodation or 'bed spaces' rose over the decade from 1971 and 1981, and persuading visitors to stay longer (to the ultimate benefit of the residents) was a key part of the City Plan prepared in the early 1980s to determine policies over the following ten years.

The modern city remained best known for its image as a tourist centre, and the visitor of the 1980s could be forgiven if he or she made the same assumptions as

many of those who came to Bath in the eighteenth and nineteenth centuries. The long-established tradition of Bath as a place without general trade or industry, entirely dependent on serving the needs of the visitors, was perhaps perpetuated by the layout of the city and the concentration on the interests of the tourists. In the 1980s, the industrial manufacturing strand employed 20 per cent of the total working population, but modern industry was located in the western riverside area, which had been the industrial district of the city since the late eighteenth century. Moreover, the main locations of the most important sectors of the service industries were also sited way beyond the tourist trail: the Royal United Hospital at Combe Park, the University at Claverton Down, the MOD departments at Foxhill, Ensleigh and the Warminster Road, were all in districts peripheral to the central area. The average tourist was likely to arrive by train at Bath Spa station, or by coach or by car, to visit the major tourist attractions in the central area and perhaps trek up through Georgian Bath to the Costume Museum in the Assembly Rooms. At least half of them would also visit the shops. They might well leave Bath with an image of the city as little more than a monument to the architecture of the eighteenth century, its earlier history represented solely by the Roman Baths and its contemporary functions encapsulated in the shops and the Tourist Information Centre.

Table 10 *Numbers of visitors to various tourist attractions, 1978–1980*

Site	1978	1979	1980
Roman Baths/Pump Room	793,664	709,364	679,891
Bath Abbey	250,000 *	–	–
Museum of Costume	207,287	120,168	174,194
Victoria Art Gallery	30,742	29,374	36,750
Holbourne Menstrie Museum	–	20,374	21,205
Bath Postal Museum	–	5,000 *	5,750
Bath Bookbinding Museum	3,232 *	3,000 *	2,000 *

* Estimated numbers.

Source: Data from English Tourist Board 1981, Table 1, p. 74, City Plan, Mid-Stage Report, Bath City Council (November 1982).

Another continuity with the past was apparent in the attitudes of permanent residents towards the tourists and, more particularly, to council policies perceived as being in the interests primarily of visitors. While many local people liked the 'variety and bustle', others believed that the city was 'tourist dominated', and unpleasantly crowded in July and August. Some residents questioned the amount of money that the council deemed necessary to spend in order to sustain the 'tourist city', and the large proportion of the local budget (as well as outside investment) that was spent on the central area of Bath. Such debates are reminiscent of similar conflicts of interest in the nineteenth century: those who administer modern Bath face the same difficult task in seeking to balance the needs of residents and tourists to the benefit of all.

Heritage city CHAPTER 9

T HE ROLE of successive corporations and councils in developing Bath
has been controversial from the days of John Wood's complaints in the
early eighteenth century about the corporation's failure to implement some of
his ambitious plans. There is also a well-established tradition of ambivalence
towards the leisure function of the city, and of conflicts of interest arising
between residents and visitors. Long before 'town planning' in the modern
sense existed, the corporation was able to exercise considerable influence on the
built environment because of its ownership of land and property within the city
limits. As the power of the local authority increased over time, so it often became
the focus of resentment or protest whenever it was perceived to be favouring
the interests of the tourist trade over the needs of the permanent population.
Moreover, residents themselves could disagree over the pattern of local authority
expenditure in different parts of the city.

None of this was unique to Bath but it does seem that the special character of
the city, and its role in the life of the nation, fostered both an awareness of its
'heritage' value and a sensitivity over its image that was somewhat exceptional
in early twentieth century Britain. In this chapter we identify some key policy
and planning issues from the 1920s onward, before considering the views of
preservationists and others about the future of post-war Bath, and commenting
on the various images of the city revealed by a public consultation exercise
carried out by the council in the early 1980s. In conclusion, we note some of
the discrepancies between the image and reality of Bath in the 1990s and on into
the twenty-first century.

Whose city? Planners, preservationists and people[1]

During the inter-war period the council pursued initiatives which increased its
powers of control over development in and around the city. Local Acts of 1925
and 1937 empowered the council to regulate the design of new buildings and the
materials used in their construction. In the first of these, the use of Bath stone
was insisted upon at the expense of Victorian red brick. The Act of 1937 also
provided for the listing of all buildings erected before 1820, and required planning
permission to be granted for any alterations to listed properties. Moreover, in
1929 the local authorities of Bath, Bristol and the surrounding areas took the
unusual step of commissioning an outline regional plan for the district. This was
undertaken by Patrick Abercrombie and B. F. Brenton, who, in their report in

1930, identified Bath as 'a compact city in a setting of beautiful country specially to be preserved'.[2] The novel 'green belt' measures put forward in this regional plan were incorporated into the Bath and District Planning Scheme of 1933, which was way ahead of national legislation on planning typical of the 1950s and 1960s. There was a further examination towards the end of the war. Abercrombie, working with the city engineer and the planning officer, prepared a specific 'Plan for Bath' that was published in February 1945.

This was a bold scheme for post-war reconstruction, expansion and development of the city. The suburbs were envisaged as fourteen neighbourhoods. There were to be shopping precincts, open plazas, five more bridges over the Avon, a new hospital and technical college, modern hotels, a recreation ground and lidos, a grand concert hall and a major development of the riverside in Walcot. Vision and optimism were not in short supply in the mid-1940s, but money and materials were. Repairing bomb damage and increasing the housing stock took priority over plazas and recreation grounds in the immediate post-war years, and Abercrombie's 1945 plan was overtaken by national legislation. Only some modest parts of it, such as the technical college, were incorporated in the twenty-year development proposals that the city authority was required to submit to central government under the terms of the Town and Country Planning Act of 1947, which also established

A view of Queen Square presented in a heavily embossed lincrusta mount, adding a luxurious touch likely to appeal to visitors in search of a 'quality' souvenir.

QUEEN SQUARE, BATH.

statutory protection for listed buildings. It led to the designation of nearly 2,000 buildings in Bath as Grade 1 or Grade 2, and a further 1,000 or so listed as Grade 3. There were, in addition, many hundreds of other buildings that would probably have been listed as worthy of preservation if they had been in a city with a less rich architectural history than that of Bath.[3]

In Bath, as elsewhere, the pace of redevelopment and new building gathered momentum from around the mid-1950s, but by then concern was growing about the adverse impact on towns of increasing motor traffic and the extent of demolition. Concern for the historic urban centres, in particular, grew stronger in the 1960s. In 1966 the Minister of Housing and Local Government announced an investigation aimed at discovering 'how to reconcile our old towns with the twentieth century, without actually knocking them down'. Bath, Chester, Chichester and York were chosen as case studies for this enquiry, because all four were recognised as cultural assets but also – with the growth of mass tourism – as economic assets to the nation.[4]

At local level, the council had commissioned Colin Buchanan and Partners in 1964 to carry out a Planning and Transport Study of Bath. The principal feature of the report (published in 1965) was what came to be known as 'Buchanan's tunnel', which was proposed to run under the north-central part of the city to take east–west traffic through Bath. Publication of Buchanan's Plan intensified the debate over preservation, but the slow processes of government meant that its implementation was not an immediate prospect. The plan was not debated by council until the summer of 1971.[5] Meanwhile, virtually wholesale demolition was under way in those parts of Bath the council had designated as comprehensive development areas. Local controversy over planning policies in the city led to the setting up of a public enquiry in 1972, but this was cancelled before the hearing began and in its place the Secretary of State for the Environment instigated joint consultations between Bath City Council, Bath Preservation Trust, and the County Council.

> 'IF YOU WANT TO KEEP GEORGIAN ARTISANS' HOUSES, THEN YOU WILL HAVE TO FIND GEORGIAN ARTISANS TO LIVE IN THEM.'
>
> BATH CITY ARCHITECT (ATTRIB.)

The powers of the local council had, however, been eroded by increasing centralisation since the 1940s and they were diminished further when the Local Government Act of 1972 was fully implemented two years later. Thereafter Bath was merely a 'district' within the new County of Avon. It retained the right to use its coat of arms, to call itself a city and to have a mayor, but control of education and highways passed to the county. Moreover, the city's hospitals were now controlled by the West Wiltshire Health Authority, and the council was no longer wholly responsible for water supply or sewage and refuse disposal.[6] Bath's future was henceforth to be determined primarily by the Avon county structure plan. Since the late 1970s a policy of minimal growth for the city has been in place, and preservation has been integral to subsequent plans and proposals for the city. The city council has nevertheless remained the focal point of criticism

Sir (Leslie) Patrick Abercrombie

Patrick Abercrombie (1879–1957) was born in Sale, Altrincham, one of a family of nine. His father, William (who died before 1909), was from Fife and became a Manchester stockbroker and businessman, with literary and artistic interests. His mother, Sarah Anne Heron (died c.1916) was from Yorkshire. In 1887 Lynngarth, a new family home, was built in Ashton by the Leicester architect, Joseph Goddard. The arts and crafts interiors left a strong impression on the young Patrick Abercrombie. He was educated at Uppingham School, Leicestershire (1893–96), and at the Realschule, Lucerne, Switzerland. In 1897 Abercrombie was articled to a Manchester architect while he attended evening classes at Manchester School of Art. On completion of his articles, he moved to Liverpool, and lived until 1936 in the Birkenhead area. In 1907, he was appointed as a junior lecturer in school of architecture at Liverpool University, and so began his long and distinguished career in civic design and town planning.

In 1909 Abercrombie became a research fellow and edited the *Town Planning Review*, the first journal of its kind in Britain. His fellowship took him abroad every year to France, Germany and Italy, and these travels fed into his vision of the symbiotic cultural and social interdependence of the city-region. This informed his writing and civic design practice. He was appointed as professor of civic design in 1915, a post he held for twenty years. Abercrombie was a leading consultant throughout the inter-war years and worked prolifically. Stratford-on-Avon, Sheffield, east Kent, the Bristol and Bath region, Cumbria, Gloucestershire and the Thames Valley were all subjects he worked on in the 1920s and 1930s. In 1933 he published *Town and Country Planning* which brought his ideas to a wider public. His London plans, published in 1943 and 1944, were probably his greatest achievements. Working with others in the field, Abercrombie addressed the key problems of traffic congestion, poor housing, inadequate and poorly distributed open space. One important feature of *The Greater London Plan* in 1944 was the recommendation for the movement of more than a million people to a ring of new towns beyond the green belt and the first generation of new towns followed legislation in 1946. Abrcrombie's plan for Plymouth in 1943, a city intensively bombed during the war, involved a comprehensive replanning to create a traffic-free zone in the city centre. Unfortunately, the architecture failed to match the boldness of the concept and the wider regional dimension of the scheme was lost. His plan for Bath in 1945 was a bold, utopian scheme of rebuilding after extensive bombing damage, but was largely ignored in practice.

Abercrombie was knighted in 1945 and received many professional honours in Britain and abroad. He died in Berkshire in 1957. His embracing vision rested on the acceptance of the planner as expert, which began to be rejected by the community participation movement of the 1960s.

Source: *Oxford DNB* (2004), pp. 79–82.

from residents. The debate over conservation and development has a long history in Bath, but the emergence of an organised preservation movement in the early twentieth century almost certainly owed something to the growing popularity of the city in the Victorian and Edwardian eras as a place of genteel residence. The wealthy or comfortably off newcomers, with the advantages of education and a leisured life style, were a potentially articulate pressure group and many of them were likely to be more sympathetic to conservation than to radical change. The first organisation dedicated to preserving the city's architectural heritage, the Society for the Preservation of Old Bath, was established as early as 1908.

The phrase 'old Bath' apparently meant 'Georgian Bath', to conservationists and councillors alike. Public consultation by means of a local referendum preceded the local acts of the inter-war years, and the powers that the council obtained related to new buildings and to those pre-dating 1820. A neo-Georgian style was approved for the new premises of the Royal Literary and Scientific Institute in Queen Square in 1932. The council undertook some improvements that modified 'Georgian Bath' between the wars, including rebuilding the corners of Kingsmead Square and making a new thoroughfare from St James Street to Southgate Street. The eighteenth-century Kingston baths, south of the abbey, were levelled and the area was paved over to form the present courtyard. No controversy over these measures has been recorded, but proposals by the council (under the 1937 Act) for substantial changes to Walcot Street and to move the Royal National Hospital for Rheumatic Diseases to a new site generated some heated debate and public opposition.[7] A local referendum would have taken place had it not been for the outbreak of war in 1939, which put an end to development for the duration.

The 1945 Abercrombie Plan was received by the general public with moderate enthusiasm, although the scale of demolition that it would have entailed and the impact of a proposed ring road (following the lines of the old city walls) brought some opposition. Until the early 1960s, however, reconstruction and the repair of war damage took priority over long-term development. Buildings in the Paragon, the Circus, the Crescent, and in Queen Square were made good. The Abbey churchyard was substantially rebuilt, the Assembly Rooms were again restored and opened to the public in 1963. Publication of the Planning and Transport Study in 1965 marked the beginning of some fifteen years of intense debate over Buchanan's tunnel. It was regarded by the Ministry of Housing and Local Government as an acceptable solution to Bath's traffic problem, and it was supported by the majority of councillors and also the architectural correspondent of the *Bath Chronicle*. But public opinion was sharply divided over the road plan. The debate broadened to encompass the consequences of council policy in the comprehensive development areas, and conservation in general, and in the 1960s the council altered some of its policies in response to public opposition. Beauford Square (*c.*1730), Kingsmead Square (1730s) and New Bond Street (1806–10), for example, were all saved from demolition or radical modification by the campaigning conservationists. Buchanan's tunnel and accompanying plans

opposite
The Abercrombie plan. Sir Patrick Abercrombie's plan for Bath, 1945, proposed a utopian post-war reconstruction of the city, including the building of an embankment along the river and redevelopment of the area between Walcot Street and the Avon.
BY COURTESY OF BATH CENTRAL LIBRARY, BATH & NORTH EAST SOMERSET COUNCIL

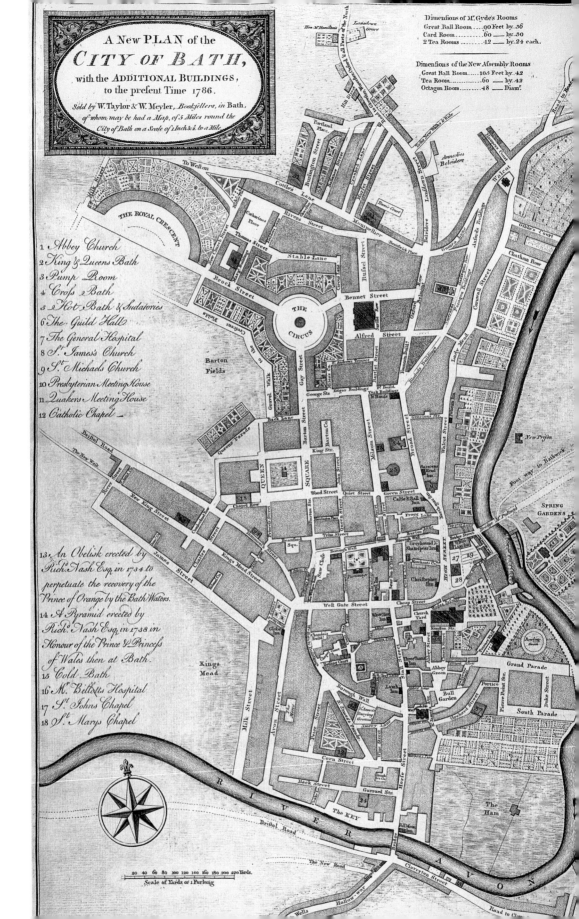

A New PLAN of the
CITY OF BATH,
with the ADDITIONAL BUILDINGS,
to the present Time 1786.

Sold by W. Taylor & W. Meyler, Booksellers, in Bath,
of whom may be had a Map, of 5 Miles round the
City of Bath on a Scale of 1 Inch & ⅜ to a Mile

Dimensions of Mr. Gyde's Rooms
Great Ball Room ....90 Feet by 36
Card Room ....60 — by 30
2 Tea Rooms ....12 — by 24 each.

Dimensions of the New Assembly Rooms
Great Ball Room .....105 Feet by 42
Tea Room..............60 — by 42
Octagon Room ....48 — Diamr.

1 Abbey Church
2 King & Queens Bath
3 Pump Room
4 Cross Bath
5 Hot Bath & Sudatories
6 The Guild Hall
7 The General Hospital
8 St. James's Church
9 St. Michaels Church
10 Presbyterian Meeting House
11 Quakers Meeting House
12 Catholic Chapel

13 An Obelisk erected by
Richd. Nash Esq. in 1734 to
perpetuate the recovery of the
Prince of Orange by the Bath Waters.
14 A Pyramid erected by
Richd. Nash Esq. in 1738 in
Honour of the Prince & Princess
of Wales then at Bath.
15 Cold Bath
16 Mr. Bellotts Hospital
17 St. Johns Chapel
18 St. Marys Chapel

Scale of Yards or 1 Furlong

above Old Bond Street in the heart of Bath. Public interest in the preservation of Bath's buildings and townscape began in earnest at the beginning of the twentieth century and culminated in the establishment of the Bath Preservation Trust in November 1934. It is interesting to list the names and (where known) the occupations and social standing of the Trust's founder members: Horace Annesley Vachell of Widcombe Manor (a writer of popular novels); Thomas Sturge Cotterell, MBE, JP (chairman) of 21 Pulteney Street and a member of the city council; R. N. Green-Armytage of 5 Queen's Parade (barrister); James Calder of 10 Lansdown Crescent; John Shirley-Fox of 3 Lansdown Crescent (portrait painter); Sir Alexander Waldemar Lawrence, Baronet; Annie Florence Tylee; George E. Hughes of 15 Gay Street (solicitor with Collins & Hughes); Charles Peers; A. Leonard Fuller of 9 Gay Street (a distinguished Fellow of the Royal College of Surgeons); Major Francis J. Staynor. Clearly in these early years the issue of Bath's heritage appealed primarily to members of the social elite, although by the 1970s there was a significantly broader social base for the Save Bath campaigns.

PHOTOGRAPH: CARNEGIE, 2004

left Marketing and promoting the tourist and heritage attractions of Bath is nothing new, as this 'New Plan of the City of Bath' from 1786 shows.

BY COURTESY OF BATH RECORD OFFICE

were officially abandoned in 1979, on the grounds of escalating estimated costs, but the issue had attracted attention in the national press and the outcome could be claimed as a victory for the conservation lobby.[8]

Changing attitudes in the country as a whole, as well as local events and circumstances, contributed to the growing strength of the preservation movement in Bath. In the first post-war decades an either/or attitude to conservation and development was commonplace. In the climate of the times, restoration, renovation and redevelopment for new uses were rarely considered as viable alterations to rebuilding. Those who shared the view that redevelopment was a welcome sign of progress would no doubt have agreed with the comment attributed to the city architect of Bath, that 'If you want to keep Georgian artisans' houses, then you will have to find Georgian artisans to live in them'.[9] To others it seemed an act of cultural vandalism to clear away aesthetically pleasing old buildings, particularly when they were replaced by what some regarded as the depressingly utilitarian bus station, the Snow Hill high-rise flats, the 'hen coops' of Holloway, and what has been described as the 'vulgar mass-produced monotony of the Marks & Spencer's and Woolworth's building'.[10] Concern for the built and natural environment has increasingly come to be shared by growing numbers of people from all social classes, as better education and rising living standards have raised the general level of awareness of cultural and aesthetic values. Consequently, the either/or attitude was gradually superseded by concepts of sympathetic development, good modern architecture and the conversion of old buildings for new uses.

In Bath the conservation issue was given added weight by the publication in 1973 of *The Sack of Bath*, in association with the Bath Preservation Trust, which was formed in 1934 following the demise of the earlier Old Bath Preservation Society. It was further strengthened by a proliferation of new organisations, including the Bath Action Group, the Bath Environmental Campaign and the Bath Amenity and Transport Association, which represented between them a wide spectrum of opinion in the debate about Bath's future.

Such groups, and many other sympathisers, took part in the 'Save Bath' campaign of the 1970s, which culminated in the council adopting the main proposals of the campaigners in the 'Saving Bath' plan of 1978. *The Sack of Bath* became something of a key text, an influential book in which the authors vehemently condemned the consequences of planning in Bath:

> Today artisan Bath is largely rubble. Acres upon acres of the Georgian City's minor architecture have been flattened in the course of a decade and a half ... The set pieces – Royal Crescent, the Circus, Milsom Street, the Pump Room, and so on – stand glorious and glistening (some have been restored and cleaned) for tourists to come and see in their thousands every year. But now

'TODAY ARTISAN BATH IS LARGELY RUBBLE. ACRES UPON ACRES OF THE GEORGIAN CITY'S MINOR ARCHITECTURE HAVE BEEN FLATTENED IN THE COURSE OF A DECADE AND A HALF ...'

they have become like mountains without foothills, like Old Masters without frames. The Bath of the working classes, the Bath which made Beau Nash's fashionable resort possible has been swept away ... In few places has the notion of 'urban renewal' been applied with such destructive vigour as here, or with such callous disregard for the finer subtleties of urban charm.[11]

Those who actively participated in the campaign to 'Save Bath' – by lobbying MPs and government ministers, by organising public meetings and marches, and other strategies of protest – were an articulate minority. They came from diverse backgrounds, including students and housewives, businessmen and professional people, bodies such as the Young Liberals, and at least one former city councillor as well as the retired city engineer who had been part-author of the Buchanan Plan of the mid-1960s. The majority of Bath's citizens were silent in the great debate over its future.[12] An attempt to canvass their opinion was made, however, in an exercise in public consultation during the early 1980s, as part of the preliminary work on preparing a city plan setting out the council's policies and proposals for Bath in the decade from the mid-1980s to the mid-1990s. A number

A pre-war aerial view of the Circus and Royal Crescent. Visitors and residents can now see such views for themselves, because Bath has become a centre for air-balloon enthusiasts. Several companies offer flights over the city and ascents, from Victoria Park, attract interested crowds.

'DO WE PRESERVE
BATH AT THE EXPENSE
OF THE NEEDS OF THE
RESIDENTS?'

CITY PLAN, 1982

of organisations were invited to comment on what should be included in the plan, and local papers published the text of a publicity brochure about the project. A wide range of interests was represented by the organisations consulted, which included conservation and environmental groups, charities, housing associations, women's groups, and such diverse bodies as the Rotary Club and the University of Bath. In total 194 replies were received by the council, of which 140 were letters or comments submitted by individuals.

The good intentions of the authorities were stated in the prologue to the mid-stage report on the City Plan (November 1982), in which it was acknowledged that planning for the future of Bath entailed recognising the expectations placed upon the city by a wide spectrum of people. The fundamental question, familiar to corporations and councils of earlier centuries, was also set out: 'Do we preserve Bath at the expense of the needs of the residents?' Some conservationists might reply by agreeing with Adam Fergusson (co-author of the *Sack of Bath – and After*) that 'those who live in and enjoy the beauties of an eighteenth-century town should not expect the amenities of Harlow New Town or Hemel Hempstead'.[13] but it is highly likely that the majority of Bath's residents would concur with the council's assumption that they expect 'the same opportunities and facilities as those in any similarly sized town in Britain'.

In trying to satisfy the conservationists while also seeking to meet the needs of the resident population, the business community, and the tourists, those who administer Bath are subject to certain restraints and influences. Physical expansion is curtailed by the minimal growth policy and the green belt around the urban boundaries. What little land there is available for development is concentrated at the periphery, and is designated primarily for industrial use. There are now 5,000 listed buildings in Bath and the whole of the city centre is a conservation area, constituting the largest single such area in the whole country. As in the past, there is a widespread belief that tourism and the retail sector with which it is closely associated are vital to the prosperity of Bath.

These factors have direct consequences in several interrelated ways. The council is reluctant to release land set aside for industrial usage, as this would affect its efforts

A statue of 'Edward the Peacemaker', Edward VII, in Parade Gardens.
PHOTOGRAPH: CARNEGIE, 2004

'Bog Island' fountain, Terrace Walk. The fountain, by Pieroni and dating from 1859, stood in Stall Street until 1989 when it was moved to the traffic island created by demolition and road widening in 1933. Underground public lavatories, later converted to a nightclub, gave the site its popular name.

PHOTOGRAPH: CARNEGIE, 2004

to maintain economic diversity and provide local jobs by attracting manufacturers and small businesses to its industrial estates. Coupled with the minimal growth policy, this accounts in part for the unmet demand for housing in Bath – particularly for relatively cheap 'starter homes'.[14] The former mining village of Peasedown St John has been developed as a dormitory town to house the 'overspill' of Bath's population. The council's concern to maintain the character of Georgian Bath can lead to disputes between home-owners and the planning department over such matters as the colour of external paintwork. There is also tight control over shop frontages, advertising, and street furniture. In general, retail projects likely to draw trade away from the city centre are opposed by the council. Pedestrianisation and park-and-ride schemes have been introduced to make the central shopping area more attractive, but traffic restrictions on central streets have not been universally welcomed by traders. The controversial installation of bollards in Milsom Street saw the council criticised not only for the inconvenience caused, but also the results were seen as both expensive in the loss of trade and an ugly addition to Bath's main shopping street.

Decisions made by the council clearly affect the perceptions that Bathonians have of their city and, as in the nineteenth century, there are those who believe that the official concerns of the council do not coincide with the requirements of the residents. Many of the respondents to the consultation exercise of the early 1980s considered there was 'a difference in the care and direction of resources to the affluent Georgian Bath and the city centre compared to the outer areas'. Moreover, there existed a strong feeling that if many of the suburban problems occurred centrally, they would be dealt with promptly and effectively. Allied to these views there was also a conviction among some of the respondents that 'a snob element tends to linger in Bath', exemplified by a professional couple living off

'OF COURSE, NOBODY WHO IS ANYBODY LIVES SOUTH OF THE RIVER.'

293

the Lower Bristol Road who recalled being told, 'Of course, nobody who is anybody lives south of the river'.

In reality social segregation is probably not as marked in central Bath and the inner suburbs as it was in the past. Some Georgian houses in the upper town are in multiple occupation, let out to students and young working people. Victorian artisan dwellings, however, have become desirable residences, beyond the means of the contemporary equivalent of an artisan and are now likely to be lived in by middle-class home-owners. The central Abbey ward remains one of sharp contrasts, encompassing both the Circus and the council flats off Kingsmead Square, but the most extreme social divide in modern Bath is between the central conservation area and the council estates rarely seen by visitors to Georgian Bath. In the early 1980s more than a quarter of the population lived in council-housing estates (now run by the Somer Housing Association), located mainly in the south-west sector of the city some three kilometres from the centre. One aim of the City Plan was to consider the needs of residents in outer Bath, for when it was being prepared community centres, branch libraries, banks and other facilities were conspicuously few in outlying neighbourhoods. People living in such places had to travel into the centre not only to enjoy the general amenities of the city but also to obtain some essential services.

There was clearly a class dimension involved in local perceptions of Bath as 'two cities', but the underlying conflict was seen as the competing interests of residents and tourists. A number of residents held the view that 'the balance ... at present, veers too much towards the tourists', and it was suggested that: 'The people of Bath are turning against the tourists because the powers that be appear to think more of the tourists than the residents'. Comments on visitors to the city ranged from 'tourists are our life blood' to 'the ordinary people of Bath do not benefit from tourists'. The question of tourism evoked some muddled images of the city. While some people saw Bath as 'a Tourist Centre first and foremost', others spoke of it as primarily residential ('one of the pleasanter towns in which to live') and there were those who feared that tourism might destroy the 'special character' of Bath. One conclusion drawn in the report published in November 1982 was that the comments of respondents suggested the possibility of having a clear image of Bath, and that the management of the city would be 'effective, efficient and economic' if it was conducted in accordance with that image. The acknowledged difficulty with that suggestion, however, would be in deciding 'whose image of the city to pursue'. The diversity of the city was obscured in earlier times, by its dominant image as the resort of fashion or a place of genteel residence, and the differing images evoked by modern Bath seem to imply that its complexities were still not fully recognised in the 1980s. In that decade Bath was, in reality, a provincial city with a historic past and a variety of functions. Twentieth-century day-trippers had succeeded 'the quality' and the seasonal visitors, but Bath was widely known as a major international tourist resort. Yet it could also be accurately defined as any one of the following: a residential city, home to a population of some 80,000; a sub-regional shopping centre serving upward of a quarter of a million people; a sub-regional medical centre with extensive hospital facilities; a centre for further and higher education; a principal administrative base for the Ministry of Defence. In seeking to understand Bath, diversity remains a more useful concept than any dominant image.

Into the twenty-first century

Some 4 million tourists visit Bath each year. What brings them to the city, and accounts for it being one of the most popular tourist locations outside London, was set out in an official guide of the early 1990s:

> For almost two millennia, the city of Bath has welcomed visitors of all kinds: the sick, seeking a cure from the healing waters, the wealthy seeking entertainment, and today's visitors, drawn by the legacy of that past. This includes some of the most spectacular Roman remains in Britain and a city unique in being almost exclusively Georgian. Bath is one of the best-preserved Georgian cities in the world. Such is its importance that in 1988 the whole city was designated a World Heritage site, the only one in Britain ... Today the city attracts visitors from all over the globe and the atmosphere sparkles with cosmopolitan life. Some of the world's greatest actors and musicians perform here and even the streets are alive with entertainers. Bath has become an international cultural centre, as well as a world heritage city.[15]

The tourist who strays beyond the central area might question the description of Bath as being 'almost exclusively Georgian', and few who visited the city in the

A tour bus on the Royal Crescent.

early 1990s could fail to notice that its streets were alive with beggars as well as buskers. As in the past, the guides present a selective image of Bath with which to attract potential visitors. Similarly, today's residents can feel harassed by the sheer numbers of visitors, in ways that are reminiscent of nineteenth-century encounters.

For some permanent residents of the World Heritage City, the compensations of living in a particularly beautiful built environment are offset by the inconveniences of making one's home in a major tourist resort. During the season, life in Bath can take on the quality of a film set, when groups of camera-clicking tourists crowd the streets. At other times, Bath literally becomes a film set aided by the Bath Film Office that has successfully attracted a series of high profile films and television series to make use of the architectural backdrop for costume drama. Crowds of locals flock to watch the stars of films like *Vanity Fair* (shot in June 2003), and a lucky few join in the fun as film extras. Tourism makes a particular impact on those who live in Georgian Bath, such as residents of the Royal Crescent, who are typical of others in their uneasy relationship with the tourists. A voluntary agreement between bus operators and the council theoretically limits the number of guided tours along the Crescent to nine per hour, but the agreement is often breached at peak times, when as many as twelve tourist buses an hour – or one every five minutes – may rumble along the street.

The chairman of the Royal Crescent Society has expressed concern about the deteriorating condition of the road, and the volume of traffic causes damage to the stonework of the Grade 1 listed buildings. Some residents accept that, 'If you choose to live in the Royal Crescent you should expect to have your house used as a tourist attraction', but most would like tour buses to be limited to five an hour, if not banned completely.[16]

The Crescent has also been the focal point for another clash of interests in the city. As part of the Bath Festival, open air concerts were held in the Victoria Park in 1992 and 1993, when the international stars José Carreras and Dame Kiri Te Kanawa performed. The lawn in front of the Royal Crescent was used as seating space for the concerts, but this prestige event was modified in 1994 when four residents used an ancient power of veto to refuse to allow the same arrangement as in previous years. The chairman of the Royal Crescent Society told the local press that the majority of residents were happy to share their 'front garden' with others once a year, and the minority of objectors were castigated by one householder as 'selfish snobs'.[17] It is somewhat ironical that one Royal Crescent resident should call others 'snobs', and particularly so in this context, for the festival is an annual event that brings with it evidence of latent class hostility in Bath. The International Festival of Music and the Arts brings top-quality performers to the city, much good publicity, and many 'cultural tourists'. Its organisers (Bath Festivals Trust) make efforts to appeal to a wide range of tastes, and 'fringe' events are intended to bring entertainments within the reach of all. Yet every year the onset of the festival is accompanied by what has became another annual event, a spate of letters to the press complaining about high ticket prices and elitism.

The nineteenth-century social divide between upper town gentry and the

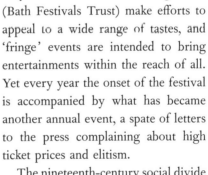

'THE FESTIVAL IS MAINLY FOR THE UPPER CLASS, WHO WANT TO LISTEN TO MORBID CHAMBER MUSIC ... WE MUST PLEASE THE SNOBS IN ROYAL CRESCENT, CIRCUS AND LANSDOWN ...'

left The Royal Crescent (with number 1, the Bath Preservation Trust's principal museum, at the far right of this photograph) provides an elegant backdrop to concerts and other events staged in the Victoria Park below.
PHOTOGRAPH: CARNEGIE, 2004

297

lower town working classes persists and is given expression in diatribes like the following, written by a resident of Twerton: 'Bath Festival is mainly for the upper class, who want to listen to morbid chamber music, and the likes of it. The festival is run at a loss each year, and they still carry on with it. We must please the snobs in Royal Crescent, Circus and Lansdown'.[18] Moreover, the best intentions of the organisers can be regarded as patronisingly offensive. The idea of setting up a 'soapbox' in the Abbey churchyard (as part of the Festival in 1994) was intended to add something definitely local to an event acknowledged to be 'full of imported culture', but instead of turning Bath's town square into a Hyde Park corner the soapbox provided a forum for councillors, businessmen, and clergymen.[19] One incensed resident, particularly put out by a 'sermon' from the soapbox, wrote to the *Bath Chronicle* to complain that setting the day, the time, the agenda, the speakers and the order of the speakers was 'more akin to an annual congress of a totalitarian regime, than anything symbolising free speech'.[20]

Ten years later, in August 2003, the Three Tenors – José Carreras, Placido Domingo and Luciano Pavarotti – gave another highly acclaimed concert in Victoria Park, raising £15,000 for charity. It was generally recognised as a great coup for Bath, despite the predictable complaints of a few begrudgers. In the same year, against a background of a critical report of management of the Bath Festival and continuing a financial deficit, a renewed attempt to incorporate all the festivals into an umbrella organisation promoting Bath as a 'festival city', prompted public resistance from the organisers of the International Guitar Festival. Other events in Bath's cultural calendar include the Literature Festival, the Film Festival and the Mozart Festival, each enjoying a separate identity while sharing booking arrangements through the festival office. Tim Joss, director of Bath Festivals Trust (before his departure in 2004) resisted the charge of elitism and remained upbeat about the prospect of the city of festivals concept forming a partnership between the Arts Council, Bath and North East Somerset Council and the Bath Festivals Trust. Marketing the city for the twenty-first century remains a challenge, just as it was for the city fathers of the early nineteenth century. On the other hand, some attempt has been made to incorporate all the people of Bath in the annual celebration. The opening night of the International Music Festival – the city's biggest free party – was voted Best Bath Event in 2003. Youth orchestras and a long overdue inclusion of jazz events have broadened the appeal of the music offered to the public.

THE AVERAGE HOUSE PRICE IN BATH [2003] ... WAS £207,287 ... AVERAGE MALE EARNINGS WERE RECKONED TO BE ABOUT £24,000 PER ANNUM.

Another persistent feature from the nineteenth century and earlier is the extremes of wealth and relative deprivation, if not absolute poverty, that continue to co-exist in Bath. These are particularly evident in the housing sector. The recession of the late 1980s stemmed the influx of wealthy new residents, but in the early 1990s the housing market showed signs of a slight recovery. Grade 1 listed houses are costly to purchase and expensive to maintain. Consequently, few complete period town houses come on the market (only five of the thirty houses in the Royal Crescent remain in single occupation) but, nonetheless, local estate agents were reporting renewed interest by the summer of 1994 from London commuters and by investors from Hong Kong, South Africa, North America and Europe. Houses in the Crescent were selling for some £850,000 to £975,000 in 1993 and 1994. The asking price for a five-bedroomed town house in Lansdown in 1994 was £290,000, and £245,000 for a Grade 1 listed house in St James Square. A Bath purchasing agent described his clients as 'well-heeled thirty-somethings looking for a permanent home in the £400,000 plus range'.[21] but such prices remained well beyond the reach of most of Bath's residents.

By 2003, house price inflation in Bath, saw even greater inequality in housing provision. Figures released by the Halifax Building Society in December recorded a total of 22 million-pound homes sold in Bath and North East Somerset since 1995, making Bath one of the top markets for million-pound homes outside London. Estate agents, Crisp Cowley revealed that a house in the Circus in 1982 would have cost around £125,000. This compares with a renovated house at the same address selling in 2002 for over £2 million.

Houses available on the market at the higher price range in 2003 included, a Grade 1 listed town house in Great Pulteney Street advertised for £1.5 million (where even a one-bedroom flat was selling for £220,000), and a four-bed Georgian town house in Cavendish Crescent offered for sale at £1.1 million. In the middle range, a four-bedroom Edwardian terraced house on Poets Corner, Bear Flat, was listed at £345,000, a five-bedroom, 1930s semi-detached on Newbridge Road (possibly built for around £750) had an asking price of £240,000 and two-bedroom flats were on offer at between £180,000 and £260,000 in Brock Street and Henrietta Street. The cheapest properties available were one-bedroom apartments; one in Twerton at £85,000, and one in Thomas Street (in need of decoration) at £105,000. It was reported that the average house price in Bath during April to June 2003 was £207,287. At the same time, average male earnings in Bath were reckoned to be about £24,000 per annum, slightly less than the national average. Key workers, nurses, teachers and firemen, were being priced out of the housing market in Bath. Head teachers lamented that some posts were difficult to fill as a result. By late 2004, the heat had gone out of the housing market, and there were predictions in the press of a future decline of twenty per cent in house prices.

Bath still contained sub-standard homes, lacking basic amenities or in a state of severe disrepair, co-existing with listed buildings in the World Heritage City. Housing reports issued in 1994 revealed that some 3,500 homes in Bath were unfit for habitation and a further 3,400 were in need of essential repairs.[22] Out of a total of 34,100 households surveyed, 10,007 were defined as 'in housing need'. Of these households, 117 lacked basic amenities such as a bath, inside toilet or hot water supply. A further 1,845 had to share facilities with another household, and 2,688 were in accommodation that was over-crowded.[23]

In the report of Avon County Council's Social Stress Study (published in

1994) two parts of the city – Abbey ward and Twerton ward – were classified as areas of social and economic deprivation. The criteria by which social stress was measured were criticised in the press by a councillor, photographed in the Circus, who declared 'I think it is an insult to the people who live in the Abbey ward'. The city centre, however, is not a homogeneous district of Georgian architecture and contemporary affluence. As in the nineteenth century, it remains one where the extremes of wealth and poverty are particularly apparent. The classification of working-class Twerton as deprived was accepted by the local press, as 'perhaps more predictable': 'Families are used to the description. They are also used to seeing little done'.[24] The former council estates in and around the city are benefiting from improvement schemes, and the council has powers to issue orders for repairs to private landlords, but the age of the city's housing stock means that poor housing is likely to be a feature of Bath for some time to come. About 40 per cent of houses in the city were built before 1891, and a further 16 per cent date from before 1850.[25]

In addition to those of its population living in sub-standard accommodation, Bath has a number of homeless people. In the early 1990s the problem was of sufficient scale to prompt action by the council, the churches, and various charities. A night shelter (initially funded by a £100,000 capital grant from the council) was established, and voluntary bodies organised 'soup runs' to those sleeping rough. During National Housing Week of 6–12 June 1994 the press gave publicity to a proposal to launch a 'deposit bond scheme' with the aim of helping 100 people a year to move into privately rented accommodation. Another organisation, the Bath Resettlement Service, was also active in helping the homeless. The reappearance of beggars on the streets of Bath was a feature of the early 1990s, closely associated with the rise in the numbers of the homeless caused by the effects of recession and government policies which restricted the right of young people to state benefits. The authorities' response to this phenomenon evokes reminders of past efforts to clear the streets of beggars, for fear of frightening away trade. Genuine humanitarian concern undoubtedly exists for the 'deserving

Part-funded by a huge Millennium Commission contribution of £7.78 million in 1997, the £23 million Bath Spa project has – at the time of going to press in 2006 – not yet opened to a bemused public. There is genuine admiration for the modern design, with its spectacular glass frontage and roof-top pool, but long delays and an accident-prone history have given rise to wry amusement at the embarrassing gap between the glowing rhetoric of the public relations effort and the grubby reality of the work, not yet done, by the private contractors.

BY COURTESY OF BATH CENTRAL LIBRARY, BATH & NORTH EAST SOMERSET COUNCIL

poor' of today, and this was reflected in the response of some councillors, clergymen, the local MP, and several local residents to Prime Minister John Major's remarks in May 1994 about 'offensive and unjustified' beggars. Indeed, a police inspector commented on the liberal tendencies of 'a substantial proportion of people' in Bath, and recalled some members of the public giving money to beggars even as the 'offender' was being cautioned by a policeman.[26] Nonetheless, a complaint that has echoed down the centuries was reiterated in a letter to the *Bath Chronicle* in June 1994, in which the writer expressed the view that 'a lot of the begging here is a con trick' and went on to ask 'why do beggars only appear in the honey-pot areas?' The affluence of Bath, with its comfortably-off residents and its numerous wealthy visitors, has traditionally been a 'honey-pot' attracting the poor in search of charity. Alarmist news reports of beggars making easy money on the streets are nothing new either, and similarities with the past are also discernible in the efforts of the authorities to regulate street life, and to discriminate between the 'deserving' and 'undeserving' poor.

By the summer of 1994, aggressive begging had been stamped out by the 'strenuous efforts' of the council and the police. The activities of some of Bath's beggars in the early 1990s (most of them young, often accompanied by large dogs, and not always sober) did undoubtedly amount to harassment, and their presence was an irritation if nothing more to many residents and visitors. For retailers and those involved in the tourist trade, they also posed a genuine threat to business by directly intimidating some passers-by and deterring others from frequenting the central areas. However, the available evidence suggests that the numbers of aggressive beggars were few, but that somewhat extreme measures were taken to suppress them. The combined efforts of the council and the police included a more rigorous enforcement of existing laws and the introduction of a by-law prohibiting the drinking of alcohol in public places. As part of this initiative the *Big Issue* magazine for the homeless came to Bath. Those who sell the *Big Issue* (and earn money by retaining a proportion of their takings) are issued with an official badge, which is withdrawn if complaints are made against the vendor: it clearly identifies them as the new 'deserving poor'. Nevertheless, local residents complain regularly of running the gauntlet of *Big Issue* vendors in walking through the central streets of the city.

The regulation of street life has been a perennial concern of the authorities throughout Bath's history, and today the buskers as well as the beggars are subject to social control. They operate under an agreed code of practice, and in 1993 the Guild of Buskers was formed to give a voice to the street entertainers of Bath. They seem to be popular with the tourists and they feature in much of the publicity that advertises the city, but complaints from city-centre residents and shopkeepers about noise levels and affronts to public decency led to greater restrictions on their activities in the summer of 1994. Thereafter performing in the streets after 10 pm was banned, and the press reported that the police would be given powers to 'crack down on any dress, actions or words by buskers which are likely to cause alarm or distress to the public'.[27] On one celebrated occasion embarrassment was caused to American visitors in the Pump Room, who were confronted by the outdoor spectacle of near-naked street entertainers in Abbey churchyard, distracting them from drinking their afternoon tea.

Criminal activity in the city is another perennial feature, with modern overtones. Bath has its share of petty crime and urban disorder, but violent events such as murder are rare. Vehicle-related offences were the predominant crime problem in Bath during 1990, when theft of and from motor vehicles accounted for a third of total crime.[28] Car crime continued into the new century, while the theft of mobile phones became a new offence prompted by fashion and technological advance. The court reports in the local press are a catalogue of vandalism, shoplifting, benefit fraud, drink- and drug-related offences, and prosecutions for using televisions without a licence. The map location of weekly burglaries became a new feature reported in the *Bath Chronicle*. Inner city rioting is unknown in Bath, although in 1992 an incident on one of the suburban council estates escalated into a major disturbance, during which some forty youths stoned a bus, set fire to a car, and smashed windows in houses and shops, before the police gained control of the situation.[29] (This took place in Twerton, which has a reputation reinforced by repetition: the disturbances of 1992 were recalled in a press report of 1994, about planned improvements to the estate.) Arson attacks on cars have persisted on council estates and there has even been the odd incident of lead-pipe bombs being found in city schools. A few shops in Bath have been burgled by 'ram raiders', but the metal blinds that protect retail premises in many towns have not been allowed to disfigure the Georgian city. The installation of roller shutters requires planning permission, and the view of the planning authority is that such shutters could 'destroy the appearance of the street to the detriment of both the residents and the tourists, who like to window-shop in the evenings and at weekends'.[30] The police constantly reassure the public that crime in general has fallen during recent years (some 7 per cent within Bath and North East Somerset between 2002 and 2003), with particular reductions in the number of domestic burglaries, stolen cars, robberies and thefts from vehicles. The fear of crime remains greater than its recorded incidence.

The retail sector of the economy was badly affected by a decline in trade as the recession deepened, in the early 1990s. High rents and business rates forced out many retailers from the shopping complexes built in the 1980s. About 6 per cent of the city's shops were empty in May 1993. Shop after shop closed down in the Colonnades complex until by June 1994 only one tenant, the Tourist Information Centre, remained in the development.[31] The recession also deterred investors from redeveloping various sites in the city, including the Empire Hotel beside the Guildhall.

In the mid-1990s future prospects improved. Plans to rejuvenate the spa were set in motion, the Empire Hotel was converted into expensive luxury accommodation, and an 'Ideas for Bath' exhibition at the Hot Bath Gallery attracted much interest. Yet the mood was also one of anxiety and uncertainty. The Ministry of Defence decision, finally made in June 1995, to close its Foxhill site and relocate some 1,600 jobs, caused concern because of its consequences for local employment.

The city also faced uncertainties in other areas. Political change occurred in Bath after some fifty years of Conservative dominance. The city consistently returned a Conservative MP at every general election from 1945 until 1992, when the electorate rejected Chris Patten in favour of a Liberal Democrat, Don Foster. The revival of Liberalism in Bath also gave the city a Liberal Democrat council, which made some controversial decisions and thereby prompted a long-overdue renewal of public interest in municipal politics. The reorganisation of local government, in order to create a few unitary authorities, swept away Avon County Council, and the Bath and Wansdyke councils combined to become Bath and North East Somerset in 1996, thus posing problems of identity for both the people of Bath and those living in and around Radstock, Keynsham and the Chew Valley. Tensions between the perceived interests of Bath and those of the old Wansdyke district remained a key theme embracing local issues, posing the question of the long-term viability of Bath and North East Somerset as a political entity. In two successive elections, the Bath and North East Somerset electorate have produced hung councils, with no single party exercising power. Perhaps it is too early to offer a judgement on the effectiveness of the cooperation across the party divide in the new executive council. Local politics offers voters the unedifying spectacle of constant sniping between individual councillors in the letter columns of the local press, and a perpetual barrage of criticism from council taxpayers who denounce the excesses and failures of council policies. We might speculate whether Bath and North East Somerset Council will have the short-lived fate of the unlamented Avon Council. The position of mayor of Bath has survived as a ceremonial post, sitting uncomfortably alongside a new post of chairman of the council. Bath citizens feel a loss of identity within Bath and North East Somerset, a feeling that has been exploited by the 'back to Bath' movement led by an ex-mayor of the city. Outside the city in north-east Somerset, there is considerable resentment against expenditure in Bath regarded as extravagant and wasteful.[32]

New schemes and a new Bath

The plethora of development schemes proposed for Bath promise a new Bath for the twenty-first century. Yet the age-old tension between the needs of residents and those of tourists remains a central concern in the implementation of plans designed to improve the fabric and amenities of the city. Serious problems have to be addressed and the solutions need to be successfully incorporated into major developments. First among these is the poor quality of transport provision in and around the city. Overseas visitors encounter a transport infrastructure that is well below the best standards of continental Europe. The train services from London continue to be some of the worst in the country. Frequent delays infuriate daily commuters to London, visitors and local residents. The persistence of the wrong time on Bath Spa station clock provides a fitting symbol of the poor service available to train passengers. Furthermore, the palliatives that have been employed to reduce congestion, new signs, one-way systems, various park and ride schemes and a half-hearted pedestrianisation, have had only a marginal effect on traffic flow while managing to irritate city retailers. Improved transport provision remains a key objective in new plans for the development of the city.

The key new development plans, the Spa, the Southgate Shopping Centre, and Western Riverside, will collectively transform the look of the city and contribute substantially to its future prospects. With the approval of the Lord Chancellor for the title of the 'New Royal Bath', the Spa is almost complete while the other two schemes are still in the planning or even pre-planning stage and are set to rumble on for many years to come. Part-funded by a Millennium Commission contribution of £7.78 million in 1997, the £23 million Bath Spa project has evoked a mixed response among the local citizenry. Some have certainly shared the excitement of the council executive director, Nicole O'Flaherty, at a prospect of bringing back to public use a facility that was used 2,000 years ago. There is genuine admiration for the modern design, by Sir Nicholas Grimshaw, with its spectacular glass frontage and roof-top pool. However, the long delays in the opening of the Spa and an accident-prone history in its completion have given rise to wry amusement at the embarrassing gap between the glowing rhetoric of the public relations effort and the grubby reality of the work, not yet done, by the private contractors. This reached a high point with the arrival of the Three Tenors at Bath in August 2003 for their concert in front of the Royal Crescent. This was timed to coincide with the opening of the Spa. They were duly filmed at the roof-top pool, but the opening was again delayed. Apparently, the wrong paint had been used and the work had to be done again. The contractors were forced by legal injunction to allow new contractors in to re-paint the interior. Due to open in the year 2000, Bath Spa will not open until sometime in 2006.

The combination of Bath and North East Somerset Council and private developers has not proved an efficient or harmonious partnership. With the same uncomfortable bedfellows – the council and private contractors – signed up for much more ambitious schemes for the Southgate Shopping Centre and Western Riverside, the prospects for budget overspend, disputes over project management, and continual delays, seem all too likely. The Southgate scheme

An attentive crowd enjoying the performance of one of Bath's street entertainers, at a prime location beside the Pump Room.

BATH CENTRAL LIBRARY, LOOSE PICTURES COLLECTION

is now seen to be an urgent priority if Bath is to compete with rival shopping centres in Bristol and Swindon. The prospect of replacing the ugly centre built in the 1970s with a more aesthetic development to include shops, offices, housing, and the bonus of an integrated transport system connecting the railway and bus stations, has widespread support. Yet, even at an early stage of planning, concessions have had to be made to the developer, Morley Fund Management, over the commitments originally made of £2.9 million towards the city's transport plans. Approval of the scheme was reached in the summer of 2003, but given the experience with Bath Spa, it would be over optimistic to envisage trouble-free progress in the implementation of the Southgate development.

Plans for Western Riverside, the biggest brownfield development site in the South West, also became clearer in November 2003 when a proposed starting date of the end of 2006 was announced. Artistic impressions of the plans to transform 50 acres of derelict land to the west of the city conjure up the exciting prospect of integration between the existing fabric of Bath's historic buildings with modern world-class architecture and design. The important project spearheaded by Bath and North East Somerset Council, Grosvenor Estates and the South West Regional Development Agency includes high-quality, high density and mixed-use urban development providing vital homes, shops, offices, leisure and community facilities. It is hoped that the scheme will create 10,000 new jobs in Bath. Inevitably, in the selling of the scheme to the public, eager anticipation competes with a certain wariness over long delays experienced in the past. The prospect of a scheme involving an ultimate new build of over three million square feet, a Light Rapid Transit system, a river taxi service, new cycle ways and new open spaces have to be tempered by the long duration of between 15 and 20 years predicted for the completion of the scheme. A spokesman added a sober note to public relations rhetoric in admitting the nature, scale and complexity of the project presented a number of significant challenges: 'The end result will be worthwhile, even if the journey is sometimes uncomfortable.' He predicted that the success of the scheme depended on the commitment and patience of the local community. A great deal rides on its ultimate success, not only for Bath, but for the wider region of north-east Somerset.

Alongside local re-organisation, Bath's civic leaders need to think on a more international scale, making full use of the city's rich diversity and history to create a more sophisticated appeal to visitors from around the world. Many tourists make a depressingly brief visit to the Pump Room and the Roman Baths, purchase a cheap souvenir in Bath Mementos and then depart quickly on the coach to Oxford or Stratford. This produces little cultural or commercial gain for the city, at the heavy price of more annoyance to residents. Bath has always had to respond to changing circumstances and will do so again, albeit reluctantly in the future.

A current example of the popular resistance to change is posed by the expansion of student numbers at Bath University and at Bath Spa University, which became a full university in 2005. While being very different institutions, one a leading research-based university, mostly in science subjects, the other a teacher-led institution specialising in the Humanities, Creative and Performing Arts and Education, they have both grown impressively through popular demand in an expanded higher education sector. This has created a strong pressure on housing provision in Bath. Oldfield Park, with 30 per cent of properties occupied by students, is only the most visible of areas now dominated by a student presence. Local residents have proved highly vocal in their protests at the presence of large numbers of students in their midst. Strong objections have been raised against threats to the green belt at Claverton Down where the University of Bath proposes to build more facilities and accommodation, even to the extent of a suggestion from one angry resident that the university should move completely out of Bath, instead of building merely a new campus at Swindon. Bath Spa University's plan for new student housing on the old Hygate Gear site on the Bristol Road also met with fierce opposition from local residents. The scheme was approved on appeal, yet the need for more student housing remains as the numbers continue to rise in line with government targets. The importance of the financial input into the local economy, from the presence of students and staff, has been calmly put forward by spokesmen for the universities, and there is some recognition of the contribution made by students to employment, charitable and sporting activity in the city. However, these general considerations appear to have less force than the threat of encroachment. The irony is that every medium-sized city in the country without a university is keen to have one for the financial benefits alone. Bath is fortunate to have two such institutions, albeit relatively small in total student numbers.

Such competing interests within the city highlight the difficulties in planning for the future. Could a positive way forward be found in harnessing the most important visions of past centuries as models for developing the city for the twenty-first century? Remembering the architectural and aesthetic vision of John Wood (father and son) in the eighteenth century, recognising the unifying purpose of Jerom Murch's civic gospel of the Victorian period and drawing on the utopian planning of Patrick Abercrombie after the Second World War, would set the precedents. What is required is a new vision that draws on the rich legacy of the city's past for the benefit of its present and future citizens – a difficult task as earlier historic attempts have shown. There are some grounds for qualified optimism in the City of Bath World Heritage Site Management Plan, published in November 2003. At least some lessons have clearly been learnt from the disastrous mistakes committed in the 1970s with 'the Sack of Bath' and the new building that never rose above the nondescript and the ugly, representing a betrayal of Bath's architectural heritage. Now conservation is king. What is less clear is the conflict between the acknowledged responsibility to preserve the city's outstanding historic townscape and archaeological remains and the pressing needs of its citizens who wish to live in a thriving, living city. The intention is to use Bath's status as a World Heritage Site to support and further the vitality of the local community. It does gloss over the age-old tension between the needs of visitors and residents and possibly underestimates the resistance to change still prevalent among sections of the population. A popular perception is that the funding of grand schemes such as the new Bath Spa comes at the expense of less glamorous provision, old people's day centres, youth clubs, and improving the facilities available for those living on the fringes of the city and in other parts of north-east Somerset.

What seems likely is that commercial imperatives will continue to foster images of Bath that support the generation of tourist money, images that can sit uneasily alongside the realities for people who live in the city.

Acknowledgements

Our enthusiasm for the study of Bath history has been shared with our own undergraduate and postgraduate students at Bath Spa University, formerly Bath College of Higher Education, and we have drawn on their research as well as our own in the writing of this book. Inevitably, in a full history of Bath, we have consulted the work of specialists in the Roman, medieval, and Stuart periods, Barry Cunliffe, Peter Davenport and John Wroughton, as well as scholars who have written on more modern aspects of the city's past, notably R. S. Neale, a pioneer in the social history of Bath. In addition to the many books written on Bath, the volumes of Bath History, edited by Brenda Buchanan, have provided an important source of specialist articles.

Two other sources have proved invaluable in tracking down illustrations and information on buildings: James Lees Milne and David Ford's *Images of Bath*, and Michael Forsyth's *Bath*, in the Pevsner Architectural Guides series.

We would like to acknowledge the advice and guidance given to us on the illustrations as well as the text in local libraries, archives and specialist collections. Our thanks go to Colin Johnston, the Head Archivist and to Lucy Powell, his assistant, at the Bath Record Office in the Guildhall; to Stephanie Round, the Local History librarian at Bath Central Library and assistant Helen Button; to Ruth Moppett at the Victoria Art Gallery; to Eleanor Murphy at the Bath Preservation Trust; to staff at the University of Bath Library and the Newton Park Library at Bath Spa University; to Stephen Clews, the curator of the Roman Baths Museum; to Peter Martin, the head verger at Bath Abbey; to Stuart Burroughs at the Museum of Bath at Work; and to Cathryn Spence at the Building of Bath Museum. We are most grateful to Jane Jones, of the School of Historical and Cultural Studies at Bath Spa, who provided invaluable assistance in processing the text.

A special debt of gratitude is owed to Alistair Hodge and his team at Carnegie Publishing, who took an active interest at every stage of production, but also took on a leading role in the research, selection and production of the illustrations. This expertise in illustrations has given the book an important dimension that not only complements the written text but offers the reader fresh images of the city, many previously unpublished, and with a quality of production that is greatly superior to that usually offered to the public. In particular, the inclusion of early maps of the city will add immeasurably to local knowledge of medieval and early modern Bath. The many modern photographs capture Bath in all its diversity, in all its magnificence, and at the same time including the unsavoury side of its fascinating history.

Notes and references

Note to Introduction

1. R. S. Neale, *Bath: A Social History, 1680–1850, or A Valley of Pleasure, yet a Sink of Iniquity* (London, 1981), p. 1.

Notes to Chapter 1: Origins and early history

1. P. Cresswell (ed.), *Bath in Quotes: A Literary View from Saxon Times Onwards* (Bath, 1985), p. 19.
2. Information on the local topography, landscape and geology is taken from Michael Aston and Rob Iles (eds), *The Archaeology of Avon: A Review from the Neolithic to the Middle Ages* (Avon County Council, n.d., *c.*1985) and Mick Aston, 'The Bath Region from Late Pre-historic to the Middle Ages', *Bath History*, i (1986), pp. 61–89.
3. John Haddon, *Portrait of Bath* (London, 1982), p. 19.
4. Charles Moore, 'On the Middle and Upper Lias of the South-West of England', *Proceedings of the Somerset Natural History and Archaeological Society*, vol. 13 (1865), p. 128, cited in Angus Buchanan and Neil Cossons, *Industrial Archaeology of the Bristol Region* (Newton Abbot, 1969), p. 101.
5. John Haddon, *Portrait of Avon* (London, 1981), pp. 23–4.
6. Jane Austen, *Persuasion* (first published 1818; paperback edition, Ware, Herts, 1993), p. 19.
7. Daniel Defoe, *A Tour Through the Whole Island of Great Britain* (1724–26) (Harmondsworth, 1971), p. 359.
8. See R. S. Neale, *Bath*, on Wood's version of the Britannic myth: chapter 6, 'Ideology and Utopia', III, pp. 186–90. For more recent works on John Wood see Tim Mowl, *John Wood: Architect of Obsession* (Bath, 1998) and Kirsten Elliott, *Myth-maker: John Wood 1704–1754* (Bath, 2004).
9. Aston, 'The Bath Region', pp. 66–7.
10. *Ibid*, p. 68.
11. *The Victoria County History of Somerset* (1904), vol. 1, p. 83.
12. Unless otherwise indicated, all archaeological information is taken *passim* from Michael Aston and Rob Iles (eds), *The Archaeology of Avon*.
13. Aston, *Bath Region*, p. 67.
14. Barry Cunliffe, *Roman Bath Discovered* (Stroud, Gloucestershire: 2000), pp. 10–12.
15. Peter Davenport, 'Town and Country: Roman Bath and its Hinterland', *Bath History*, v (1994), pp. 7–33, p. 10. See also Aston, 'Bath Region', pp. 69–73 on the Roman period.
16. Our main sources on Bath as the spa town Aquae Sulis are Barry Cunliffe, *Roman Bath*, *passim*, and articles by Peter Davenport cited in the references below.

17. Peter Davenport, '*Aquae Sulis*: The Origins and Development of a Roman Town', *Bath History*, viii (2000), pp. 7–23, p. 8.
18. *Ibid*, pp. 11–13.
19. *Ibid*, pp. 15–17.
20. Davenport, 'Town and Country', p. 13.
21. Davenport, '*Aquae Sulis*', p. 21.
22. R. S. O. Tomlin, 'Voices from the Sacred Spring', *Bath History*, iv (1992), pp. 7–24, p. 16.
23. Jean Manco, 'Saxon Bath: the Legacy of Rome and the Saxon Re-Birth', *Bath History*, vii (1998), pp. 27–54, pp. 31–2.
24. Barry Cunliffe, *Roman Bath* (Batsford/English Heritage edn, 1995), p. 103.
25. *Ibid*.
26. Cunliffe, *Roman Bath* (Batsford/English Heritage edition), p. 109.
27. Davenport, 'Town and Country', p. 109.
28. *Ibid*, pp. 15–21.
29. Aston and Iles, *Archaeology of Avon*, p. 60.
30. *Ibid*, p. 65.
31. Cunliffe, *Roman Bath* (Batsford/English Heritage edn), p. 109.
32. Aston and Iles, *Archaeology of Avon*, p. 67.
33. Davenport, Town and Country, pp. 21–2.
34. Cunliffe, *Roman Bath* (Stroud, 2000 edition), p. 143.
35. Aston and Iles, *Archaeology of Avon*, p. 69.
36. *Ibid*, p. 70.
37. The poem is quoted in many of the books on Bath. The earliest copy in existence, made in the tenth century, was presented to Exeter Cathedral in 1050 by Leofric, its first bishop.
38. Peter Davenport, *Medieval Bath Uncovered* (Stroud, 2002), pp. 22–4.
39. *Ibid*, p. 24.
40. Manco, 'Saxon Bath', p. 32.
41. Peter Davenport, 'Bath Abbey', *Bath History*, ii (1988), pp. 1–26, p. 1.
42. Davenport, *Medieval Bath*, pp. 34–5.
43. John Haddon, *Bath* (Bath, 1973), pp. 37–8.
44. Peter Davenport, *Bath Abbey*, pp. 34–5.

45. Manco, 'Saxon Bath', p. 37.

46. Kenneth Hylson-Smith, *Bath Abbey: A History* (The Friends of Bath Abbey, Bath, 1988), pp. 55–6.

47. Manco, *'Saxon Bath'*, pp. 47–8.

48. *Ibid*, p. 39.

49. *Ibid*, pp. 40–2.

50. *Ibid*, p. 50.

51. Davenport, *Medieval Bath*, p. 63.

Notes to Chapter 2: Norman Conquest to 1700

1. John Haddon, *Bath* (Bath, 1973), p. 40.

2. Peter Davenport, *Medieval Bath Uncovered* (Stroud, 2002), p. 71.

3. *Ibid*, pp. 71–2.

4. Peter Davenport, 'Bath Abbey', *Bath History*, ii (1988), pp. 1–26, p. 8.

5. Kenneth Hylson-Smith, *Bath Abbey: A History* (The Friends of Bath Abbey, Bath, 1988), p. 71.

6. Davenport, *Medieval Bath*, p. 74.

7. Robert Bell, 'Bath Abbey: Some New Perspectives', *Bath History*, vi (1996), pp. 7–24, p. 18.

8. Hylson-Smith, *Bath Abbey*, p. 71.

9. Davenport, 'Bath Abbey', p. 11.

10. Quoted in Haddon, *Bath*, p. 46.

11. Austin J. King and B. H. Wells, *The Municipal Records of Bath, 1189 to 1604* (London, Bath; n.d., *c.*1900), p. 42.

12. Davenport, *Medieval Bath*, p. 99.

13. Elizabeth Holland, 'The Earliest Bath Guildhall', *Bath History*, ii (1988), pp. 163–80, pp. 163–5.

14. Davenport, *Medieval Bath*, p. 99.

15. King and Watts, *Municipal Records*, pp. 14–15.

16. Davenport, *Medieval Bath*, p. 120.

17. *Ibid*, p. 108.

18. *Ibid*, p. 107.

19. *Ibid*, p. 172.

20. Barry Cunliffe, *The City of Bath* (Gloucester, 1986), p. 89.

21. Davenport, *Medieval Bath*, pp. 109–10.

22. Holland, 'The Earliest Bath Guildhall', p. 168.

23. Jean Manco, 'Bath and "The Great Rebuilding"', *Bath History*, iv (1992), pp. 25–51, p. 41.

24. R. W. Dunning, *A History of Somerset* (Bridgewater, 1987), p. 17.

25. Hylson-Smith, *Bath Abbey*, pp. 100–1.

26. *Ibid*, p. 101.

27. Cunliffe, *City of Bath*, p. 91.

28. Davenport, *Medieval Bath*, p. 166.

29. *Ibid*, p. 168.

30. Hylson-Smith, *Bath Abbey*, p. 119.

31. *Ibid*, pp. 120–1.

32. Davenport, 'Bath Abbey', p. 22.

33. Hylson-Smith, *Bath Abbey*, p. 121; Davenport, *Medieval Bath*, pp. 65, 137.

34. Davenport, *Medieval Bath*, p. 171.

35. Hylson-Smith, *Bath Abbey*, p. 123.

36. Holland, 'The Earliest Bath Guildhall', p. 169.

37. Sylvia McIntyre, 'Bath: The rise of a Resort Town, 1660–1800', in Peter Clark (ed.), *Country Towns in Pre-industrial England* (Leicester, 1981), p. 222.

38. John Wroughton, *Stuart Bath: Life in the Forgotten City, 1603–1714* (Bath, 2004), pp. 25–6.

39. John Wroughton, *The Civil War in Bath and North Somerset* (Bath, 1973), pp. 58–84.

40. John Wroughton, 'Puritanism and Traditionalism: Cultural and Political Division in Bath, 1620–1662', *Bath History*, iv (1992), pp. 52–70, p. 55. See also Wroughton, *Stuart Bath*, for a more detailed account.

41. Wroughton, *Stuart Bath*, pp. 39–41; Wroughton, *Civil War*, *passim*; see also Robert Dunning, *The Monmouth Rebellion. A Complete Guide to the Rebellion and Bloody Assize* (Wimborne, 1984).

42. Wroughton, *Stuart Bath*, pp. 39–40. Copies of the original warrant (16 November 1685) are held at Bath Reference Library. Copy dated July 1786: AL374A; copy made *c.*1800: AL374B.

43. Manco, 'Bath and "The Great Rebuilding"', pp. 26–7.

44. Davenport, *Medieval Bath*, p. 145.

45. Manco, 'Bath and "The Great Rebuilding"', pp. 46–7.

46. McIntyre, *Bath*, p. 201.

47. Wroughton, *Stuart Bath*, pp. 9, 57; Wroughton, *Civil War*. All that follows on life in seventeenth-century Bath is drawn from Wroughton's chapter one, 'Bath on the Eve of War', pp. 1–17. For a more detailed account of this period see Wroughton, *Stuart Bath: Life in the Forgotten City, 1603–1714* (Bath, 2004).

48. Christopher Morris (ed.), *The Journeys of Celia Fiennes* (London, 1947), p. 21.

49. Manco, 'Bath and "The Great Rebuilding"', pp. 26–9.

50. McIntyre, 'Bath', pp. 202–3.

51. Wroughton, *Civil War*, pp. 9–10.

52. McIntyre, 'Bath', pp. 202–3.

53. *Ibid*.

54. John Wroughton, *An Unhappy Civil War. The Experiences of Ordinary People in Gloucestershire, Somerset and Wiltshire, 1642–1646* (Bath, 1999), pp. 165–7.

55. For a full discussion of puritanism in Bath and religion in the city after the restoration, see Wroughton, *Stuart Bath*, chapter 14, 'Religious Life', pp. 167–91.

56. Jean Manco, 'The Cross Bath', *Bath History*, ii (1988), pp. 49–84, pp. 64–5.

57. Bryan Little, *Bath Portrait* (Bristol, 1961), p. 31.

58. Roger Rolls, *The Hospital of the Nation: The Story of Spa Medicine and the Mineral Water Hospital at Bath* (Bath, 1988), p. 2.

Notes for Chapter 3: Frivolity and fashion, 1700–1820

1. R. S. Neale, *Bath: A Social History 1680–1850, or A Valley of Pleasure, yet a Sink of Iniquity* (London, 1981); David Gadd, *Georgian Summer: The Rise and Development of Bath* (Newbury, 1987).

2. Princess Amelia's journey is described in Benjamin Price, *The Benevolent Man, A Life of Ralph Allen of Bath* (Harvard University Press, Cambridge, Mass., 1967); information on boat services between Bath and Bristol is taken from this source, p. 25.

3. Neale, *Bath*, p. 118.

4. C.W. Chalklin, *The Provincial Towns of Georgian England. A Study of the Building Process, 1740–1820* (London, 1974), pp. 182–6. The role of international and national credit is emphasised by R. S. Neale, but see Chalklin, *Provincial Towns of England*, for detailed analysis of regional and local investment in urban development in Bath and other towns between 1740 and 1820. On investment in the Bath Turnpike Trust and other information about capital investment in the Bath region, see B. J. Buchanan, 'The evolution of the English turnpike trusts: lessons from a case study,' in *Economic History Review*, 2nd series, xxxix, 2 (1986), pp. 223–43; 'Aspects of capital formation: some insights from North Somerset, 1750–1830', *Southern History*, vol. 8 (1986), pp. 73–93.

5. Neale, *Bath*, p. 151.

6. *Ibid*, pp. 165–209.

7. Tobias Smollett, *The Expedition of Humphry Clinker* (1771; Harmondsworth, 1983), p. 63.

8. Anon., 'Bath – A Simile' (1779), quoted in Neale, *Bath*, p. 205.

9. Sylvia McIntyre, 'Bath: The Rise of a Resort Town, 1660–1800', in Peter Clark (ed.), *Country Towns in Pre-industrial England* (Leicester, 1981), table 22, p. 226.

10. Neale, *Bath*, p. 180.

11. McIntyre, 'Bath', p. 225.

12. *Ibid*, p. 226.

13. Chalklin, *Provincial Towns*, pp. 182–3.

14. *Ibid*, p. 78.

15. *Ibid*, p. 78

16. *Ibid*, p. 78.

17. Neale, *Bath*, p. 148.

18. Buchanan, 'The evolution of the English turnpike trusts', pp. 231–2.

19. Letter of Fanny Burney to her sister Hetty, quoted in Maggie Lane, *A City of Palaces: Bath through the eyes of Fanny Burney* (Millstream Books, Bath, 1999), pp. 47–8.

20. Brian Little, *Bath Portrait* (Bristol, 1961), p. 80.

21. Neale, *Bath*, pp. 40–1.

22. McIntyre, 'Bath', pp. 208–10.

23. R. W. Dunning, *A History of Somerset* (Bridgwater, 1987), p. 80.

24. Daniel Defoe, *A Tour Through the Whole Island of Great Britain* (1724–26) (Harmondsworth, 1971), p. 360.

25. From Christopher Anstey, 'A Farewell to Bath' in *The New Bath Guide* (London, 1767), in Paul Cresswell, *Bath in Quotes. A Literary View from Saxon Times Onwards* (Bath, 1985), p. 69.

26. Roger Rolls, *The Hospital of the Nation: The Story of Spa Medicine and the Mineral Water Hospital at Bath* (Bath, 1988), p. 80.

27. Thomas Haynes Bayly, *Amenities of Bath* (London, 1820).

28. McIntyre, 'Bath', pp. 204–6.

29. Smollett, *Humphry Clinker*, p. 68.

30. Graham Davis, 'Entertainments in Georgian Bath: Gambling and Vice', *Bath History*, i (1986), pp. 1–26.

31. Smollett, *Humphry Clinker*, pp. 78–9.

32. *Miseries of Human Life or the Groans of Samuel Sensitive and Timothy Testy* (London, 1806), p. 87.

33. Chalklin, *Provincial Towns*, pp. 52–3.

34. Jane Austen, *Persuasion* (Ware, Herts, 1993), p. 19.

35. Anon., 'A Step to the Bath with a Character of the Place', 1700, quoted in Neale, *Bath*, p. 12.

Notes to Chapter 4: The lower orders, 1700–1820

1. R. S. Neale, *Bath, A Social History 1680–1850, or A Valley of Pleasure, yet a Sink of Iniquity'* (London, 1981), pp. 49–94; Sylvia McIntyre, 'Bath: the rise of a resort town, 1660–1800' in Peter Clark (ed.), *County Towns in Pre-industrial England* (Leicester University Press, 1981).

2. Bath Library, Grosses' Glossary, *The Beggars of Bath* (1790).

3. R. Rolls, *The Hospital of the Nation: the Story of Spa Medicine and the Mineral Water Hospital at Bath* (Bath, 1988), p. 9.

4. Rolls, *Hospital of the Nation*, p. 77.

5. Neale, *Bath*, pp. 70–9.

6. M. Brown and J. Samuel, 'The Jews in Bath', *Bath History*, i (1986), pp. 150–72.

7. Trevor Fawcett, 'Black people in Georgian Bath', *Avon Past*, 16 (Spring 1993), pp. 3–9.

8. McIntyre, 'Bath: the rise of a resort town', p. 215.

9. Trevor Fawcett, 'Eighteenth-century shops and luxury trade', *Bath History*, iii (1990), pp. 49–75, p. 49.

10. Bath Record Office, Poor Law Settlement Examinations, 7 September 1764.

11. McIntyre, 'Bath: the rise of a resort town', p. 238.

12. Louis Simond, *Journal of a Tour and Residence in Great Britain* (1810–11), in Paul Cresswell (ed.), *Bath in Quotes: A Literary View from Saxon Times Onwards* (Ashgrove Press, Bath, 1985), p. 83.

13. Bath Record Office, Poor Law Settlement Examinations, 21 May 1763.

14. Jan Chivers, 'In the midst of life' – sudden death in Bath, 1776–1835: a study of the Coroners' Examinations and Inquisitions', MA, Local and Regional History, Bath Spa University College, 1997.

15. Bath Record Office, Coroners' Inquests, 14 April 1783.
16. Graham Davis, 'Entertainments in Georgian Bath: Gambling and Vice', *Bath History*, i (1986), pp. 1–26.
17. Bath Record Office, Coroners' Inquests, 6 March 1815.
18. Steve Pool, 'Radicalism, loyalism and the "Reign of Terror" in Bath, 1792–1804', *Bath History*, iii (1990), p. 120.

Notes to Chapter 5: Genteel residence, 1820–1914
1. R. Mainwaring, *Annals of Bath* (Bath, 1838), p. 262.
2. Bath Library, 'Bodies and Souls: a discursive paper with Glimpses of the City of Bath' (1864).
3. Bath Library, A letter to the mayor of Bath on the causes of the present declining condition of the city, LUD HUDIBRAS (Bath, 1840).
4. S. Gibbs, *The Bath Visitant* (Bath, 1844), pp. 56–7.
5. E. Yates, 'A Week in Bath', *The World*, 8 April 1891.
6. *Ibid*.
7. *The Guide Through and Round Bath* (1900), p. 10.
8. Bryan Little, *Bath Portrait* (Bristol, 1961), pp. 92–3.
9. *Ibid*, p. 99.
10. *Bath Chronicle*, 4 December 1890.
11. R. Warner, *A History of Bath* (Bath, 1801), p. 344.
12. *Bath Guide* (1900), p. 7.
13. Bruce Crofts, *Forgotten Year: News from Bath in 1882* (Bath, 1982), pp. 4–5.
14. R. Mainwaring, *Narrative of the Progress of an epidemic disease which appeared at Bath in the autumn of 1832* (Bath, 1833); see also Clive Charlton, 'Cholera in Bath, 1832–1866', MA in Local and Regional History Dissertation, Bath Spa University College, 2001.
15. Bath Library, *The Denunciad up to date*, by Cynic, dedicated to the Bath Corporation, in 2 parts (1898, 1902), p. 7.
16. *The Original Bath Guide* (1830), p. 51.
17. Bath Redivivus, *St Stephen's Review*, 29 October 1887.
18. John Wroughton (ed.), *Bath in the Age of Reform 1830–1841* (Bath, 1972), pp. 59–66.
19. *Ibid*, pp. 67–9.
20. *Ibid*, pp. 74–7.
21. Barry Cunliffe, *The City of Bath* (Gloucester, 1986),

Notes for Chapter 6: A city at work, 1820–1914
1. R. S. Neale, 'The standard of living, 1780–1844: a regional and class study', *Economic History Review*, 19 (1966), p. 592.
2. *Ibid*, p. 593.
3. Duncan Harper, *Bath at Work* (Bath, 1989), p. 7.
4. Mary Ede, 'Bath and the Great Exhibition of 1851', *Bath History*, iii (1990), pp. 139–58.
5. Harper, *Bath at Work*, p. 91.
6. Hugh Torrens, *The Evolution of a Family Firm: Stothert & Pitt of Bath* (Bath, 1978). See also Ken Andrews and Stuart Burroughs, *Stothert & Pitt: Cranemakers to the World* (Stroud, 2003).
7. R. S. Neale, *A Social History 1680–1850, or A Valley of*

19. *Ibid*, pp. 114–37, from which information in the following section is chiefly drawn. See also Neale, *Bath*, pp. 310–15.
20. Neale, *Bath*, pp. 50–6, 63–9.
21. John Cam Hobhouse, 'Snug Lying' from *Wonders of a Week at Bath* (1811), in Cresswell, *Bath in Quotes*, pp. 80–1.

pp. 157–60.
22. *Ibid*, p. 160.
23. *Ibid*.
24. Crofts, *Forgotten Year*, p. 4.
25. Cunliffe, *City of Bath*, pp. 160–2.
26. Roger Rolls, *The Hospital of the Nation: The Story of Spa Medicine and the Mineral Water Hospital at Bath* (Bath, 1988), p. 84.
27. Cunliffe, *City of Bath*, pp. 163–5; see also Barry Cunliffe, 'Major Davis: Architect and Antiquarian', *Bath History*, i (1986), pp. 27–60.
28. Visit to Bath (London Doctors), 18 January 1913, pamphlet B914.238, VIS, Bath Library.
29. *Bath and District Shilling Guide Books* (London, c.1916), p. 60.
30. *Ibid*.
31. *The World*, reprinted in *Bath Chronicle*, 20 April 1876.
32. G. P. Davis, 'Image and reality in a Victorian provincial city: a working-class area of Bath, 1830–1900', PhD thesis, University of Bath (1981), pp. 83–4; see also Elizabeth Trotman, 'The employment of female domestic servants, 1851–1881, with special reference to the City of Bath', BEd Hons Dissertation, Bath College of Higher Education (1984).
33. Armistead Cay, *The Mayoralty of George Woodiwiss, Esq., JP, DL. Mayor of Bath, November 1897* (Bath, 1898), p. 65.
34. *Bath Chronicle*, 11 November 1869.
35. 'Penelope's Diary', *Bath and County Graphic*, 7 June 1897.
36. *Ibid*, 27 October 1897.
37. *Shilling Guide Books*, pp. 48–59.

Pleasure, Yet a Sink of Iniquity (London, 1981), p. 271.
8. Torrens, *Stothert & Pitt*, pp. 55–6.
9. Harper, *Bath at Work*, pp. 70, 91–2.
10. Elizabeth Trotman, 'The employment of female domestic servants, 1851–1881, with special reference to the city of Bath', BEd Hons dissertation, Bath College of Higher Education (1984), pp. 39–40.
11. *Ibid*, p. 10.
12. J. S. Bartrum, *The Personal Reminiscences of an Old Bath Boy* (Bath, 1910), p. 46, copy in Bath Library.
13. Kenneth R. Clew, *The Kennet and Avon Canal* (Newton Abbot, 1968).
14. Martin Hemmings, 'Bath and its Communications', in

J. Wroughton (ed.), *Bath in the Age of Reform, 1830–1841* (Bath, 1972), pp. 67–78.

15. *Ibid*, p. 72.

16. The Somerset Coal Canal was also bought by the GWR, in 1904, and a new GWR branch line was constructed over most of its course. See Clew, *Kennet and Avon*, and *The Somersetshire Coal Canal and Railways* (Newton Abbot, 1970).

17. Census Enumerators' books, St Michael's Parish, Bath, 1861 (National Archives), Kew.

18. Bath Library, Bath Directory, 1893.

19. Bath Record Office, Annual Reports of the Chief Constable (1885–1894).

20. Neale, *Bath*, p. 269.

21. R. S. Neale, 'Economic conditions and working class movements in the city of Bath, 1800–1850', MA dissertation, University of Bristol (1963), p. 6. Neale was inclined to make generalisations in distinguishing between the city's parishes, thus obscuring their complexities. He defines Lyncombe and Widcombe as 'poor' and emphasised its industrial aspects when in reality it was both industrial and suburban. Similarly, Neale saw Walcot as a suburb of the wealthy, but the size and economic diversity of the parish meant that it did not match entirely either category of 'inner-city' or 'suburban' parish.

22. *Bath and Cheltenham Gazette*, 20 November 1821.

23. *Ibid*, 19 August 1820; 5 September 1821.

24. *Bath Chronicle*, 22 January 1852. For the Irish in eighteenth- and nineteenth-century Bath, see Graham Davis, 'Social Decline and Slum Conditions: Irish Migrants in Bath's History', *Bath History*, viii (2000), pp. 134–47.

25. Trotman, 'Employment of female domestic servants', pp. 29–30.

26. See Jay Winter (ed.), *The Working Class in Modern British History* (Cambridge, 1983), pp. 171–9.

27. G. Sanger, *Seventy Years a Showman* (1910), quoted in Kellow Chesney, *The Victorian Underworld* (London, 1970), p. 33.

28. Bath Record Office, Bath Watch Committee Minutes, 6 vols, 1836–1900. Evidence is drawn specifically from Minutes 1861–99, in G. P. Davis, 'Image and reality in a Victorian provincial city: a working-class area of Bath,

1930–1900', PhD thesis, University of Bath (1981), p. 48.

29. Davis 'Image and reality', p. 301.

30. *Doing Good: A Brief Memoir of the late Mr George Cox of Bath*, by David Wassell (1862), p. 30.

31. Louie Stride, *Memoirs of a Street Urchin*, ed. Graham Davis (Bath, 1984), pp. 7–8.

32. Neale, *Bath*, p. 271.

33. Bath Record Office, Walcot Parish Valuation List (1862).

34. *Bath Chronicle*, 2 April 1863.

35. *Ibid*, 6 November 1876.

36. *Ibid*, 22 August 1867.

37. Medical Officer of Health Report (1907), p. 25.

38. R. B. Hope, 'Educational developments in the city of Bath, 1830–1902, with special reference to its inter-relations with social and economic change', PhD thesis, University of Bristol (1970), p. 143.

39. *Ibid*, p. 166.

40. Board of Education Report (1902), pp. 11–12, in Hope, 'Educational developments', p. 166.

41. Report of the Interdepartmental Committee on the Employment of Children Act 1903, Parliamentary Papers, 1910, vol. xxvii, Bath Tabular Statements, Appendix (pp. 534–41), pp. 502–9.

42. Neale, 'The standard of living', pp. 590–606, and *Bath*, pp. 77–81, 282. His main sources were the Account Books of Overseers of Highways (Walcot) for the period 1809–32 (in Bath Library), and retail price lists published in the *Bath and Cheltenham Gazette* from 1812 to 1844. The average number of labourers employed by the Highway Surveyors in the first weeks of January, May and September from 1780 to 1851 was only 11.3, although the actual numbers ranged from nil to 89.

43. P. Mathias, *The First Industrial Nation: An Economic History of Britain 1700–1914* (London, 1969), p. 378.

44. Neale, *Bath*, pp. 289–91.

45. *Ibid*, p. 291.

46. Davis, 'Image and reality', pp. 379–448.

47. Medical Officer of Health Annual Reports (1910), pp. 14–15. See also Clive Charlton, 'Cholera in Bath', MA in Local and Regional History, Bath Spa University College, 2002.

48. *Ibid*, MOH Reports.

49. *Ibid*, pp. 56–7.

Notes to Chapter 7: Voice of the people, 1820–1914

1. John Wroughton (ed.), *Bath in the Age of Reform, 1830–1841* (Bath, 1972).

2. R. B. Hope, 'Educational development in the city of Bath, 1830–1902, with special reference to its inter-relations with social and economic change', PhD thesis, University of Bristol (1970), p. 91.

3. The main source for this section is R. A. Neale, *Bath: A Social History, 1680–1850, or a Valley of Pleasure, Yet a Sink of Iniquity* (London, 1981), particularly chapter 10. Quotations in the text are those used by Neale (unless otherwise indicated) and his references to sources are

given in the notes.

4. *Bath and Cheltenham Gazette*, 16 March 1820.

5. *Bath Journal*, 12 June 1829.

6. Wroughton, *Bath in the Age of Reform*, pp. 21–3.

7. *Bath and Cheltenham Gazette*, 18 October 1831.

8. *Ibid*, 8 November 1831.

9. Wroughton, *Bath in the Age of Reform*, p. 24.

10. For a full account of Roebuck's career in Bath, see Neale, *Bath*, pp. 346–83.

11. Wroughton, *Bath in the Age of Reform*, p. 25.

12. Neale, *Bath*, p. 348.

13. For more information on local Chartism see Asa Briggs (ed.), *Chartist Studies* (London, 1959; repr. 1972), chapter vi.
14. *Bath Guardian*, 9 June 1838, quoted in D. Nicholls, 'Chartism: a local study', BA Combined Studies dissertation, Bath College of Higher Education (1986), p. 85.
15. *Bath and Cheltenham Gazette*, 19 December 1837.
16. Briggs, *Chartist Studies*, pp. 187–8, 190.
17. Wroughton, *Bath in the Age of Reform*, pp. 105–6.
18. On the Anti-Corn Law League, see J. Y. Ward (ed.), *Popular Movements, c.1830–1850* (London, 1970).
19. Briggs, *Chartist Studies*, pp. 342–3; Wroughton, *Bath in the Age of Reform*, pp. 18–19.
20. *Bath Chronicle*, 8 July 1841.
21. Bath Record Office, parliamentary election results for the city of Bath.
22. *Bath Chronicle*, 9 January 1902.
23. Wroughton, *Bath in the Age of Reform*, pp. 82–4.
24. Neale, *Bath*, p. 364.
25. 'The Fussletons in Bath: A series of poetical letters' (Bath, 1836), p. 4, quoted in Alexander E. Kolaczkowski, 'The Politics of Civic Improvement: Bath 1835–1879, with special reference to the career of Sir Jerom Murch', PhD thesis, University of Bath (1995), p. 109.
26. Neale, *Bath*, p. 364.
27. G. P. Davis, 'Image and reality in a Victorian provincial city: a working-class area of Bath, 1830–1900', PhD thesis, University of Bath (1981), p. 297 and n. 82.
28. A. M. Press, *Liberal Leaders of Somerset* (1890),
29. Davis, 'Image and reality', ch. 8, pp. 503–92.
30. *Bath Chronicle*, 11 August 1864.
31. Letter from J. Murch, *Bath Chronicle*, 26 April 1866.
32. C. S. Barter, 'Report on the Sanitary Condition of the City and Borough of Bath during the years 1867 and 1868' (1869), p. 14, Bath Library.
33. *Bath Chronicle*, 24 March 1864.
34. *History of the Bath Waterworks*, published by order of the Council (Bath, 1878) (authorship attributed to the Revd C.W. Shickle), Bath Library.
35. *Bath Chronicle*, 16 May 1895; *Bath Year Book* (1896), Bath Library.
36. See above, chapter 5, pp. 85–6.
37. *Bath Chronicle*, 13 December 1890.
38. See Derek Fraser (ed.), *The New Poor Law in the Nineteenth Century* (London, 1976); for Bath, see Davis, 'Image and reality', pp. 264–71; also Revd. Spencer,' The Working of the New Poor Law in the Bath Union, or a Peep into the Board Room at Walcot', *Bath Tracts* (1836), and Augustus G. Barretté, 'A Few Plain Facts', *Bath Tracts* (1837), Bath Library.
39. Spencer, 'The Working of the New Poor Law', p. 12.
40. British Parliamentary Papers, 1851 Census, Great Britain. Report and Tables on Religious Worship, England and Wales. Table F, p. cclii: Religious Accommodation and Attendance in Large Towns.
41. All information on the school board taken, unless otherwise indicated, from Hope, 'Educational development'.
42. Minutes, Church School Managers' Union, 23 March 1876; 20 April 1876; quoted in Hope, 'Educational developments', p. 128.
43. School Board Chronicle, vol. lviii, 1897, p. 320 quoted in Hope, 'Educational developments', p. 161.

Notes to Chapter 8: Twentieth-century Bath

1. A. J. P. Taylor, *English History, 1914–45* (Oxford, 1977), p. 2.
2. In replies to a questionnaire on Bath's war effort, the total number of recruits was given as 'direct enlistment 2,969; grouped men 6,813; Military Service Act 1,431'. The first two categories were probably all volunteers, and the remaining 1,431 were conscripts. Bath Record Office, World War I, Mayor's Business Papers, File CL 10/2.
3. Louie Stride, *Memoirs of a Street Urchin*, ed. G. Davis (Bath, 1985), p. 15.
4. Lord and Lady Temple gave over Newton Park House to the military for the duration. It was described in magazine articles as 'Lady Temple's Hospital', to which she donated two Ford ambulances. See G. Davis, *The Langtons at Newton Park, Bath* (Bath, 1985).
5. Bath Record Office, 'Bath War Hospital 1914–1929', copy of talk given by Kate Clarke to Weston History Group (1993), Ref. PP 626.
6. Bath Record Office, World War I, Mayor's Business, File CL 10/2.
7. *Ibid.* No figures are given for women employed in occupations other than munitions production. For some experiences of one of Bath's nurses, see Bath Record Office, 'Letters of a VAD' (photocopies) written by Kathleen Ainsworth (1892–1982) to her parents in Swindon, Bath War Hospital, 1916–17, PP 627.
8. Bath Record Office, World War I, Mayor's Business, File CL 10/2,.
9. Stride, *Memoirs of a Street Urchin*, p. 15.
10. Anne Part, 'The development of the school medical service: a case study of Bath, 1913–1939', *History Papers III* (Bath College of Higher Education, 1980–81), p. 23. The article is based on Part's unpublished BEd dissertation (1980) of the same title.
11. John Haddon, *Portrait of Bath* (London, 1982), p. 25.
12. Stride, *Memoirs of a Street Urchin*, p. 38.
13. The restored Assembly Rooms were reopened by the Duchess of Kent in 1938, only to be gutted by fire in the bombing raids of 1942. Haddon, *Portrait of Bath*, p. 25.
14. John K. Walton and Cliff O'Neill, 'Numbering the holiday makers: the problems and possibilities of the June census of 1921 for historians of resorts', *The Local Historian* 23, 4 (November 1993), p. 20.
15. Barry Cunliffe, *The City of Bath* (Gloucester, 1986),

p. 168.

16. Stride, *Memoirs of a Street Urchin*, pp. 38–9.

17. In his Annual Reports, 1919–39, the MOH consistently estimated that 10 per cent of the population were employed in the industrial sector.

18. For example, in the 1921 census, hotel-, inn- and lodging-house keepers, publicans and beer-sellers, were assigned to the 'Food, Drink and Tobacco' category, but there were included in the 'Personal Service' category at the 1931 census.

19. *Somerset Guardian*, 29 January 1937.

20. Dr J. Blackett (MOH for Bath, 1919–45), 'Fifty years of public health and social welfare in a county borough, Bath, 1895–1944', unpublished MA dissertation (1949), p. 186, no awarding institution identified; copy held at Bath Library is stamped 'Degree conferred 5 July 1949'.

21. Bryan Little, *Bath Portrait* (Bristol, 1961), p. 109.

22. Annual Report, MOH (Bath), 1934, p. 10.

23. Part, 'Case Study of Bath', p. 22.

24. *Ibid*, pp. 7–8 and appendix 1, p. 240; for York see B. S. Rowntree, *Poverty and Progress* (London, 1941).

25. Annual Report, MOH (Bath), 1919–39.

26. Blackett, 'Fifty years of public health and social welfare', p. 13.

27. *Ibid*, p. 193.

28. For a brief account of inter-war housing see Stephen Constantine, *Social Conditions in Britain, 1918–1939* (London, 1983), pp. 23–32.

29. Annual Report, MOH (Bath), 1919, p. 24.

30. Part, 'Case Study of Bath', p. 23.

31. Blackett, 'Fifty years of public health and social welfare', pp. 186–7.

32. In 1918–19, 28 unions were affiliated to the Trades and Labour Council.

33. *Bath Chronicle*, 15 May 1926. Reports from *Bath Chronicle*, 4–15 May, on the strike.

34. Bath Trades and Labour Council, Minute Books, University of Bath Library, Special Collections: Co-op Archive.

35. *Ibid*, Delegate Rolls, 1918–19; 1930, University of Bath Library, Special Collections.

36. Miscellaneous papers found in the Trades and Labour Council archive (not catalogued) include a letter from the Bath Unemployed Association, dated 10 February 1936, and a press cutting of the editorial column of the *Bath and Wiltshire Chronicle and Herald*, 14 February 1936. The BUA wrote to urge the Trades Council to exclude the press from its meetings, apparently because of critical newspaper comments on the role of the BUA in raising the issue of 'underpayment' to some railway workers.

The charges were proved to be without foundation.

37. Letter from Bath Labour Party to Bath Trades Council, 20 September 1932. The Co-op Archive (Bath Trades and Labour Council), University of Bath Library, Special Collections.

38. Blackett, 'Fifty years of public health and social welfare', p. 186.

39. Niall Rothnie, *The Bombing of Bath* (Bath, 1983), p. 10. For more recent research on the military aspects of the Bath blitz, see John Penny, 'The Most Devastating Baedeker Blitz', MA in Local and Regional History, Bath Spa University College, 1998.

40. Blackett, 'Fifty years of public health and social welfare', p. 186.

41. Census (England and Wales), County Reports, Somerset (1951), Table A, Population Change mid-1931 to mid-1951, p. xiv.

42. Rothnie, *Bombing of Bath*, p. 10.

43. Little, *Bath Portrait*, p. 109.

44. See Rothnie, *Bombing of Bath*; M. Wainwright, *The Bath Blitz* (Bath, 1992). For more detailed research on the Civil Defence in Bath, see George Scott, 'Bath and the Baedeker Firebomb Débâcle', MA in Local and Regional History, Bath Spa University College, 2000, and Katherine Hollingsworth, 'Bath Civil Defence 1939–1943: The Unfortunate Consequences of Local Authority Control', MA in Local and Regional History, Bath Spa University College, 2002.

45. Blackett, 'Fifty years of public health and social welfare', p. 189.

46. Brian Collecot, private collection. The authors are indebted to Dot and Roy Holmwood for passing on this source.

47. *Ibid*.

48. Juliet Gardiner, *Britain, 1939–1945* (London, 2004), pp. 518–19.

49. Bath Trades and Labour Council, delegate rolls, Co-op Archive, University of Bath Library, Special Collections.

50. The City Plan, mid-stage report (November 1982), Bath City Council, p. 37.

51. Unless otherwise acknowledged, all information in this section is taken from the City Plan (November 1982).

52. Little, *Bath Portrait*, pp. 108–21.

53. GOAD *Shopping Report* (1986), Bath Library.

54. Roger Rolls, *The Hospital of the Nation, The Story of Spa Medicine and the Mineral Water Hospital at Bath* (Bath, 1988), pp. 162–3.

55. The City Plan (November 1982), p. 73: evidence based on data from survey conducted by South Western Industrial Research Limited in 1972–73.

Notes to Chapter 9: Heritage city

1. 'Whose city' was asked rhetorically in the prologue to the City Plan (3), Mid-Stage Report (November 1982). Bath City Council.

2. Christopher Pound, *The Genius of Bath: The City and the*

Landscape (Bath, 1986), pp. 93–4.

3. Adam Fergusson and Tim Mowl, *The Sack of Bath – and After* (Michael Russell Publishing Ltd in association with Bath Preservation Trust: first published 1973; extended

edition published 1989).

4. Barry Cunliffe, *The City of Bath* (Gloucester, 1986), p. 173.

5. John Haddon, *Portrait of Bath* (London, 1982), pp. 168–75.

6. *Ibid*, pp. 33–74.

7. *Ibid*, p. 25.

8. *Ibid*, p. 29.

9. *Ibid*.

10. Cunliffe, *The City of Bath*, p. 12.

11. Fergusson and Mowl, *The Sack of Bath*, p. 62.

12. Haddon, *Portrait of Bath*, p. 29.

13. Fergusson and Mowl, *The Sack of Bath*, p. 62.

14. A housing report in 1994 stated that 1,200 new homes were needed to meet housing demand in Bath, *Bath Chronicle*, 19 October 1994.

15. *Official Visitor Guide*, 1993.

16. *Bath Chronicle*, 9 June 1994.

17. *Ibid*.

18. *Ibid*, 12 June 1994.

19. *Ibid*, 3 June 1994.

20. *Ibid*, 9 June 1994.

21. *The Guardian*, 'Weekend', Property Section, 21 May 1994.

22. *Bath Chronicle*, 24 May 1994.

23. *Ibid*, 19 October 1994.

24. *Ibid*, 9 September 1994.

25. *Ibid*, 24 May 1994.

26. *The Guardian*, 'Society' (article by Tim King, 'Those who pass by', on begging and homelessness in Bath), 14 September 1994.

27. *Bath Chronicle*, 24 May 1994.

28. Avon and Somerset Constabulary, Annual Report of the Chief Constable (1990), Bath Library.

29. *Bath Chronicle*, 24 May 1994.

30. *Ibid*, 9 August 1993.

31. *The Guardian*, 'Weekend', 21 May 1994.

32. *Bath Chronicle*, 10 June 1994.

Further reading

Books and reports

Patrick Abercrombie *et al.*, *A Plan for Bath* (Bath, 1945).

Ken Andrews and Stuart Burroughs, *Stothert & Pitt: Cranemakers to the World* (Stroud, 2003).

Christopher Anstey, *New Bath Guide* (Bath, 1830–32 edition).

A. Barbeau, *Life and Letters at Bath in the XVIII Century* (London, 1904).

C. S. Barter, *Report on the Sanitary Condition of the City and Borough of Bath during the years 1867 and 1868* (1869), Bath Library.

B. S. Bartrum, *The Personal Reminiscences of an Old Bath Boy* (1910), Bath Library.

Anne Borsay, *Medicine and Charity in Georgian Bath: A Social History of the General Infirmary, c.1739–1830* (Aldershot, 1999).

Peter Borsay, *The Image of Georgian Bath, 1720–2000* (Oxford: 2000).

Benjamin Boyce *The Benevolent Man: A Life of Ralph Allen of Bath* (Oxford, 1967).

Asa Briggs (ed.), *Chartist Studies* (London, 1959; repr. 1972).

C. W. Chalklin, *The Provincial Towns of Georgian England: A study of the building process, 1740–1820* (London, 1974).

Paul Cresswell (ed.), *Bath in Quotes: A Literary View from Saxon Times Onwards* (Bath, 1985).

Bruce Crofts, *Forgotten Year: News from Bath in 1882* (Bath City Council, 1982).

Barry Cunliffe, *Roman Bath Discovered* (Tempus edn, Stroud, 2000).

——, *The City of Bath* (Gloucester, 1986).

Peter Davenport, *Medieval Bath Uncovered* (Stroud, 2000).

Graham Davis, *The Langtons at Newton Park, Bath* (Bath, 1980; 2nd edn 1985).

——, *Bath beyond the Guide Book. Scenes From Victorian Life* (Bristol, 1988).

——, 'The scum of Bath: the Victorian poor', in Barry Stapleton (ed.), *Conflict and Community in Southern England* (Stroud, 1992), pp. 183–98.

——, 'Beyond the Georgian façade: The Avon Street district of Bath', in Martin Gaskell (ed.), *Slums* (Leicester, 1990), pp. 144–85.

Daniel Defoe, *A Tour Through the Whole Island of Great Britain* (1724–26) (Penguin English Library edition, Harmondsworth, Middlesex, 1971).

Robert Dunning, *The Monmouth Rebellion, a Complete Guide to the Rebellion and Bloody Assizes* (Wimbourne, 1984).

John Eglin, *The Imaginary Autocrat: Beau Nash and the Invention of Bath* (London, 2005).

Kirsten Elliott, *Myth-maker: John Wood, 1704–1754* (Bath, 2004).

Trevor Fawcett and Stephen Bird, *Bath: History and Guide* (Stroud, 1994).

Adam Fergusson and Tim Mowl, *The Sack of Bath – and After* (Michael Russell Publishing in association with Bath Preservation Trust, extended edn, 1989).

Michael Forsyth, *Pevsner Architectural Guides: Bath* (London, 2003).

Derek Fraser, *The New Poor Law in the Nineteenth Century* (London, 1976).

David Gadd, *Georgian Summer. The Rise and Development of Bath* (Newbury, 1987).

S. Gibbs, *The Bath Visitant* (Bath, 1884), Bath Library.

Thom Gorst, *Bath: An Architectural Guide* (London, 1997).

John Haddon, *Portrait of Bath* (London, 1982).

Duncan Harper, *Bath at Work* (Bath, 1989).

Kenneth Hylson-Smith, *Bath Abbey: A History* (The Friends of Bath Abbey, Bath, 1988).

Walter Ison, *The Georgian Buildings of Bath* (London, 1948; 2nd edn, Kingsmead Press, Bath, 1980).

J. Lees-Milne and D. Ford, *Images of Bath* (Richmond-upon-Thames, 1982).

Bryan Little, *The Building of Bath* (London, 1947)

——, *Bath Portrait* (Bristol, 1961).

R. Mainwaring, *Annals of Bath* (Bath, 1838)

——, *Narrative of the Progress of an epidemic disease which appeared in Bath in the autumn of 1832* (Bath, 1833).

Sylvia McIntyre, 'Bath: the rise of a resort town, 1660–1800' in Peter Clark (ed.), *Country Towns in Pre-industrial England* (Leicester, 1981), pp. 198–244.

L. Melville, *Bath under Beau Nash – and after* (London, 1926).

Tim Mowl, *John Wood: Architect of Obsession* (Millstream Books, Bath, 1988).

R. S. Neale, *A Social History 1680–1850, or A Valley of Pleasure, Yet a Sink of Iniquity* (London, 1981).

K. Needell, *Printed Maps and Plans of the City of Bath, 1588–1860* (London, 2001).

Benjamin Price, *The Benevolent Man, A Life of Ralph Allen of Bath* (Cambridge, Mass., 1967).

Christopher Pound, *Genius of Bath: The City and Its Landscape* (Bath, 1988).

Roger Rolls, *Hospital of the Nation: The Story of Spa Medicine and the National Mineral Water Hospital at Bath* (Bath, 1988).

Niall Rothnie, *The Bombing of Bath* (Bath, 1983).

R. A. L. Smith, *Bath* (London, 1944).

Tobias Smollett, *The Expedition of Humphry Clinker* (Penguin English Library edition, Penguin Books, Harmondsworth, Middlesex, 1983).

Louie Stride, *Memoirs of a Street Urchin*, ed. Graham Davis (Bath, 1984).

Andrew Swift, *All Roads Lead to France: Bath and The Great War* (Bath, 2005).

Hugh Torrens, *The Evolution of a Family Firm. Stothert & Pitt of Bath* (Bath, 1984).

M. Wainwright, *The Bath Blitz* (Bath, 1975; Bath, 1992).

J. T. Ward (ed.), *Popular Movements c.1830–1850* (London, 1970).

John Wood, *A Description of Bath* (2nd edn, Bathoe & Lownds, London, 1765).

B. Wriston, *Rare Doings at Bath* (Chicago, USA, 1978).

John Wroughton (ed.), *Bath in the Age of Reform, 1830–1841* (Bath, 1972)

——, *The Civil War in Bath and North Somerset* (Bath, 1973)

——, *King Edward's School at Bath, 1552–1982* (Bath, 1982)

——, *Civil War Trail Around Bath* (Bath, 1993)

——, *An Unhappy Civil War. The Experiences of Ordinary People in Gloucestershire, Somerset and Wiltshire, 1642–1646* (Bath, 1999)

——, *Stuart Bath. Life in the Forgotten City, 1603–1714* (Bath, 2004).

Journals

Mick Aston, 'The Bath region from late prehistory to the middle ages', *Bath History*, i (1986), pp. 61–89.

Robert Bell, 'Bath Abbey: Some new perspectives', *Bath History*, vi (1996), pp. 7–24.

Robert Bennet, 'The last of the Georgian Architects of Bath: the work and times of John Pinch', *Bath History*, ix (2002), pp. 87–103.

Stephen Bird, 'The earliest map of Bath', *Bath History*, i (1986), pp. 128–49.

Philippa Bishop, 'Beckford in Bath', *Bath History*, ii (1998), pp. 85–112.

Mike Bone, 'The rise and fall of Bath's breweries, 1736–1960', *Bath History*, viii (2000), pp. 106–33.

M. Brown and J. Samuel, 'The Jews in Bath', *Bath History*, i (1986), pp. 150–72.

Brenda J. Buchanan, 'Aspects of capital formation: some insights from North Somerset, 1750–1830', *Southern History* 8 (1986), pp. 73–93.

——, 'The evolution of the English turnpike trusts: lessons from a case study', *Economic History Review*, 2nd series, xxxix, 2 (1986), pp. 223–43.

——, 'The Great Bath Road, 1700–1830', *Bath History*, iv (1992), pp. 71–94.

——, The Avon Navigation and the Inland Port of Bath', *Bath History*, vi (1996), pp. 63–87.

R. Angus Buchanan, 'The bridges of Bath', *Bath History*, iii (1990), pp. 1–21.

——, 'The floods of Bath', *Bath History*, vii (1998), pp. 167–88

——, 'Bath: University City', *Bath History*, ix (2002), pp. 160–80.

John Catell, 'Edward Snell's diary: a journeyman engineer in Bath in the 1840s', *Bath History*, ix (2002), pp. 104–25.

Barry Cunliffe, 'Major Davis: architect and antiquarian', *Bath History*, i (1986), pp. 27–60.

Peter Davenport, 'Bath Abbey', *Bath History*, ii (1988), pp. 1–26.

——, 'Town and Country: Roman Bath and its hinterland', *Bath History*, v (1994), pp. 7–23.

——, 'Aquae Sulis: The origins and development of a Roman Town', *Bath History*, viii (2000), pp. 7–26.

Graham Davis, 'Entertainments in Georgian Bath: gambling and vice', *Bath History*, i (1986), pp. 1–26.

——, 'Social decline and slum conditions: Irish migrants in Bath's History', *Bath History*, viii (2000), pp. 134–47.

——, 'Sir Jerom Murch and the "civic gospel" in Victorian Bath', *Journal of Liberal Democrat History*, Issue 37 (winter 2002–3), pp. 14–17.

Mary Ede, 'Bath and the Great Exhibition of 1851', *Bath History*, iii (1990), pp. 2–9.

Trevor Fawcett, 'Dance and teachers of dance in eighteenth-century Bath', *Bath History*, ii (1988), pp. 27–48.

——, 'Eighteenth-century shops and the luxury trade', *Bath History*, iii (1990), pp. 49–75.

——, 'Black people in Georgian Bath', *Avon Past*, 16 (1993), pp. 2–9.

Sally Festing, 'Charles Richter and Bath Cabinet Makers: the early years', *Bath History*, vii (1998), pp. 146–66.

Michael Forsyth, 'Edward Davis: nineteenth-century Bath architect and pupil of Sir John Soane', *Bath History*, vii (1998), pp. 107–28.

Elizabeth Holland, 'The earliest Bath Guildhall', *Bath History*, ii (1988), pp. 163–80.

Mac Hopkins-Clark, 'A change of style at the Theatre Royal, 1805–1820', *Bath History*, iv (1992), pp. 136–54.

Jonathan Kinghorn, 'Privvie in Perfection: Sir John Harrington's Water Closet', *Bath History*, i (1986), pp. 173–88.

John Kite, '"A Good Bargain": the struggle for a Public Library, 1850–1924', *Bath History*, iv (1992), pp. 136–54.

Alex Kolacjkowski, 'Jerom Murch and Bath Politics, 1833–1879', *Bath History*, vi (1996), pp. 155–73.

Robin Lambert, 'Patrick Abercrombie and planning in Bath', *Bath History*, viii (2000), pp. 172–96.

Jean Manco, 'The Cross Bath', *Bath History*, ii (1988), pp. 49–84.

——, 'Bath and "The Great Rebuilding"', *Bath History*, iv (1992), pp. 25–51.

———, 'Saxon Bath: the legacy of Rome and the Saxon rebirth', *Bath History*, vii (1998), pp. 27–54.

Briggitte Mitchell, 'English spas', *Bath History*, i (1986), pp. 189–204.

Tim Mowl, 'A trial-run for Regent's Park: Repton and Nash at Bath, 1796', *Bath History*, iii (1990), pp. 76–89.

R. S. Neale, 'The standard of living, 1780–1844: a regional and class study', *Economic History Review*, XIX (1966), pp. 590–608.

Chris Noble, 'The New Gaol in Bathwick (1772–1842)', *Bath History*, ix (2002), pp. 64–86.

Steve Poole, 'Radicalism, loyalism and the "Reign of Terror" in Bath, 1792–1804', *Bath History*, iii (1990), pp. 114–37.

Roger Rolls, 'Bath cases: care and treatment of patients at the Bath General Hospital during the mid-eighteenth century', *Bath History*, ii (1988), pp. 139–62.

Jane Root, 'Thomas Baldwin: his public career in Bath, 1775–1793', *Bath History*, v (1994), pp. 80–103.

R. S. O. Tomlin, 'Voices from the sacred spring', *Bath History*, iv (1992), pp. 7–24.

Nicholas von Behr, 'The cloth industry of Twerton from the 1780s to the 1820s', *Bath History*, vi (1996), pp. 88–107.

Owen Ward, 'Isaac Pitman and the Fourth Phonetic Institute', *Bath History*, vii (1998), pp. 129–45.

Robin Whalley, 'The Royal Victoria Park', *Bath History*, v (1994), pp. 147–69.

John Wroughton, 'Puritanism and Traditionalism, cultural and political division in Bath, 1620–1662', *Bath History*, iv (1992), pp. 52–70.

Unpublished dissertations and theses

J. Blackett, 'Fifty years of public health and social welfare in a county borough, Bath 1895–1944', MA dissertation, no awarding institution identified (1949). Copy held at Bath Library.

Joy V. Burt, 'Oldfield Park West and East Twerton in the late Nineteenth-century: A comparative study', MA in Local and Regional History, Bath Spa University College, 2001.

Jan Chivers, 'In the midst of life' – sudden death in Bath, 1776–1835: a study of the Coroners' Examinations and Inquisitions', MA Local and Regional History, Bath Spa University College, 1997.

Clive Charlton, 'Cholera in Bath', MA in Local and Regional History, Bath Spa University College, 2002.

Tricia Curr, 'A Peep into Two Prisons', MA in Local and Regional History, Bath Spa University College, 2002.

G. P. Davis, 'Image and reality in a Victorian provincial city: a working-class area of Bath, 1830–1900', PhD thesis, University of Bath (1981).

Katherine Hollingworth, 'Bath Civil Defence 1939–42: The Unfortunate Consequences of Local Authority Control', MA in Local and Regional History, Bath Spa University College, 2002.

R. B. Hope, 'Educational developments in the city of Bath, 1830–1902, with special reference to its inter-relations with social and economic change', PhD thesis, University of Bristol (1970).

Mac Hopkins Clark, 'Bath Theatre Royal', MA in Local and Regional History, Bath Spa University College, 2002.

V. J. Kite, 'Libraries in Bath, 1618–1964', thesis presented for the Fellowship of the Library Association (1966).

Alexandra E. Kolaczkowski, 'The Politics of Civic Improvement: Bath 1835–1879 with special reference to the career of Sir Jerom Murch', PhD thesis, University of Bath (1995).

R. S. Neale, 'Economic conditions and working-class movements in the city of Bath, 1800–1850', MA dissertation, University of Bristol (1962).

D. Nicholls, 'Chartism: a local study', BA Hons Combined Studies dissertation, Bath College of Higher Education (1986).

Anne Part, 'The development of the school medical service: a case study of Bath, 1913–1939', BEd Hons dissertation, Bath College of Higher Education (1980).

Ann Partridge, 'The Dolemeads: a study of early municipal housing in Bath', BEd Hons dissertation, Bath College of Higher Education (1980).

John Penny, 'The Most Devastating Baedeker Blitz', MA Local and Regional History, Bath Spa University College (1998).

J. Saunders, 'Hotel provision in Bath, 1851–1891', BEd Hons dissertation, Bath College of Higher Education (1980).

George Scott, 'Bath and the Baedeker Firebomb Debacle', MA in Local and Regional History, Bath Spa University College (2001).

Elizabeth Trotman, 'The employment of female domestic servants, 1851–1881, with special reference to the city of Bath', BEd Hons dissertation, Bath College of Higher Education (1984).

P. M. Wadsworth, 'Leisure in nineteenth-century Bath', MA dissertation, University of Kent (1977).

Elizabeth White, '"Fallen on Hard Times": Mrs Partis and her College for Distressed Gentlefolk', MA in Local and Regional History, Bath Spa University College (2001).

Index

Index entries in *italic* type refer to illustrations or to information within captions or text boxes